# Reflections on International Tourism

# Developments in Urban and Rural Tourism

edited by

Mike Robinson
Richard Sharpley
Nigel Evans
Philip Long
John Swarbrooke

UNIVERSITY *of*
NORTHUMBRIA *at* NEWCASTLE

*Sheffield Hallam University*

2000

©The Centre for Travel & Tourism, Centre for Tourism and the Authors

ISBN 1 871916 50 X

First published 2000

Cover Design by Tim Murphy Creative Solutions

Published in Great Britain by
the Centre for Travel and Tourism in association with
Business Education Publishers Ltd.,
The Teleport,
Doxford International,
Sunderland   SR3 3XD

Tel:   0191 525 2400
Fax:   0191 520 1815

*British Cataloguing-in-Publications Data*
*A catalogue record for this book is available from the British Library*

Printed in Great Britain by Athenaeum Press, Gateshead

# Preface

Tourism continues to reach out in to space and time. Implicit within the trite phrase of 'tourism is the world's largest industry', it *appears* that everyone is either a tourist or a potential tourist, everywhere is someone's destination and no human activity is immune from the fleeting glimpses of transient eyes. Appearances, of course, can be deceptive.

Ironically, change, movement, development and growth are the norms that characterise a phenomenon that many still see as an opportunity to slow down, relax and do little. The new millennium will undoubtedly see more tourists, more tourism, more travel, more impacts, more to market, more to manage. Core human traits of creativity and curiosity, desires to consume and commune, along with the need to survive, remain as the fundamental, and often conflicting, drivers for this thing we label tourism. Tourism is an important subject of academic inquiry *precisely* because it is an extension of our humanity and the cultures we inhabit, and because of the rapidity of change and growth that now typifies it.

This series of six volumes arose out of a major international conference held at Sheffield Hallam University, UK, in September 2000. Organised by the Centre for Travel and Tourism, University of Northumbria and the Centre for Tourism Sheffield Hallam University, **Tourism 2000: Time for Celebration?** was designed to reflect on, evaluate and anticipate the growth and development of tourism from its roots in pilgrimage and exploration, to its present and future role as a vast and complex social and cultural activity, a diverse international industry, and a focus for academic discourse. The conference attracted tremendous interest from academics, policy makers and practitioners from across the world and in itself was a touristic experience. These books contain 173 of nearly 200 papers presented at the conference.

The importance of this series lies in its diversity as well as its dimensions. We believe it to be important that authors from differing disciplines, perspectives, nationalities and cultures are able to reflect on the many facets of tourism. With diversity, however, comes problems of categorisation and hard editorial decisions. We trust that in the main we have managed to produce a reasoned and manageable breakdown of papers.

The production of one book can generate a plethora of problems. Not surprisingly the production of six volumes involving so many contributors and from such a diversity of locations has not been without anguish. Differing interpretations of the word 'deadline' is a common source of editorial angst! Technology too, though we are indebted to it, has frequently been the object of derision – the email delivery failure, the server that is down, the lost file, the scrambled text, and the ever popular 'pressing the wrong button.'

Fortunately there are those amongst us that appear to take problems in their stride and who sail on through the waves of worry. Thanks must go to Richard Shipway for his help in chasing the most elusive of authors. Thanks also to Jill Pomfret for her help in the editing process and to Amanda Miller for her assistance. Central to this bout of thanks are the staff at Business Education Publishers Ltd (BEP), who have been down this road with us many times now and continue to deliver a service second to none. Without the professionalism, commitment and good humour of Andrea Murphy, Moira Page and everyone who has worked on this series at BEP, you would not be reading this.

Finally our thanks go, as ever, to all the contributors to the series. Reflections on International Tourism provides a home for over 200 researchers, thinkers, critics and practitioners from nearly forty countries who have been through the processes of contemplation and reflection – those precious intellectual spaces between doing and being.

The important thing that all our authors now offer us through the work contained in these pages, is an invitation for you, the reader, to engage in your own process of reflection.

Mike Robinson
Sheffield, 2000

# Introduction

Traditionally, the countryside and the city have, both physically and structurally, represented polar opposites. Not only have they been characterised by significant environmental and geographical distinctions, but they have also embraced diametrically opposed social, cultural, economic and political systems. In particular, the 'typical' elements of rurality – close-knit communities bound by tradition and kinship, working within an agrarian economic system and bound by political structures reflecting the traditional dominance of the landowners – have contrasted starkly with the modern social structures, cultural values, economic systems and political processes of urban life. In the specific context of tourism too, the countryside and the city have (with the exception of culturally/historically important centres or purpose-built urban tourist centres, such as seaside resorts) long represented distinct, separate spaces. The countryside was (and still is) a place to escape to, a tourism/leisure space offering a refuge from modern, urban life.

More recently, however, particularly in post-industrial, postmodern societies, the distinctions between urban and rural areas have become less apparent. Although a semiotic gulf remains between them, their contrasting socio-cultural, economic and political structures and institutions have, to a great extent, become de-differentiated. The countryside, for example, has become a living space for urban workers and non-agrarian industries are now supporting rural economies whilst, in many cities, specific districts are referred as 'villages' within the urban environment.

Of particular relevance, urban areas are no longer places to escape from, but tourism destinations; they have become places to go to. Indeed, although treated separately in the literature – and recent years have witnessed a dramatic increase in the number of texts addressing the issue of urban tourism in particular – the countryside and the city are, in effect, two sides of the same tourism coin. Over the last two decades or so, both urban and rural areas have experienced a variety of similar social and economic problems, including increasing unemployment, a decline in the traditional industrial/economic base and environmental degradation, and both have turned to tourism as a potential panacea to these ills. In the countryside, tourism is the new cash crop; in the city, the provision of tourist services is the new industry. In either case, however, the objective is the same.

Not surprisingly perhaps, rural and urban areas also face similar issues, challenges and problems in the planning and management of tourism. In general, the countryside has long been a highly popular tourism destination, suffering associated pressures and consequences. Urban tourism is, according to most commentators, a major growth area in tourism and, as a result, towns and cities experience similar tourism-related problems. More specifically, the countryside and the city also share problems in the context of, for example, environmental sustainability, funding for tourism projects, governance, the commoditisation of culture/heritage and so on. Therefore, not only is it important that, given the widespread dependence on tourism as a vehicle for socio-economic regeneration, both urban and rural tourism should be the focus of in-depth investigation and research. It is also entirely appropriate that, as here, they are combined within a single volume.

The issues and challenges associated with urban and rural tourism development are many and varied and, as the contributions to this book demonstrate, researchers are addressing increasingly focused or specific themes. Nevertheless, the overarching debate regarding the potential regenerative role of tourism remains apposite as urban and rural areas alike place greater reliance on tourism (in whatever form, from temporary festivals and events to more permanent attractions) as a means of achieving socio-economic development or revitalisation. That is, the potential benefits of tourism are not always realised – not all rural areas are suitable or able to take advantage of tourism development, whilst the hoped-for growth in tourism has not always materialised in some towns and cities – and, therefore, a critical analysis of the regenerative/economic benefits of tourism remains an essential foundation for inquiry into more specific issues.

What, then, are these specific and current themes and issues in urban and rural tourism development? Essentially they can be grouped under two broad headings, namely, the environmental and socio-cultural consequences of tourism development, and the planning/management/marketing of tourism. Within each of these, there are a variety of sub-themes, many of which are addressed in this book. The environmental/socio-cultural consequences of tourism relate to both direct impacts upon the local environment and society and the problems or conflicts that arise from the transformation in the use or function of urban / rural areas. Direct impacts include the consequences of particular events/activities on the physical environment or local communities, such as motor rallying, whilst the change in function of rural and urban areas from places of production (agriculture/forestry or industry/manufacturing) to places of consumption (for example, walking/mountain climbing in the countryside, or shopping, dining out or visiting theatres, museums or heritage centres in towns and cities) gives rise to a number of challenges. In particular, the development of tourism as a new use of space leads to conflicts between tourists and local communities, the commoditisation of heritage and, more generally, the contestation of urban/rural space.

Within the tourism planning/management/marketing theme, a number of specific issues are of direct relevance to both urban and rural tourism development. The politics of management remains a primary problem, in particular the balance or partnership between the local community, private and public sector players within the overall context of governance. Whilst integrated governance is considered desirable, particularly as public sector funding remains a significant ingredient of many rural/urban projects, local communities may feel they have lost control of development. At the same time, debate continues to surround the benefits of so-called 'lame duck' or flagship projects (frequently sponsored or supported by the public sector) as tourist attractions and their longer-term contribution to local regeneration. The controversy surrounding the Millennium Dome in Greenwich, London is a particularly visible and well-publicised example.

Related to this, the effective management of tourism development remains a challenge, particularly in rural areas. Frequently, local communities or businesses lack the experience, knowledge or resources for the effective management and marketing of tourism. Developing tourism entrepreneurship, therefore, is a vital consideration in tourism development whilst, in both rural and urban areas, the pooling of resources, or networking/collaboration schemes are considered an effective means of overcoming a lack of financial or expertise resources. This is certainly the case in remote rural areas. More generally, planning and management issues also include transport management (currently an important agenda item in both urban and rural tourism destinations) and visitor management techniques as elements of an overall integrated approach to the sustainable development of tourism.

Finally, the marketing, branding or image creation of urban and rural tourism destinations is a contemporary issue that is related to the problems of host-guest relationships or tourist and urban/tourist space conflicts. The creation of brand images has proved to be successful in the promotion of both cities and rural areas and there are various means of achieving such an image. Nevertheless, the brand image may not always be commensurate with reality or local communities' desired image and, therefore, there is a need for research into the longer term consequences of developing place images as tourism marketing tools.

Inevitably, there are many more specific issues and topics that are of relevance to the development of either or both rural and urban tourism. However, the papers in this book address the main themes that have emerged as understanding and knowledge of the problems and processes of urban/rural tourism development has grown. Furthermore, they also make a significant new contribution to that body of knowledge.

# Table of Contents

# The making of a Cairo: The city of one thousand and one nights

*Heba Farouk Ahmed*

University of California, USA

## Abstract

The French Expedition to Egypt in 1798 had awakened in Europe a new taste for antiquities. By the nineteenth-century, a visit to Egypt had become very popular for European and American tourists and travellers. They not only came to see and experience the country, but to acquire something different beyond travel. To spend the winter in Egypt meant more than just a trip to the East, where it became equivalent to a certificate of belonging to the right social class.

Through the nineteenth-century we see a change in the notion behind travel, where travellers' interests began to turn away form antiquities to other aspects of the country: the Egyptian landscape; the scenes of Cairo; and the manners and customs of the people. Visitors wrote back home telling families and friends how Egyptian towns and cities were compared to those at home, as those, back home, were longing to learn more about the 'Magic of the East.' It is clear that the travellers who came to Cairo, had a certain idea about the Orient, and accordingly wrote from that perspective. These travellers were looking for certain things about which they had read or heard about either at home or on their way to Egypt. Nineteenth-century tourists desired more than what was available for them, and accordingly produced their works from that imaginary perspective. In many cases they responded to Cairo and other Egyptian cities in different ways.

In this paper, I show how Cairo was produced in travellers' writings and books as an 'imaginary' city, and/or a different city from what they had expected to see. Stanley Lane-Poole starts his book *The Story of Cairo* by referring to "The Two Cities" that he further named the 'European' and the 'Egyptian' Cairo. That was also common in many other works written in the latter part of the nineteenth-century, where terms like 'new', 'modern', and/or 'westernised' appeared in contrast to 'old', 'Islamic' and 'medieval' Cairo. Since then until today, this 'duality' of Cairo was to be reiterated as a fact in most scholarly research covering the Cairo of the nineteenth-century. This paper suggests that this notion of 'duality' was an imported foreign concept, and did not reflect the Cairo that they had encountered. Despite the existence of two physically distinct parts of the city that, as noted by Lane-Poole, made up the city, I will demonstrate that Egyptians/Cairenes perceived it as one whole city. I argue that this dual vision imposed by foreigners (mostly Europeans) had been based on their frame of reference in their own cities, whereas for Egyptians (mostly natives rather than the westernised elite), Cairo still appeared to them as *the* city. They even named Cairo 'Misr al-Mahrushah' (The Guarded Egypt). The paper will carry a comparative approach contrasting the different views of how the city appeared and was portrayed by the different travellers, and how some of them saw it as representing the city of the *Arabian Nights*. Egyptians' writings are also analysed to portray their view of themselves and their city in different terms.

In all these cases, it appears that a different Cairo had been manufactured in the non-Arabic literature where foreign travellers attempted to rationalise Cairo and its people into a western view of order and pattern.

## Nineteenth century 'cultures of travel'

*"Narratives of Egyptian travel being already sufficiently abundant, I have not attempted to add another to the list. The scope of this volume is wholly different. It consists, for the most part, of notes of conservations with Egyptians. . . . What has been told to me may not always have been the truth, but at all events it has been that which my informants wished me to believe. . . . The conclusions at which I have arrived differ so widely from the views prevalent in England, that I believe shall be doing a real service to the cause of truth and charity by putting them on record."* (Taylor, 1888: v)

*"Countless travellers have made their way up and down the Nile . . . and these travellers have left us, as for no other region for so long a time, a record of their passage. . . . Travellers' accounts, written by the common foot soldier as well as the great Napoleon himself, offer a unique glimpse of Egypt as it was being discovered by the modern traveller."* (Kalfatovic, 1992:ix)

European travel to the East was a discourse that had been adopted by many travellers as it became central to class and gender formation. As John Urry suggested, travel changed in the nineteenth-century from an opportunity for discourse to travel as "eyewitness observation," within which there was developed a visualisation of experience and the development of the "gaze." (Urry, 1990) Grewal explained that whether travel is a metaphor of exile, mobility, difference, modernity, or hybridity, it suggests the particular ways in which knowledge of the Self, society, and nation was, and is, within European and North American culture, to be understood and obtained, (Grewal, 1996), and I would further add how it had been applied to the East. Several scholars today are questioning the 'authenticity' of those works, and looking into different ways to decipher the forms of 'travel' discourse.

It is during that time that the West had come to live as though the World were divided into a realm of mere 'representations', and a realm of the 'real' and accordingly became divided into the West and non-West. To understand travel and tourism in the nineteenth-century is to examine the travellers' experiences, writings and how they had produced cities by private interests in travel literature.

# Encounters

Contemporary literature, both foreign and Arabic, on nineteenth-century Cairo provides very little information on the city and the encounter of the natives with their 'modern' city. From reviewing western literature and travellers' accounts produced in the nineteenth-century and early twentieth-century, it appears that many travellers hardly had any contact with the public and the bulk of the population, and their writings described mainly the princely households. In this paper, I show how Cairo was produced in travellers' writings as an 'imaginary' city, or how they desired the city in a certain manner different from what they had encountered. I compare different foreigners'/travellers visions of 19th century Cairo, and contrast these descriptions with those of some Cairenes. Although the material consulted for this comparison is quite different, yet it is important to identify how the city had been perceived and described by those different groups. For the foreigners and travellers the sources would be mostly traveller accounts, city guides, letters and memoirs; and for the natives, novels, newspapers and various topographies.

Many of the books published on Cairo and written by foreigners in the nineteenth-century were grouped under the category/subject: travel and description, or manners and customs, and/or guidebooks. In many cases, travellers read these books on their way to Egypt, and sometimes on their *dahabieh* (Nile boat) going up the Nile to be prepared for what to look for and what they would eventually see. Surprisingly, many of those readers decided to write their own version about Egypt in general, and Cairo specifically, depending on their own experience. However, in many of these cases, the writings had been about their experience in the city as a reaction to, or in contrast with what they had read about and imagined rather than what they have seen.

For this paper, I analyze the works of Stanley Lane-Poole, Edwin De Leon, and Lady Duff Gordon to show the impact of the 'culture of travel' on the way Cairo was portrayed in travelers' literature. Although there is a vast array of literature produced by travelers and tourists, I chose these three for several reasons. First, they have all resided in Cairo for extensive periods of time, rather than just pass by it as tourists, or as 'birds of passage.' Second, they have all witnessed the transformations that had been taking place as a result of Khedive Ismail's (1863-1879) efforts to modernize the city, and each one of them had reacted differently to the changes. Finally, they represent diverse groups of foreigners and travelers. Stanley Lane-Poole was a British, who held different positions in Cairo during the British occupation and wrote several books on Cairo; Edwin De Leon, was a former American Consul-General in the 1870s; and Lady Duff-Gordon, was an English woman who had come to Egypt for treatment as she escaped from the weather of Europe.

In many of these narratives, travelers' chose to portray Cairo as representing the city of the *Arabian Nights*.[1] Hundreds of Englishmen and women as well as Americans knew the stories and grew up reading them since they were translated to French and English in the eighteenth/nineteenth-century[2], and accordingly came to Cairo with the idea about the 'exotic' Orient. The stories have flourished through history, as every story is about fascinating, crazy people faraway where the real seemed less than the imagined. It is known that many of the characters in *The Arabian Nights* are fictions of a storyteller's imagination, however, some of them lived and actually had the adventures related in the stories.

As travel to Egypt became common among travellers in the nineteenth-century, several artists and writers became concerned with the life of contemporary Egyptians, and the Muslims as they were with the remains of ancient Egypt. There was a great interest in the Orient and its culture, which produced a large group of writers on Cairo and Egypt. In many cases, disentangling the elements of fantasy from reality in their works was often far from straightforward, as many authors wrote lyrically about the Romantic Orient without having ventured there. (Starkey, 1998) That also parallels the time when narratives about cultures were becoming very popular, and writers competed in producing those works. Although the travellers' motivations have been different, however, that was when nineteenth-century 'urban tourism and experience' was a wide spread phenomenon. At that time, Cairo was on the list of the elite and foreigners that aspired to be well travelled. Although one gets useful information from examining these different works, yet reading and relying on those interpretive narratives and descriptions of the city produced at the time becomes problematic. On one hand, we get a clear description of the city from their writings, but on the other hand, the story seems incomplete without the points of view of the native Egyptians.

## Stanley Lane-Poole's[3] Cairo: The 'dual' city

Stanley Lane-Poole is among those scholars who had published extensively on late nineteenth-century Cairo. He started his career on Cairo by editing his uncle's (Edward W. Lane) work describing the city in the 1820/30s that he named *Cairo: Fifty Years Ago*. He also worked as a teacher, and his final position in Cairo was as a member of the Comité (Commission for the Preservation of Arab Monuments). Besides editing Lane's book, he wrote two books *Cairo: Sketches of its History, Monuments, and Social Life* (1898), and *The Story of Cairo* (1906), as well as other books on Islam.

Lane-Poole in his book *The Story of Cairo*[4], although written after residing in the city for twenty years, refers to the streets of Muslim Cairo (he also referred to it as Egyptian Cairo) as hardly spoilt, and to him it was in a great degree the city of the *Arabian Nights*. He starts the book by explaining that Cairo in the fullest sense had been a medieval city, where it still retained at the beginning of the twentieth century much of its medieval character. He refers to Cairo of his time as "The Two Cities" that he further named the 'European' and the 'Egyptian' Cairo. To him the city was also changing but not in all aspects, where he alludes to the improvements introduced in the city within the last twenty years, the time of the British occupation. To him, if it were not for the work of the British during the occupation, the city would have been frozen and never developed. He writes:

> *"We have given them public order and security, solvency without too heavy taxation, an efficient administration, even-handed justice, the means of higher education, and above all to every man his fair share of enriching Nile."* (Lane-Poole, 1906)

According to Lane-Poole, Cairo never acquired any order before actual colonialism where its people were illiterate, lacked all urban amenities, and *only* acquired them after their contact with the Europeans. He referred to those reforms as "the reforms of the Firengy [foreigners]". In reality, as will be demonstrated in the second part of the paper, the reforms and the 'project of modernity' were much underway earlier on before the presence of the British.

In contrast to the above statement, Lane- Poole himself also questioned all the new urban amenities introduced in the city to the natives where he had written:

> *"[T]hen all this fiddling with water and drains and streets; what is it all for? . . . [having] put pipes and patent traps and other godless improvements into the mosques, will one's prayers be better than they were in the pleasant pervasive odor of the old fetid tanks? The streets are broader, no doubt, to let the Firengis roll by in their two horsed 'arabiyas and splash the Faithful with mud."* (Lane-Poole, 1906, viii)

From this it is clear that 'modernity' as we know it was good for Europeans, and foreign residents but not for Cairenes. When talking about 'natives' he refers to that true Cairene as "the same man whom we saw keeping shop or taking his venture to sea in the faithful mirror of the *Arabian Nights.*" Although living in the city for almost two decades, it is still the characters of the *Arabian Nights* from the Middle Ages that appeal the most to Lane-Poole to represent the original natives.

Throughout his different works, Lane-Poole's "Two Cairos" were distinct in character, though but slenderly divided in site. The 'Egyptian Cairo' is that of the natives' quarters and the bazaars, whereas, to him, European Cairo knew little of its medieval sister. He later explains that in European Cairo, there are signs that another Cairo, an Oriental Muslim Cairo, existed not far away. (Lane-Poole, 1906) To him, there were characteristic sights in Cairo in which old and new were oddly blended, and only connected by means of a street. Al-Muski Street seemed to be the cutting fissure between the two cities.

Lane-Poole had a different reading to the city where he explained how the older quarters were not something worth experiencing, but rather to be viewed from a distance. He wrote:

> *"It is in the bazaars that one feels most the shock of contact with the unfamiliar; but, in a less intimate yet deeply impressive way, to drink in the full inspiration of the Muslim city one must climb to the ramparts of the Citadel about sunset and slowly absorb the wonderful panorama that spreads below and around. . . All in that wide range beneath the eye is of the East Eastern. . . Here we realise Cairo for the first time as a city of the Middle Ages, and more than that, a city with an heritage from the dawn of history."* (Lane-Poole, 1906: 26-31)

It is very clear how he turned Cairo to be a 'museum', or on display, to be just viewed and looked at as a 'picturesque' scene from the top of the hill. In addition, he also portrayed the trip as: "unhappily, to get there one usually passes along the most terribly defaced street in all Cairo." It is a bit confusing as in that case, he is not referring to the narrow streets of the medieval quarters but to Muhammad Ali Boulevard[5], where he was criticising the project and the opening up of the street in the older quarters, and made it a point to remind the reader that it happened before "England took the reins of Egypt."

Again, Lane-Poole referred to the experience of getting to Cairo as "approaching a city which was still to all intents the city of *Arabian Nights*." Although he traces the stories of *The Arabian Nights* to their origins in Persia and India and Baghdad, he also confirms that it was in Cairo where these famous tales took their definite shape. In his analysis to the stories, he explained that the topography portrayed in those stories is that of Cairo, that of the Caliph's city, and the society they describe was precisely that "orthodox Muslim society of the Cairene type."[6] We also learn about the "Thousand and One Nights" in other parts of his book where he wrote about Cairene merchants and directly related it to the characters of the Nights. He referred to these different characters assuming that all readers were familiar with them,[7] (Lane-Poole, 1906, 265) and accordingly wove the characters of the *One Thousand and One Nights* into his own story of Cairo.

His other work *Cairo: Sketches from its History, Monuments and Social Life* also starts by reminding the reader of the co-relation between Cairo and the dreams of the *Arabian Nights* of the travellers' childhood where he explained that every step in the old quarters of the Mohammedan city told a story of the famous past. (Lane-Poole, 1898) He wrote:

> *"A few streets away from the European quarter it is easy to dream that we are acting a part in the veracious histories of the Thousand and One Nights, which do, in fact, describe Cairo and its people as they were in the fourteenth century."*
> (Lane-Poole, 1898: 2)

He explained that the older quarters were the stage for the stories as "in its very dilapidation the city helps the illusion." In that same sense, it is this 'illusion' that becomes the subject matter of Lane-Poole's works, and helps him establish the "dual" city. To make a clear distinction between the tourists, foreigners, elites and the natives, he explained how thousands of tourists, mounted on thousands of donkeys, explored the native quarters every winter, however they did not belong to European Cairo, they were "birds of passage", and not inhabitants of the city. The foreigners actually living in his "European Cairo" did not ride donkeys, but were only dragged to the bazaars at rare occasions, and with reluctance by the importunity of some enthusiastic visitor.

He also explains that the "blessed conservatism" of the East was behind maintaining much of the old city in its beautiful ruinous unprogressive order. Lane-Poole refers to al-Ghuriyyah as one of those larger but narrow streets which is distinguished with the name of *shari'* or thoroughfare. The streets of the older quarters were so narrow as Lane-Poole explained: "[W]atch the throng passes by: the ungainly camels, laden with brushwood or green fodder, which seem to threaten to sweep everything and everybody out of the street." (Lane-Poole, 1906: 8)

Lane-Poole described his second city "European Cairo", by tracing its origins to the times of the Ottomans in the sixteenth-century, where the Amirs and Beys resided in that area, and started to develop it. He claimed that the mosques of Egypt suffered damage and demolition, not under the Ottomans, but under Muhammad Ali. He explained that this was due to Muhammad Ali's regime where he laid hands on the Waqfs or religious endowments that for many centuries had been in trust for the maintenance of the mosques and colleges of Egypt. (Lane-Poole, 1906)

Lane-Poole affirmed that it was the Europeanising movement in the nineteenth-century, "inevitable, and in many ways most desirable" that had brought with it a large destruction of mosques and other historic buildings that impeded carriage traffic or stood in the way of the new streets and squares which the viceroys of Egypt planned with little or no regard to existing antiquities. According to the official documents available at the Cairo National Archives, these assertions can be challenged in many aspects regarding the implementation of the physical aspects of the modernisation plan. Lane-Poole described the new quarters of the city as:

> *"The limits of the modern additions are only too plain, but the street improvements of the reigning dynasty happily do not extend to the old Fatimy quarter, . . . the modern additions extend only from the Ezbekiyya to the river, and consist of a number of parallel boulevards and* rondes places, *where ugly western uniformity is partly redeemed by some cool verandahed villas and the grateful shade of trees."* (Lane-Poole, 1898: 7)

Lane-Poole explained that not only did the buildings in the Frank quarters give a European impression, but also half the people in the streets wore European dress, modified in the case of native officials and others by the red fez, and coat. Also, the street lamps were familiar as those of their native isle back in their countries.

Between his two works, Lane-Poole entitled the new addition in Cairo once as "European Cairo", and another time as "England's work in Egypt" thus attributing all the credits, and development in the city to the British. He referred to the changes that occurred during the fifty years previous to writing the book, and accordingly compared Cairo of his time to that of his uncle Edward W. Lane. Yet with all the changes regarding transportation and building of streets, he still criticised those developments as "dusty, rattling, and old-fashioned," (Lane-Poole, 1898, 283) thus portraying his dissatisfaction with the quality of service.

He further described the new quarters of the city where the European hotel, in that case he was referring to Shepherd's Hotel, was the meeting place for all of Frankish Cairo. In the surrounding area in Azbakiyyah were European shops that displayed their plate-glass windows. Lane-Poole explained that foreigners/travellers/or non-natives had to go some distance before they could find the picturesque cupboard-shop of the East. Also, if those travellers desired, they could "hear a French opera and see a French ballet in a theatre exactly resembling those [they] left behind in London." Not only that but they can also go around, if they chose, "in as European a manner as through Switzerland." (Lane-Poole, 1898, 288)

It is not clear which Cairo he belonged to or admired. On one hand, he praised his European Cairo as it was pushing the city and Egypt forward towards development, and on the other hand, he also criticised those works and showed that they were just cheap imitations of those in Europe. He also pointed out that Egyptians were not sensitive to the Arab monuments, and demolished many in the process of modernising the city, as well as neglected others. Lane-Poole also explained the important role of the Comité for the Preservation of the Monuments of Arab Art, of which he was a member. According to Mahdy (Starkey, 1988) the Comité's role was about the construction of an exotic theme park, a Disneyesque world designed to bring the *Arabian Nights'* fantasy to life.[8]

From Lane-Poole's perspective, two main points appear in all of his writings. First, Cairo was a 'dual' city that he referred to as the Egyptian, and the European. However, using this dichotomy, I would refer to them as "The City of the Arabian Nights", and "The City of the Europeans", where the first reflected his imagination as an illusionary city and projected the *Arabian Nights* on reality, and the other represented the reality just like his cities back home. Second, the duality that he established had many facets to it: us/them; east/west; Lane's Cairo/his Cairo, and others. It is only through these dualities, that it was easier for him to visualise and comprehend Cairo, as was not seeing the reality, but rather creating the Orient.

## Lady Duff Gordon's Cairo: From the imaginary to the real

There are several reasons that led me to choose these letters among the works I am analysing for those encounters. First of all those were letters written between 1863 and 1865, at the beginning of the period of Khedive Ismail, the starting period of Cairene modernity. Second, they are letters that were not intended by their author to be published at the time she had been writing them, and thus could be used to an extent as a first hand on information on the city, without being filtered for the readers or audience. Finally, it had been written by a woman, who lived for an extensive period of time in Egypt, and had not been engaged by any means in any official position, like the other authors I have chosen to analyse their works.

Sara Austin had been the one responsible for putting the letters together in a volume that she published under the title *Letters From Egypt 1863-65*, and in her preface she pointed out some of the issues that I see worth discussing here. First, she alluded to the fact that Lady Duff-Gordon had written them while she was sick, "far from all the resources which civilised society offers to the suffering body and the weary and dejected spirit; above all, far from all the objects of the dearest affections." From this it is clear that Austin hardly had any information about Egypt and its people, and she was preparing the reader for that. Not only that, but she had also reflected on Lady Gordon's friendship with the Egyptians, and her life in Egypt by writing: "no doubt her admiration of her Arab friends will appear to many groundless or exaggerated, and the indulgence with which she regards some of their usages which are the least to our taste excessive."[9] (Lady Duff-Gordon, 1865)

In her first letter written from the Port of Leghorn, Lady Gordon explained that she was looking forward to seeing the "beauty of Cairo." However she later explained that she does not think that she would get much good out of life in an Eastern town as "the dust is intolerable, and the stuffiness in doors very unwholesome."

By the third letter, Lady Gordon had arrived where she referred to "Grand Cairo" as the place from where she had been writing. She starts by saying "I write to you out of the real *Arabian Nights* . . . Cairo is a golden existence, all sunshine and poetry, and I must add, all kindness and civility."[10] When she was invited to attend a wedding, she kept referring to the characters of *The Arabian Nights*, as if she were part of one of the stories. In her visit to the bazaar to purchase items needed for her trip up the Nile, she kept referring to "more Arabian Nights", as if the stories had been the true thing, and her trip or tour in the city was the illusion.[11] In another part, she referred to her thoughts of Noor-ed-Deen Allee (a character form one of the stories), and wondered if a jennee (Genie) would take her anywhere if she would take up her night's lodging in one of the comfortable little cupola-covered buildings.

Lady Gordon seemed hesitant at one point when writing about the streets of Cairo as she said: "I suppose I shall be thought utterly paradoxical when I deny the much talked-of dirt. The narrow, dingy, damp, age blackened, dust-crusted, unpaved streets of Cairo are sweet as roses compared to those of the "Centre of Civilisation;" moreover an Arab crowd does not stink, even under this sun" (Lady Duff-Gordon, 1865). From her experience in the city, she saw much more and read deeper meanings than what the dust on those streets had reflected. It is also clear that she had read other works on Cairo where many authors had discussed extensively the dirt and the condition of the Cairene streets.

Lady Gordon left to Upper Egypt from November 1862 and returned back to Cairo in March 1863. In her writings she referred to the city as Cairo, except when she reiterated Omar's, her dragoman, conversation where he had referred to 'Masr al-Qahirah.' It is during that part of her trip that she started describing the city, she wrote:

> *"The more I see of the black slums of Cairo, the more in love I am with it. The dirtiest lane of Cairo is far sweeter than the best street of Paris. Here there is the dirt of negligence, and the dust of a land without rain, but nothing disgusting; and decent Arabs are as clean in their personal habits as English gentlemen. As to the beauty of Cairo, that no words can describe: the oldest European towns are tame and regular in comparison . . . Cairo is the Arabian Nights; there is a little Frankish varnish here and there, but the government, the people, all are unchanged since that most faithful picture of manners was drawn."* (Lady Duff-Gordon, 1865)

From her writings, one can extract several things about Cairo. She indeed referred to the beauty of the city, but she also referred to the dilapidated condition where she explained that the days of the beauty of Cairo "are numbered", as the mosques were falling into decay,[12] and the exquisite lattice windows were rotting away, and were being replaced by European glass, however, she made it clear that "only the people and the government remain unchanged." Interestingly enough, by her nineteenth letter, she referred to it as been written from 'Masr-el-Qahirah' and in between parentheses she wrote Cairo, where she had invoked the term used mostly by the natives. She left to Marseilles for the summer and came back in the fall. At this point, she hardly mentioned the *Arabian Nights*, as in her first letters she always referred to the stories. One can deduce that her point of reference had changed based on her own experience and encounter in the city that was what had become clear in her mind. It is very apparent how she started seeing through the myth and imagination, and wanted to see the real, and be part of it.

Lady Duff-Gordon represents some of those other group of travellers, who came to the city with a preconceived idea, but managed to change their point of reference, and comprehend beyond their imagination. It is only through experience, and willingness/desire that she was able to unveil the 'imaginary' and appreciate the 'real.'

# Edwin De Leon's Cairo: Fear of losing the imaginary to 'modernity'

Edwin de Leon's book *The Khedive's Egypt*, also known as "The Old House of Bondage Under New Masters", was published in 1878 after he served as the consul-general in Egypt (1854-1860). He described his first encounter in Egypt in Port Said, on his way to Ismailiyah, by writing: "again we're confronted with civilisation," in a way that affirmed that it had not been expected. (De Leon, 1878, 20) He made that comment when his luggage had been weighed on the departure by the steamer, where he further wrote: "Orientalism also took leave of us in a chorus of lamentations, from dragomen and porters, already heavily overpaid for real or imaginary services forced upon us."

The main focus here will be on his chapter entitled 'Old and New Cairo', describing his approach to Cairo in 1869 after years of development and change. De Leon contrasts the city to what had existed before, when he visited Cairo twelve years earlier, where he wrote:

> "It is on approaching the Cairo station that the great improvement of the city and its suburbs, becomes perceptible to the visitor who has been absent for several years. He rubs his eyes, and almost distrusts his vision; for looking up the Shubra road which leads into Cairo, as well as outside the former limits of the city, where formerly stretched for miles fields under cultivation, he now sees, far as his eyes can reach, in every direction well-built and even palatial residences, surrounded by gardens, adding on new cities, for miles." (De Leon, 1878)

He went further in contrasting the old and the new where he explained that old Cairo had been formerly surrounded by high and massive walls, and entered by a wide gate, both of which had disappeared, as broad boulevards opened an easy way into the city and out to the desert. He explained that the old had given place to the new where blocks of high buildings have replaced the 'picturesque' old erections of mud and wood, and accordingly surprises the returning visitor.

De Leon further referred to the disappearance of Azbakiyyah, the pride, the glory of the city and people, as it had vanished. He explained that the new stone buildings had arcades that were an imitation of those of the Rue de Rivoli at Paris. Not only that but the old Eastern buildings[13] were gone, and that 'picturesque' was replaced by European models. When discussing the park at Azbakiyyah, De Leon pointed out the changes as being converted into a French or German tea garden, under the auspices of a French ornamental gardener. He described it as "partly on the trim Versailles model, partly in imitation of Bois de Boulogne, with its artificial lake with swans in it, and small mock-steamers for sailing over three feet of water." (De Leon, 1878: 51)

De Leon does not point out the separation of the two Cairos as sharply as Lane-Poole did, but he rather contrasts the experiences in the different parts of the city. According to De Leon, at the opposite side of Azbakiyyah, near Muski (also referred to as the street of the Frank shops) the Arab population were accustomed nightly to assemble in a circle around some favourite story teller giving them a re-hash of the "Thousand and One Nights" stories. However, that seemed like the "mirage of the desert" where the oriental sights and sounds have passed away from the vision of the traveller. Not in all cases, as De Leon referred to other travellers that were happy as "sentimental travellers" and bewailed the substitution of cleanliness and order for dirt and disorder.[14]

De Leon referred to 'Ismailiyyah quarter', one of the new quarters, as "entirely a new creation, and is one of the prettiest portions of the city," where the Khedive's policy had been different regarding that area of the city. He encouraged the erection of good houses for the European and Europeanised residents, as well as he attracted new ones from abroad where he offered to give building lots to every person who would build a house of a fixed value, rising in proportion to the estimated worth of the gift. Accordingly, there had been lots that were mapped out in the rear of the hotels, where there were no buildings, on the outskirts of the city, and "a new town of several thousands of houses occupied the site." Some of the houses were palatial, with very little of the Eastern element perceptible about them.

With all these changes and 'improvement' of De Leon's "favourite city" (using his own words), he expressed that for that climate the old system of narrow streets, and exclusion of too much sunshine, together with the old plan of Eastern building, were best suited to the climate, place and people. De Leon had both praised and criticised the Khedive for his efforts in 'modernising' Cairo, where it is very clear form his writing how he had feared losing the Orient to 'modernity.'[15] It is as if he wanted Cairo to remain as the "authentic," and should not be approached by modernisation to maintain that illusion.

## The Natives' Cairo

*Once through the gate, the Pasha was entranced by the beautiful view and the splendour of the place. He was quite overcome with pleasure, he said, "Which ruler in this land owns this land?"*

*"It's public property," Isa Ibn Hisham replied. "It doesn't belong to any single person. The government created it as part of public service facilities for all classes of people to stroll in."*

*They started walking around the various parts of the garden, looking at the leafy trees, luxuriant branches, and pretty flowers. The pasha was shuddering for joy at the incredibly beautiful vista offered by this lush plantation . . . . We searched for somewhere to sit down for a rest and found a bench on the patio. The following conversation ensued as the occasion demanded.*

*Pasha: "Why isn't this place thronged with people" Why aren't they walking around looking at the beautiful views and taking advantage of the shade? You've just been telling me that the government has opened it up to anyone passing by. So why are the only people I can see those foreigners over there wearing their distinctive clothes with their wives and children by their side? Has the government reserved this place for Westerners and banned Egyptians from using it? Up till now, I haven't noticed a single Egyptian since we came in."*

Isa: *"The government doesn't discriminate between one nationality and another. Egyptians, it seems, have grown accustomed to scorning spiritual pleasures and utterly disregard them. It's as though Egyptians have put themselves into some kind of prison and confined their thoughts about the universe entirely to material things.*

Pasha: *"May the Creator and Maker be exalted! How is it that Egyptians have got into this habit of disregarding the enjoyment they can get from a blessing like this, by this I mean the observation and study of all kinds of things? The situation seems to have gone so far that foreigners have developed a liking for it and have far outshone the Egyptians.'*

Isa: *" As far as I can see, the only reason for it that Egyptians are consistently lazy. They can't be bothered to stimulate the innate feeling hidden deep inside them or to cultivate it through practice, meditation, and constant repetition. Foreigners, on the other hand, have devoted particular attention to this type of practice; they take the trouble to cultivate such traits, and it has become one of their most sophisticated arts. They have also developed a passion for ancient relics. They compete with each other to acquire them and go to excessive lengths to keep them exclusively to themselves.* (al-Muwaylihi as translated in Allen, 1992)

I started this section with that dialogue between two Egyptian characters to show another encounter with the 'modern' city, but in that case, it is with their own city. The work is structured around a minister of war from the time of Muhammad Ali (1805-1841) who is resurrected from his grave, and meets with the narrator, a contemporary Egyptian, who serves as his guide to a Cairo that is rapidly being transformed into a cosmopolitan metropolis with an administration heavily indebted to French and British influence.

## Al-Tahtawi's, Mubarak's, and al-Muwaylihi's Cairo: Misr al-Mahrusah (The Guarded Egypt/Cairo)

In this part, I show how Cairenes wrote about their city. I focus on how they portrayed the city not as a dual city, nor as the city of the *Arabian Nights*, but as Cairo (or Misr al-Mahrusah/The Guarded Egypt). The writings that I chose to analyse are by three Egyptian authors: Rifa'ah al-Tahtawi, Ali Mubarak, and Muhammad al-Muwaylihi. They produced different works in the form of journals, newspaper articles, novels, and topographical studies. Those three Egyptians have also travelled to Europe and produced accounts about the West to open the eyes of the natives to what had been taking place there. They had also brought back observations and varied perceptions of the West (Starkey, 1998). In my analysis, I focus on the different ways that those writers had chosen to represent the city. It is through the analysis of those works that we get a clear picture of Cairo, and its relationship with Europe. Those writers/intellectuals had been deeply involved in the affairs of the country, where they had a hand in directing the country's administrative, intellectual, political and urban set-up.

Starting with Rifa'ah al-Tahtawi[16], who had witnessed the transformation of Cairo, one gets another reading of the process of change. al-Tahtawi's *Takhlis al-Ibriz*, and *Manahij al-Albab al-Misriyyah* are among many works that he had written during his career. In *Takhlis al-Ibriz*, al-Tahtawi wrote about his trip to Paris, and described the everyday life in the West, where he had presented a factual account of European civilisation to the reader. He wrote about Parisians' relations to each other and the built environment, the order of the cities, the State and the government and the constitution. He also described the geography of the place, portrayed the population, customs, clothes, theatres, education and culture.

Al-Tahtawi described the open/outdoor public spaces in Paris, and compared them to the *maidans* of Cairo, and explained that some of them are of the same width, but more advanced in the level of cleanliness. He kept reminding the reader that whatever he was presenting might be strange and different from the natives' customs, but he was by no means exaggerating. To keep the reader on track and to some extent familiar with whatever he was presenting, he alluded to similarities and/or differences in Cairo where it was not explicit in all cases. In his description of Paris, in reference to Cairo, he wrote:

> " . . . *Some of the advantage that we see here is how they put the sewage system underground to supply the baths at the different locations of the city with water from the river, and also to the various tanks. This is simple as compared to Egypt where there they fill up the tanks with water that was carried and transferred by camels . . .Also, there is a major difference between the taste of the water from the Seine and that from the Nile, if they purify that of the Nile before they use it, it would be better than any medicine.* " (al-Tahtawi, 1849) [my translation]

Al-Tahtawi also acknowledged the beauties of Cairo where he wrote that if Misr (which is also Cairo) did indeed acquire the tools and skills of 'modernity', it would have been the Sultanate of all cities, and the leading city of the world. At different points, it is not clear whether al-Tahtawi wanted Egypt to adopt the French system as is or not. Al-Tahtawi's trip to Paris shaped his way of thought and intellectual career for the following decades until he died in 1873. In his other writings, al-Tahtawi supported the efforts for modernising Cairo, and had not described Cairo by any means as a 'dual city', nor as the city of *The Arabian Nights*. He focused at length on a cultural definition of Cairo and Egypt within a broader framework of world civilisations and history.

Ali Mubarak[17] had also studied in France in the 1840s, and when he returned back to Egypt, he held several administrative positions including Minister of Public Works and Minister of Education. He was also a writer where he had written a novel of four parts *Alam al-Din* (1882), a major biographical/topographical work *al-Khitat al-Tawfiqqiyah* (1889, twenty volumes that cover the history and geography of Egyptian cities), and several other books.

*Alam al-Din*[18] is a novel of an Azhari Shaykh who travels with an Englishman to Europe, and with whom he discussed in detail the positive and negative aspects of the two civilisations. The book's purpose was clearly educational, where Mubarak wrote about Arab and Egyptian history. It is structured around conversations between the Shaykh, his son, and the British orientalist. Many of the chapters (*musamarat*) are theoretical in nature, in the form of either a discourse between members, or a lecture by one of them to the others. Although Mubarak had chosen 'imaginary' characters for his stories, it is through them that we get a clear picture about Cairo and Egypt by comparing what they were seeing and hearing about the West with their own city.[19] Mubarak had written extensively about the new urban amenities (railroad, telegraph, postal service, opera house, theatres and parks) that had been introduced in Cairo, however, he did not refer to Cairo as a 'dual' city. (Mubarak, 1882) He had acknowledged the introduction of those new aspects of 'modernity,' and indeed believed that it did not alienate the urban culture, and the Cairene population.

Mubarak's other work *al-Khitat al-Tawfiqqiyah al-Jadidah*, does not deal only with Cairo but with all of Egypt. The sources were various, from traditional Arabic accounts, to those of European travellers, to maps, property records, and others. Although he referred to several of those tourists, yet his Cairo was not a 'dual' one. He explained that it had been divided into eighths (*athman*), for administrative purposes. Each eighth was divided into quarters, where there had been a variety of types of local types, and each district had its own economic and social personality. He also pointed out that there had been some inequality between the various districts, which is common in many cities. The *Khitat* is an important source as it provides social, religious, and architectural dimensions of life in nineteenth-century Egypt. Mubarak stated in his introduction that he was motivated to write in order to keep knowledge about the architectural and technological accomplishments of past generations from being lost to the collective memory.

Although Mubarak had incorporated some of the travellers and foreigners writings on Cairo, however, he made it a point to explain that he was aware that European orientalists were actively engaged in appropriating Egypt, its cities, its history, and its monuments for themselves and their governments. Several scholars (Berque, Campo, Baer, Hunter) have explained that the *Khitat* is a device for counteracting European intellectual appropriation of the land and for documenting the nationalist claim that Egypt was for the Egyptians.

As for Muhammad al-Muwaylihi's *Hadith Isa ibn Hisham*[20] (written in 1898, and published in 1907), it reflects a realistic portrayal of segments of Egyptian society (Allen, 1992). He had also written in particular about the reign of Khedive Ismail. He referred to many aspects of the society at the time, where he wrote about the clash of East and West, traditionalism and modernism in religion. Al-Muwaylihi, unlike al-Tahtawi and Mubarak, wrote about Egypt's situation in the latter part of the nineteenth-century where there had been an attempt to apply French law and an adapted European legal system, yet, he explained that that would have been applied on the 'whole,' rather than on a part, or segment of the city.

All of these narratives were attempts by their authors to provide information about the East in relation to the West for the Egyptian reading public. However, in doing so, most of them used comparative methods so as to make it easier for the reader to comprehend the extents of differences. In another work, Duse Mohamed refers to his account *In the Land of the Pharaohs: A Short History of Egypt* as a history of Egypt written from a native's point of view, and accordingly delivers it "as one having authority." In this sense, he explains that he aims to reveal the reality of that history as a statement of facts as Europeans, in their own version, of the city had used information imparted by the natives for native destruction. Furthermore, he explained that many Europeans who have resided in Egypt in the late nineteenth-century, or have spent some time there, seemed to have carried on the tradition of writing about Egypt form an authoritative point of view. (Mohamed, 1911)

# Conclusion: The effect of the 'one thousand and one nights'

As several scholars had explained, European travellers went to Egypt to bring back a picture of the 'exotic,' a nineteenth-century tradition that had been initiated and inspired by Napoleon's expedition. Very few studies had examined the 'culture of travel' in pre-colonial situations, which indicates that contemporary literature needs further attention.

As have been demonstrated, many of the above foreign writers alluded to, referred and or covered in depth the story of Cairo as that of "One Thousand and One Nights." Although at first hand it seemed that that was all what they knew about the East, and built as their frame of reference, however, in many of these writings we see it appearing over and over again. To them it was the 'real', and the reality became the 'imaginary'. In many cases the writers portrayed what they had imagined and desired, rather than what they were witnessing and experiencing.

It is this unfamiliarity with certain aspects of Cairo, and their imaginary blue print of the Oriental city that made it appear, or I would rather say, made writers portray it as a 'dual city'. In some of these cases, writers alluded to the different areas/districts of the city as different cities, however, contemporary scholars have interpreted those writings as descriptions of a dual city, and reiterated it. As a result, most of the literature dealing with nineteenth-century Cairo described the city in those terms, where travellers characterised it as a 'dual' representation of a single culture.

Although both Lane-Poole and De Leon have been comparing the old and the new Cairo, their points of reference were different. For Lane-Poole, he based all his works on comparing Cairo to Edward Lane's description of the city in the 1830s, whereas De Leon, was comparing it to what he had experienced before. Also, Lane-Poole had been writing from the position of being an Englishman during the British colonial period who had had a hand in some of the changes taking place, and thus clarifying his position, and explaining his role with the Comité. De Leon, on the other hand, an American consul-general, was writing to reflect on some of the works introduced by Khedive Ismail. Another point that I would like to highlight is that the 'duality' that appeared in many of these works stemmed from the authors' familiarity with their own cities, not only in terms of physical and urban form, but also in terms of social status.[21] In many ways, the expression 'dual city' was a European category of thought that they applied on the situation of Cairo without exerting effort to comprehend the unfamiliar structure of that city. One can argue that those travellers exerted more effort in reconstructing the Oriental picture, rather than documenting the reality.

# Endnotes

1.  *The Arabian Nights* were literally told stories, spoken stories, one a night for a thousand nights, and then one final night. In these stories, imagination, memory, invention, humor, mischief, laughter and anything else one may want to think of were included. The stories are about the Caliph Harun al-Rashid who was the ruler of Baghdad, the capital of Mesopotamia, which is now the country of Iraq, on the Persian Gulf in southwest Asia.

2.  Saroyan explains that the stories were another kind of Bible, social rather than religious, another kind of people's guidebook in matters of heart, head, body and spirit. It was first translated to French in 1704 by Antoine Galland, and then translated to English in 1811 by Jonathon Scott.

3.  Stanley Lane-Poole played different roles in the administration of Cairo at the turn of the twentieth-century.

4.  The Story of Cairo was written in 1902, and published in 1906. At that time, Lane-Poole was a professor of Arabic at Trinity College, Dublin.

5.  Muhammad Ali Boulevard was a street that linked the different quarters of Cairo, Azbakiyyah and the Citadel. Many scholars describe it as a true example of 'Haussmannization'. I challenge this assertion in other work.

6.  Lane-Poole, Stanley (1906), The Story of Cairo, (J. M. Dent and Co.) p. 261. He further gave a detailed account about the time when the Arabian Nights had been written. He explained that they were written for the people, for the audiences who gathered in coffee-shops to listen to the professional reciter, for the large uneducated middle class of Cairo.

7.  Lane-Poole wrote: "The Thousand and One Nights are full of such successful ventures. Did not the Second Shaykh who led the Two Black Hounds, describe how we then prepared merchandise and hired a ship and embarked our goods, and proceeded on our voyage for the space of a whole month, at the end of which we arrived at a city where we sold our merchandise."

8.  Several scholars (Hampikian, Bierman) have written extensively about the works of the Comité where they pointed to their active role in conservation projects. Although the Comité did extensive work, however, there were several other committees established earlier that carried on similar projects, and Lane-Poole never referred to in his works.

9.  Austin explained that she was determined to omit some of the passages that illustrated the manners and morals of the Arabs, however she discovered that to do so would be to rob the volume of much of its value.

10. In another part (p. 80) she wrote that "If anyone tries to make you believe any nonsense about "civilisation" in Egypt, laugh at it. The real life and the real people are exactly as described in that most veracious of books, the 'Thousand and One Nights.' The tyranny

is the same, the people are not altered; and very charming people they are." In another part (p. 96) she also referred to the Arabian Nights were she explained that she thought of her servant, Omar, as Badr-ed-Deen Hasan, another one of the characters of the stories.

11. Lady Gordon made it clear in many sections of her letters that none of the people she ran into, begged at all, or asked for baksheesh. This is a point that was repeated over and over again in many of the traveller accounts.

12. In a later section, she wrote that if she could afford it, she would have a sketch of a beloved old mosque of hers, "falling to decay", with three palm-trees growing in the middle of it. She further added that she would have a full book as everything was exquisite, and all was going.

13. He described those Eastern buildings as having latticed windows, and entrances beneath by a small door pierced in a thick wall, through which one passed into an inner open court in which was tethered a donkey, passing up a flight of narrow winding stone steps to enter the house. However, when he later visited these have changed based on European models that were square, formal, uniform, "hideous-looking imitations of the ugliest architecture in the world." (p. 51)

14. In that case, he is not opposing the changes as he wrote: "Much sentimental rubbish has been written about this improvement of Cairo; but in a sanitary and progressive point of view, no sensible man or woman, however sentimental can deny the improvement and growth of Cairo under the demolishing tendencies of the Khedive." He refers to many amenities of the European culture that had been introduced in Egypt including modes of transportation and carriages; smoking cigarettes and cigars; European fashions.

15. In his description of the Khedive and his achievements, De Leon alludes to the duality in his character too. He explained that the Khedive lived in a fashion partly European, partly Eastern, "European as to cuisine and mode of taking his meals, the latter of which he does in company with the chief members of his household, his chamberlains, private secretaries."

16. Rifa'ah al-Tahtawi was among those few native Egyptians to be admitted to official positions in the government. His major contribution to the reform was in the 'cultural' field. His contributions in the field of history had been immense.

17. Ali Mubarak had a relationship to and participation in the government. At that time, he was responsible for engineering the construction of Khedive Ismail's several projects, including palaces, streets, bridges, irrigation ditches, etc.

18. Alam al-Din is a four-volume work of fiction.

19. Al-Qadi explained that Mubarak aimed at using that form to be free to express his sharp ideas primarily about the East, and also about the West. Furthermore, she sought that Mubarak did not want to be "informative" but rather "instructive", and for that "descriptions" were not sufficient, where "judgments" were mandatory.

20. al-Muwaylihi uses Isa ibn Hisham, and the Pasha, along with the umda (mayor), and a playboy where he discusses a variety of institutions, social groups, and classes within Egyptian society.

21. Lady Gordon made this point clear where she wrote that one must come to the East to understand absolute social equality. She clarified that point by explaining that although there is no education, yet she found no reason why the donkey boy who ran beside her may not become a great man, as all Muslims are equal.

# References

Ahmed, L. (1978), *Edward W. lane: A Study of His Life and Works and of British Ideas of the Middle East in the Nineteenth-Century* (London: Longman).

Allen, R. (1992), *A Period of Time – A Study of Muhammad al-Muwaylihi's Hadith Isa ibn Hisham,* (Oxford: Ithaca Press).

Al-Shayyal, Gamal al-Din (1958), *al-Tarikh wa al-Muarikhun fi Misr fi al-Qarn al-Tasi' Ashr* (Cairo: Maktabat al-Nahdah al-Misriyyah).

Al-Tahtawi, Rifah Rafi (1849), *Takhlis al Ibriz fi Talkhis Bariz* (Cairo: Matba'at Bulaq), 2nd edition.

Berque, J. (1972), *Egypt: Imperialism and Revolution* (London: Faber and Faber).

Crabbs, J. A., Jr. (1984), The Writing of History in Nineteenth-Century Egypt: A Study in National Transformation (Cairo: AUC Press).

De Leon, E. (1878), *The Khedive's Egypt* (New York: Harper and Brothers, Publishers).

Grewal, I. (1996), *Home and Harem: Nation, Gender, Empire, and the Cultures of Travel* (Durham and London: Duke University Press).

Kalfatovic, M. R. (1992), *Nile Notes of a Howadji: A bibliography of Travellers' Tales from Egypt, from the Earliest Time to 1918,* (London: The Scarecrow Press).

Lady Duff-Gordon (1865), *Letters from Egypt* (London: Macmillan and Co.).

Lane, E. W. (1836), *An Account of the Manners and Customs of the Modern Egyptians, Written in Egypt* during the years 1833, 34 and 35, 2 volumes.

Lane, E. W. (1839-41), *The Thousand and One Nights*, commonly known in England as *The Arabian Nights' Entertainments*, translated in 4 volumes.

Lane-Poole, S. (1898) *Cairo: Sketches of its History, Monuments and Social Life* (London: J. S. Virtue).

Lane-Poole, S. (1906), *The Story of Cairo* (J. M. Dent and Co.).

MacKenzie, J. M. (1995), *Orientalism: History, Theory and the Arts* (Manchester: MUP).

Mitchell, T. (1988), *Colonising Egypt* (Cairo: AUC Press).

Mubarak, A. (1882), *Alam al-Din* (Alexandria: al-Mahrusah).

Mubarak, A. (1889), *al-Khitat al-Tawfiqiyyah al-Jadidah li-Misr al-Qahirah wa Muduniha wa Biladiha al-Qadimah wa al-Mahrusah*, 20 vols. (Bulaq: al-Matbah al Kubra al-Amiriyyah).

Saroyan, W. (1966), *The Arabian Nights*, for young readers, (New York: Platt and Munk).

Starkey, P. and Starkey, J. eds. (1988), *Travellers in Egypt* (London: I. B. Tauris).

Taylor, I. (1888), *Leaves from an Egyptian Note-Book* (London: Kegan Paul, Trench and Co.).

Tucker, J. E. (1986), *Women in Nineteenth-century Egypt* (Cairo: AUC Press).

Urry, J. (1990), *The Tourist Gaze: Leisure and Travel in Contemporary Societies*, (London: Sage Publications).

# City cultures as the object of cultural tourism 2000

*Patricia M Avery*

University of Wales Institute, UK

## Abstract

This paper starts from the premise that cultural tourism is not a panacea for economic problems, nor is it a recent new device to attract more tourists and consequently more money. The danger is that it is assumed that regeneration and urban revitalisation equals cultural tourism. There is a paucity of evidence, confirmed by a number of studies, such as those by Bianchini and Parkinson, that direct economic benefit has accrued from cultural industry strategies in Western European cities. The difficulties that need to be addressed if we are to create an urban environment fit to live in in twenty years time will largely depend upon the emphasis placed upon the cultural dimension rather than on purely economic grounds. A related problem is that of tourism on which cities are basing their economic strategies may well not guarantee long-term economic viability since they are increasingly forced into urban competition by the use of 'flagship' enterprises and the creation of cultural quarters.

This study strives to present a conceptual approach to examining city cultures, and, in particular, cultural quarters, of the challenges that lie ahead for cities to be able to compete world wide amidst the challenges of the new millennium.

The drive to renew Britain's cities, policies and programmes for urban regeneration will be discussed, focusing on the example of Temple Bar, Dublin, and asks whether lessons can be learned from this model. It is argued that whilst the focus for much research on urban regeneration have focused on an economic or functional emphasis, it is possible to switch to a more cultural and aesthetic emphasis. One of the central themes of this paper is that there has been a blurring of boundaries between the notions of culture; culture as 'a way of life' (the anthropological sense), and culture as the arts, spiritually elevating cultural products and experiences (high culture).

It can also be argued that on a global level we are witnessing the end of the dominance of a few metropolitan centres of artistic and intellectual life, with new forms of cultural capital, and a wider range of symbolic experiences on offer within an increasingly globalised (and more accessible) field of world cities. In this paper, the issue of how to formalise the collective representation of the legitimate interests of today's corporate consortia, without destroying the creative leap of the imagination which alone can breathe life into a concept and ensure that it will continue to refresh the spirit for generations to come, will be questioned.

In the attempt to draw people back to inner cities or to attract tourists, the imperative should be the same; that of creating a city, not merely of post-modern centres of consumption, play and entertainment, but as a means to build bridges through mobilising culture, not merely to become 'lures for capital', but by propelling culture to greater importance within the contemporary and future city.

# Introduction

The arts and cultural tourism are a relatively new area of study in economics, an area largely ignored by the founding fathers of economic theory, Adam Smith and Alfred Marshall. Essentially, the issue of the role of art and culture in economic development cannot be entirely separated from the questions of public support and resource allocation. However, since the early eighties, the case for using tourism to promote economic development in cities has been widely discussed. (Law, 1993) Deindustrialisation, unemployment and growing global competition, need to be constantly renewing their economies or face decline and death. Hence, over the last decade or so, many European towns and cities, conscious of growing competition from other cities and the need to redevelop and stimulate their economic activities and attract visitors, businesses and investors, have been launching urban regeneration schemes, in which culture, leisure and tourism play a central role There has been a proliferation of such schemes across Europe, particularly in ports, waterfronts and other run-down areas, which are centred primarily around museums, theatres, opera houses, urban theme parks, and more recently, large leisure cultural complexes.

One of the central themes of this paper is to question assumptions often made by both tourism and cultural organisations that such projects can be a panacea for economic problems essentially through attracting more visitors, despite little evidence that direct economic benefit always follows in the wake of such projects. Difficulties associated with developing mega complexes of this type are numerous such as the sheer scale of the operation, reconciling the wide range of objectives and interests and the prohibitive costs of carrying out market research, to name but a few. Even more disturbing, perhaps, is the lack of a framework for effective tourism and cultural partnerships, and for effective public-private sector partnerships. A case study of Temple Bar, Dublin, is presented, which highlights some of the issues and challenges posed by using culture, in particular, the cultural quarter, to promote Temple Bar, as an exemplary model for future development elsewhere. The likely role that culture and cultural tourism might play in making and maintaining a pluralistic culture in the new millennium is discussed, and it is suggested that it is the economics of culture that will determine the outcome of this project. It is concluded that investment in such projects is motivated by the opportunity to gain 'cultural capital' for a place, both to enable it to appear attractive to the service classes who act as the main employees of these new industries and who are the main consumers of these industries, as well as gaining direct image benefits.

# The convergence of tourism and culture

Cultural tourism cannot be understood as simply a 'new' market trend .According to Richards (1996) the growth of cultural tourism can better be explained as a consequence of wider social and economic trends, which mark either the period of 'late modernity' or postmodernity', depending on the terminology you prefer (Harvey, 1989).The consumption of tourism and culture is now organised by the 'tourism industry' (Smith, 1988) and the 'cultural industries'(Shaw, 1991b; Wynne,1992). The resulting changes in the organisation of production have created a whole new breed of attractions and intermediaries who supply culture specifically for tourist consumption, a phenomenon dubbed the 'heritage industry' by Hewison (1987). Indeed, these changes have implications for existing cultural attractions as well as newer ones. Using culture as a vehicle for tourism development and promotion is also becoming an important element of public policy (Richards). A notable development is the transformation of former productive spaces into areas of cultural tourism consumption. At the same time, consumption of all forms of culture has expanded, as the democratisation of culture and growth of middle class have opened up 'high' culture to a wider audience. As tourism and cultural consumption have grown, so the relationship between tourism and culture has also been transformed. Furthermore, many of the activities being expanded, such as culture and sport, with a consequence of this being that a blurring of boundaries between the 'high' arts and popular arts, has occurred. Postmodernity has reaffirmed this blurring of boundaries' and entails a resultant rejection of all the cultural manifestations of modernity as passe, and here the term 'culture' would be extended to include wider cultural production.

Featherstone (1991) points to rise of the term 'postmodernism' and the implications of the alleged shift towards the post-modern which serves to highlight the significance of culture in a dual emphasis upon (1) the emergence of new techniques of cultural production and reproduction which transform everyday experiences and practices, and (2) the questioning of the deep cultural coding of modernity in which knowledge was given foundational status in the sense that science, humanism, Marxism, or feminism claimed or aspired to offer humankind authoritative guidelines for both knowledge of the world and practical action within it.

# A cultural economy?

The rising tide of European policy interest in the economic dimension of the arts is a relatively recent development. Previously, concerns had centred more on cultural democracy and on the conditions and terms of work for those employed in the arts. It became apparent only as recently as 1983 at the Munich Research Workshop on 'Financing of Cultural Policy' (Myerscough 1988) that the economic importance of the arts was attracting an interest across Europe. More recently, the argument has moved on to higher ground, by relating the role of the arts to the fact that we live in an era of industrial restructuring characterised by the growing importance of the service industries (especially in the areas of finance, knowledge, travel and entertainment), and of industries based on new technologies exploiting information and the media. According to the Policy Studies Institute Report 'The Economic Importance of the Arts in Britain' by John Myerscough, 1988. "The success of cities in the post-industrial era will depend on their ability to build on the provision of services for regional, national and international markets. By the same token, regional policy must concentrate on attracting service industries as a more urgent aim than winning manufacturing plant." It goes on to say that the arts fit naturally into this frame, with the more specific questions being posed, being not so much whether the arts have an economic dimension, but rather, what is the specific and distinctive economic contribution the arts can make?

Amongst the specific objectives of the study, was the importance of cultural tourism and its contribution to the national economy, including the areas of possible development. Since this study was carried out, there has been increasing emphasis on developing urban regeneration schemes linked to cultural initiatives. According to Middleton (1991) an Arts Council report 'An Urban Renaissance' listed eighty initiatives. However, as he warns, euphoria can too easily set in. To put the case for the arts on a purely economic basis is to diminish their essential nature. There is no question but that they can provide a strong sub-structure for the renewal process, can generate energy and commitment locally to give coherence to the community.

## Evaluating the claims

The hypothesis that the arts, as cultural resources, contribute to various aspects of economic growth and development and the quality of life, is central to this paper. By cultural resources, we mean: cultural amenities that result directly or as externalities from art, artistic values, and artistic events; the economic impact of the arts industry; and cultural processes for achieving human development. These properties are derivative from the explicit objectives of artists and arts institutions. While considerable interest has been expressed in the idea of the arts as cultural resources and the role that they play in societal development, written works are scarce and tend to be advocacy position statements. The same could be said of the paucity of literature of the contribution of the arts to tourism and urban regeneration and urban/regional development.

The predominant research has focused on the economic impacts on the community of local non-profit arts institution. Considerable research was undertaken by arts councils in the United States, consisting of at least forty case studies. Typically, the primary form of export for the local arts industry is measured by the extent to which tourists visit or attend local arts institutions and events. (Hendon, 1980).Even though the local arts industry can generally take its products to distant consumers, the industry's ability to generate and support tourist trade locally is emphasised in these studies.

Most studies try to equate arts expenditures with export demand and multiplier effects with cause and effect. Typically, the economic impact studies are not content with the multiplier effect, or what Cwi calls an induced effect. To local arts spending is added the complementary expenditures made by arts consumers- expenditures for transport, restaurants, parking ,hotels, and so forth- and this total is subject to the multiplier effect. As Hendon argues, even if this kind of multiplier effect is limited only to scientific analysis of tourists' demand for local arts, an almost unanswerable question of cause and effect is implied: is the local arts industry generating even part of the tourism, or is it, like parking service, merely responding to it? It is clear what the local economy must do to meet the demand of the distant consumers. This is less clear for any service industry that must attract the customer to the locality in order to export its output. With tourism, it is almost totally vague. Arts institutions and activities will be only one of many attributes and amenities that rather inexplicably define "the product" demanded by tourists.

Other questions are (1) why do culture consumers choose to travel to exercise their demand, and (2) to what extent can an expanded local arts industry induce net new levels of cultural tourism at the regional or national level, rather than increasing the community's share of a constant market?

Pick (1996) goes further in disputing the claims of the optimistic picture of tourism and the benefits it brings to the arts. The conventional view is that arts attractions brought high-spending tourists into locations which benefited economically from spending. There were some anxieties about the overcrowding and pollution tourism seemed to bring, but they were usually brushed aside by organisations such as the British Tourist Authority. (1979):

> *The arguments for 'developing' precincts in inner cities simply for the purposes of attracting profitable tourists, has been widely heard in recent years. Usually, argues Pick, it is presented as if a government's sole interest in promoting the arts must be commercial. "It is not infrequently supported by 'impact studies' which purport to show that the overall spending generated by, for example, attracting tourists to a new arts festival- that is, spending in local hotels, bars, restaurants, transport services, etc- means that overall, investment in arts facilities which attract tourists yields handsome profits".*

Pick is equally critical of impact studies, emphasising that among their weaknesses are that when calculating the 'profits' by these means, the considerable costs of building new roads, parks, hotels and arenas are sometimes falsely amortised across several years of public expenditure. No calculation is made of the 'displacement factor' whereby local transport is disrupted, local retailers are sidelined and many locals leave the area to spend their money somewhere else because of the noise and crowds the new festival attracts. There is also a considerable 'knock-on' effect on local cultural activities which are not part of the mainstream event or festival. For example, local arts administrators in Vancouver calculated it was at least three years before they regained their local patronage after the disruptive effects of *Expo 86.*

Pick argues that it might be more useful to look at the commercial value of tourism by different means, such as a 'base line' impact study. This does not simply look at the spending generated by a new cultural attraction, but looks rather more at where the money ends up- that is, who actually gets the profits. By this second, more sophisticated analysis one cannot claim that the spending of tourists at a new arts festival is generating profits for the locality, if the money spent is actually enriching far distant corporations who own the hotels, restaurants, transport services, etc.

The truth may well be that encouraging tourism sometimes brings disadvantages, and that some of these disadvantages are economic. (Pick, 1996). Britain's own experience gives us useful evidence of this. In 1979 Britain's tourist account' (the balance between what incoming tourists spend in Britain and the British spend abroad) showed a slight profit. In 1980 it began to go into the red. By 1982 11,600,000 visitors to Britain spent £3,184,000,000 while Britains made 20,600,000 trips overseas and spent £3,650,000,000 - an average overall loss of £466,000000. Making the usual assumption that cultural spending is about 4% of total tourist spending the net loss to the arts on that year was some £20 million, In each succeeding year the loss on the 'tourist account' has inexorably risen, and now stands at more than £3.6 billion a year, representing an annual cultural loss to Britain of some £150,000,000.

Examples of wider cultural engagement within government policy frameworks have involved the Arts Council with urban regeneration, social reconstruction, the economic impact of the arts, and the arts contribution to tourism and the export effort.

Studies commissioned by the Arts Council included The Economic Importance of the Arts (Policy Studies institute, Myerscough 1998) which attempted for the first time to quantify the economic impact of the arts and to provide verifiable data to be used by the arts funding structure to argue for additional resources.

Similarly, the contribution of the arts to tourism and the export effort as part of the economic (described as business) case for an increased slice of the public purse was also developed. This is evidenced in the Arts Council of Great Britain's "A Great British Success Story". It claimed that tourists in 1984 brought £5,319m to Britain, and 60% of those in a survey that year confirmed that they were attracted to the country by the galleries and museums, with 35% by theatre and a further 22% by music. 14 years later, similar but more sophisticated claims have been made this time by the Department of Culture, Media and Sport in its Creative Industries Mapping Document with, for example, an aggregate value of exports estimated at £7.5bn.

However perhaps the real argument about tourism and the cultural economy lies more in cost benefit analysis, which looks at the cultural harm tourists may do. They will look at the cultural phenomenon known as 'falsification by tourism', which occurs when theatres simplify their dramatic, dance and musical offerings simply to please the tourists; when galleries show art works more to do with cultural PR than with the statements real artists are making; when museums selectively show artefacts that harmonise with the picture the tourist authorities want to give rather than the truth. It can then be said that even if the country's tourism account shows a net profit, something else, at least as valuable as the balance of payments, is still being destroyed.

The arts have provided conventional economics and institutional economics with almost as much difficulty as has religion. The trouble, however, does not permit rejection, for art obviously falls within the goods and service categories and therefore should be encompassed by economics. (Troub, 1980). As a multidimensional affair, art can be usefully examined from a number of perspectives; as a consumer good, as a production activity, as a private and/or public capital good, as technology, as concept, as action, as an instrumental approach to metaphysics, and so on. In past decades, conventional economics has accorded little attention to the arts and has included some rather curious notions about the association between the arts and the economy; but over the past several years conventional economics has focused on the arts industries with growing frequency.

According to Troub, what has emerged is an economics *of the* arts (economic analysis of demand and supply characteristics of various arts industries and of associations with other industries and the economy), *in* the arts (analysis of resource allocation decisions in arts administration), and *for* the arts (analysis of the case for public support, the efficiency of various levels and types of support, and so on). Analysts have drawn on consumption, production, industrial organisation and welfare theories, as well as other concepts in the conventional inventory. Difficulties, however, are sometimes encountered, and as Netzer noted, "Almost everyone considers the arts something different from the goods and services that we leave to the mercies of the marketplace" (1978, p. 15).

Over the decades economists working from the conventional perspectives of the discipline and the minority group labelled institutionalist have frequently viewed with one another with disdain, if not hostility. One of the several sources of conflict is mutual misunderstanding. It could equally be said that similar misunderstandings take place between the economists and the artists. Economics is looking at art through its own marginally tinted glasses, and art is beginning to look back with a jaundiced (but elegantly presented) eye.

In examining the relationship of the arts to urban development, Shananhan (1980), suggests that we may minimise some problems of definition if we consider urban development to have three components:

1. economic, emphasising the importance of the industry mix for a vital local economy;

2. physical development, encompassing the importance of the physical environment as the skeleton of the urban fabric; and

3. human development, emphasising the importance of meeting the total set of human needs.

Obviously, any strategy for setting developmental objectives requires an integration of these three aspects.

In making any evaluation of the claims of what the arts and cultural industries can do for cultural tourism and vice versa, it might be helpful to attempt to define what we mean by the arts. The term "the arts" is used ubiquitously in making these claims; the arts are loosely identified as:

1. an industry in which institutions and organisations are functioning as businesses interrelated with other local businesses;

2. broad-based to rather specific cultural amenities; or

3. cultural education, tools, and processes (Shanahan 1980).

Some of the claims that the arts contribute to revitalising urban centres have been better thought out than others. Some of the implied development resources are intangible and not empirically verifiable. In some cases, just how the tool can be increased or changed, let alone utilised, is unknown. What is clear is that the potential for the arts to be any one of these three development tools is almost entirely removed from the usual objective of artists and arts organisations- the achievement of artistic excellence. The single exception is the profit motive of the commercial portion of the arts industry.

Overall, the main linkage question is whether programme objectives designed to achieve artistic excellence can also be made to contribute directly to economic growth and development and an improved quality of life. Of course, the converse also applies: if these derivative objectives are emphasised, how can the achievement of artistic excellence be left uncompromised? There are no clear-cut answers to these questions, just as there is limited and uneven verification of the development potential of the arts.

However, several recent reports attempt to evaluate the role of the arts in economic growth and development, especially on the regional or local basis. The arts industry, it is generally agreed, is said to be capable of direct and immediate contributions to the local economic base- to the level of and trend in economic performance and the quality of life for individuals. Can the arts, as an industry like any other industry, be a part of the growth sector capable of producing net additional spendable income and jobs at the same level? If so, what part of the metropolitan region is most affected? These short term direct economic impacts have been researched extensively in some places, although empirically little is known about how the arts compare to other service industries in terms of contributing to import substitution. And what happens in the longer run? What determines the potential of an urban economy to sustain its growth and development as new industries and populations are born and old ones disappear? What happens as established industries have the opportunity to relocate or reallocate their industry activity? How can the arts, viewed as the set of development tools, influence these choices?

More importantly still, is the implication that these factors have the capability to hold or attract new generations of the population. And because of the decentralisation of the work place and suburbanisation of the population, it is important to include in the analysis the peculiar economic problems of the urban'centre.

## Arts industry, creative industries or cultural industries?

From the mid-1980s, the concept of 'cultural industry' was linked increasingly to various social-democratic projects of urban regeneration in British cities. These strategies were inspired by theoretical developments in the political economy of communications and culture Worpole states that 'In any programme of urban and civic renewal, getting the economic base right is going to be a key ingredient'' including, for him, cultural industry in the broadest sense. The difficulty here is that the cultural industry can become an exceptionally elastic concept, ranging from art and craft workshops all the way across to mass-market retailing, shopping as a creative pursuit.

The increasing emphasis on the commercialisation and the economic value of the arts and culture coincided with the use of the term 'cultural industries' to define this sector. The broader view of the arts was adopted by Myerscough (1988), who split the economic activities associated with arts and culture into three constituent parts:

1.  presentation of arts events and attractions (museums and galleries, theatres and concerts);

2.  production and distribution of performances by mechanical means (through broadcasting and the cinema);

3.   creation of cultural items for sale (books, pictures, discs and videos, craft items).

The activities under these headings make up the major economic contribution of cultural industries. It is interesting to see that the narrow view of arts referred to by Wynne as 'high culture' is the smallest of these sub-sections in economic terms.

Considerable interest has been aroused in the United Kingdom (UK) with regard to the economic role and function of the creative industries. This has been stimulated largely by the "New Labour" government and, for example, its representation of the nation to the world as 'Cool Britannia".

Chris Smith, Britain's New Labour Secretary of State for Culture, Media and Sport, indicated early in his ministry that the creative industries were a growth sector of the UK economy, and stated that

> *"It is incumbent on the government, in partnership with industry, to take active steps to promote economic growth in the creative and cultural sector. If we do not do so, then others will reap the economic reward"* (Creative Industries Task Force 1998).

The creative industry concept has as a result been enshrined in one of four key policy themes for the Department of Culture, Media and Sport (DCMS) - i.e. economic value. The other three themes, access, excellence and education, are the predictable interests of any Labour government, and Chris Smith reinforces this interpretation:

> *"as ensuring that the full economic and employment impact of the whole range of creative industries is acknowledged and assisted by government"* (Smith 1998).

Other examples of wider cultural engagement within government policy frameworks have involved the Arts Council with urban regeneration, social reconstruction, the economic impact of the arts, and the arts contribution to tourism and the export effort.

Local economies are changing: traditional industries are continuing to decline and jobs and growth are coming from different directions including cultural industries. In the past such activity was often derided as not creating real jobs or wealth. Yet today it is claimed that the Creative and Cultural Industries generate £57bn of wealth, with over 1,5000,000 people working in this sector. Yet there are some crucial tests for those heralding the brave new world of creative and cultural industries. Are jobs in these industries replacing the loss of traditional work? Are communities really being empowered by creative and cultural industries?

Smith confirmed that collecting and analysing data on the creative industries is problematic, and that claims made in the past are difficult to substantiate (Creative Industries Task Force Mapping Document 1998). Rather worryingly, a similar view was expressed as long ago as 1970 in the UNESCO report, Cultural Policy in Great Britain, which stated: *"Britain has undertaken little long range planning of any kind so far, not studied methods in other countries, nor taken much care over cultural information. Statistics in the whole field covered by this report are hard to come by, hard to compare, and hard to rely on."*

Nevertheless, the DCMS went ahead with an audit in 1998 and published the Creative Industries Mapping Document, which made the claim that these industries generated £57 billion revenues, with employment of circa 1 million, as described in Table 1.

**Table 1**

| Activity | Revenues (£m) | Employment |
|---|---|---|
| Advertising | 4,000 | 96,000 |
| Architecture | 1,500 | 30,000 |
| Arts and Antiques | 2,200 | 39,700 |
| Crafts | 400 | 25,000 |
| Design | 12,000 | 23,000 |
| Designer Fashion | 600 | 11,500 |
| Film | 900 | 33,000 |
| Leisure Software | 1,200 | 27,000 |
| Music | 3,600 | 160,000 |
| Performing Arts | 900 | 60,000 |
| Publishing | 16,300 | 125,000 |
| Software | 7,500 | 272,000 |
| Television and Radio | 6,400 | 63,500 |
| **Total** | **£57 billion** | **circa  1,000,000** |

*Source*: Mapping highlights, DCMS 1998

There remains, however, a proven need for accurate data to enable the monitoring and evaluation of the effectiveness of public policies directed towards the creative industries, but also for the regional social and economic strategies being established by the newly formed Development Agencies for England. Similar needs exist for the devolved arrangements in Wales and Scotland.

The Arts Council of Great Britain's arts economy strategy traditionally encompassed the traditional art forms; dance, drama, literature, music, visual arts and film. Newcomers to this portfolio were broadcasting and video, now a recognised part of the arts establishment.

Economics, was now driving the national, regional and local funding agendas. With the advent of the cultural industries, and arts economy, there was also an increasing awareness of the impact and speed of change being generated by new technology, particularly information technology and new media.

As a result, there was inevitably another attempt at defining the arts, which in this case was drawn from the Public Law 209 of the 89th United States Congress, "the term 'arts' includes, but is not limited to

> *"music (instrumental and vocal), dance, drama, folk art, creative writing, architecture and allied fields, painting, sculpture, photography, graphic and craft arts, industrial design, costume and fashion design, motion pictures, television, radio, tape and sound recording, the arts related to the presentation, performance, execution and exhibit of such major art forms, and the study and application of the arts to the human environment."*

This definition was also endorsed by the Education, Science and Arts Committee of the House of Commons in its 1982 report on funding the arts.

With the addition of heritage, libraries, restoration, antiques trade, printing, publishing, advertising and digital media, a 'new arts' definition begins to emerge which is increasingly cultural.

It seems as though the endemic British disease of pragmatism and additionality has again prevailed, with the arts worthy of public funds alongside sports, heritage, tourism and media. Government has then defined creative industries as "those activities which have their origin in individual creativity, skill and talent, and have a potential for wealth and job creation through the generation and exploitation of intellectual property." (Creative Industries Task Force 1998).

The sectors which have been identified within this definitional framework are:

> *"advertising, architecture, the art and antiques market, crafts, design, designer fashion, film, interactive leisure software, music, the performing arts, publishing software, television and radio"* (Creative Industries Task Force 1998).

However, there remain problems in how to categorise the creative and/or cultural industries. Given the difficulties of definition referred to earlier, and the 'fluidity' of the sector, it is predictable that the conventional categories used in the UK and Europe, standard industrial classifications (SIC) and standard occupational classifications (SOC), have proved imprecise tools for measuring the cultural and creative industries.

Unsurprisingly then, as there are further difficulties encountered when quantifying the cultural and creative industries, which do not stem from the general definitional debate. These can be broken down as

(i)   no coherent national categorisation of the cultural industries

(ii)   a lack of accurate primary data.

Attempts have been made, largely since the early 1980s, by Myerscough (1988), Cultural Trends, Policy Studies Institute (1989-93), O'Brien and Feist (1995) and Pratt (1997), as well as the Department of Culture, Media and Sports, to arrive at suitable categorisations for the sector. Much of the statistical evidence, however, used by the public sector agencies and government departments is traced to national census data, the Department for education and employment's labour force survey, and new earnings study, along with several studies by the Office for National Statistics. Eurostat, on behalf of the European Union, has also been generating information in this field. It is, however, in reality, secondary data with all the inherent weaknesses of such an approach. (Roodhouse, 1999).

# The role of the cultural industries in the economic regeneration of cities

During the 1980s and 1990s cultural industries and cultural policies have been developed by many cities facing major changes and decline in their local economies. Indeed, cultural initiatives now form an integral part of the economic regeneration strategies of many cities in the UK, Europe and North America not only for their role as contributor to the local economy, but in recognition of their importance as an economic catalyst and in projecting a locality's identity at a time of intense national and international inter-city competition for jobs, investment and visitors.

Although there is no blueprint, as such, local economic strategies generally emphasise the role of the cultural sector in all or a mix of the following:

- Re-positioning a city's image

- Attracting and retaining inward investment;

- Acting as a catalyst for economic regeneration;

- Stimulating urban vitality.

Cultural organisations, especially when touring, can positively reflect a locality's status, connecting cultural excellence with a city's wider business competitiveness in the minds of (potential) investors and visitors. (Policy Research Institute). However, the impacts of cultural policies are most clearly visible in the re-imaging strategies of some cities, as inter-urban competition is based less on natural resources, location and past reputation and more on the ability to develop and project spectacular place images and symbols as a means of attracting investment, highly skilled workers and visitors (Harvey 1988, 1989, 1990).

Figure 2.1 presents a typology of city image transformation, and illustrates the role of the cultural industries in the 'transitional' strategies of indicative European cities.

**Figure 2    A Typology of City Image Transformation**

| City Trajectory | | Cities |
|---|---|---|
| Declining and obsolete | →Reborn, lively and modern | Glasgow, Manchester, Bilbao, Liverpool |
| Provincial | →Innovative and cosmopolitan | Antwerp, Barcelona, Montpelier, Rennes, Grenoble, Karlsruhe, Seville, Nimes |
| Wealthy, but culturally Underdeveloped | →Wealthy and culturally sophisticated | Frankfurt, Rotterdam, Provincial Italian Cities |

*Source*: Adapted from LEDA (1995)

Typically, the cultural sector has been exploited by urban centres and policy makers to reposition a locality after a period of economic decline and restructuring. For instance, the role of cultural industries and policies in re-defining and improving Glasgow's external city image is now well documented (Booth and Boyle 1993). In Liverpool the development of prestigious cultural facilities and amenities has also been used as a means of projecting a positive city image. However, in recent years the wider strategic importance of the cultural sector has been emphasised. Indeed, in Merseyside's Objective 1 Structural Programming Document, a strategy that guides spending of £630 million over five years, the arts, culture and media industries are identified as one of the key 'drivers of change' responsible for realising the plan's strategic vision of becoming a

> *'prosperous European City Region with a diverse economic base, 'which provides access to employment for all sections within the local community, which develops its people, their skills, talents and well-being, and emphasises its role as a gateway between Europe and the rest of the world, establishes it as a Region of learning, arts and cultural excellence and innovation, and establishes it as a Region of environmental excellence that supports a high quality of life"* (Commission of the European Communities 1994).

Furthermore, the city's successful Regional Challenge Bid in 1995 to develop its New Media Factory and the opening of the Liverpool Institute for Performing Arts are cultural initiatives that are consistent with its mission to become a City of Learning with the ability and capacity to produce leading-edge products and services.

Similarly, the development of links between the cultural industries and new media and information technologies is a strategy that has been adopted by many European cities, such as Rennes, Montpellier, and Grenobles,, and presents an image of innovation and dynamism. In Karlsruhe, for example, the city council and state government have re-established the link between science and art by developing a Centre for arts and Media Technology, linked to a college of design (Landry and Bianchini 1995). It seeks to harness the potential of new developments such as computer animation, music and performing arts to produce commercial applications that will strengthen the city's economic base.

Wealthier cities like Frankfurt are consolidating their competitive advantage by tackling the gap between their high economic status and relatively low cultural standing as cities such as Barcelona, Milan, Paris and Berlin gear-up to compete as international centres of culture, finance and innovation (Bianchini 1993).

However, using cultural products per se to develop a city's competitive advantage by making it distinct from other cities in the national and global hierarchy maybe rendered moot by competing or alternative innovations arising elsewhere. Furthermore, if a local cultural policy is not linked to an economic and social development strategy that aims to meet both local and external needs it may have the counter productive effect of producing socially wasteful investments which compound, rather than ameliorate, underlying structural problems (Harvey 1988,1989).

Cultural policies are also used as a vehicle to support inward investment activity by offering the 'quality of life' desired by urban elites (for example Boogarts 1990, Griffith 1991, 1993, Booth and Boyle 1994, Lofteman and Nevin 1994), and increasingly by some cities as a marketing weapon when selling themselves as places for capital investment (Kearns and Philo 1993). Indeed, many local and regional development agencies in the UK have become ever more concerned with projecting positive cultural images in their promotional campaigns designed to attract mobile international investment. A trend that was confirmed in a recent study of UK development agencies, which found that a quarter of all agencies surveyed gave a primary focus to cultural factors in their marketing work, with all giving such factors a secondary emphasis (Griffith and Williams 1992).

## Cultural quarters

The cultural industries have played a significant role in the physical and environmental renewal of many cities in North America and Europe. In several UK cities cultural quarters and areas with a critical mass of arts activities have also generated positive impacts on the physical environment. For example, Sheffield's Cultural Industries Quarter, Birmingham's Custard Factory, the Northern Quarter in Manchester, Dean Clough in Halifax and the Kirklees Media Centre in Huddersfield to name only a few. The most recent addition came with the announcement that the £127 million Lowry Centre, located in the Salford Quays development, would receive £65 million from the Arts Council, Millennium Commission and National Heritage Memorial Funds. This project demonstrates the potency of the cultural sector as an agent of regeneration. The Centre which will incorporate the Lowry Gallery, a 1,600 seat auditorium, a 400 seat theatre and the Salford University's National Industrial Centre for Virtual Reality (Salford City Reporter 1996). The Centre's also expected to attract 700,000 visitors a year, creating 250 jobs directly and a further 1,500 indirectly and stimulate £60-70 million in private sector investment (Manchester City Council 1994). However, the positive environmental spillover and trickle-down effects are usually confined to the area under development (Law 1994).

The role of the cultural sector in developing urban tourism is a major feature of city economic development strategies as fierce inter-city rivalry to attract discerning visitors requires the provision of more differentiated leisure and art forms (Urry 1995). To attract visitors to Birmingham the city has emphasised the development and promotion of prestigious cultural organisations- City of Birmingham Symphony Orchestra, the Royal Ballet and D'Oyly Carte Opera companies and repertory theatre. And the physical cultural infrastructure- the £300 million Symphony Hall located the £1800 million International Convention Centre, the £57 million National Indoor Arena and the £260 million Brindley Place Festival Marketplace development (Loftman and Nevin 1994).

Other cities have also used planned programmes of festivals and events to raise their national and international profile with visitors, drawing on their cultural and community heritage. For instance, the Edinburgh Festival is estimated to generate £44 million of direct expenditure by visitors which supports 1,700 (fte) jobs in Scotland (Edinburgh City Council 1995). City of Drama 1994 in Manchester attracted 2 million visitors to paid events and injected £36 million into the local economy (Manchester City of Drama 1995).

Cultural amenities, festivals and public art can attract and retain residents, workers and visitors to urban centres, but they are especially important to the development of a city's evening and night-time economies. That is where economic, social and cultural transactions and activities are encouraged to take place over longer periods of time and beyond the confines of the 9-5 day. The extent to which people engage in activities after 5p.m. to constitute the evening economy will depend on the diversity and depth of cultural, retail and leisure provision (Policy Research Institute 1998).

The cultural sector is now often included within the urban regeneration of cities to address wider economic, social and cultural objectives. At a time of intense inter-city competition, the most successful cities are those which can reconcile (and satisfy) the social and economic needs of residents with the need to exploit their inherent or finessed competitive advantages as places attractive to investors, highly skilled workers and visitors.

## From culture to economics

The economic motivation for public investment in arts and culture has been a major focus of government policy in many parts of Europe in recent years. Tourists make an important contribution to the economic importance of the arts and increasingly culture and the arts are increasingly an important part of tourism strategies. It is, however, at the level of the city that most interest has been generated in the economic importance of cultural tourism.

Bianchini argues that there are two particular categories of European cities where cultural tourism is a primary objective of cultural policy. The first of these is 'declining cities'. These have used cultural policy to support strategies for the diversification of their economic base and the reconstruction of their image. New investment in inner city arts and cultural projects became the means for reconstructing the external image of many European cities. The aim here was to attract new investment and to generate physical and environmental renewal through service industries expansion, with investment in the arts a major catalyst for economic development. Included within this category he includes Glasgow, Sheffield, Liverpool, Birmingham, Hamburg, Bochum, Rotterdam, Lille, and Genoa. (Richards 1996).

The second category Bianchini refers to are those cities where cultural tourism is particularly important are termed 'cultural capitals'. These are cities which are recognised as major cultural centres but which have had to invest heavily in cultural infrastructure just the same because of competition from other European cities. They are investing to maintain their lead in the European league table. Included in this category are London, Edinburgh, Paris, Copenhagen, Amsterdam, Berlin and Rome. Prestigious projects such the Musee d'Orsay, the Museum of Science and Technology, the Louvre Pyramid, and the Opera at La Bastille in Paris in the 1980s in Paris are prime examples.

Richards (1996) maintains that in the past, culture and tourism were regarded as separate spheres, and cultural institutions in particular fought hard to avoid the supposedly negative impacts of visitor orientation and commercialisation. However, the dichotomies between culture and economy and culture and tourism have been increasingly hard to maintain. The collapse of distinction between culture and economy is marked by a growing exploitation of cultural resources for commercial ends. Indeed, interestingly, Richards argues that the heritage attractions identified by Hewison (1987) in the UK in the mid-1980s can now be seen as the precursor of a much wider commercialisation of cultural resources, which is summarised in the concept of the 'cultural industries' (Wynne, 1992).

Economic motives have been given further prominence by a growing dissatisfaction with traditional policies for stimulating cultural participation. Art and culture are becoming increasingly interchangeable with sport and tourism, as elements in an overall destination marketing mix. However, critics are the increasing emphasis on economic considerations of the arts are many. Justin Lewis (1990) has sought to resolve the contradictoriness of an economic rationale for public policy in 'the arts' by insisting upon *cultural purpose,* not only aspirationally but also in making sense of what actually happens. Lewis (1990:130) argues that the economic case put by the likes of Rees-Mogg (1985) and more substantially by John Mysercough (1988) is flawed when taken to its logical conclusion: "If we wanted an arts funding strategy based upon economic benefit, we would *not* spend the money in the way we do now. The arts are funded according to particular aesthetic judgements, not on the basis of tourism and industrial strategy."

One of the many dangers include the considerable problems of coordination for public sector agencies. The fragmentation of cultural tourism supply, covering as it does public, private and voluntary sectors, and a wide range of tourism, heritage and arts organisations, makes it hard to ensure that all sectors of the cultural tourism 'industry' are working in concert. (Richards 1996). Policy-makers will need to ensure that a coordination function is not solely dictated by the predominantly economic logic of performance indicators but that the public sector also retains a function in ensuring access to culture and promoting a climate in which cultural creativity can flourish.

The contribution made by art and sports activity to the local economy and society is set to win greater recognition through the local cultural strategies now being drawn up as part of a new government scheme. There are now plans for all councils to draw up strategies for the support and development of cultural activities and creative industries. The aim is to encourage councils to devise a cultural strategy which not only responds to what the community wants, but helps boost the economy and encourage regeneration. The government wants the local cultural strategies to link to other local plans, and take into account relevant national and regional agendas.

A steering group drawn from the Department of Culture, Media and Sport, the Department of the Environment, Transport and the Regions and the local Government Association has drawn up guidance on the preparation of the new cultural strategies. It lists the benefits of such strategies as including a clear rationale for supporting activities, bringing culture to centre stage in local authorities, helping to deliver best value, promoting partnerships and acting as a lever for obtaining external funding.

The aims are far reaching. As well as taking on board developments in the Lottery grant allocation process and the Best Value regime, the themes of quality, access, raising standards and the promotion of cultural sector jobs are expected to be central to these strategies.. At the moment, most local authorities either take a service specific approach to delivering cultural strategies, or a thematic approach.

The idea of creating cultural quarters in towns and city centres is gaining favour as a way of securing the economic benefits of the flourishing arts-led industries. Sheffield, along with a growing number of other towns and cities, has in practice been very much looking to replace jobs in old industries with new "culturally" based pockets of activity in specific, and often very tightly defined locations close to the urban centre, including the National Centre for Popular Music.

As we have seen, culture, in the context of urban development, has quite a loose definition, covering not just high art such as opera, drama or classical music, but also areas such as media, communications, film, pop music, 'learning' and art. Southwark's recreation of the Shakespearean traditions of London's Bankside and Wolverhampton's nightlife strategy illustrate two ends of this spectrum.

Tourism has only recently become an item on the economic agenda of many inner-city local authorities. The London Borough of Southwark (LBS), which is immediately south of the River Thames, opposite the City of London, St Paul's Cathedral and the Tower of London, was slower to adopt positive tourism development policies than many other inner London Boroughs, despite having a number of established attractions. (Tyler 1999). Since 1993, however, policy initiatives have sought to establish a major cultural quarter for London on the south bank of the Thames. This includes, through hundreds of millions of pounds of investment in infrastructure, attractions and services, two new tourism clusters within the LBS, known as Bankside and the Pool of London. A third adjoining cluster known as the South Bank is in the neighbouring London Borough of Lambeth. promoting itself as the 'Millennium Mile', London's dramatic riverside, it is regarded by many as London's newest landmark.

As Tyler points out, the London Borough of Southwark has not always embraced the tourism industry as it does today. At present major cultural attractions, accommodation and infrastructure projects are underway within the north of the borough. These include the Tate Gallery of Modern Art Extension and the Globe Theatre, Wine World Experience, London Bridge Experience and other attractions. Several mid-range hotels are now being built while the multi-million pound Jubilee Line extension links Southwark, for the first time, directly to the West End of London.

The Council Officers Working Report on tourism was published as a committee paper in November 1988, and took a wide-ranging view of tourism, recognising that tourism may help Southwark become a better place to live and work. It also recognised that market-led tourism development was underway as a result of the LDDC's development policies, and that planning for tourism could help to mitigate any negative effects of unbridled development. It concluded:

> *Tourism is not a panacea for Southwark's economic and unemployment problems. It could, however, be a key strand in a development strategy for the borough...*

The Cross River Partnership (LBS together with the Borough of Lambeth, the City of Westminster and the City of London and other key public sector organisations) seeks to develop Bankside and the South Bank as a major new destination helping to relieve tourist congestion within the centre of London by developing a 'cultural quarter for London', improving the infrastructure and landscape of the area.

Indeed, this positive strategy symbolises how far Southwark Council have moved towards tourism over the last decade, although the job is far from finished the momentum now seems unstoppable. Southwark Council, along with its partners, would now seem to be creating London's new cultural quarter through what Bob Coomber (Chief Executive Officer, London Borough of Southwark) calls 'Sense with Vision'.

A major show of proactive leadership was to invest £2 million of the Council's money in a feasibility study to help convince the Tate Gallery's trustees that Bankside Power Station was the right choice for its new extension. The report concluded that the site would help generate 430-1000 jobs for the residents of Southwark and £16-35 million turnover for the trustees (McKinsey and Co.1994).

The concept is a logical extension of the widely accepted process of replacing jobs in manufacturing with those in the service industries. But a particular feature is he interest in the concept of creating specific "cultural quarters", or "cultural industry quarters", where a particular set of skills is used as the springboard for wider regeneration. Such ideas are quickly gaining currency in regeneration circles. The EDAW consultancy say it has never been so busy drawing up strategies for cultural quarters in towns across the country- meeting a demand, it says, which is fuelled by a recognition that cultural quarters can bring in the jobs as well as the tourists (Economic Development, in Urban Environment, 25 June 1998).

It is currently working in Sheffield, Birkenhead, Salford and Glasgow and Belfast on such schemes.

> *"Of course we are trying to integrate culture with all the rest of the other things, but there is a recognition that it can stand alone as a fulcrum for investment in a very specific area,"* says Doug Wheeler, director at EDAW's Glasgow office.

> *However, he warns that 'in cultural quarters you need a very specific urban management regime, related to mixed-use, planning, landscaping and residential development'.*

Paul Skelton, cultural team leader at Sheffield City Council, says the best results come when as many cultural businesses as possible are packed into a limited area, backed up with a lot of support services. "Over time this results in a sort of pressure cooker effect".

A strategy drawn up along these lines for Belfast envisages the redevelopment of the Cathedral Quarter, building on the arts businesses, including groups of performing artists already there. The overall plan is to use culture as the catalyst for environmental renewal, to attract capital spending up to £40m, and to generate new economic activity.

Both Wheeler and Sheffield's Paul Skelton believe that the right noises are finally coming out of the government, recognising the importance of culture in regeneration, through the funding of arts and culture in National Lottery grants, as well as the creation of specific projects such as the New Audiences schemes to help bring the arts to a wider range of organisations (UET 30 April 1998). The setting up of the Creative Industries Task Force to oversee links between government and the industries in 1997 is also seen as positive.

However, Skelton remains sceptical about the Government's motives, and warns that cultural quarters must remain distinct pockets of activity in towns and cities to have the biggest impact. " In a sense the Government is trying to bask in the reflected glory of schemes already up and running. It must not turn into an alphabet soup of competing agencies and perspectives. At a local level the result would be an extreme fragmentation of policy-steering any sort of coherent agenda through this maze will be difficult and time consuming".

# Case study: Temple Bar, Dublin

Temple Bar is a living community, in which residents, artists, cultural organisations and small businesses have co-existed for many years. A plan for the demolition of the area to make way for a transport centre in the 1980s was replaced by a plan to revitalise the area as the Cultural Quarter of Dublin City as a result of community action by this community.

In 1991, Temple Bar Properties was set up by Government to oversee the renewal of the area, and the company then made a proposal to Government for the capital funding of a programme of cultural developments, to be co-funded by the ERDF and the Irish-Government exchequer. This proposal is built on the existing cluster of cultural and artistic activities in Temple Bar, consolidating and expanding on what had already emerged spontaneously.

## Temple Bar's cultural quarter

Temple Bar is Dublin's cultural quarter. One of Europe's most innovative and successful urban renewal projects, it is a vibrant, living community, in which residents, artists, visitors, cultural organisations and small businesses co-exist. The Temple Bar area covers about 28 acres, located in the centre of Dublin and is bounded by the south quays of the River Liffey, Dame Street, Fishamble Street and Westmoreland Street. Temple Bar is Dublin's 'old city' precinct. No other part of Dublin has such a concentration of historical, architectural and archaeological features.

The area was first developed in the 18th and 19th centuries. However, by the 1970s and 1980s, it had begun to fall into decline. Through community pressure, a plan to turn the area into a central bus depot was defeated and the government launched the Temple Bar initiative as a flagship project to mark Dublin's year as European City of Culture in 1991. The Temple Bar urban renewal project began as a vision articulated by diverse groups of local, cultural and business organisations, architects and conservationists, who recognised the importance of the area.

The Temple Bar Cultural Quarter represents a concentration of predominantly contemporary arts and cultural practice; living artists, new media, experimental work in all artistic forms, including theatre, film, music, design and all of the visual and plastic arts. It is the belief of Temple Bar Properties that this rich diversity, concentrated in a small area, is the basis on which the cultural quarter will renew itself, and in turn, the cultural life of the community it serves.

## Policy

The cultural policy of Temple Bar Properties is to work with artists, cultural organisations and any other interested bodies to realise he development of Temple Bar's Cultural Quarter, building upon what has already taken place spontaneously in the area, and maximising this opportunity for cultural innovation and experimentation. This has found expression not only in the infrastructural programme, but also in a range of supporting initiatives, which have served to develop both the wider cultural agenda, and also the specific developmental needs of local artists, cultural organisations and cultural entrepreneurs.

The main cultural work of Temple Bar Properties 1991-1996 has been the devising and implementation of a programme of capital development, in close collaboration with artists and cultural organisations. Some of these organisations were already based in Temple Bar, some were based outside the area, and others were newly developed within Temple Bar Properties itself.

## Aims and Objectives

The objectives published by the company in 1992 are:

- The urban renewal of the Temple Bar area;

- The consolidation and development of cultural activity in Temple Bar;

- The regeneration of a resident population within Temple Bar;

- The expansion of interesting retail outlets and service industries in Temple Bar;

- The marketing of Temple Bar with the aim of attracting an increasing amount of business, activity and people to the area on a year-round basis;

- The improvement of the Temple Bar environment in co-operation with the appropriate authorities;

- To contribute to the creation of employment and economic growth.

Temple Bar Properties embarked on a two-phase development programme. Phase One ran from start-up in 1991 until 1996 and Phase Two ran from 1996 until 1999. The first phase involved the implementation of the EU Urban Pilot Project which agreed a number of agreed initiatives, including the development of the Irish Film Centre, infrastructural improvements and pedestrian routes, marketing, research and planning for the urban renewal of the area . This phase saw the realisation of many specific objectives. Numerous buildings and sites were re-developed; cultural centres were developed or refurbished; residential apartments were built and sold; retail units were let and sold; human resources and training initiatives were delivered, and a supporting strategic, environmental community and marketing plan around all of these initiatives was implemented.

Phase Two: 1996-1999 concentrated on the area west of Parliament Street also bounded by the Liffey Quays, Fishamble Street and Lord Edward Street. New development took on board the results of he archaeological investigations in the area and the requirement for substantial residential development in scale with the medieval pattern of the site which lay within the original city walls. In addition, the aim was to encourage and nurture a sense of "public ownership" of the cultural quarter through a strategy of promoting accessibility and participation in the activities, events, cultural centres and facilities of the area, the maximisation of employment opportunities, and the development of partnerships with the inner-city community organisations.

## The organisations, partnerships and stakeholders

To date, Temple Bar has experienced an intensive revitalisation programme. This has been realised because of the vital participation, on many levels, of people, partners and stakeholders, including local organisations, cultural organisations, state, semi-state and statutory bodies, business organisations and European organisations. The private sector too has played a most important role in the renewal of the area.

The financing has been equally complex, involving a combination of private and public sector funding. There is a broad mix of uses in the area- in the private sector, apartments, shops, hotels, bars, etc, and, in the public sector, cultural centres, streetscape improvement schemes, and the Green Building. The programme is aimed at catering for local residents, for Dubliners in general, and, of course, for foreign visitors. The provision of facilities has been undertaken with respect for the existing building stock and taking into account financial and heritage constraints, but it is the cultural aspect that has been of paramount concern in the development.

## The cultural programme

Particularly since the 1980s, cultural activity has been at the heart of Temple Bar's character. It has been the policy of Temple Bar Properties to integrate a recognition of the unique qualities of the area's heritage- history and contemporary- into all aspects of the development programmes.

While Temple Bar Properties has been centrally involved in the capital programme for the cultural centres, the company is equally conscious of the need for sustainable cultural businesses to operate the buildings. The cultural programme undertaken in Phase One, therefore, comprises the development of coherent business plans for the centres, integrated with the relevant initiatives in training and job creation, and other promotional supports. The development of the cultural mix in Temple Bar has been a strategic one. The plan was to consolidate the cultural uses which already existed while developing new complementary initiatives to realise a more complete and sustainable 'cultural quarter' Over the Phase One development, the mix of cultural centres and organisations is as follows:

*Cultural Organisations which already existed in Temple Bar*

1. The Irish Film Centre

2. Temple Bar Gallery and Studios

3. The Gallery of Photography

4. Temple Lane Studios

5. Sound Training Centre

6. Project Arts Centre

*Established Cultural Organisations new to Temple Bar*

7. Music Base

8. Dublin's Viking Adventure

9. DIT School of Photography

10. Photographic Archive of the National Library of Ireland

11. Black Church Print Studio and Original Print Gallery

12. Association of Artists in Ireland

13. Gaiety School of Acting

*New Cultural Organisations, initiated by Temple Bar Properties*

14. DESIGNyard, The Applied Arts Centre in Temple Bar

15. Arthouse, the Multi-Media Centre for the Arts

16. The Ark, A Cultural Centre for Children.

It is Temple Bar Properties' aspiration that Temple Bar will provide a working model of urban renewal for other development initiatives in Ireland and Europe. The European Commission has recognised this flagship project as an important model for future urban development in Europe. In this wider international context there is enormous interest in studying, evaluating and monitoring the processes and outcomes of the development. In the context of Dublin city, people are supporting the idea that the city will have its own inner-city enclave which has character and diversity to match the most interesting areas in cities world-wide. All of these factors, it was hoped, will come into clearer focus as Phase Two developed and as the realisation of a diverse yet integrated cultural quarter becomes a reality.

Phase One witnessed an innovative but practical investment in the cultural infrastructure of Temple Bar. It also realised the first part of a vision which integrated commercial, social and public activity and participation into that cultural mix. Over the coming years, Temple Bar Properties will continue to promote the cultural renewal of the area building on these strengths so as to sustain the integrity and viability of Temple Bar as a living part of the city. In the context of the programme and design and construction of Phase Two, Temple Bar Properties pledge to further involve artists and applied designers in a collaborative process which is integral to the innovative design of public spaces.

## Culture or conflict?

There are substantial challenges when culture is used to spearhead an urban renewal project.; 'the gentrification' of other areas is well documented. The proposal to concentrate on culture in the Temple Bar project originally came from Temple Bar's own cultural community who, fed up with leaking roofs and having seen the uncertainty which was created by earlier proposals for the area, seized the opportunity to propose permanent homes in Temple Bar for their organisations. Paradoxically, the fact that proposals which originated from the cultural community have been realised has given rise to unease within that community about the dangers posed to artistic creativity by State intervention. By stating that where the infrastructure is in place one expects better delivery of the finished artistic project', Colm O'Brian has pointed to a challenge facing the Temple Bar cultural community, which is as significant in its way as the threat of a bus station obliterating the area.

Other conflicts, or apparent conflicts, will be influential in the future of Temple Bar, and these must be taken into account of in any analysis of the redevelopment. (Magahy, Temple Bar Properties). Magahy believes that there is a creative tension between apparently conflicting uses and users of the area- for example, residents and publicans, commercial and not-for-profit enterprise, culture and tourism- which will in fact ensure the sustainability of he area. However, she is certain that a kind of 'area democracy' will maintain a balance, whereby one sector will not preside over another. 'Temple Bar has always been about contradiction and multiple uses, and the area is robust enough to sustain a high level of apparent conflict.

## On reading Temple Bar

Temple Bar is more than a series of discreet projects, and the fact that the overall project of renewal is still incomplete makes it difficult to form a comprehensive judgement. "In any event Temple Bar will never be 'finished', like Paris, it will continue to metamorphose over time as new uses place different demands on it". (Magahy). What is clear is that Temple Bar as a project is a large and ambitious one. It is perhaps now possible to see that much of the energy and imagination which has driven the individual elements has derived from the collective vision of the project as a whole. This is certainly the case of the whole being greater than the sum of its parts.

Today, Temple Bar forms a necessary heart to Dublin which it lacked and always needed if the city was to prosper. It has achieved this in physical terms, but also in revising perceptions of Dublin- a city until lately divided into independent mental zones. It has linked up the map in some way. Significantly, it has been achieved without the destruction of another quarter of the city; it has not replaced anything, but added to the overall.

The Temple Bar project raises as many questions as it answers, about the meaning of urban renewal, the approach to renovating the city, the new architecture, how the future of Dublin is taking shape, what it will contain. In McGonagle's view, Temple Bar is not just innovative urbanism or property development, economic regeneration or a series of cultural initiatives. "It is both a reflection of and a contribution to contemporary Irish society, and ultimately has to be tested as such" Its reading, therefore, cannot be limited to the limitations of any single strand of its programme. It is not a question of good or bad buildings or spaces, or of specific projects recognisable as art, bit of a holistic enterprise whose complete totality is more than the sum of its parts. (McGonagle 1996). It has been well argued elsewhere that Temple Bar includes all the elements of urban regeneration, cultural initiatives and public art, but it is the combination of these elements and Temple Bar's composite nature, originating in the instinctive and unsentimental economic action of artists, which amounts to a summary of the issues- dangers as well as opportunities- which face Ireland in the new Millennium.

## Cities: Buildings and people

Matt McNulty, Director-General of Bord Failte, argues that the success of Temple Bar is due to the approach which was founded on a respect for historic and architectural elements "Within an overall leadership and integrated vision, it permitted diversity and imagination, and drew benefits from both. One of its ground-breaking achievements is that it brought purpose and progress to an area where there were a myriad of different agendas and divergent interests. And it did so within an empowering transparency and constant public debate which was welcomed and vigorously engaged in."

Furthermore, McNulty argues that the Temple Bar project was unique and untried in Ireland, in that it would be led not by commerce, but by tourism, culture and the arts, and so the birth of the concept of a 'cultural quarter' for Dublin took shape. Benefits, for him, were not just to the tourism economy of the city, but to conservation, culture and the arts. "One of its determining strengths was that in tourism, cultural and arts terms, it gave practical expression to the technique of 'clustering', which understands and builds synergetically on many related elements."

However, Professor Leo Klaassen believes that policy-makers should bear in mind a caveat:

> *"Tourism should be largely disregarded as a factor in the process of urban renewal, not because it is not worthwhile, but because in the hierarchy of values, it comes long after the requirements of a loving local community which wants to be something else than just the keeper of a museum."*

He argues that disregarding tourism is not being against tourism; it is just to the contrary. When a historic town has been renovated according to sound ideas and principles, and has sought to provide for the local community, tourism will come anyway as a bonus. Tourism and local interests are far from opposed in the sphere of urban regeneration.

The example of Temple Bar is a case in point. In a country relying largely on rural tourism, the idea of such a 'culture hub' in the inner city of Dublin, so close to the mythical Trinity College, has transformed the function of the city on tourists' maps. Dublin has become a real destination for cultural tourism in Dublin. Even more unbelievable for a country of emigration. Temple Bar and the facilities available there have made Dublin a destination sought after by European artists and intellectuals looking for a pleasant cultural; environment in which to live and work.

# Conclusion

Temple Bar has capitalised on an existing core of artistic ventures to renew an old and historic area of the city, bringing in new long-term jobs and adding to the city's cultural life. Urban renewal projects such as Temple Bar have a value not only as a means of restoring physical capital, but perhaps even more importantly in generating social capital based on creativity and communality. Investment in culture is paying off in Ireland, where a study by Coopers and Lybrand has recently shown that 'culture employs 33,800 people in the country (70% full-time) who are generating an output of 441 million punts out of which subsidies represent less than 12% of revenues.

This highlights how the financial investment for the renaissance of Temple Bar is part of a more general strategy for Ireland to make culture a source of jobs and revenue, not just a pastime.

Is culture then equivalent to economic destiny? Fukuyama does not go so far. 'Culture is not an unbending, primordial force, but something shaped continuously by the flow of politicians and history'. However, culture can be something more than this. As we have seen in discussing its impact on the urban scene, it can be the engine for economic, social and environmental transformation of the space in which we live. 'Culture is not passive, rather it is one of the fastest growing and most labour-intensive industries in advanced nations. The expansion of leisure time and the growing demand for heritage, art, entertainment and cultural consumption are reshaping the function of cities and urban areas alike. Investments in art and aesthetic activities are viable and profitable in post-capitalist, knowledge-based economics' (Arzeni 1996).

The city is man's greatest collective artefact, and sometimes his greatest collective work of art. A city provides a framework for human activity and must needs change to meet the changing needs of those who live and work in it. Responsive to every nuance of demand, the city all the time adapts itself accordingly. Cities generate activity, and wealth, on an enormous scale, and new cultural spaces are increasingly seen as ways to bolster their economies through tourism. The experience of places like Covent Garden, one of the most popular tourist attractions in London after the Tower, showed that tourists do not make up the majority of those who now throng the area. A 1982 survey by the Greater London Council showed that nearly sixty per cent of visitors were Londoners. Covent Garden needed a new economic generator, and it has got one. What is important in the last analysis, is that Covent Garden has brought back to the capital an experience taken for granted in most big cities but long lost to Londoners themselves: the simple pleasures of eating, drinking, shopping, meeting friends, listening to music, watching the world go by, in an open-air setting designed for the purpose. The Masterplan for the South Bank in London has been described by architect Rick Mather as being an 'opportunity to create one of the most exciting and welcoming arts quarters in the world. Marcus Binney, *The Times* architecture correspondent, said: "After almost 50 years, the vision of a cultural centre on the river, buzzing with activity, could finally be realised". Mather describes his new cultural park as *"the best site in London"* and hopes it *"will become the new central square for the city"*.

Projects such as the Walsall Art Gallery, the Baltic Flour Mill and the Lowry Centre have, as part of lottery and European funding conditions, prepared advance economic impact studies which will continue as part of the monitoring after opening. The Lowry has become something of a catalyst for a regeneration project, which, together with other developments should create 11,000 jobs by the time the Imperial War Museum opens in 2004. Cultural and heritage attractions generated an estimated £5bn for the UK economy (British Tourist Authority 1998) However, as Ylva French and Sue Runyard warn, we must be careful not to overstate the impact cultural facilities have on the local economy. 'Only when all other critical factors including location and marketing are in place can a major exhibition or new venue can be expected to generate jobs and new spend". What is needed now in the UK is an extensive economic impact study on museums, galleries and cultural spaces, putting the local economic impact studies into context and 'showing that investment in arts and heritage can provide the best possible investment for a healthy national economy, as well as providing an invaluable educational, recreational and cultural resource for local communities' In the city of today, there should be no place for 'them' and 'us'; we are all responsible. As Middleton (1987) pointed out, we get the surroundings we deserve. " One does not have to be one hundred per cent determinist to believe that, if *we* shape our cities, so do *they* in some measure shape us. In working to give them grace and dignity, to make them a pleasure to live in, we are not only enriching day-to-day life for ourselves. We are helping to design the future of a civilised society.' That is the measure of the challenge we face.

# References

Adair, G. (1992), *The Postmodernist Always Rings Twice; Reflections on culture in the 90s*. Fourth Estate. London.

ACCIS Report. (1994), *The business of culture*. Ministry of Culture, Tourism and Recreation for the Advisory Committee on a Cultural Industries Sectoral Strategy.

Arts Council (1985), *A Great British Success Story: an invitation to the nation to invest in the arts*, London: Arts Council of Great Britain.

Arts Council (1993), *A Creative Future: National Arts and Media Strategy*, London: HMSO.

Arzeni, S. (1996), *Culture as Innovative Force*. in Temple Bar: The power of an idea. Temple Bar Properties.

Bianchini, F. (1993), *Culture, Conflict and Cities: Issues and Prospects for the 1990s*, in Parkinson, m. and Bianchini F (Eds), Cultural policy and Urban Regeneration: The West European Experience. University of Manchester Press, Manchester.

Bianchini, F. and Parkinson, M. (1993), *Cultural Policy and Urban Regeneration: the West European Experience*, Manchester: Manchester University Press.

Boogarts, I. (1990), *A New Urban Planning Tool Kit: Are Investments in the Arts and Culture New Tools for Revitalising the City?* Paper presented to the 6th International Conference on Cultural Economics, UMEA, Sweden.

Booth, P. and Boyle, R. (1994), *See Glasgow, See Culture*, in Parkinson, M and Bianchini, R. (Eds) Cultural Policy and Urban Regeneration: The West European Experience, University of Manchester Press, Manchester.

Corner, J. and Harvey, S. (1991), *Enterprise and Heritage; Crosscurrents of National Culture*. Routledge. London and New York.

Cwi, David. In Hendon, W. S. Shanahan, J. L. and MacDonald, A. J. *Economic Policy for the Arts*. Abt Books. Cambridge, Massachusetts.

Deakin, N. and Edwards, J. (1993), *The Enterprise Culture and the Inner City*. Routledge. London and New York.

Dublin, The Temple Bar Area - A Policy for its Future (1985), A report complied by the Dublin City Association of An Taisce.

Featherstone, M. (1991), *Consumer Culture and Postmodernism*. Sage Publications.

French, Y. and Runyard, S. (Feb. 2000), 'Show Me the Money' in *The Marketing and Public Relations Handbook for Museums, Galleries and Heritage Attractions*. The Stationery Office.

Fukuyama, F. (1995), *Trust: The Social Virtues and the Creation of Prosperity*. The Free Press, New York.

Grabler, K. Maier, G. Mazanec, J. A. and Wober, K. (1997), *International City Tourism; Analysis and Strategy*. Pinter. London and Washington.

Green, M. and Wilding, W. (1970), *Cultural Policy in Great Britain*. UNESCO.

Griffiths, R. (1991), *The Role of Cultural Policy in Urban Regeneration*, Paper presented at Seminar on 'Revitalising City Centres and Restructuring Industrial Cities', University of Lodz, Poland.

Griffith, A. and Williams, A. (1992*), Culture, Regional Image and Economic Development in the United Kingdom*, World Futures, 33, pp 105-29.

Harvey, D. (1988), 'Voodoo Cities', *New Statesman and Society*, 30 September.

Harvey, D. (1989), *The Urban Experience*, Blackwell, Oxford.

Hendon, W. S. Shanahan, J. L. and MacDonald, A. J.(eds) (1980), *Economic Policy for the Arts*. Abt Books, Cambridge. Massachusetts.

Hewison, R. (1987), *The Heritage Industry: Britain an a Climate of Decline*, London: Methuen.

Kearns, G. and Philo, C. (Eds) (1993), *Selling Places: The City as Cultural Capital, Past and Present*. Pergamon Press, Oxford.

Landry, C. and Bianchini, F. (1995), *The Creative City*. DEMOS, London.

Law, C. (1994), *Urban Tourism: Attracting Visitors to Large Cities*. Mansell, London.

Law, C. M. (ed) (1996), *Tourism in Major Cities*. International Thomson Business Press.

Lawson, Price. (1986), *A Report on the Economic and Employment Benefits to be Gained by the Borough from Tourist Related Development,* a report for the Southwark Chamber of Commerce.

Lewis, J. (1990). *Art, Culture and Enterprise*, London: Routledge.

Local Cultural Strategies, (1999), *Department for Culture*, Media and Sport.

Loftman, P. and Nevin, B. (1994), Prestige Project Developments: Economic Renaissance or Economic Myth? A Case Study of Birmingham, *Local Economy*, Volume 8, No 4 pp 307-325

London Borough of Southwark, (1988), *Towards a Strategy for Tourism:* Report of the International Working Party.

London Borough of Southwark, (1995a), *Tourism Strategy for Southwark.* A Report to the Regeneration and Environment Committee.

London Industrial Strategy,. (1985), The cultural industries. *London Industrial Strategy*, 11.

London Tourist Board, (1993), *Tourism Strategy for London: Action Plan 1994-97,* London: LTB.

Lury, C. (1997), Consumer Culture. Polity Press.

McGonagle, D. (1996), *Temple Bar; The Power of an Idea.* Temple Bar Properties Ltd.

McGuigan, J. (1996), *Culture and The Public Sphere.* Routledge. London and New York.

McKinsey, and Co. (1994), *Assessing the Economic Impact of the Tate Gallery of Modern Art at Bankside (Version 2),* Report for the London Borough of Southwark and The Tate Gallery.

Middleton, M. (1991), *Cities in Transition; The regeneration of Britain's inner cities.* Michael Joseph. London.

Middleton, M. (1987), *Man Made The Town.* The Bodley Head. London.

Myerscough, J. (1988), *The Economic Importance of the Arts in Britain.* Policy Studies Institute.

O'Brien, J. and Feist, A. (1997), *Employment in the arts and cultural industries. An analysis of the Labour Force Survey and other sources.* Arts Council of England.

O'Connor, B. and Cronin, M. (1993), *Tourism in Ireland; A critical analysis.* Cork University Press.

Pick, J. (1991), *Vile Jelly; the Birth, Life, and Lingering Death of the Arts Council of Great Britain.* Brynmill.

Pick, J. (1980), *The State of the Arts,* Eastbourne: City Arts/John Offord.

Policy Studies Institute, (1998), *Cultural Trends*, 28, London. Policy Studies Institute.

Policy Research Institute, (1994), *The Media industry in Leeds: A Sector Study.* Leeds Metropolitan University, Leeds.

Pratt, A (1999), *The Creative Industries in the UK: National, Regional and Local Dimensions and the problems of value and governance.*

Richards, G. (1996), *Cultural Tourism in Europe.* CAB International.

Rojek, C. and Urry, J. (1997), *Touring Cultures; transformations of travel and theory*. Routledge. London and New York.

Roodhouse, S. C. (2000), *Strategic Aspects of Cultural Policy; A Misinformed Strategy: The Creative and Cultural Industries Contribution to the UK Economy*. Paper presented to the FOKUS-ACEI Joint Symposium, Vienna.

Shanahan, J.S. (1980), *Economic Policy for the Arts*. Abt Books. Cambridge, Massachusetts.

Salford City Reporter, (1996), *'Grant Announced Towards Spectacular Centre for the arts at the Quays'*. 29 February.

Sheffield City Council, (1995), *Sheffield Cultural Industries Quarter: a Summary of Policy and strategy*. Sheffield City Council, Sheffield.

Smith, C. (1995), *Creative Britain*. Faber and Faber Limited, 2, 10-11.

Temple Bar, (1996), *The Power of an Idea*. Temple Bar Properties.

Temple Bar. Cultural Quarter, (1996), Temple Bar Properties.

The Employment and Economic Significance of the Cultural Industries in Ireland, (1996), *Summary Report*. Temple Bar Properties.

The Creative Industries Task Force, (1998), *Creative Industries. Mapping Document*. Department for Culture, Media and Sport, 2,3,6.

The Arts Council of Great Britain, (1985), *An invitation to the nation to invest in the arts. A Great British Success Story*. The Arts Council.

The Arts Council, (1988), *Better business for the arts. An introduction to the Arts Council Inventive Funding Scheme for arts organisations*. The Arts Council.

Throsby, D. (1994), The Production and Consumption of the arts: A View of Cultural Economics, *Journal of Economic Literature*, Volume 32,pp 1-29.

Troub, R. M. (1980), *The Arts in Economics: Conventional, Institutional, and Neoinstitutional*, in Hendon, W. S., Shanahan, J. L. and MacDonald, A. J. Economic Policy for the Arts. Abt Books. Cambridge, Massachusetts.

Urry, J. (1990), *The Tourist Gaze*, London and Newbury Park: Sage.

Urry, J. (1995), *Consuming laces*. Routledge, London.

Williams, R. (1981), *Culture*. Fontana Paperbacks.

Worpole, K. (1991), *'Trading Places- 'The City Workshop'* in Fisher, M. and Owen, U. eds, Whose Cities? London and New York: Penguin.

Wynne, D. and O'Connor, J.(1995), *'City Cultures' and the "New Cultural Intermediaries"*, paper presented to British Sociological Association Annual Conference, Leicester; April.

Zukin, S. (1988), *Loft Living - culture and Capital in Urban Change*, London: Century Hutchinson.

# Rural community-based tourism in Sabah: A case study of Bavanggazo Long House, Kudat

*Awangku Hassanal Bahar Pengiran Bagul*

University of Malaysia Sabah, Malaysia

## Abstract

The tourism industry in Malaysia has recently become one of the country's most important economic activities. The recently instituted Brunei-Indonesia-Malaysia-Philippines-East-ASEAN-Growth-Area (BIMP-EAGA) also has realised the potential of tourism as an important means of diversifying and fostering their economies. Sabah, as one of the states in Malaysia and a member of BIMP-EAGA, is blessed with unspoiled nature and variety of interesting ethnic groups. The state government of Sabah realised these resources' potential and promotes nature and culture for the tourism industry. Village tourism is promoted in Sabah where tourists can stay and experience village activities, enjoy meals of local produce, witness cultural dances and purchase handicrafts. This paper is focused on Bavanggazo Village. It is situated in the North of Sabah, is surrounded by jungle and is where the Rungus ethnic group live. Several villagers of Tinangol Village (adjacent to Bavanggazo Village) developed the idea of Bavanggazo Long House Kudat in 1992. They grouped together and created a new village i.e. Bavanggazo Village and collectively built a long house that caters to the tourists and was named Bavanggazo Long House. It was managed and financed by the family involved with the objective of improving their socio-economic status. Sabah Tourism Promotion Board or STPC and some local tour operators also assisted them in terms of marketing. It proved to be popular with both day and overnight visitors from Malaysia and overseas. In 1996, Bavanggazo Long House subcontracted its management for the duration of three years to a local tour operator, leading to conflicts among the family involved with the project. This paper will explore the development of the community-based tourism project of Bavanggazo Long House. It will address the issues of operations, employment of the families involved, management, distribution of benefits among families, management subcontracts to the local tour operators, environment conservation and the preservation of Rungus heritage and culture.

# Introduction

It has been an exciting last decade for the tourism industry in Malaysia where it has enjoyed rapid growth and survived the recent economic downturn. Sabah, one of the states in Malaysia, has also enjoyed growth in tourism with many developments in the urban and rural areas. With its natural and cultural diversity as the main assets in tourism, the Sabah government promoted Sabah's nature and culture as the state's main product. This is reflected in the latest Visit Sabah 2000 campaign where the buzzword is Sabah – Natur(e)ally!

There has been a lot of government encouragement for entrepreneurs especially in the rural community to set up small and medium scale tourism enterprises in the rural area. The most recently published Sabah Tourism Master Plan, or STM (1996) stated that an important goal of tourism development in the rural areas is to maximise community participation and distribution of socio-economic benefits to the rural communities. One of the main strategies to improve the living standard of the rural population in Sabah, in the context of tourism development, is the promotion of community enterprise. It is a collective activity initiated by the community themselves to raise socio-economic standards, improve their environment and subsequently uplift their quality of life. Based on the concept of self-help, mutual help and common ownership, the community enterprise concept encourages the participation of the local community in conceptualising their development needs and in the decision making over control of scarce economic resources (IDS/COMMMACT 1998).

Generally, there are several activities for the rural community in the Sabah tourism sector in Sabah (Teo, 1998). These are:

- Accommodation (including homestay programme, lodges, bed and breakfast)

- Home visitation for meal (including lunch, tea, dinner)

- Production and sale of handicrafts

- Full and part-time Employment (guides, dancers, boatmen, housekeepers, waiter, general worker)

- Making and sale of foods and beverages

- Carpentry services (boats, jetty, benches)

- Supply of petrol, diesel and gas

- Leasing/sale of land

Although most of the opportunities stated above are based on individual or family enterprises, they are also applicable for collective economic activities initiated by a community. This is due to the fact that the rural community is a 'big family' itself. Inter-marriages among community members are quite common. This is very true with the

Bavanggazo village community (Appendix 1). Most of the villagers are related to each other and most of them lived together in one long house (Appendix 2).

## Bavanggazo village and the Rungus people

Bavanggazo village is located approximately 130 km north of Kota Kinabalu (the capital city of Sabah) in the Matunggong sub-district, Kudat (Appendix 3). The Bavanggazo village area was formerly under another village, Tinangol Village, and was formally registered as a village by villagers who already owned land in this part of the Tinangol Village. Bavanggazo (*lit.* big river) got its name from a river that runs past through the area.

The people who live in Bavanggazo village are called the Rungus. They are the sub-tribe of the Kadazandusun indigenous ethnic group. There are only 40,000 Rungus people in the whole of Sabah and they can be found only in the Kudat and Bengkoka Peninsula at the northern tip of Sabah. The Sabah Tourism Promotion Corporation[1] promotes the Rungus tribe as very rare, as its population is marginal in the context of world population. Almost all the villagers are farmers and many of its women are quite renowned in their handicraft making skills.

## The development of Bavanggazo Long House Homestay Programme

In 1992, several villagers from Tinangol Village were selected by the Sabah Tourism Promotion Corporation to construct a replica of a Rungus long house for the Malaysia Fest celebration held at Malaysia's capital city, Kuala Lumpur. The villagers were overwhelmed with the tremendous response and interest from visitors to their long house exhibition. This initiated the idea to turn a long house into a tourist attraction. Meetings were conducted among the villagers to discuss the idea. The discussion extended to the Ministry of Tourism Development, Environment, Science and Technology. In the end, Sabah Tourism Promotion Corporation conducted a feasibility study and gave a positive result.

In early August 1992, the construction of the first long house with nine rooms was started. It was done collectively by the families involved using local materials such as tree barks and palm leaves, which were mostly free (Appendix 4). The use of electricity was deliberately excluded to provide an authentic traditional village environment (Appendix 5). Water supply came from two natural water reservoirs on the top of Gumantong Hill[2]. At this stage, Bavanggazo Long House was promoted as a homestay programme. The villagers stayed at the long house, which accommodated tourist at the same time. A souvenir shop was also constructed for the villagers to put up their handicrafts or local produce for sale. A jungle trail was established and selected villagers were appointed as trail guides.

At the beginning of the project, Sabah Tourism Promotion Corporations played an important role in promoting the Bavanggazo Long House. It established marketing channels through many Sabah based tour operators and travel agents. It also managed to organise a fund raising dinner to fund the project, and received positive response. The appointed manager of

Bavanggazo Long House was sent to field study, notably to the Sarawak Cultural Village[3] to learn the management of a tourist site.

In 1995, with the positive progress of the Bavanggazo Long House, the Sabah Government provided funds to build another 10-room long house and a modern communal bathroom facility. The second long house was exclusively for tourists. Nevertheless, tourists still can opt to stay with the villagers at the old long house.

In 1997, another fund was provided to Bavanggazo Long House for the construction of another seven-room long house and a two-room jungle hut. The hut was situated in the middle of the jungle on top of Gumantong Hill. This hut provides the jungle ambience for the more adventurous tourists who wanted to get close to nature.

## The management of Bavanggazo Long House

When the project first started, nine families from Tinangol Village were involved and they already had cultivated land in the area of Bavanggazo. They formed a committee and meetings were held every month to review the project. The chairman of the Bavanggazo Long House Project Committee also holds the position of Manager of the Bavanggazo Long House. He is the key person of the project, who also acts as an intermediary between the villagers (or committees) and other stakeholders. Surplus revenue, after all expenses were paid, would be put into a long house fund. The fund was established for the maintenance and welfare of those involved in the Bavanggazo Long House project. Involvement of tour operators and the Sabah Tourism Promotion Corporation was limited to providing advice. Some funds were also made available for the purpose of promoting the Bavanggazo Long House.

In June 1997, there was a drastic change in the management of Bavanggazo Long House. The first and second long house management was contracted out to a tour operator based in Kota Kinabalu. The villagers still managed the third long house. This arrangement would only be for a period of three years, from 1 June 1997 till 1 June 2000. Under this arrangement, the tour operator would be entitled to 85% of any revenue derived from the first and second long house operations. Ten percent of the profits received per year by the tour operator would be put into the long house fund as a gesture of goodwill.

The management contract was arranged between the manager of the Bavanggazo Long House and the tour operator. The arrangement was approved and arranged by the manager alone without any agreement from the committees. The majority of the villagers did not approve of the single-handed hand-over of the project to an 'outside' company, thereby turning their efforts from a 'community enterprise' initiated and managed by themselves into an employer-employee relationship. However, the pivotal role assumed by the manager and his skills and contacts made it difficult for the members to challenge his position. The manager still retained his position under the new management.

Few changes were made under the management of the tour operator. The most important changes made were to job structures (Appendix 6). As a important example, dance performers were paid monthly rather than after every performance. Another example was for the housekeepers to receive fixed incomes rather than commissions based according to the number of tourists, as before.

The owner of the tour operator usually visits Bavanggazo Village once a month to supervise the long house operations. The manager has to report once a month to the tour operator on matters pertaining to the operations of long houses and their financial performance.

However, due to the decreasing tourist arrivals, the project did not perform well financially. Therefore, the tour operators failed to pay the villagers their salaries on time and in full amount. Disputes over payments arose quite often. In November 1998, the agreement was revoked and replaced with a new one. The new agreement entitles the villagers 75% of the revenue and the 25% to the tour operator.

# Impacts of community-based ecotourism

## Economic benefits

Economic benefits from community-based tourism to Bavanggazo Village were derived from direct employment, part time job as musician or dancer (Appendix 7,8,9 and 10), production and sale of handicrafts as well as from the making and sale of food and beverages. The villagers also receive a percentage of the profit from the operation of the Bavanggazo Long House project.

However, the change of the management in 1997 reduced the direct benefits to the villagers. Dancers and musician used to earn RM10 per dance. They were usually paid right after the performance. After the new management took over, two different wage rates were introduced. The dancers are now to be paid RM5 per dance on a pre-booked performance, and RM10 per dance for on-the-spot performance. The new management, however, paid at the end of the month.

There are two souvenir shops in Bavanggazo Village. Both owners of the shops allow other villagers to put up their products for sale at the shops (Appendix 11). According to the souvenir shopkeepers, approximately 80% of products sold in the shops are traditional Rungus handicrafts/produce. Revenue from handicraft sales from the souvenir shops amounts to an average monthly gross income of about RM1, 000. With registered 25 participants in either of these shops, the average income from the sale of handicraft is about RM40 per month.

Some villagers are put in charge of any extra service required by tourists who stayed at the long houses. Usually, there will be somebody who is in charge of the cooking. Three meals per day usually cost RM25 per person. A laundry service is also provided upon request and the rate is negotiable.

The actual economic benefits are minimal and only supplementary to most of the participating family households. Only two to four families gained sufficient income from the project.

## Environment

The villagers both from Tinangol and Bavanggazo Village learnt that there were plans to turn the upper parts of Gumantong hill, which were under the jurisdiction of the Department of Forestry, to a plantation of *acacia* trees to be owned and managed by SAFODA. This plan will further degrade their water catchment area. Gumantong hill is seen by the villagers, apart from being a source of water, as an integral part of their tourism project. They offer guided treks for tourists through the forest and have plans to upgrade and extend the trails. Furthermore, in 1997, they built a two-room jungle hut on top of Gumantong Hill in order to diversify their accommodations and cater for more adventurous tourists.

The villagers of Tinangol Village responded by writing a letter of complaint. Villagers of Bavanggazo Village with an even higher stake in the conservation of the forest, reacted more furious. They went directly to the office of SAFODA in a neighbouring village and demanded the suspension of the plantation project.

The outcome of these protests is not clear yet. Nevertheless, the tourism project has provided an additional strong argument to conserve an important catchment area for Tinangol and Bavanggazo Village.

## Community

Preservation of some aspects of the Rungus heritage and culture was revitalised with the advent of the Bavanggazo long house project. Most of the villagers left behind their beliefs and culture when the first of many villagers was christianised in 1959 by Protestant missionaries. One of the many good examples of heritage and cultural preservation would be the preservation of the aspects of marriage ceremonies. Marriages after 1959 were mostly held at the church with couples wearing modern clothes. After the Bavanggazo Long House project started, some marriages of Bavanggazo villagers now follow the traditional Rungus marriage ceremony (Appendix 12). This is done largely to provide a cultural experience for the tourists, tour operators and outside agencies that involved in the project.

Conflict between the Tinangol and Bavanggazo villagers surfaced after the long house was constructed. Villagers from Bavanggazo Village started to disrupt the water supply from Gumantong Hill to Tinangol Village for their consumption. Since Gumantong Hill is the only available source of water for both villages, it was agreed in a meeting between the two villages that they would share the water source without disrupting each other's supply. Therefore, villagers from Bavanggazo Village secured funds to purchase a water tank and to install their own link to the common water collection site.

However, this agreement to share the water source at Gumantong Hill led to a new conflict. Villagers from Bavanggazo Village installed a 4-inch pipe to link the water collection site with their water tanks whereas Tinangol Village is linked with a 2-inch pipe. The smaller pipe to Tinangol Village supplies water for more than 100 families whereas the larger pipe supplies water for only about 20 families. Villagers from Tinangol village were dissatisfied as they saw this as an unfair implementation of their agreement.

# Summary and conclusion

This study on Bavanggazo Long House project aims to establish how far it has contributed to (i) the socio-economic development of the village community, and (ii) the self-help potential of the villagers promoted by the community enterprise.

In terms of economic development, the project provides a reasonable main and supplementary income for a number of villagers and has created some employment opportunities, although the wages are rather low.

The development of the project, from its beginning was an initiative taken by a group of villagers to implement management structure, which shifted control of the project to an outside agency. This manifested an already existing dependency pattern. The dependency of the project participants on the manger has been supplemented with a dependency on an outside tour agent. As such, the initiative taken by the villagers of Bavanggazo Village has not led to an improvement in their 'self-reliability'.

Support from outside institutions such as the Sabah Tourism Promotion Corporation, the Sabah State Government and tour operators, has failed to turn a village-based initiative into a successful community enterprise. Individual interest at the local level, as well as a diversity of interest of outside supporters, have hindered the elaboration of a more comprehensive approach to the development of the tourism project in Bavanggazo Village, and have failed to turn it into a successful collective economic activity.

The proposed plan by SAFODA to turn the top of the Gumantong Hill into an acacia tree plantation can seriously degrade a water catchment area. Villagers, especially from Bavanggazo Village, based their resistance to this plan on the importance of the catchment area as a source of water supply for both villages, and in the case of Bavanggazo Villagers, as an important attraction for tourists. The Bavanggazo Long House project provided a strong argument for the SAFODA plan to be suspended. It is believed that Bavanggazo Long House project may make a considerable contribution to the protection of the forests on Gumantong Hill.

However revival of some aspect of Rungus heritage and culture is a positive impact of the Bavanggazo Long House project. If the project is successful and expanding in the future, perhaps, more aspect of heritage and culture can be revived.

# Endnotes

1.  Marketing arm for Ministry of Tourism Development, Environment, Science and Technology, Sabah.

2.  A water reservoir is solely for Bavanggazo Village while the other one is shared with Tinangol Village.

3.  A tourism development project under Sarawak Economic Development Corporation. It is one of the most successful cultural tourism project in Malaysia and the only living museum in the world.

4.  Sabah Forestry Development Authority.

# References

Appel, G. N., (1994), The Rungus Dusun in: King, V. (ed.), *World Within: The Etnic Groups of Borneo*. Kuala Lumpur, S. Abdul Majeed and Co.

Bagul, H. (1999), A Small-Scale Tourism Enterprise: A Case Study of Bavanggazo Village, Kudat. *International Conference on Small and Medium Enterprises At New Crossroads: Challenges and Prospect*. 28-30 September 1999, Universiti Sains Malaysia, Penang.

Institute For Development Studies (Sabah), (1995), Bumiputera Participation in the State's Tourism Sector. *IDS Discussion Paper No. 5*. Kota Kinabalu, IDS.

Institute For Development Studies (Sabah) And Commonwealth Association For Local Action And Economic Development (Malaysia), (1998), 'Background' to *the Seminar on Community Enterprise: The Way Ahead*. Kota Kinabalu, Kuala Lumpur, IDS and COMMACT.

Sabah Tourism Promotion Corporation, (No date), *The Rungus and Their Longhouse Lifestyle*. Kota Kinabalu, STPC.

Schulze, H. And Suratman, S. (1999), *Villagers in Transition – Case Studies from Sabah*. Kota Kinabalu, Universiti Malaysia Sabah.

State Government of Sabah. (1997), *Sabah Tourism Master Plan – Main Report*. Kota Kinabalu, Ministry of Tourism and Environmental Development.

# Appendix 1

**Bavanggazo Village**

# Appendix 2

**A Traditional Rungus Long House**

# Appendix 3

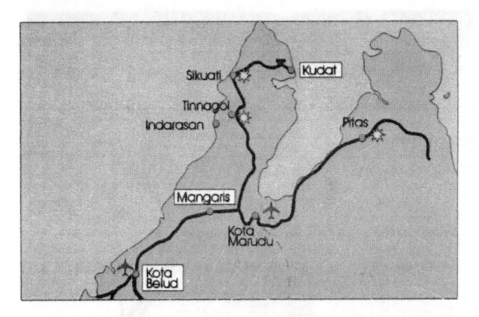

**The Location Of Kampung Tinnangol Which Is Adjacent To Kampung Bavanggazo**

*Source:* Sabah Tourism Master Plan 1997

# Appendix 4

**The Interior of a Traditional Rungus Long House**

# Appendix 5

**Electricity is Deliberately Excluded to Create an Atuthentic Traditional Village Ambience**

## Appendix 6

| Before New Management | | | After New Management | | |
|---|---|---|---|---|---|
| Job Title | Job Description | Income Per Month (Rm) | Job Title | Job Description | Income Per Month (Rm) |
| Manager | Oversees the whole operation, marketing | 500 | Manager | Overseas the whole operation and report to The tour operator monthly | 500 |
| Assistant Manager | The second person after the manager. He will take over the management in the absence of the manager | 500 | Assistant Manager | The second person after the manager. He will take over the management in the absence of the manager. He also has to report to the tour operator. | 500 |
| Housekeepers | In charge of the maintenance of the long house (bedrooms and kitchen) | RM1.75 per tourists* | Housekeepers | In charge of the maintenance of the long house (bedrooms and kitchen) | 250 |
| Maintenance Man | In charge of lighting and bathroom facilities | As above | Maintenance Man I | In charge of lighting and bathroom facilities | 120 |
| | | | Maintenance Man II | In charge of surrounding area | 50 |
| | | | Gardener I | In charge of lawn | 50 |
| | | | Gardener II | In charge of lawn | 50 |

## Appendix 7

**Mongiggol Sumandai – A Traditional Rungus Dance Performed by a Group of a Man and Three Women**

## Appendix 8

**The Dance Performance are Performed by Four Groups of Dancers, Which Were Formed at The Beginning of Bavanggazo Long House Project**

# Appendix 9

**Magunatip – Another Type of Rungus Traditional Dance Performed for the Tourists**

# Appendix 10

**Gong – A Major Musical Instrument in Traditional Rungus Dance**

# Appendix 11

**Trying on a Traditional Rungus Dress i.e. Banat, on Sale at the Souvenirs Shop**

# Appendix 12

**Rungus Women in full Traditional Costumes in a Rungus Wedding Ceremony**

# Sports events and tourism: Effects of motor car rallying on rural communities in mid Wales

*Paul Blakey, Martin Metcalfe,*
*John Mitchell and Peter Weatherhead*

Warrington Collegiate Institute, UK

## Introduction

The purpose of this research is to examine the effects of motor car rallying on rural communities, using Mid Wales as a case-study region. It is intended that ultimately this will take an holistic approach, considering economic, cultural, social and environmental effects of the sport. The research presented in this paper represents only a part of this larger (and on-going) project. It focuses on the social effects of motor car rallying, in particular concentrating on attitudes of residents in the study area towards those who visit the area both to participate in, and watch, car rallying. Impetus for such research comes from an interest in the sport of motor car rallying, a realisation of the growing prominence of sports tourism – the context within which the research is set - as an emerging academic discipline and an understanding that sports events, whatever their scale, may equally have advantages and disadvantages for rural as well as urban areas.

Motor sport, including car rallying, has a high profile in the UK due to media coverage, political controversy and sponsorship legislation. Recent incidents such as the death of a young spectator at a rally in Northumberland serve only to heighten this profile. Approximately fifteen car rallies of differing size and status are held in the study area alone each year, from locally organised club rallies to the Network Q Rally of Great Britain. Each of these events attracts varying numbers of participants and spectators. The paper identifies and discusses issues regarding the social effects of the sport on the residents of the area, particularly examining the attitudes of residents to rally in the community of Llanidloes in Mid Wales.

## The confluence of sport and tourism

As a background to the study, and to set the context in which the research has been carried out, the nature of sports tourism will be discussed. Tourism and sport are now firmly established in British society, both as industries and phenomena, and also regarding their study and research in higher education. There are obvious links between the two areas - it has long been appreciated that the tourism impacts, in economic, social, cultural and environmental terms, of 'blue-riband' events (e.g. Olympic Games, Football World Cup) can have long term effects on specific localities (Law, 1993; Standeven and De Knop, 1999). However, it is only recently that the interest in the field of sports tourism has developed and dramatically increased. Despite a general lack of text book material, increasingly more journal articles are being produced on sports tourism, and from a growing range of academic backgrounds (Gammon and Robinson, 1998). Initiatives such as the internet-based Journal of Sports Tourism have aided the development of sports tourism, yet it is important to acknowledge that as an area of academic study it is still very much in its infancy. Much of the research into sports tourism published to date has concentrated upon either an historical appreciation of sports tourism (see early issues of the Journal of Sports Tourism) or a discussion of the conceptual nature of sports tourism and the characteristics of the sports tourist (see, for example, Gammon and Robinson, 1997; Delpy, 1998; Gibson, 1998a). Additionally, regional studies have more often than not provided broad overviews of sports tourism at a national scale. Articles in the Journal of Sports Tourism have focused upon India (Ko Sasi, 1995), Spain (Miranda and Andueza, 1997) and the Dominican Republic (Coniston, 1999), amongst others.

Studies regarding the impact of sports tourism have tended to come from outside the UK and have in the main concentrated on the economic effects of individual sports on host regions in terms of income generation and tourism potential (Turco, 1998; Sofield and Sivan, 1994). More specifically reports published by UK Sport outline the importance of sports events in the UK, especially as income generators through tourism expenditure (UK Sport, 1998 a, b). This is supported by their own research into the benefits of hosting sporting events. In this research, an analysis is presented of the economic impacts of events such as the 1997 European Junior Swimming Championships, the 1997 World Badminton Championships and the 1997 Weetabix Women's British Open Golf Championships, amongst others (UK Sport, 1999). They conclude by stating:

> *"The decision to invest in major events – particularly by local authorities through strategies aimed at achieving economic development and its attendant benefits – is often perceived as being controversial. Sport, leisure and tourism are some of the few industries which are on long-term growth patterns and there are rewards to be had by investing in events as part of local development of these sectors"* (UK Sport, 1999, p.16)

There appear to be clear economic benefits, then, from the attraction of sports events that have tourism potential. It is also clear that in most sports it is not only the spectators that may be classed as tourists but the competitors also. In the context of rallying, this can be seen to include drivers, support teams, mechanics, marshals and so on. As Gibson suggests, there are three major types of sport tourism: nostalgia sport tourism, active sport tourism and event sport tourism (Gibson, 1998b), and car rallying may be seen as a sport where this model is appropriate. However, some of the reluctance of local authorities and other agencies to attract sporting events, as expressed in the quote above, may be more associated with the hidden social and environmental costs, rather than the visible economic benefits. It is for this reason that this research seeks to present a more balanced perspective by considering an holistic view. This paper considers social aspects of sports tourism events, in particular examining the attitudes of the residents to the rally when it is 'in town'. Further 'instalments' will consider economic, cultural and environmental aspects.

# Motor sport and car rallying

The Royal Automobile Club (RAC) was founded in 1903 and is technically the governing body for all motor sport in the United Kingdom. The Royal Automobile Club Motor Sports Association Limited (RAC MSA) has been a separate body from the RAC since the late 1970's and is responsible for the administration and control of motor sport rules. With the Motor Sports Council, who make the rules, the RAC MSA govern most forms of four-wheeled motor sport in the United Kingdom, including car rallying (RAC MSA, 1993). Rallies vary in scale from small locally organised club rallies through to major events such as the Network Q Rally of Great Britain. UK Sport (1998b, p.2) suggest three defining features of a major event:

- The event involves competition between teams and/or individuals representing a number of nations;

- The event attracts significant public interest, both at home and overseas, through spectator attendances and media coverage;

- The event is of international significance to the sport(s) concerned, and features prominently on their international calendar.

Clearly the Network Q Rally, formerly known as the Network Q RAC Rally and the British stage of the FIA World Rally Championship, fulfils the criteria stated above. As a special stage rally, it has far more emphasis placed on car preparation, speed and driver ability when compared to other forms of rallying (RAC MSA, 1993). A special stage rally can be defined as:

> "A rally consisting of a number of special, competitive (timed) stages (sections) to which competitors have exclusive access, each being over half a mile in length, on off road sites (though these can be either sealed or unsealed), joined by non competitive sections, which may or may not use the public highway".
> (Elson, Buller and Stanley, 1986, p28)

The Network Q Rally of Great Britain 1999 covered a total of 1155.7 miles and included 239.2 miles of competition over 22 timed special stages. It claims to be the biggest sporting event of any kind in the UK with over 1 million 'live' spectators and almost 11,000 volunteer officials. These numbers alone indicate a huge tourism potential. Moreover, media coverage is substantial; over 3 million viewers watched a single broadcast of the 1998 rally on BBC 2's 'Top Gear' programme. Additional coverage is provided by the terrestrial channels in both sports and news programming, and cable and satellite channels such as Eurosport and Sky Sports (The Western Mail, 20/11/99). A full day of competition, the middle day of the three day rally, occurs in Wales and the Welsh forests. In Mid Wales, Myherin and Sweet Lamb are each used for two stages of the competition.

# The study region: Llanidloes and the forests of mid-Wales

As the highways of England, Scotland and Wales may not be closed for special stages of rallies they tend to be run over private, Ministry Of Defence and Forestry Commission land, with disused airfields, stately homes, parks, water company and local authority land also being used, though to a lesser extent (Elson et al, 1986). As Colin Wilson of the RACMSA explains:

> *"Many British rallies use Forestry Commission gravel roads through some of Britain's most beautiful countryside but the drivers pay to maintain these roads".*
> (1996, p. 9)

The Forestry Commission was established under the 1919 Forestry Act to make good timber depletion from the First World War and since 1992 has formally been ascribed a dual role. Firstly, as the national Forestry Authority, it advises on and implements the policies of the government of the day and promotes the interests of forestry in general (Forestry Commission, 1992). Secondly, Forest Enterprise manages 40% of Great Britain's forests (1.1 million hectares) and is responsible for timber production amounting to 4.7 million cubic metres per year (Forestry Commission, 1997). Forest Enterprise is also responsible for the provision of recreational opportunities and conservation, and is committed to a policy of public access allowing the freedom to roam throughout its' woodlands subject to safety, conservation and legal constraints. In excess of 1700 recreational facilities are provided by Forest Enterprise, who also encourage the development of specialised sports and recreational activities which aim to act in harmony with the forest environment (Forestry Commission, 1992). Sites in England, Wales and Scotland owned by the Forestry Commission are used on a regular basis for stage rallying contributing around £750,000 per annum which, after timber production, is the Forestry Commission's second highest source of income (Wilson, 1996).

Forest Enterprise manages a number of large forest areas in Mid Wales. Hafren Forest is located on the eastern slopes of Plynlimon. The forest covers 40 square kilometres between the summit of Plynlimon and the market town of Llanidloes. Myherin forest is situated to the south of the A44 which runs between Aberystwyth and Llangurig. Both forests are used regularly for rallying and between the two is situated the Sweet Lamb sheep farm which is used for rally car testing, as a rally stage and as a popular spectator point. Both forests are well known as difficult stages for a number of rallies, including the Network Q competition (Weatherhead, 1999). Llanidloes was chosen as a focus for the research because it is the closest settlement of suitable size to these forest areas. It is a small market town with a population of around 4,000. A report produced by local planners in Montgomeryshire, and reported in the Cambrian News newspaper suggests that this population is characterised by an older population and a relatively small family size. The town is situated in a very rural area, yet with significant employment in the manufacturing industry. In comparison with the national average for Wales, it has higher than average percentages of older workers and retired people and correspondingly less in the 25 to 35 age group. The town is also characterised by higher than average levels of both car availability and home ownership together with a low recorded level of unemployment. Recent figures suggest that this runs at just 1.7% in the town, compared with the Powys average of 3.5% and the Wales average of 5% (Cambrian News, 18/11/99).

# Methodology

The method employed to examine the attitudes of rallying on the residents of these communities was a questionnaire survey. This was designed with a range of both open and closed questions in order to elicit suitable responses (Veal, 1992; Cohen and Manion 1997,). The questionnaire was piloted in neighbourhoods surrounding The Three Sisters Motor Racing Park, near Wigan, to check comprehensibility and to check whether responses would provide the required information. In the light of the pilot survey, minor amendments were made to the instructions to respondents, and the order of questions. A map-based dwellings count of Llandiloes was carried out from a 1:25,000 Ordnance Survey map in order to estimate the number of questionnaires needed. As a result, 1,000 questionnaires were distributed by hand to almost every household in the study area during the weekend of November 20th 1999, when the Network Q Rally was held. In accordance with the guidelines of Cohen and Manion (1997), a first class envelope, addressed to a named individual, was attached to the questionnaire to encourage completion and return. Additionally, each questionnaire included an invitation to return the document and enter a free prize draw to win a £30 gift voucher as a further incentive.

It was clear towards the end of questionnaires distribution that the number needed had been underestimated. As a result, although all 1,000 questionnaires were distributed, roughly 100 dwellings did not receive a copy; these dwellings were located in the eastern part of the town. Decisions were taken at the time to distribute to every other dwelling in this part of the town, rather than each dwelling, which had been done previously. Given this, future studies will seek to develop a more precise method of estimation of units needed.

# Initial findings

The 178 useable questionnaires returned equates to a response rate of 17.8%. This sample consisted of 62% males, 38% females. A further breakdown into age revealed 60% of respondents to be over 45 years of age, with the largest single category being over 65 (29.1%) and the smallest being 19-24 years (4.6%).

Almost all respondents (99.4%) stated that they were aware of rallying taking place in the local area. However, more than half (53%) never go to watch the sport. Of those who do watch, the forest is the most popular viewing point. Local residents were asked to state any direct contact they had with rally visitors (for example, spectators, mechanics, drivers, marshals). 81% reported no contact and 19% reported contact, predominantly through working in a local shop/garage or some other form of contact e.g. friends/relatives who participate in the sport.

Frequency data revealed a favourable attitude towards rally participants (marshals, drivers, car crew, other officials), with 46.4% responding positively and 16.2% responding negatively. The attitude towards rally spectators revealed a similarly weighted but opposite response, with 48.4% stating a negative attitude and 24.2% a positive attitude. Respondents stated their reasons for such attitudes towards rally participants and spectators and these revealed a number of common elements (see Table 1).

The research group categorised the stated reasons into clusters giving each one an appropriate label. These labels were selected wherever possible using words or phrases taken from the questionnaire responses. In some instances this process proved to be straightforward (e.g. bringing *trade* to the area) and in other cases the process was more open to interpretation (e.g. rally spectators were considered to be a *nuisance*; represented by "locals avoid driving", "locals find driving dangerous", traffic", "difficult to get to work").

The most emotive was expressed in the 'negative to spectators' quadrant. This consisted of a large number of respondents making statements such as "speeding on our narrow lanes", "doing handbrake turns" (*driving recklessly*); "think they are Colin McCrae", "treat road as racetrack" (*imitate rally drivers*); "leave rubbish", "park where they like", "use forest as a toilet", "upset community" (*lack of respect for locals*). Such strong feeling is somewhat countered by the 'positive to participants' quadrant. Here statements such as "events well marshalled", "drive sensibly and safely", "are professional" (*act responsibly*); "cause minimum inconvenience", "issue resident's pass", (*considerate*) were reported. Considerably fewer responses were received for the 'negative to participants' and the 'positive to spectators' quadrants. Within the former category, "ignorant", "don't consider locals" (*inconsiderate*) were views expressed and within the latter, "loyalty in all weather", "shows people interested in the sport" (*enjoy motor sport*).

**Table 1    Clusters of attitudes towards rally participants and spectators (n = responses)**

| Spectators (positive attitudes) | Participants (positive attitudes) |
|---|---|
| • Enjoy motor sports (n = 2) | • Act responsibly (n = 17) |
| • Bring trade to area (n = 5) | • Bring trade to area (n = 15) |
| • Freedom of choice (n = 3) | • Support motor sports (n = 9) |
| • Well behaved (n = 2) | • Friendly (n = 6) |
|  | • Considerate (n = 11) |
| **Spectators (negative attitudes)** | **Participants (negative attitudes)** |
| • Drive recklessly (n = 41) | • Nuisance (n = 6) |
| • Imitate rally drivers (n = 19) | • Inconsiderate (n = 11) |
| • Lack of respect for locals (n = 21) | • Noisy (n = 3) |
| • Minority spoil it for majority (n = 11) | • Disturb rural life (n = 4) |
| • Nuisance (n = 10) |  |
| • Noisy (n = 4) |  |

To provide further interpretation of results, selected cross-tabulations were implemented from which several main effects were observed. A relationship was found between the hosts level of contact and attitude to rally spectators (p < .01). Where there was direct contact with visitors more positive than expected attitudes to spectators and less negative attitudes than expected were expressed. Conversely, where there was no direct contact with visitors, a more negative than expected attitude towards spectators and a less positive than expected attitude was evident. In addition, a relationship was found between level of contact and attitude to rally participants (p<.01). Where direct contact with rally visitors existed, a more positive than expected attitude and a less negative than expected attitude to rally participants was expressed. Where there was no direct contact with rally visitors lower than expected positive attitudes and higher than expected negative attitudes to participants were found.

Thus, the results show that host's attitudes towards sports tourists, both spectators and participants, is significantly influenced by the level of contact. The hosts attitude to rally spectators and participants is positively affected by direct contact. No contact with rally spectators and participants negatively affects the hosts perceptions/attitudes. A relationship was also found to exist between gender and attitudes to rally sports tourists (spectators (p<0.2) and participants (p<0.1)). Males were more positive and less negative in their attitudes towards participants. Females were less positive and more negative towards participants. Similarly, in their attitude to spectators, males were more positive and less negative and females were less positive and more negative. Thus the results show that males are more likely to display a positive attitude towards the sport and females more likely to show a negative attitude.

It was evident that a relationship existed between the age of the host and their attitude to rally participants (p<0.1) and spectators (p<0.01). Those in the 0-34 year age group showed a more positive and less negative attitude to participants than expected. Those over 55 years old showed a more negative and less positive attitude to participants. Similarly, the 0-34 year olds showed a more positive and less negative attitude towards spectators, however, it was the 35-54 year age group who expressed a less positive and more negative attitude towards rally spectators. Therefore, younger members of the Llanidloes area are more tolerant of rally participants than other age groups and the middle aged group were less tolerant of rally spectators than other ages.

Furthermore, a highly significant difference (p< 0.001) was found in the attitude of local residents towards rally spectators and rally participants. Where a positive attitude to participants was expressed respondents displayed a more positive and less negative attitude towards spectators. Where a negative attitude to participants was evident, a less positive and more negative view of participants was expressed. Therefore, hosts who have a positive attitude to spectators also have a positive attitude to participants. Conversely, hosts who have a negative attitude to spectators also view participants unfavourably. Thus, it would appear that members of the host community do not discriminate between rally participants and rally spectators. They perceive the two to be the same. However, as indicated in the cluster attitude quadrants, there is some evidence that distinctions are made between participants and spectators.

## Attitudes to rally visitors in Llanidloes: Preliminary thoughts

The social relationship between sports tourists, as represented by rally participants and spectators, and their hosts can be discussed with reference to Butler's (1974) theorised model of host attitudinal/behavioural responses to tourist activity (adapted in Mathieson and Wall, 1992). Hosts with a passive attitude / behaviour are represented in the current research by the 822 non-respondents. Without further research it is difficult to determine whether this large group has a positive, negative or neutral view towards rally visitors. This represents the 'silent majority', who, according to Mathieson and Wall (1992) "accept tourism and its impacts because of the benefits it brings or because they can see no way of reversing the trend" (p.139-140).

The 178 residents of Llanidloes who responded to the questionnaire represent the active hosts of Butler's (1974) model, expressing a positive, negative or neutral attitude/ behaviour towards rally visitors. Favourable support of sports tourist activity is represented primarily by the participants "behave responsibly" and "bring trade to the area" clusters. Opposition to sports tourist activity is represented primarily by the spectators "driving recklessly", "imitating rally drivers", and "lacking respect for locals" clusters. Within this quadrant extreme examples of negative opinion were expressed such as "a bunch of w***k*rs", "petrol heads", "hand brake turns", "litter", "use forest as toilet", "treat road like racetrack" and "shop broken into". Such aggressive opposition to sports tourist activity corresponds to the concept of xenophobia proposed by Mathieson and Wall (1992), who contend that with continued expansion of facilities to satisfy tourist demands hosts attitudes may become increasingly antagonistic and eventually reach "xenophobic proportions". Although the level of facility expansion in Llanidloes is not an issue it is suggested that the resident's attitudes have, in some cases, reached this extreme level, and exceeded a threshold of tolerance. This is in part due to the behaviour of rally sports tourists. As indicated in the figures presented above the negative attitudes of hosts are directed towards rally spectators specifically rather than the participants.

At the opposite end of their scale, Mathieson and Wall (1992) refer to host's feelings of euphoria at the prospect of tourism development and associated benefits to the area. Although sports tourism development has been minimal in Llanidloes the positive attitudes expressed by the host community reflect an awareness of the benefits of rallying to the area as evident in responses such as "good for an otherwise subdued local economy", "brings trade to the area" and "winter visitors". However, in a small number of cases the impact of the rally caused members of the host community to alter their usual behaviour, for example "keep kids off school" and "don't go out when rally in progress" were mentioned. The negative responses of the host community towards rally spectators suggests that a cultural difference exists between the hosts and some sports tourists. However, further research needs to be carried out to verify this because the modes of behaviour implied by respondents may be different to their actual behaviour.

Results indicate that direct contact with rally visitors gives a more positive attitude of the host community towards the rally spectators and participants. Where there is no direct contact, it may be inferred that negative attitudes expressed are based upon indirect contact, such as observing reckless driving or seeing indiscriminate parking or other potential sources such as the media or local gossip. Based upon the assumption that rally events will continue to be staged in the Llanidloes area, there are crucial implications for the MSA. Contact, in addition to current PR activity, between event officials and the host community needs to be maximised. The positive aspects of the sport need to be further emphasised and steps taken to minimise the inconsiderate conduct of spectators. Perhaps the organisers could, through specific rally and other media, and official programmes, convey key messages of 'good conduct' to potential spectators, and thereby limit conflict between the host community and the sports tourists. However, it is recognised that, unlike many organised sports, the control of much spectator behaviour lies outside the authority of the MSA, and therefore many spectators may be difficult to reach. This is all the more significant because spectator behaviour has the potential to be the greatest influence on host attitudes towards the sport.

Finally, with regard to age, it is not a simple matter of older hosts being less tolerant of car rallying than younger hosts. Whilst younger members of the host community do express a more positive attitude to both rally participants and spectators negative attitudes are split between middle and older age groups. Also gender has a clear influence on attitudes towards car rallying. It is unclear as to the basis of females' attitudes towards the sport. Sport generally is perceived more to be an area of male activity (Messner and Sabo, 1990; Hargreaves, 1994) and car rallying would seem to fit this pattern. Furthermore, if host's attitudes are based upon media representations of car rallying, local gossip or indirect contacts with the sport e.g. witnessing reckless driving, then females may be more 'influenced' by exposure to such occurrences.

## Conclusion

The findings presented here go some way to identifying the intangible effects of motor car rallying on the rural community of Llanidloes. Based on a relatively small number of respondents clearly the sport, and in particular the sports tourists, create both positive and negative feelings within the host community. It is evident that increased interaction between individuals in the host community and sports tourists would probably assist in the process of fostering greater harmony at particular times of the year. Additionally it is quite possible that attitudes to rally visitors may be different if tested at times other than when the rally is 'in town'.

Further research is also suggested regarding the clarification of the concept of 'contact' when examining interaction between visitors and the host community. Also, research is required to determine the range of attitudes towards different types of visitor (e.g. tourists visiting for a short summer break), and so provide greater insight into the socio-cultural effects of tourism in general and sports tourism in particular.

## References

Butler, R. W. (1974), Social Implications of Tourist *Development Annals of Tourism Research* 2/2, pp.100-111, in Mathieson, A and Wall, G (1992) *Tourism: Economic, Physical and Social Impacts* Longman, Harlow, Essex.

Cohen, L. and Manion, L. (1997), *Research Methods in Education* (4th Edition) Routledge, London.

Cambrian News (1999), 'Llanidloes Has Ageing Population and Smaller Families' Cambrian News, 18/11/99.

Coniston, R. (1999), Dominican Republic Looks to Sports Tourism *Journal of Sport Tourism,* 5/3, 1999.

Delpy, L. (1998), An Overview of Sport Tourism: Building Towards a dimensional Framework *Journal of Vacation Marketing,* 4/1, 1998, pp.23-38.

Elson, M. J., Buller, H. and Stanley, P. (1986), *Providing for Motor Sports: From Image to Reality* Study 28, Sports Council, London.

Forestry Commission (1992), *The Forestry Commission of Great Britain* H.M.S.O., Edinburgh.

Forestry Commission (1997), *Forestry Commission: Annual Report Highlights, 1996-1997* H.M.S.O., Edinburgh.

Gammon, S. and Robinson, T. (1997), Sport and Tourism: a Conceptual Framework *Journal of Sport Tourism,* 4/3, 1997.

Gammon, S. and Robinson, T. (1998), The Development and Design of the Sport Tourism Curriculum with particular reference to the BA (Hons) Sport Tourism Degree at the University of Luton *Journal of Sport Tourism,* 5/2, 1998.

Gibson, H. (1998a), Active Sport Tourism: Who Participates? *Leisure Studies,* 17, pp155-170.

Gibson, H (1998b) The wide World of Sport Tourism Parks and Recreation, 33/9 September 1998, pp. 108-115.

Hargreaves, J. (1994*), Sporting Females: Critical Issues in the History and Sociology of Women's Sport* Routledge, London.

Ko Sasi, V. (1995), Sports Tourism in India *Journal of Sport Tourism,* 2/2, 1995.

Law, C. (1993), *Urban Tourism: attracting Visitors to Large Cities* Mansell, London.

Mathieson, A. and Wall, G. (1992), *Tourism: Economic, Physical and Social Impacts* Longman, Harlow, Essex.

Messner, M. A. and Sabo, D. F. (Eds) (1990), *Sport, Man and the Gender Order* Human Kinetics, Champaign.

Miranda, J. and Andueza, J (1997), The Role of Sport in the Tourism Destinations Chosen by Tourists Visiting Spain *Journal of Sport Tourism,* 4/3, 1997.

RAC Motor Sports Association (1993a), *Starting Motor Sport* RAC Motor Sports Association, Slough.

RAC Motor Sports Association (1993b), *Operations Manual* RAC Motor Sports Association, Slough.

RAC Motor Sports Association (1993c), *RAC MSA Yearbook* RAC Motor Sports Association, Slough.

Sofield, T. H. B. and Sivan, A. (1994), From Cultural Festival to International Sport: the Hong Kong Dragon Boat Races *Journal of Sport Tourism,* 1/3, 1994.

Standeven, J and E. Knop, P. (1999), *Sport Tourism* Human Kinetics, Champaign.

Turco, D. (1998), Travelling and Turnovers: Measuring the Economic Impacts of a Street Basketball Tournament *Journal of Sport Tourism,* 5/1, 1998.

UK Sport (1998a), *Major Events: A Blueprint for Success* UK Sport, London.

UK Sport (1998b), *A UK Strategy: Major Events* UK Sport, London.

UK Sport (1999), *Major Events: The Economics* UK Sport, London.

Veal, A. J (1992), *Research Methods For Leisure and Tourism* Longman/ILAM, Harlow, Essex.

Weatherhead, P. (1999), Introduction and background for research into the effects of stage rallying on the environment. *Department of Leisure and Sport Research Journal (Edition 2), Warrington Collegiate Institute, Warrington.*

Western Mail (1999), 'McRae Has Point To Prove' The Western Mail, 20/11/99

Wilson, C. (1996), Leisure at the Limit. *The Leisure Manager, April/May, 9.*

# The economic impact of tourism - A critical review

*David J Egan and Kevin Nield*

Sheffield Hallam University, UK

## Introduction

The adoption of tourism as an economic development strategy has not been without debate and questioning. The justification of large-scale public investment via EU Regional Development Funds, Development Agencies, etc, has led to numerous impact studies. The essential premise underlying the use of tourism in economic development is the economic advantage which is measured, or at least impact studies attempt to measure:- the number of jobs created; the kind of jobs created; the impact tourism has on the maintenance of amenities; and physical regeneration plus the more nebulous benefits of the impact of tourism on the image of the area and its general attractiveness to economic investment.

A key development in the 'coming of age' of tourism in the eyes of policymakers was undoubtedly the development of tourist multiplier models as first developed by Archer (1973) in his study of Anglesey, 'The Impact of Domestic Tourism'. This model and developments of it have been applied by a wide range of authors in the 1970s and 1980s – Archer (1976, 1977a, 1977b) ; Henderson (1975); Wheller and Richards (1974); Vaughan (1977); Archer, Shea and Vane (1974). The attraction to policymakers is that here is a technique that will produce figures on the income and employment impact of tourism including the indirect and induced effects. Thus, claims for the number of jobs or income can be shown courtesy of a scientific study.

Such a study was undertaken for the Department of Environment Inner Cities Directorate, 'Tourism and the Inner City : An Evaluation of the Impact of Grant Assisted Tourism Projects', which concluded that, "Tourism projects have had a positive net impact on the areas in which they have been undertaken" (Department of the Environment 1990). The 20 projects they examined created 1200 permanent jobs and 348 seasonal or casual jobs, plus indirect employment. In the case of the Albert Dock and Merseyside Maritime Museum they estimated the secondary effects created an additional 70% over and above the direct jobs at the project, whereas in the case of Hull Marina and Post House, they estimated that secondary jobs accounted for an additional 44% of jobs. These secondary effects are referred to as the multiplier effect and measured by the multiplier.

It cannot be over-emphasised how important the development and use of tourist multipliers has been in the education of policymakers in the importance of tourism at the national and sub-national level. Moreover, it has acted as a catalyst for the belief that tourism can and should be part of the regeneration of run-down urban areas in the UK. A typical example would be the plans for the Dearne Valley in South Yorkshire, a former coal mining and steel-producing region where the opportunities for tourism development are a key part of the plans for economic redevelopment. One of the more obvious examples of the importance and apparent success of tourism in economic regeneration has been in old industrial cities with a poor image and scarred landscapes, as illustrated by the urban tourism movement from the old industrial cities of "Baltimore, Cleveland, Detroit and Pittsburgh in the USA and Bradford, Birmingham, Liverpool and Manchester in the UK, to cities like Duisburg and Lyons in continental Europe". Law (1993).

In a matter of a couple of decades we seem to have come from a position where tourism was written off by policymakers and researchers as an unimportant part of economic regeneration because the jobs were seasonal and part-time, almost to the other end of the spectrum where tourism is seen as an important export industry for cities and sub-national areas and most of the jobs are permanent.

In this paper we are going to develop a critique of the multiplier technique as applied to tourism studies which will suggest that the contribution of tourism to economic regeneration is over-stated and over-estimated.

# The multiplier concept

The concept of the multiplier is based upon the recognition that sales from one firm require purchases from other firms within the local economy, that is the sectors of an economy are interdependent, the key being that a change in the level of final demand for one sector output such as tourism will not only affect that particular industry but also all the other sectors which supply goods/services to the tourism sector and in turn to the other sectors that supply goods/services to those sectors.

Thus because firms in the local economy are dependant upon other firms for their supplies any change in tourism expenditure will bring about a change in the local economy's level of economic activities, comprising production, household income, employment and government revenue. The concept of the tourism multiplier is the measure of the ratio of the changes i.e. the change in income, employment or output to the change in tourist expenditure. The impact can be divided between the direct, indirect and individual effects.

It is well known that the value of any tourism multiplier is meaningless unless one understands the methodology used to estimate it and the type of multiplier involved. Cooper et al (1998) describe five types of multipliers: - transactions (or sales multiplier); output multiplier; income multiplier; employment multiplier; government revenue multiplier.

In terms of methodology Cooper et al (1998) describe the four major techniques which have been employed to measure the value of the tourist multiplier, these being base theory, Keynesian Multiplier, ad hoc and input-output. It is generally recognised that input-output is the preferred methodology but that the data requirements are so large that in many cases they are impracticable to use. This led Archer ( 1973 ) to develop the ad hoc multiplier that lies between the Keynesian multiplier and input-output in terms of sophistication and data requirements.

It is well recognised that there are a range of weaknesses in and limitations to multiplier models, in particular data deficiencies, restrictive assumptions and operational limitations and supply constraints.

In this paper we are criticising not so much the methodology of the multipliers but how methodological limitations of the multiplier and the interpretation of the results may overstate the importance of tourism in the process of economic regeneration.

Our starting point is the economic base multiplier, these days usually ignored on the grounds that the model is far too simplistic to be accurate in calculating tourism multiplier values. However, the theory underlying the economic base multiplier gives us a useful way of analysing the relationship between the so-called export sector and the local sectors of an economy.

An early debate on the role and importance of the export sector in sub-national economies between North (1955, 1964) and Tiebout (1956, 1964) raises a number of key points fundamental to the role of exports in regional economic growth.

The economic base model starts from the premise that economic activity can be separated into three sectors/stages, often referred to as the Fisher Clark thesis (Fisher 1935; Fourastie 1949). According to this theory of economic development there is a 'natural' process of industrialisation starting with the primary industries (e.g. agriculture, fishing, forestry and mining) which then evolves into manufacturing/secondary economic and then into the service/tertiary sector. The underlying assumption appears to be that services are in some sense 'parasitic' and contribute little to the growth of local and regional economies. (Kaldor 1966). At the extreme Fourastie (1947), for example, argues that if a regional economy develops the tertiary sector beyond the level at which it can be supported by the primary and secondary sectors this will cause economic decline rather than growth.

The debate concerning deindustrialisation throughout the 1980s reflects this view of an export-base world (Drennan 1992; Goe and Shanahan 1991; Harrison and Bluestone 1988).

The fundamentals of an economic-base/export-base theory is the paradigm that an area needs to generate export sales in order to grow, thus the rationale of dividing economic sectors into basic or non-basic within the economic base multiplier. The 'basic' industries have to consist of the primary and secondary sectors, particularly the extractive industries and manufacturing industry, whereas the service sector is perceived as non-basic, that is industries that serve only the local market. An extreme view is that the service is wholly dependent on the wealth generated by the high-wage manufacturing sector.

However, the growing dominance of the service sector has led to a wide-scale criticism of the simplistic assumptions underlying economic base theory (Begg 1993; Marshall and Wood 1992; Williams 1996). The growing view appears to be that such a dichotomy of basic and non-basic is incorrect (Curry 1987) or that the service industries are now too diverse to be explained by the crude basic/non-basic dichotomy (Daniels 1993; Goe and Shanahan 1990), the argument being that the basic/non-basic dichotomy cannot adequately capture the heterogeneous nature of many service activities that in practice possess widely different economic characteristics. Some services, for example, are obviously export sectors in the sense that much of their production is sold outside the home region e.g. call centres and, as has been argued for a long time, tourism.

Williams (1996) argues that the basic sector should not be recognised as comprising any activity which earns export income for the region via the sale of tangible and intangible services such as tourism. Although recently postulated, this view underlies the concept of the tourist multiplier, and a very early tourist economic base multiplier by R R Nathan and Associates (1966) was used to calculate the short-run employment effects created by tourism expenditure in each of 375 counties and independent cities of Appalachia.

If we consider reviews of tourism multipliers from Archer ( 1977 ) 'Multipliers State of the Art' to Cooper et al (1993) in the mainstream textbook 'Tourism Principles and Practice', the basic formulae are the same starting with economic base multipliers, moving on to ad hoc multipliers and finishing with input-output multipliers. We do not intend to get into a debate about the superiority of one type of multiplier over another, but rather to make the point that underlying all the multiplier models is an implicit assumption that tourism, in the case of tourism multipliers, is an export sector in the sense of the economic basic/non-basic dichotomy - that is a change in tourism expenditure brings about a change in the rest of the economy.

However the basic/non-basic dichotomy is no different from the debate between North and Tiebout in the 1960s. The debate to us seems to have missed the fundamentals of the basic/non-basic dichotomy by concentrating on trying to justify a simplistic taxonomy of economic activity epitomised by C William's (1996) classification of 'basic' consumer services such as tourism and regional shopping malls. Ioannides and Debbage (1998) note that classifying tourism as a basic consumer service may be misleading because others have suggested that some sections of the tourism industry can be sold to other firms as a producer service (Begg 1993; Bull and Church 1994).

This highlights our fundamental analysis, the debate as to whether tourism is a basic or non-basic has long been won. A more interesting question - whether all aspects of tourism activity should be defined as basic - is the real question to our mind. Let us take a mainstay of tourism employment - hotels - which account for approximately 25% of tourism employment - to illustrate this proposition. To estimate the impact of a new tourism project which included, say, a new hotel, the orthodox approach would be to use either an ad-hoc multiplier or input-output multiplier to calculate the income and jobs created by the project, the estimate would cover the direct, indirect and induced effect of the investment. The jobs and income would be attributed to the tourism project and our hypothetical example would further add to the case for using tourism as a tool of economic regeneration. However if our hotel was a business hotel where the majority of the clientele were business persons visiting a wide range of existing firms in our local economy the question then arises whether the hotel is an export-base activity as normally assumed or is rather part of the non-export service sector. This distinction is vital because it changes the hotel from being an engine of local economic growth to an activity that is dependent on the prosperity of the existing economy, therefore the significance of the tourism project to the regeneration of the local area would be greatly overestimated by the orthodox multiplier analysis. If all tourist activity cannot be regarded as basic, research to date on the contribution of tourism to economic regeneration will have been overstated. To illustrate this point lets us consider the case of Sheffield.

# Sheffield case study

Sheffield is a prime example of a former industrial city whose wealth was based on the traditional basic industry of steel and engineering now trying to regenerate its economy on the back of the service sector, particularly tourism linked with the development of a range of sports and leisure facilities.

This policy has seen unemployment in Sheffield fall from over 15 %, with pockets within the city of more than 35%, in the 1980's to 6.2% today. This recovery has definitely been led by the service sector with jobs being created in banking and insurance (particularly call centres), retail (the giant shopping mall of Meadowhall and call centres again), transport and education at the expense of the traditional employment in the manufacturing sector. Hotels and Catering have played a major part in the regeneration of the Sheffield economy in the period 1996-97, accounting for 1,300 new jobs, a 15.7% increase in this sector although Sheffield shows a Location Quotient of 0.91 showing it is under-represented compared to the UK economy as a whole.

The policy would appear to be a success when looking at the current boom in new hotels under construction or planned for the city centre. In the past 5 years, the city has seen five major new hotel developments. These developments involve major players within the industry and include Stakis (now Hilton) and Ibis, with a number of hotel developments in the pipeline including a £5million development for the Exchange brewery site and £14 million proposal for a Sheffield University hotel. However, one aspect of this success is rather strange - most of these hotel developments are what we would perceive as business hotels, i.e. a producer service rather than a consumer service. Obviously the demand for the hotels in practice tends to be a mixture of both business, mainly mid-week, and leisure use at weekends. Indeed occupancy rates in Sheffield vary from 80 - 100% midweek to 20 - 30% at weekends. The importance of the business use is further reflected in the price differentials, where midweek rates may be 25 - 33% higher even when quoted on rack, and undoubtedly demonstrate that the core business is business use.

If most of their customers are business customers, the question we are raising is - is the hotel a basic or non-basic activity?

This we feel is the real value of the basic/non-basic dichotomy rather than the simplistic taxonomies of economic activity as a method of analysing the importance of a new development to the economic development of an area. Our argument is that in the above example the hotel development should be regarded as non-basic because without the existing economic activities whether they be primary, secondary or tertiary activity, business people would not travel to Sheffield, therefore there would be no demand for hotel beds and therefore no demand for new business hotels.

There are important implications for the use of tourism development in economic regeneration if as we would suggest the current use of tourism multipliers over emphasises the contribution of tourism and specifically hotels to local economic growth. This is of particular significance in the light of the growing reliance of tourist developments in the furtherance of economic growth in many former industrial areas desperately looking for economic recovery.

# References

Archer, B. H. (1973), *The Impact of Domestic Tourism*, Bangor Occasional papers in Economics Number 2, University of Wales Press, Cardiff.

Archer, B. H. (1976), Uses and abuses of multipliers, in Gearing, G. E., Swart, W. W., and Var, T., (eds), *Planning for Tourism Development: Quantitative Approaches.* Praegar, New York: 115-132.

Archer, B. H. (1977a), *Tourism in the Bahamas and Bermuda: Two Case Studies,* Bangor Occasional Papers in Economics Number 10, University of Wales Press, Cardiff.

Archer, B. H., (1977b), *Tourism Multipliers: The State of the Art,* Bangor Occasional Papers in Economics Number 11. University of Wales Press, Cardiff.

Archer, B. H., Shea, S. and Vane, R. (1974), *Tourism in Gwynedd: An Economic Study.* Institute of Economic Research, University College of North Wales, Bangor.

Begg, I. (1993), 'The Service sector in regional development', *Regional Studies* 27,8: 817-25.

Bull, P. J., and Church, A. P. (1994). 'The Geography of employment change in the hotel and catering industry of Great Britain in the 1980's: a subregional perspective, *Regional Studies* 28,1:13-25.

Cooper, C. et al. (1998), *Tourism Principles and Practice*, Longman, Harlow.

Department of the Environment, (1990).

Drennan, M. P., (1992), 'Gateway Cities: The Metropolitan Sources of US Producer Service Exports', *Urban Studies* 29,2: 217-35.

Fisher, A. G. B. (1935), *The Clash of Progress and Security,* Macmillan. London.

Fourastié, J. (1949), *Le Grand Espoir du XXe Siécle,* Paris,

Goe, W. R., and Shanahan, J. L., (1991), 'A conceptual approach for examining service sector growth in urban economies: issues and problems in analysing the service economy', *Economic Development Quarterly* 4,2: 144-53.

Harrison, B. and Bluestone, B. (1988), *The Great U-Turn,* Basic Books, New York.

Henderson, D. M. (1975), *The Economic Impact of Tourism: A Case Study in Greater Tayside,* Research Report No 13. Tourism and Recreation Research Unit, University of Edinburgh.

Kaldor, N. (1966), *Causes of the Slow rate of Growth in the United Kingdom,* Cambridge University Press, Cambridge.

Law, C. (1993), *Urban Tourism: Attracting Visitors to large Cities*, Mansell.

Marshall, J. N., and Wood, P. A., (1992), 'The role of services in urban and regional development: recent debates and new directions', *Environment and Planning A* 19:575-96.

Nathan, R. R. and Associates Inc. and Resources Planning Associates,(1966), *Recreation as an Industry*, a report prepared for the Appalachian Regional Commission, Washington, D.C.

North, D. C. (1955), 'Location Theory and Regional Economic Growth' reprinted from the *Journal of Political Economy*, Vol, 63 ( June 1955) in Friedmann. J., and Alonso. W., (1964) *Regional Development and Planning*: A Reader: 240-255.

North, D.C. (1964),'A Reply' in Friedmann. J., and Alonso. W., (1964) *Regional Development and Planning: A Reader:* 261-264.

Tiebout, C. M. (1956), 'Exports and regional Economic Growth' reprinted from the *Journal of Political Econom*y, Vol, 63 ( April 1956), in Friedmann. J., and Alonso. W., (1964) *Regional Development and Planning: A Reader* pp 240-255.

Tiebout, C. M. (1964), 'Rejoinder' in Friedmann. J., and Alonso. W. (1964), *Regional Development and Planning: A Reader:* 261-264.

Vaughan, R. (1977), *The Economic Impact of Tourism in Edinburgh and the Lothian region.* Scottish Tourist Board, Edinburgh.

Wheller, B. and Richards, G. (1974), *Tourism in Cardiganshire: An Economic Study,* Wales Tourist Board, Cardiff.

Williams, C. C. (1996), 'Understanding the role of consumer services in local economic development: some evidence from the Fens', *Environment and Planning A* 28: 555-71.

# The Forest Recreation European Network: A proposed interdisciplinary forum for forest recreation and tourism research and policy analysis

*Xavier Font*

Leeds Metropolitan University, UK

## Introduction

This paper will discuss the proposal of developing the Forest Recreation European Network (FREN), currently being evaluated under the European Commission's Framework Programme 5. The proposal is to run a three year networking scheme involving over 45 members of staff in 16 European universities, research institutes and governmental organisations, with the common goal of addressing the problems of rural sustainable development, diversification and employment by promoting the value and impact of recreation and tourism to multiple-use forest management.

If the FREN bid does succeed, it will achieve the above objectives through interdisciplinary scientific and management transfer of expertise in analysing the economic, environmental and social impacts of forest recreation and tourism, their role and potential for rural development. At a policy level, it will contribute to the assessment of rural, forest, conservation and recreation European policies against national conditions. At a user level, it will encourage in the diversification of forest businesses by providing information on business opportunities, guidelines and good practice examples, and it will contribute to the implementation of environmental management systems in forest recreation and their integration with biodiversity and forest management programmes.

Whether the proposal is successful or not, the rationale behind it is still valid and the members of this bid will endeavour to find the funds to carry out such collaborative work. The paper will primarily focus on the rationale for proposing a network, including its Community added value, contribution to EU policies and social objectives, and the innovation elements of proposing a network like this one. It will then outline the network objectives and expected achievements, the proposed packaging of the workplan and the consortium of FREN members. This paper concludes that this network is a good value method to disseminate and encourage good practice and joint research in rural land management through the encouragement of sustainable tourism and recreation.

## Why forest tourism and recreation are crucial to the development of rural Europe

Europe has a problem of devaluation of rural economies, and the changing role of rural areas from producers of agricultural products to stewards of lifestyles, landscapes and traditions (Robinson, 1990; Petty, 1998). Tourism and recreation have an important role to play in transforming rural economies from the primary to tertiary sector (Eagles & Martens, 1997; Marcouiller, 1998). At the turn of a millennium it is time for reflection regarding the role of tourism in society. This paper takes the positivistic approach that it is time to celebrate and embrace the potential of tourism and recreation as key elements of rural development, yet this has to be done within the limits of sustainable development, and with the assistance of cross-country and inter-disciplinary expertise. This will ensure tourism is not only short term market-led, but also responsive to the considerable needs of deprived rural areas and the long-term impact on rural landscapes and communities.

FREN will be presented in the context of a changing Europe, the current actions taken at pan-European level and its possible contribution. The New Rural Development Policy (NRDP) and the Common Agricultural Policy (CAP) encourage maximising the added value of forest and agricultural land (European Communities, 1999; European Commission, 1999a; 1999b). The NRDP emphasises the need to create a stronger agricultural and forestry sector, as well as improving the competitiveness of rural areas through diversification and multi-functional farm holdings and looking for new sources of income. Forested land produces low economic returns, yet it has a crucial environmental, as well as aesthetic value to Europe (Scrinzi et al, 1995; Font, 1999a; Council of Europe, 1995), and it is necessary to ensure it has a stronger role in rural development, hence contributing to the principles of the Common Agricultural Policy (European Communities, 1999a). Yet these policies need new methods to help in their implementation, and a network like the one here proposed can do so by disseminating the benefits of forest recreation and tourism to forest managers.

The NRDP stresses the need to decentralise policy responsibilities and make them relevant to specific rural conditions (European Commission, 1999a; 1999b). Yet decentralisation has to be equipped with mechanisms for cross-country communication and dissemination of good practice and positive outcomes, and it needs to take place within a framework of European standardisation. A network is necessary to provide the Community with information relating to the value of recreation and tourism to forest holdings in different countries, hence furnishing Community decision makers with information for rural and forest policy development and the evaluation of grants for rural land management. This network can then be used by policymakers as a discussion and testing ground for future policies, since the experts involved in this proposal have proven their ability to contribute to national and regional policies.

How can an international interdisciplinary network contribute? By promoting the full value of forests for the provision of services to forest management where and when these are appropriate, developing an understanding of the impact of forestry and conservation policies and practices to forest recreation and tourism, writing guidelines for forest recreation and tourism feasibility assessment, collecting examples and expertise on the management of sustainable recreation and tourism businesses in forests, assessing the future of forest recreation and tourism, and suggesting how the European Commission can develop new instruments or adapt the current ones. The development of a network of this type will also generate extra added value to the dissemination of the potential of tourism and recreation in forest areas, since networking engages further relevant national and regional stakeholders by involving them in the discussion and dissemination of good practice and the potential impacts of tourism and recreation.

Raising the profile of multiple use of forests and sharing information regarding the potential economic, environmental and social impacts of tourism and recreation in forests will allow forest owners to consider multiple use alternatives. This will contribute to the Community social objectives in four areas:

- **Economic**. Ensuring the preservation of the European forests by providing alternative sources of income other than from timber production (Dubgaard, 1998; English & Thill, 1996; Horak, 1997; Hulmi, 1999). Tourism and recreation can generate income from charges made for entry, parking, participating, hiring equipment, as well as for services provided on site (Font & Tribe, 2000). Methods to encourage willingness to pay by visitors will be a key element of the work carried out by this network (Bateman *et al*, 1996; Bennet & Tranter, 1997).

- **Employment and entepreneurship**. Recreation and tourism are renowned for their employment potential amongst women and young people, traditionally underrepresented in the forestry industry. New sources of income encourage entrepreurship within the rural communities, which is a key source of social sustainability (Hulmi, 1999; Bostedt & Mattsson, 1995). Because recreation and tourism are less susceptible to changes in prices controlled externally, the forest owner is more likely to be able to forecast income and be accountable for his/her actions. Forest owners will be more likely to be more entrepreneurial, since they will be more responsible for generating its own revenue, rather than relying on European grants for their income.

- **Environment**. The introduction of recreation and tourism to forest management aims to allow forest owners to preserve a permanent forest cover, forest biodiversity, protection of endangered species, carbon sequestration and watershed quality, crucial to the environmental quality of the countryside. The introduction of visitors to the forest will encourage a more rational management of the forest resources through selective felling, diversification of forest stands and species, and smaller clearings. Visitors will bring their own environmental impacts, and management options for the minimisation of negative impacts will be thoroughly discussed in this network (Broadhurst, & Harrop, 2000; Bornemeier *et al*, 1997; Collins, 2000; Hunter & Green, 1995; Liddle, 1997).

- **Social**. Increasing numbers of visitors to the countryside have created an added pressure for leisure spaces away from the daily urban pressures. Forests have the ability to absorb larger number of visitors than the open countryside, by screening different activities and amenities. Providing managed forest settings for the enjoyment of the public will increase the quality of life of residents, and participation in outdoor activities is a crucial element of a healthy lifestyle (Curry, 1994; Lang, 1995; Sharpley, 1996; Bennet, & Tranter, 1997).

Organising a European-wide Forest Recreation Network is an innovative way to encourage the multiple management of forests. Bringing together forest and recreation specialists can benefit both sectors, and the reasoning behind organising a network as the way to encourage joint discussion between sectors that traditionally do not collaborate.

Forest recreation and tourism have received little attention in the past and only when considered as an addition to the production of timber (Broadhurst & Harrop, 2000). Recent European and national policy developments and timber certification schemes include recreation as one of the elements of sustainable, multi-purpose forest management, and society as a whole is placing recreation challenges to forest managers (Sheiring, 1996; Forest Stewardship Council, 1996; FFCP, 1998; Forest Authority, 1998). For those forest owners not aiming for timber certification, market pressures will force them to look for complementary or even alternative ways to generate revenue, and recreation and tourism can be such sources. The promotion of tourism and recreation in forests will provide opportunities for forest owners to generate revenues, placing less pressure on the European premiums to cover losses from afforestation and set aside land. This should encourage forest owners to focus on a more selective, sustainable production of timber and overall forest management.

Yet the forestry industry does not have the knowledge nor the skills to turn their forest from a timber producing site to a safe setting for visitors to participate in activities without damaging the environment and also generating revenues (Font, 1999a; Font & Tribe, 2000; Skuras, 1996). Only large forest estates will have the funds to employ dedicated recreation officers, and therefore it is necessary to train foresters in recreation issues (Tomkins, 1990; Flynn *et al*, unpublished). The forestry industry requires information on how to implement sustainable recreation and tourism, how this can provide alternative income and up to which extent it can be compatible with timber production. This information needs to come at different levels: raising awareness of the potential of recreation and tourism, providing a platform for the discussion and sharing of ideas, published guidelines based on good practice, and a help desk that allows one to one communication, amongst others (Font *et al*, unpublished). Although there are some good examples at national level (in Britain, see Forestry Commission 1990a; 1990b; 1992a; 1992b; 1994; in Finland, Metsähallitus, 1998), these are not transferred and validated across borders and industry players tend to repeat similar work.

From the tourism point of view, the demand for ecotourism and outdoor recreation is increasing and the pressures on land use are becoming more obvious, both in developed and developing countries (English & Thill, 1996; FNNPE, 1993; Hammit & Cole, 1998). Forested land has traditionally been considered as of lower economical value than agricultural land, and the main output has been the production of timber. Yet a large part of the ecotourism experience and the recreational landscapes depend on the maintenance of forested land, and forests are crucial pockets of biodiversity conservation (Aplet *et al*, 1993). Forests are part of the countryside that visitors enjoy, sometimes the purpose of the visit and other times just the setting for recreational activities, but little tourist revenue reaches forest owners, despite the fact that this revenue is much needed (Dedieu, 1995; Font & Tribe, 2000).

Increased pressure for recreational land, especially in protected areas, places forested land in a prime position to cover this gap, because forests can screen tourist activities and absorb large numbers of visitors. Yet recreation and tourism usually take place in the most fragile environments, which can place new environmental pressures on delicate ecosystems. Although valuable research has been carried out on the environmental impacts of recreation of tourism specifically to public forest parks, this has not crossed national borders and has not been applied to different forest typologies (Hamitt & Cole, 1998; Liddle, 1997; Tribe *et al*, 2000). It is especially important that guidelines for designing outdoor recreation sites reach private forest owners. The potential of forest-based tourism and recreation becomes evident when considering the high value they have in North American forest management, where the Society of American Foresters has a working group on recreation and the USDA Forest Service plays a key role in the country's enjoyment of the outdoors. Members of FREN have strong relationships with these groups and can benefit from their experience, yet there is very little transfer of expertise across European countries and dissemination of good practice, which has lead to an ad hoc list of pockets of innovation. Creating a network solves the short term problem of lack of communication, which in turn will contribute to solving the long term rural diversification and lack of competitiveness.

Since there is little international research on forest recreation and tourism, proposing a network is the most adequate method to ensure a flexible, multi-disciplinary approach to covering the problem. The different members of the FREN network have experience in carrying out research in relation to the impact of recreation to forest management and forest ecology, and the specific characteristics of forest-based recreation and tourism. Scientific and management expertise is required from the following disciplines: forestry, environmental management, recreation and tourism and applied economics. Yet at present there are no structures to promote the dissemination of specific projects and interest groups in the subject, and experts tend to work within the predefined structures in their own discipline. Bringing together this team will allow synthesis and integration, cross-border dissemination of material, translation of documents, international comparison and standardisation of methodologies, and establish models of effective practice and their transferability across regions of the EU and avoid duplication of work already carried out. This will strengthen the Community role in forest research and bring a new angle to rural community development.

At present, the European Forest Institute, the largest pan-European body co-ordinating forest research and member of this application, has amalgamated research relating to forest science and timber technology, but recreation has generally been left aside, yet this will change through this network. An international group of International Union of Forestry Research Organisations (IUFRO) members share data relating to forest recreation, landscape and nature conservation (http://iufro.boku.ac.at/iufro/iufronet/d6/hp60100.htm), but the scope of the group and the time constraints do not allow the group to deepen in the subject. Aspects of forest related recreation are also part of the activities of working group 1 "objectives and functions" of COST-E12 "Urban forests and trees", yet the objective of this group is narrower and membership is closed. The European Commission has also been funding a three year project to develop an environmental management system award to encourage forest tourism and recreation (Tribe, 1998; Tribe & Font, 2000), which was managed by the project co-ordinator of FREN.

# The proposed network

For the reasons listed above, an international interdisciplinary team was brought together to prepare a bid for funds under the European Commission Framework Programme 5, under the "Quality of Life and Management of Living Resources" research theme. The members of the FREN network have identified seven key objectives that need to be addressed:

1.   To bring together an interdisciplinary team of policymakers and researchers in environmental and social sciences applied to multiple use of forests.

2.   To strengthen the quality of forest tourism research through international liaison and exchange of information.

3.   To promote the value of recreation and tourism as part of multiple-use forest management, and the incorporation of recreation and tourism issues in forest design plans.

4.   To share research relating to forest ecosystem management in the context of recreation and tourism.

5.   To transfer experiences relating to good recreation business practice, and specifically methods to generate revenue through recreation for forest owners.

6.   To assess the relation between European and national rural policies and forest recreation and tourism (CAP, NRDP, forest strategies, standards, protocols).

7.   To disseminate information to forest owners aiming to integrate forestry and recreation.

The objectives will be operationalised in a structured approach and ensure outcomes are achieved the above objectives by focusing the networking process on themes representing the current thinking across Europe on the priorities for tourism and recreation development in the forest context. The themes were made to match the reporting procedures of six phases, each one of six months. The proposed themes are:

1.   The value and use of recreation and tourism to forest management.

2.   The impact of forestry and conservation policies and practice to forest recreation and tourism.

3.   The potential value of forest recreation and tourism to rural communities.

4.  Guidelines for the feasibility assessment of recreation and tourism in forests.

5.  Managing sustainable recreation and tourism businesses in forests.

6.  The future of forest recreation and tourism in Europe.

The expected result of each phase will be to collect a critical mass of interdisciplinary data on each theme, generate a discussion and interpretation of the data and its transferability, and repackage this information in a usable, easy to find format for interested parties throughout Europe. This will be achieved by organising international workshops and conferences on the key themes, running national help desks, disseminating the data collected via e-mail, Internet and post, and the collection of key sources of data in theme-specific resource packs.

Each six monthly phase will be organised in a similar structure. At the beginning if a phase, each member will gather data relating to the key theme of the phase within their country, which will be shared using the FREN electronic discussion list. Data of interest to outside parties will be added to the FREN web page, translated when necessary and distributed back to specific organisations that can benefit from it. By using the electronic list, the members will contribute with their expertise to decide which information needs to become part of the FREN resource pack for the theme under review in that phase. Towards the end of each phase, one representative of each member will attend a FREN workshop organised in one of the member countries, with the objective to present the most relevant data collected for the resource pack, according to their expertise and information available in their country. Information for the pack will be collated in the six month of the phase, and further distributed via the national members in a variety of forms.

The database created by each national member will become one of the key deliverables of FREN. Each national database will be joined to form a European database of forest recreation stakeholders, key forest sites, interested parties and experts. The database will help in data gathering, data dissemination and discussion, and it will become one of the key elements of the FREN Internet page. Also each member of FREN will run a helpdesk to allow other organisations benefit from the network's expertise in implementing and developing new tourism and recreation businesses.

At the end of each phase a resource pack will be collated, including all the data free of copyright, and methods to obtain other data, around the theme. This will be the result of the information collected by each FREN member around this subject, organised and prioritised according to the discussions of members, presented at the FREN workshop towards the end of the phase. It will include positioning statements by the FREN group regarding the current situation in the topic and a list of recommendations to target decisionmakers. These resource packs may take the form of published books, manuals or working documents, depending on the format that seems more appropriate and the amount of information collected.

The FREN proposal has a truly multidisciplinary background in order to ensure all the above objectives can be achieved, and expertise is represented. Despite the fact that organisations' expertise will mean that different partners will lead the agenda behind different themes, all members will participate in each theme in order to ensure the transfer of knowledge.

The bid was prepared by a consortium of four Forest Research Stations, six faculties of agricultural economics or forest management, three faculties of tourism, two rural development government agencies, and the internationally reputed European Forest Institute. The different approaches to forest tourism and recreation ensure that the group can carry out a comprehensive analysis of the potential impacts of activities in the forest, their complementarity and feasibility. The geographical groups reflect the different socio-economic and geographical realities of rural Europe, in particular in relation to the economic and environmental value of forest management, and the role of tourism to the country's rural economy. Special emphasis has been placed in bringing together countries from the periphery of Europe to ensure a decentralised perspective to problem solving.

The consortium is organised in four regional groups: West Europe, East and Central Europe, Scandinavia and Mediterranean basin. Buckinghamshire Chilterns University College (UK) manages the overall proposal and co-ordinates the West European team, which also includes Wageningen University and Research Centre (Holland) and Dublin Institute of Technology (Ireland). The East and Central Europe team is co-ordinated by the University of Agricultural Sciences in Vienna (Austria) and includes the Czech University of Agriculture Prague (Czech Republic), the Budapest University of Economic Sciences (Hungary) and the University of Ljubljana (Slovenia). The Scandinavian team is co-ordinated by the European Forest Institute (Finland), with the Norwegian Forest Research Institute (Norway), the Institute of Local Government Studies (Denmark), and the Lithuanian Forest Research Institute as members. Finally, the University of Florence co-ordinates the Mediterranean team, including the Forest and Range Management Research Institute (both Italy), the University of Patras (Greece) the Forestry Technological Center of Catalonia and the Agricultural Research and Training Institute (both Spain).

## Conclusion

At the time of writing this paper the European Commission has not yet decided whether this project will be funded or not. Despite this, the applicants are convinced of the need of such network to ensure a cohesive development of methodologies and outcomes within Europe. Creating such network will provide the means to the economic situation of forest owners, introduce recreation issues in forest and rural policies, and establish forest recreation as a research discipline. The FREN members will promote and raise the awareness of forest recreation and tourism issues locally and nationally, collect data and disseminate it, and run national help desks for advice on the integration of recreation and tourism with forestry. Review reports, guidelines and starter packs will be collated, helpdesks available for advice, workshops organised, an Internet resource centre will be available and an e-mail discussion group established. Finally, FREN will focus on encouraging the multiplier effect of the proposed solutions to multiple use of forests.

# References

Aplet, G. H., Johnson, N., Olson, J. T. and Sample, V.A (ed) (1993), *Defining sustainable forestry*, Washington: Island Press.

Bateman, I. J., Diamand, E., Langford, I. H. and Jones, A. (1996), Household willingness to pay and farmers' 'willingness to accept compensation for establishing a recreational woodland, *Journal of Environmental Planning and Management*, Vol 39 (1): 21-43.

Bennet, R. and Tranter, R. (1997), Assessing the benefits of public access to the countryside, *Planning Practice and Research*, Vol. 12 (3): 213-222.

Bostedt, G. and Mattsson, L. (1995), The value of forests for tourism in Sweden, *Annals of Tourism Research*, Vol. 22 (3): 671-680.

Broadhurst, R. and Harrop, P. (2000), Forest tourism: putting policy into practice in the Forestry Commission, in Font, X. and Tribe, J. (Eds) (2000) *Forest tourism and recreation: case studies in environmental management*, Wallingford: CAB International.

Bromley, P. (1994), *Countryside Recreation: A Handbook for Managers*. E&FN Spon: London.

Collins, B. (2000), Implementing environmental management systems in forest tourism: the case of Center Parcs, in Font, X. and Tribe, J. (Eds) (2000) *Forest tourism and recreation: case studies in environmental management*, Wallingford: CAB International.

Council of Europe, (1995), *Forests in Europe: proceedings from the 4th Pan-European Colloquy on tourism and the environment, Warsaw, 20-21 September 1994*, Strasbourg, France: Council of Europe Press.

Curry, N. (1994), *Countryside Recreation, Access and Land Use Planning*. London: E&FN Spon.

Dedieu, J. (1995), The functions of Europe's forests- public expectations, the dangers ahead and the economics of management, in Council of Europe, *Forests in Europe: proceedings from the 4th Pan-European Colloquy on tourism and the environment, Warsaw, 20-21 September 1994*, Strasbourg, France: Council of Europe Press, 17-18.

Dubgaard, A. (1998), Economic valuation of recreational benefits from Danish forests, in Dabbert, S., Dubgaard, A., Slangen, L. & Whitby, M., (eds), *The economics of landscape and wildlife conservation*, Wallingford: CAB International, 53-64.

Eagles, P. & Martens, J. (1997), Wilderness tourism and forestry: the possible dream in Algonquin provincial park, Journal of Applied Recreation Research, Vol. 22 (1): 79-97.

English, D. B. and Thill, J. C. (1996), *Assessing regional economic impacts of recreation travel from limited survey data*, Research note SRS-2- Southern Research Station, USDA Forest Service, Asheville, USA, Southern Forest Experiment Station, USDA Forest Service.

European Commission (1999a), CAP reform: rural development, Directorate General 6, Fact Sheet CH 25-99-008-EN-C, Brussels: European Commission.

European Commission (1999b), CAP reform: a policy for the future, Directorate General 6, Fact Sheet CH 25-99-001-EN-C, Brussels: European Commission.

European Communities (1999), The Common Agricultural Policy - 1998 Review, European Union Agriculture and Development, Luxembourg: Office for Official Publications of the European Communities.

FFCP, (1998), *Draft Finnish Forest Certification Standards*, Helsinki: Finnish Forest Certification Project.

Flynn, P., Font, X., Tribe, J. and Yale, K. (unpublished), Environmental Management Systems in outdoor recreation: the case study of a Forest Enterprise (UK) site, unpublished paper, submitted to the *Journal of Sustainable Tourism*.

FNNPE (1993), *Loving them to death?: sustainable tourism in Europe's Nature and National Parks*, Grafenau, Germany: Federation of Nature and National Parks of Europe.

Font, X. (1999a), Tourism, recreation and the value of British woodland, *Symposium on British tourism: The geographical research frontier*, 21-23 Sept 1999, Exeter: RSG/ IBG.

Font, X. (1999b), Environmental management of forest tourism and recreation, *Quarterly Journal of Forestry*, Vol. 93 (2): 134-136.

Font, X. and Tribe, J. (2000), Recreation, conservation and timber production: a sustainable relationship?, in Font, X., and Tribe, J. (eds) Forest tourism and recreation: case studies in environmental management, Wallingford: CAB International, 1-22.

Font, X., Yale, K. & Tribe, J. (unpublished), Introducing environmental management systems in forest recreation: results from a consultation exercise, unpublished paper, submitted to Managing Leisure.

Forest Authority (1998), *The UK Forestry Standard*. Forestry Commission: Edinburgh.

Forestry Commission (1990a), *Forest nature conservation guidelines*. Forestry Commission: Edinburgh.

Forestry Commission (1990b), *Recofax: Recreation Planning, Design and management Information Sheets*. Forestry Commission: Edinburgh.

Forestry Commission (1992a), *Community woodland design: guidelines*. Forestry Commission: Edinburgh.

Forestry Commission (1992b), *Forest recreation: guidelines*. HMSO: London.

Forestry Commission (1994), *Forest landscape design: guidelines*. Forestry Commission: Edinburgh.

Forest Stewardship Council (1996), *Principles and criteria for forest stewardship*, Revised March 1996, edited October 1996, Oxaca, Mexico: Forest Stewardship Council.

Hammitt, W. E. and Cole, D. N. (1998), *Wildland recreation: ecology and management*, New York: John Wiley and Sons.

Horak, S. (1997), Influence of forested area in hotel vicinity on hotel accommodation prices, *Turizam*, Vol. 45 (5/6): 125-138.

Hulmi, R. (1999), Forest tourism in Finland, in Font, X (ed), (1999) *Environmental management of forest tourism and recreation*, Conference proceedings (unpublished), 21st November 1998, High Wycombe: Buckinghamshire Chilterns University College, 56-61.

Hunter, C. and Green, H. (1995), *Tourism and the environment: a sustainable relationship?*, London: Routledge.

Lang, W. (1995), Experiences in the recreational management of forests with various functions, in Council of Europe, *Forests in Europe: proceedings from the 4th Pan-European Colloquy on tourism and the environment, Warsaw, 20-21 September 1994*, Strasbourg, France: Council of Europe Press, 35-37.

Liddle, M. (1997), *Recreation Ecology*, London: Chapman and Hall.

Manning, R. E., Valliere, W. & Minteer, B. (1997), Environmental values, environmental ethics and national forest management: an empirical study, General Technical Report N. NE-232, Northeastern Forest Experiment Station, USDA Forest Service, Radnor, USA: Northeastern Forest Experiment Station, USDA Forest Service, 216-222.

Marcouiller, D. (1998), Environmental resources as latent primary factors of production in tourism: the case of forest-based commercial recreation, *Tourism Economics*, 4 (2): 131-145.

Metsähallitus, (1998), Metsähallitus sai kansainvälisen sertifikaatin ympäristöasioiden hoidosta, Press bulletin 24 March 1998, Helsinki: Metsähallitus.

Petty, J. (1998), *Living Land : Agriculture Food and Community Regeneration in Rural Europe*, London: Earthscan.

Robinson, G. (1990), *Conflict and change in the countryside: rural society, economy and planning in the developed world*, Chichester: John Wiley.

Scheiring, H. (1996), Eine funktionenorientierte, integrale Waldwirtschaft, *Forstwissenschaftliches Centralblatt*, Vol. 115 (4/5): 206-212.

Scrinzi, G., Floris, A., Flamminj, T., and Agatea, P. (1995), *Un modello di stima della qualita estetico-fuzionale del bosco*, ISAFA Comunicazioni di Ricerca dell'Istituto Sperimental per l'Assestamento Forestale e per l'Alpicoltura, Trento, Italy: ISAFA.

Sharpley, R. (1996, 2nded.), *Tourism and Leisure in the Countryside*, London: ELM Publications.

Skuras, D. (1996), Regional development of forest recreation facilities: planning decisions in Greece, *Scottish Agricultural Economics Review*, N. 9, 57-66.

Tomkins, J. (1990), Recreation and the Forestry Commission: the case for multiple-use resource management within public forestry in the UK, *Journal of Environmental Management*, Vol. 30, 79-88.

Tourfor, (2000), *The Tourfor award pack*, High Wycombe: Buckinghamshire Chilterns University College.

Tribe, J. (1998), Tourfor: an environmental management systems approach to tourism and recreation in forest areas. In D. Hall and L. O'Hanlon. *Rural Tourism management: sustainable options*. International Conference Proceedings Scottish Agricultural College: Ayr, Scotland, 561-577.

Tribe, J & Font, X. (2000), The Tourfor project and lessons for the UK woods and forest, *Access to Woodlands: threats and opportunities Conference*, Royal Agricultural Society of England and Royal Forestry Society, Warwickshire (UK) 9 March 2000.

Tribe, J., Font, X., Griffiths, N., Vickery, R. and Yale, K. (2000), *Environmental Management for rural tourism and recreation*. London: Cassell.

# Gisborne 2000 New Zealand welcomes the new millennium

*Bob Garnham*

Victoria University of Wellington, New Zealand

## Abstract

The city of Gisborne on New Zealand's east coast is situated close to the first landfall made by Captain James Cook in 1769. Mount Hikurangi at the northern end of the Raukumara range some 75 kilometres north of Gisborne has special significance for indigenous Maori. It was therefore appropriate that millennium celebrations should be held at Gisborne, the first city to see the dawn of the New Year. To celebrate the event a wide variety of activities and events took place over a period from 18 December 1999 to the end of January 2000. The largest public event was the dawn concert by Dame Kiri Te Kanawa with the New Zealand Symphony Orchestra and the Waihirere Maori Group. Whilst many of the public events involved large numbers of European New Zealanders the dawn of the new millennium held special significance for Maori. As was expected a large number of Maori who have family and tribal affiliations with the area came to take part in the ceremonial dawn event on the summit of Mt. Hikurangi. The population of Gisborne estimated at about 32 000 was expected to swell to over 200 000; the influx of such a large number of people was expected to have a considerable impact on the social and economic fabric of the city. This paper discusses some of the implications of the millennium events for Gisborne and examines their social and economic impacts.

## Introduction

By definition the millennium events that took place in Gisborne meet the criteria of hallmark events. Ritchie (1984: 2) defines them as, '[m]ajor one-time ... events of limited duration, developed primarily to enhance the awareness, appeal and profitability of a tourism destination in the short and/or long term. Such events rely for their success on uniqueness, status, or timely significance to create interest and attract attention.' Further, Hall (1992: 1) succinctly paraphrases a similar definition considering, '[h]allmark events ... are major festivals ... their primary function being to provide the host community with an opportunity to secure high prominence in the tourism market place.'

Certainly the millennium is a major one-time event for the majority of the population and its celebration is limited in its duration. Whilst the turn of each new year, decade and century is cause for celebration it is not surprising that the start of a new millennium has been greeted with world-wide enthusiasm. It has provided the incentive for a raft of promotional activities in places large and small; millennium projects abound in all manner of shape, size and cost around the globe, not least in New Zealand and Gisborne in particular. The televising of the first dawn concert of the new millennium by New Zealand's TV3 network ensured that Gisborne, and New Zealand, had a high profile.

# New Zealand and the Millennium

On 01/01/2000 the sun rose at 5.46 am NZDT, 7 minutes after striking the 1753 metre Mt Hikurangi, inland from the township of Ruatoria, 112 kilometres north of Gisborne City. Gisborne's claim to be the first city in the world to see the dawn of the new century is supported by calculations by Lechner *et al* 1997 and Wall (1999) who plot the progression of sunrise from south to north due to the inclination of the earth's axis to the plane of the ecliptic. The times of sunrise indicate that the sun rises first over the Antipodes Islands; the Chatham Islands are the first inhabited land on which the sun rises on Mount Hakepa (971m) on Pitt Island. Lechner *et al* (1997:257) calculate sunrise on Mount Hikurangi (951m) at 4:38 NZST and at Gisborne airport at 4:46 NZST (Lechner *et al* 1997: 254). Gisborne at longitude 178° east of Greenwich the closest city to the International Date Line consequently becomes the first city to see the rising sun.

In the early 14th century, the Polynesians from the voyaging canoe "Horouta", settled on the shores of the bay on which Gisborne City now stands. It became known as Turanganui-a-Kiwa (the stopping-place of Kiwa) after the captain of "Takitimu," the second canoe to land on the East Coast. The Maori name for the district, Tairawhiti, means "the coast upon which the sun shines across the waters". Captain James Cook made his first landfall on New Zealand soil at Turanga on 9 October 1769. His diary shows that he had initially named the bay in which he and his crew found themselves, "Endeavour Bay," after his ship, but subsequently altered it to Poverty Bay *"because it afforded us no one thing we wanted."* The European settlement of Turanga established in 1831 took its present name of Gisborne from the Hon. William Gisborne the Colonial Secretary in 1870. Thus Gisborne is significant to both the indigenous people of the region and the European population.

Interest in determining the first place to witness sunrise of the new millennium is stimulated from an astronomical and academic perspective and an economic aspect. In the case of the latter it is investment in a 'one-off' tourist attraction occasion. Whilst Gisborne is a small but established tourist destination the potential for capitalising on its location with respect to the dawn of the new millennium provided the incentive for promoting the city and district as *'the'* place to welcome the new year.

However, planning for millennium events in Gisborne should not be seen as a 'one-off' event but as part of a deliberate wider policy to put the city on the tourist map, and to grab a place in the sun. At a different level the celebrations provided an opportunity for the District Council to rationalise its spending on street furniture and re-imaging of the city.

# Gisborne as a tourist destination

The city is relatively isolated from the major urban centres of the North Island (Table 1), the closest cities, Napier and Hastings, are about 220 km or a 2½ to 3 hour drive to the south. Distance from other urban centres determines the city as a destination in which visitors spend several nights, it attracts very few day visitors.

**Table 1    North Island cities, population and distance from Gisborne**

| City | Population (1996 census) | Distance from Gisborne | |
|---|---|---|---|
| | | Km | Hrs* |
| Gisborne | 32 608 | 0 | 0 |
| Auckland | 992 000 | 504 | 7 |
| Hamilton | 158 000 | 394 | 5 |
| Napier & Hastings | 113 000 | 225 | 3 |
| New Plymouth | 49 000 | 599 | 8 |
| Palmerston North | 74 000 | 394 | 5 |
| Rotorua | 53 000 | 287 | 4 |
| Tauranga | 82 000 | 298 | 4 |
| Wanganui | 41 000 | 468 | 6 |
| Wellington | 334 000 | 550 | 7 |

*Sources:* Statistics New Zealand; NZ AA guide
Note: * driving time assuming an average speed of 80 kph including rests

The main tourist route through New Zealand from the gateway city of Auckland runs south to the thermal attractions of the Central North Island including Rotorua and Taupo. The scenic coastal attractions of the north east area of the North Island prompted the formation of a macro-region for promotion and marketing purposes. Linking Auckland with and encompassing the Coromandel, Coastal Bay of Plenty, Eastland and Hawkes Bay the Pacific Coast Highway (PCH) is designed to attract tourists to this somewhat marginalised region. The creation of the PCH has implications for strategic planning for millennium events in Gisborne and on the east coast of the North Island. The major attractions of the region are its warm sunny climate, sandy beaches and its cultural heritage. As a scenic drive the road is narrow with few passing places but it attracts an increasing number of motor homes that present a traffic hazard to motorists.

## Planning for the millennium events

The Gisborne District Council (GDC) through the Regional Tourism Organisation (RTO) First Light Tourism Eastland (FLTE) took responsibility for co-ordinating public agencies, private organisations and commercial interests to ensure the minimum of disruption for the region over the New Year period. The 'old' organisational structure that involved many sub-groups meeting together to formulate policy recommendations for the council was replaced with a new committee in November 1998. This committee, chaired by the Mayor, was responsible for examining Civil Defence, camping areas, ambulance, rural and urban fire, water reticulation, food and liquor, transport/traffic control and parking issues. In 1998 the GDC established the Year 2000 Co-ordinating Committee in preparation for millennium events. As a full committee of the council with the statutory powers that implies its objectives were, "to effectively co-ordinate the promotion, staging and performance, of key Year 2000 and new millennium events within the Gisborne District, particularly over the period from 18 December 1999 to 9 January 2000, and within the balance of the Year 2000." The goal was to maximise the opportunities being created by the oncoming Year 2000 and new millennium celebrations, particularly as they related to the Gisborne district, its history, heritage, culture, and relationship with the international date line and the 'First to See the Light' brand.

Reporting to the Operations Sub-Group were Working Group leaders each of whom headed a committee of specialists in their appropriate fields. The working groups included accommodation, airport, communications, emergencies (civil defence), fire (rural and urban), health, human resources, inner city, law and order (police), marine, media and public relations, medical, traffic and transportation, utilities – rubbish, sewage, water. The overall aim of the planning exercise was to be over- rather than under-prepared for all eventualities.

## Aspects and scope of millennium festival planning activities

Motel and hotel accommodation in Gisborne city and district provide approximately 1500 beds, with the addition of existing homestays, farmstays, self-contained units, boarding houses, backpackers, tourist flats and cabins, etc. the number of commercial beds throughout the district is close to 3000. In addition to the commercial camping grounds along the East Coast from Opotiki to Gisborne and Gisborne City's Waikanae Beach Camp camping facilities were provided by Gisborne District Council and some private landowners including sports clubs. Freedom camping, normally available in restricted areas along the East Coast was extended but with a warden/fee system to avoid indiscriminate camping in high fire risk areas.

Local residents who intended to be away from the city over the festival period were encouraged to make any furnished homes they would be vacating available for rent or alternatively offer to host guests in their own homes. In addition to all of the above a large number of visitors would not require commercial accommodation because they would be in the city for one night only, they would provide their own tent, caravan or motor-home, or be staying with friends, or family.

## Methodology

The research for this paper was conducted through qualitative interviews of visitors to and residents of Gisborne over the period 18 December 1999 to 24 January 2000. The social impact survey utilised a questionnaire based on Doxey's Irridex to determine residents' attitudes to the events. They were asked to respond to 18 questions indicating their attitude on a five point Likert Scale. Two surveys were completed of a random sample of 200 people; the first round completed prior to Christmas, when the celebrations were expected to bring over a 100 000 visitors to the city. A second round, visiting the same sample of people was completed after the conclusion of the main events. Residents were also given the opportunity to comment on the events and on Gisborne's preparedness for them.

Economic impacts of the events on the city were assessed through face-to-face interviews with a random sample of visitors to the city during the period between Christmas and January 8. Using a questionnaire approach visitors were asked for their reasons for visiting the city and region, their normal place of residence, mode of travel, and expenditure on accommodation, food and beverage, shopping and transport while in the city and/or region.

Independent research carried out by Architects, Planners, Resource Managers Ltd., (APR) and the GDC Year 2000 Project Manager, validated the fieldwork findings in that the results were consistent with their research conducted during the periods preceding and following the celebrations. The total economic impact assessment of the events was calculated on the basis of low and high estimates of visitor numbers. The application of multipliers to the high and low estimates of visitor numbers for each of the four segments of expenditure (Table 7) produces a range of estimates of the economic value of two months of celebrations over December and January. Accommodation bednight rates calculated from the field survey as $45 per capita were deemed low, calculations based on the rates printed in the *Accommodation Guide* indicated an average of $88. A post event telephone survey of accommodation operators confirmed that with the exception of three or four days over the New Year, the list rates had not been raised.

## Social impacts

For New Year's Eve 1998/99 the council closed off the town's retail centre to traffic as a test-run for the Millennium celebrations. The exercise was a success and served as a reference-point for the 1999 celebrations. The act of closing the town centre to traffic combined with a general ban on alcohol in the area was aimed at fostering a family atmosphere. The main concerns were parking (both from the Police and the GDC Year 2000 project manager admitted that locals would be resistant to the idea of 'walking a few blocks' to get to town on New Year's Eve) and encouraged people to utilise shuttle-bus services. An educational approach to the first problem and the use of security guards to enforce whatever temporary legislative measures the council adopted for the night enabled a family atmosphere to develop. Provision of a free shuttle bus service that looped through the suburbs to the town centre went someway to convincing people to leave their cars at home for the night.

The formation of a group called Odyssey's End, in 1998 and its subsidiary company, Gisborne 2000 Limited, had, as its express aim the organisation and running of a massive

Millennium concert. Odyssey's End – in reality a world-wide travel club – planned to bring 60,000 international visitors to New Zealand over the 10-day Christmas/Holiday period and send 30,000 of those to the Gisborne 2000 concert. Another 30,000 domestic concert-goers were expected, bringing the total to 60,000 at the concert, a further 30,000 visitors from overseas elsewhere in the country were expected to arrive bringing the total to around 90 000. The total projected attendance, though not all at the same time, is 180 000. Media releases of figures such as these raised doubts in the residents' minds as to how well they as individuals, and the city as a whole would cope.

The social impact of events on residential populations generally concern disruption of people's 'normal' environment by noise created by traffic and the increased number of people, congestion of local city streets and roads by tourist traffic and congestion of city pavements in the vicinity of attractions (Cheng 1990). In the case of the millennium events in Gisborne these potential problems were compounded by the statutory holiday period coinciding with potential Y2K problems. The fact that the city is relatively isolated from other urban centres and that a tourist cohort of more than double the normal residential population was expected to descend on the city prompted concern with the effectiveness of the city's infrastructure to cope with such a large influx of visitors.

Respondents demonstrated high levels of enthusiasm in anticipation of the post-Christmas events, however, overall the events did not come up to the expectations of the sample. Although prior to the events people considered that they would welcome visitors to the city the post event surveys indicated less enthusiasm than before. APR research findings indicated that there was general concern over the ability of the city to cope with increased numbers of visitors, particularly with respect to traffic, noise, litter and crime.

The GDC contracted research through a Rotorua based company APR to conduct an appraisal of residents' attitudes to the impending impact of the events. In particular residents were asked about their thoughts on the preparedness of the city for the influx of an expected 100 000 plus visitors. They were also asked to comment on the extent to which they were prepared to tolerate noise, traffic and loss of privacy that might result from an increased population. Results of the research into the perceived levels of tolerance indicates that as the events drew closer people became more aware of and concerned over noise and traffic but less concerned over the possibility of increased odour and loss of privacy (Table 2).

**Table 2**   **Percentage of residents concerned about the impact of noise, traffic, odour, and privacy**

| Issue | Noise | Traffic | Odour | Privacy | N = |
|---|---|---|---|---|---|
| July | 89.9% | 87.3% | 62.5% | 72.2% | |
| August | 85.7 | 84.9 | 60.9 | 65.5 | |
| November | 93.7 | 90.6 | 52.1 | 66.8 | 310 |

*Source:* calculated from *Gisborne District Council Millennium Survey, Market research compilation report,* APR Consultants, November 1999

The pre-event field surveys reiterated these concerns but post event surveys indicated that people considered that the city coped well; concerns over noise, traffic, litter, crime and general disruption were considered to be unfounded. Comments reveal few misgivings over the perceived preparedness of the city, the majority of respondents commented favourably on the amount of time and effort put into planning for the celebrations (Table 3).

**Table 3    Perceptions of the impacts of increased visitors on Gisborne (N=192)**

|  | Pre event score | Post event score |
| --- | --- | --- |
| To what extent will the city cope with increased traffic | 2.7 | 3.7 |
| To what extent will there be an increase in noise levels | 3.7 | 3.0 |
| To what extent will there be an increase in the amount of litter in the city | 3.9 | 2.8 |
| To what extent do you expect there to be an increase in crime | 3.7 | 2.4 |
| To what extent do you think the celebrations will disrupt the city | 3.0 | 2.6 |
| How efficient do you think the pre-planning for the event has been? | 3.1 | 4.0 |
| Enthusiasm for the events | 3.2 | 3.5 |
| Benefit to the city of Gisborne | 3.5 | 3.6 |
| Changes to the main road | 3.1 | 3.8 |

*Source:* Field survey data

Such results validate the time and expenditure invested in pre-planning for the events. Whilst there is satisfaction with the way the city as a whole coped, social impacts include the effects of closing the main street and side roads to traffic. Disruption of the 'normal' pattern of life in a small conservative city is reflected in comments on the lack of parking, perceived inadequacy of the bus service and toilet facilities for some events.

Given that many of the city's residents live away from the main venues and would probably not be involved in them, apart from a spectator role, it is not surprising that many were neutral in their enthusiasm for the celebrations (Table 4), less than a fifth of the sample indicated that they were not enthusiastic. These findings were replicated by the social impact survey of residents prior to the events and confirmed by a follow-up survey of the same people after the main events.

**Table 4    Levels of enthusiasm for the events N= 310**

| Level of enthusiasm for the events | % |
|---|---|
| Very | 37.7 |
| Neutral | 43.5 |
| Not enthusiastic | 18.7 |

*Source:* calculated from *Gisborne District Council Millennium Survey, Market research compilation report,* APR Consultants, November 1999

Ruamano 2000, organisers of Gisborne city's official dawn event to which the Government allocated one million dollars, said it was a great honour to have someone of Dame Kiri's status take part in Gisborne's official dawn ceremony. The concert, telecast live around the world, was a television event rather than a live performance for the audience. Consequently the audience expressed dissatisfaction with the venue and the fact the major performer received a fee for her appearance. It was felt that she could have provided her talents at no cost. A further area of dissatisfaction was the commentator's attitude that did not do justice to the city and concert.

# Economic impacts

The location of Gisborne ensures that visitation will almost certainly incur an overnight stay in commercial accommodation or with friends or family. Thus the stay necessitates spending on food and beverage; with the New Year celebrations it was expected that spending in this sector would be relatively high. Given that most visitors stayed in the city, due to the location of accommodation, spending on transport within the city bounds was expected to be relatively low. The fact that the celebrations were a 'one-off' event determined an expectation that spending on retail shopping, including souvenirs would be relatively high.

It is acknowledged that the degree to which the city and district can benefit financially from the increased activity, is dependent on the capability of the economy to absorb visitor expenditure – adequate stocks, adequate staff, adequate service, adequate trading hours, adequate access. In the case of Gisborne there were real fears that the city's infrastructure would not be able to cope with the pressure of a predicted 180 000 or more visitors.

## What was expected?

The initial prediction of 180 000 visitors was based on the predicted ticket sales for a concert featuring David Bowie, Split Enz and Dame Kiri Te Kanawa and other events including Te Kowhai, Servant 2000, waka taua and a number of special attractions including a motor cycle rally, cycle tour, triathlon and ocean race. The visitor cohort included a large number of international visitors in addition to a large domestic contingent. The potential impact of such a large number of visitors on a small provincial city raised concerns over the provision of accommodation and other infrastructural needs. Consequently plans were put into operation to ensure the supply of accommodation, water, waste disposal facilities, health and safety needs and the provision of a free, circular transport system to bring people into the city centre that had been closed to 'normal' traffic flow.

The need for short-term employees was identified by the servicing and hospitality industries as well as the additional staff required for infrastructure services – fire, medical, police and city utilities. Leave was cancelled and accommodation arranged for staff relocating from other regions. Advertising for 100 additional hospital staff began in June 1999. Planning for at least an additional 1100 paid positions was made, and in addition an army of volunteers was being recruited for inner city work from visitor information services to parking control.

## What transpired?

The estimation of 180 000 visitors to the city was progressively scaled down after the collapse of the much vaunted concert (Table 5). A more realistic estimate from surveys undertaken by APR Consultants in July, August and November 1999 indicate a figure of between 46 000 and 65 000. The nature of the various events and the people attending them indicates that many visitors spent a relatively short time in the city, for example of a sample of 264 people 65% stayed five days or less. As with changes in the predicted number of visitors the expected length of stay also declined from an expected 9 to an average of 6 nights (Table 6). Many visitors had minimal impact on the commercial accommodation sector as they stayed with family or friends, or as with the younger visitors in campsites.

**Table 5    Estimated number of visitors to Gisborne**

| Survey date | Estimated mean number of visitors |
|-------------|-----------------------------------|
| July 1999   | 60 500 |
| August      | 62 000 |
| November    | 50 800 |

Source: calculated from *Gisborne District Council Millennium Survey, Market research compilation report,* APR Consultants, November 1999

**Table 6   Length of stay of visitors to Gisborne December 1999 and January 2000**

|  | Number of visitors | Visitor nights | Length of stay |
|---|---|---|---|
| December 1999 | 27 900 | 245 392 | 8.8 |
| January 2000 | 27 160 | 179 679 | 6.6 |
| Survey (27/12/99 – 4/1/00) | 370 | 2812 | 6.0 |

Sources: *Gisborne District Council Millennium Survey, Market research compilation report* APR Consultants, November 1999 Fieldwork data

The individual and collective effects of a number of factors explain the decline in the expected number of visitors to Gisborne. These included a certain degree of lethargy resulting from the hype of 'millennium events,' and more especially the escalation of concert ticket prices. A general concern for infrastructure failure due to much prophesied Y2K problems discouraged people from travelling away from home, the high degree of hype that preceded the events had the effect of discouraging people, particularly those who thought the size of the crowd would detract from their own enjoyment. The cancellation of the proposed concert may well have had an effect on further reducing the number of visitors to the city. Two issues have arisen through the media's treatment of the facts: firstly, doubt has been raised over the accuracy of figures; secondly, potential visitors – especially families on holiday – may have been deterred from going to Gisborne because of concerns over high traffic volumes. Tales of over-priced accommodation certainly did not act to attract visitor numbers particularly anecdotal evidence quoting one motel charging $1 000 per room per night and others increasing their published rates by 200 to 300%. There was also concern that reports of potentially high traffic volumes deterred people from going to Gisborne. A telephone survey of accommodation operators indicated that with the exception of three or four days over the New Year normal rates were held for all of December and January.

An estimate of the crowd at midnight December 31/January 1 was put at 28 000 (*The Dominion* 2000), similar to the audience of the dawn concert. By including people who had returned home for Christmas and those who were attracted to events that took place before, during and after the dawn ceremony the estimated number of visitors is put at between 50 000 and 75 000. Taking into consideration the 60% estimated to have stayed with family or friends (APR 2000) it is not surprising that commercial accommodation did not achieve 100% occupancy rates over the period December 11 1999 to January 31 2000. The average length of stay calculated from the field survey was six nights; this included hostels and campsites as well as hotels and motels. The length of stay related not only the statutory holiday period but also annual leave taken during the school holidays. A further factor that determined the length of stay was the variety of activities and entertainment available, in this context a recurring comment from younger visitors was that there was not much to do.

Although spending on accommodation calculated at $45 is considerably lower than what was expected it can be interpreted as a consequence of the many visitors in the 20-29 age group who stayed in campsites or hostels. The bednight rate calculated at $88 (*AA Accommodation Guide* 1999) is more representative given that in general the providers of commercial accommodation maintained their normal rates for most of December – January. However, in response to the perceived increase in demand most raised them over the four days of the New Year. In retrospect the increased demand did not materialise; the occupancy rates for December and January being 31 % and 40% respectively, or 11% and 14% below the same months of the previous year. Visitor numbers of between 44 613 and 53 193 were estimated by APR (2000: 2) stayed with friends or family. The *Accommodation Monitor* (GDC 2000) recorded 53 638 bednights, an average stay of 2.26 nights, in commercial accommodation during December 1999 and January 2000. Based on these figures the total number of visitors was between 68 347 and 76 927, hence the economic value of the millennium events to Gisborne during December and January ranges from $40 mn to $44.5 mn (Table 7).

**Table 7    Estimated input of fresh money into the Gisborne economy**

| Total economic output (Minimum 68 347 visitors) | | | |
|---|---|---|---|
| | Direct $ spend | Indirect $ | Induced $ | Total $ value |
| Accommodation* | 2 413 710 | 1 520 637 | 96 548 | 2 510 259 |
| Food & beverage | 15446422 | 7 723 211 | 5 251 783 | 20 698 206 |
| Retail etc | 10047009 | 4 420 684 | 3 014 103 | 13 061 112 |
| Transport | 2733880 | 1 230 246 | 792 825 | 3 526 706 |
| Total | | | | 39 796 283 |

| Total economic output (Maximum 76 927) visitors) | | | |
|---|---|---|---|
| Accommodation** | 4 720 144 | 2 973 691 | 188 806 | 4 908 950 |
| Food & beverage | 17 385 502 | 8 692 751 | 5 911 071 | 23 296 573 |
| Retail etc | 11 308 269 | 4 975 638 | 3 392 481 | 14 700 750 |
| Transport | 3 077 080 | 1 384 686 | 892 353 | 3 969 434 |
| Total | | | | 44 477 016 |

Notes: * Accommodation based on a 'low' $45 per capita per night
      ** Accommodation based on a calculated average $88 per night
Sources: Accommodation bednights, Gisborne District Council *Accommodation Monitor*,
Statistics New Zealand
Calculated from fieldwork survey expenditure on accommodation in Gisborne
Average cost of accommodation in Gisborne, calculated from *AA*
*Accommodation Guide 1999*

The location of Gisborne ensures that visitation will almost certainly incur an overnight stay in commercial accommodation or with friends or family, the average stay calculated from the field survey was 6 nights. Given that visitors are essentially staying in the city due to the location of accommodation spending on transport within the city bounds was expected to be relatively low. The average cost of commercial accommodation in Gisborne calculated from the *AA Accommodation Guide* (1999) is about $90 per night. The fact that a visit to this destination is generally not an annual event for many people, and that there will be the only millennium for the vast majority, spending on retail shopping, including souvenirs was expected to be relatively high. The stay in a destination necessitates expenditure on food and beverage, and with the New Year celebration it was expected that spending in this sector would be relatively high, reflecting the holiday and party atmosphere of the occasion.

A further factor contributing to the relatively low spending pattern in each of the sectors was the predominance of young people (Table 8), 62% below the age of 29, who stayed in low cost accommodation but spent on food and beverages. Observations and anecdotal evidence from informal discussions with residents and visitors corroborated the age characteristics of the visitor cohort identified by the survey.

**Table 8    Age of sample population**

| Age | Total | % |
|-----|-------|---|
| Under 20 | 73 | 20 |
| 20 – 29 | 152 | 42 |
| 30 – 39 | 49 | 13 |
| 40 – 49 | 56 | 15 |
| 50 – 59 | 27 | 7 |
| 60 – 69 | 7 | 2 |
| 70 + | 2 | 1 |
| Total | 366 | 100 |

*Source:* Field survey

In addition to the historic and cultural reasons for promoting millennium celebrations in Gisborne there was a desire to boost Gisborne's economy through increasing its exposure to an international audience, and to boost tourism as an agent of increasing employment and generating income for the city and region. Residents responded positively to the perception that the events were a money-making exercise (Table 9).

**Table 9**   **Residents' perceptions of millennium events as an income generator.**

|  | Pre event score | Post event score |
|---|---|---|
| Events seen as a means of generating income | 3.7 | 3.4 |
| Visitors seen as a source of money | 3.6 | 3.6 |

*Source:* Field survey

# Conclusions

In line with Ritchie's (1984) comment that events may be used as a means of creating an awareness of the place and generating future return visits 60% of an initial sample of 168 people said that they would make a return trip to Gisborne. Of the sample 69% said that they would recommend Gisborne as a holiday destination to family and friends. Particular mention was made of the weather, and beaches and the friendliness of the resident population. Of the 67 who said they would not return 40% said that they would recommend it to family and friends. Major negative comments referred to the perception of isolation and, especially from younger visitors, that there was 'nothing to do.' The long-term benefits of tourism include repeat visits and word of mouth recommendations plus spin-off from advertising and promotion through television and the print media. Around one billion people worldwide were expected to join in New Zealand's millennium celebrations, including the Gisborne ceremony broadcast live as part of TV3 and the BBC's 2000 TODAY Millennium Day Broadcast. Accordingly the GDC await the results of the 'free' publicity and exposure the city gained as a result of its location.

The effectiveness of the city's planning for the events was highly rated by two thirds of respondents to the pre-event survey of residents, in retrospect 75% of respondents considered that the pre-planning had enabled the city to cope well with the celebrations. The findings of this research, and that of APR, clearly demonstrate the benefits of careful long-term strategic planning prior to a major event being held in a small centre.

# Acknowledgements

The author acknowledges the assistance provided Justine Hurlstone and Richard Lamb, Gisborne District Council Economic Development Unit for funding to enable the research to be undertaken and for making APR reports available. Derek Allen, Project Manager First Light Tourism Eastland and Deryck Shaw, APR Consultants, Rotorua for access to their research reports. Tourism students of Victoria University of Wellington who helped with the collection of data on which this report is based.

# References

Allen, D. Chairman, First Light Tourism Eastland, personal communications.

APR Consultants, August (1999), *Gisborne District Council Millennium Survey, Market research compilation report*, Rotorua.

APR Consultants, November, (1999), *Gisborne District Council Millennium Survey, Market research compilation report*, Rotorua.

APR Consultants, February (2000), *Gisborne District Council Post-Millennium Survey, Draft* Rotorua.

Cheng, J. (1990), Tourism: How Much is Too Much? Lessons for Canmore from Banff, *Canadian Geographer* 24 (1): 72-80.

Hall, C. M. (1992), *Hallmark Tourist Events*, Belhaven Press, London.

Lamb, R. Gisborne District Council Economic Unit, personal communications.

Lechner, P. D.; Blain, P. A; McWhirter, N. D; Kristament, I. S. (1997), An assessment of where people will witness the first sunrise of the new millennium, *The Geographical Journal*, 163 (3): 253-258.

Ritchie, B. (1984), Assessing the impacts of hallmark events: conceptual and research issues, *Journal of Travel Research*, 23 (1): 2-11.

Shaw, D. APR Consultants, Rotorua, personal communications.

*The Dominion*, 28 000 at Clock Tower, Wellington, 1 January 2000.

Wall, J. (1999), Timing the millennium: when and where? *Geography*, 84 (2): 139-146).

# The importance of integrated networking in the governance of urban tourism: Comparing evidence from England and the Netherlands[1]

*Femke Geerts*

University of Bristol, UK

## Introduction

Until quite recently tourism has been a fairly problematic subject in academia. National and local governments came to acknowledge the importance of tourism at the end of the 1980s and the beginning of the 1990s, after an earlier sceptical attitude towards the sector. Reasons for this shift in disposition have been the recognition of tourism's potential to contribute to economic development, to employment creation and more general place regeneration. However, this increased attention and sometimes even boundless belief in tourism to achieve all this, has not been mirrored in the academic world. Although there has been increased interest in tourism as a field of research, for a long time it was considered to be a problematic subject. This has changed fortunately and tourism has now cast off this 'Cinderella' status, as it is called in some literature. However, the heightened policy awareness of the role of tourism has not been matched by a growing expertise in the area of implementation nor has the increased academic interest in the subject been matched by greater understanding of the organisation and structure of tourism production.

There are several reasons why there has been comparatively little research on the organisation of the tourism system. A first and very practical explanation is that tourism is extremely difficult to define, being an activity, an industry as well as an experience. The wide range of actors directly as well as indirectly involved in tourism makes a clear demarcation of the sector's organisational boundaries complicated. A second explanation for the lack of organisational research in tourism is that the subject is rarely approached from a multi-disciplinary perspective. Placing the study of the tourism system in the context of the urban governance debate provides a much broader analytical base and can therefore help to overcome this deficiency. The main aim of this paper is to be able to provide feedback on how to improve the organisational structure of the tourism system. To this end, it is important to not only understand *how* tourism is organised but, more importantly, also *why* the tourism sector is organised the way it is. The first part of this paper attempts to determine what the influences are on the organisational structure of the tourism system. The second part of the paper introduces Amin and Thrift's concept of institutional thickness (1994; 1995) and examines six elements that contribute to the institutional thickness of a successful tourism system. It has to be kept in mind that it is not the aim of this paper to provide policy-makers with a checklist of ingredients that, taken together, will produce the ideal organisational model for every locality's tourism system. The value of the concept of institutional thickness is that it can provide guidance for those localities trying to improve the organisational structure of tourism by establishing criteria against which to evaluate the organisational capacity of their tourism system.

# Explaining the organisational structure of the tourism system

In order to be able to provide feedback on the governance of urban tourism, we need to identify what factors and conditions shape the state and structure of the tourism system and what the extent of their influence is. Investigating the organisational roots of the tourism system will enable us to make an informed judgement and evaluation of the sector's present structures as well as to make recommendations for possible improvements. The following four interrelated factors can be distinguished which determine and create the organisational structure and culture of the tourism system: the culture of governance, the culture of tourism, an element of 'inevitability' and the current state of flux of both governance and tourism. Assessing the importance of each element and establishing whether it constraints or facilitates a successful tourism network is important if we want to find out to what extent it is feasible to improve the organisation of tourism and how realistic it is to strive to achieve some sort of ideal model for tourism.

## The culture of governance

The practice of governing cities has changed beyond recognition in the last two decades (see, for example, Harvey 1989; Healey *et al.* 1995; Leach *et al.* 1994; Stewart and Stoker 1995). A complex interplay of factors has led to the emergence of a global world, enabling (or forcing) us to live, work and undertake leisure activities in a global marketplace. Traditional procedures and practices are no longer appropriate and able to deal with these global issues and organisations are therefore having to struggle to accommodate for these changes. Governing structures have changed to such an extent that we can now speak of the emergence of new organisational forms no longer based on the traditional concepts of hierarchy and bureaucracy. Urban governments are increasingly working through and alongside other participants in the city-region, with decision-making processes taking place outside of traditional local government structures. Public, private and non-profit sector organisations alike have become more open to co-operating with each other in partnerships and networks. Increased complexity of certain problems combined with a growing interconnectivity between localities has further contributed to this change in governmental cultures and structures. It is virtually impossible for any single organisation (governmental or otherwise) to effectively deal with any issue or activity on its own. This is especially true in the case of tourism, an industry and activity comprising several interlinked elements. Governmental organisations have acknowledged the fact that not only do they need to improve co-operation with external partners, but, equally important, also between internal partners. In the old culture of strong departmentalism, councils experienced great difficulty in placing tourism in any one department because of its complex nature. The new culture, with more emphasis on horizontal and vertical linkages within governments, has greatly benefited tourism, a subject that needs to be approached in an integrated manner.

Tourism has become more acknowledged by governmental organisations as a subject worthy of political attention, as a sector able to contribute to economic and social well-being and as a field that requires planning and managing. Despite this increased interest, governmental organisations are struggling to define a new role for themselves in the tourism system and are finding it difficult to justify their continued involvement in tourism. Although this dilemma is understandable, especially in a time when governments are moving from 'providing to enabling', they still have a substantial role to play in the organisation of the tourism system based on three arguments. First of all, governmental organisations need to be involved to counteract the inequalities resulting from market forces, which is understood as being a more traditional governmental responsibility. Secondly, governments should be involved in tourism not just for ideological or political justifications, but because tourism can generate monetary, economic and social benefits. Thirdly, an institutionally thick tourism system requires the involvement of all stakeholders, including the public sector. In summary, the particular culture of governance in a locality is reflected in, or even has an influence on, the wider atmosphere and identity of a city and hence also on the way it deals with tourism. It would seem that the shift from 'government to governance' with its emphasis on co-operation between internal and external partners and its more open, outward-oriented culture has greatly facilitated a move towards a more effective organisation of the tourism system. In theory at least because, as the next section shows, in practice this new structure and culture has led to an increased complexity.

## The culture of tourism

The tourism system possesses several distinct characteristics that have a decisive influence on its state, shape and structure. First and foremost, it must be acknowledged that the tourism system is made up of numerous elements, all interlinked and interdependent. The organisational boundaries of the tourism industry are extremely difficult to define involving as it does a nearly unlimited number of sectors and services from the public, private and non-profit sectors. In addition, tourism, of all the services that councils get involved in, probably crosses more departments than any other sector. Inherent to tourism's diverse nature is the degree of variation in commercialisation and professionalism that exists in the tourism industry. The majority of tourism businesses is made up of small and medium-sized firms, often criticised for their amateurism. This majority coexists with a small number of large tourism businesses, sometimes part of a national or multinational chain. While the diversity of the tourism system could present a constraint to an effective organisational structure, it is at the same time tourism's unique 'selling point'. Because of tourism's complex and fragmented nature, the main structural weakness of the industry is its inability to speak with a more co-ordinated and unified voice. It is not just this research that has come to the conclusion that the history of the industry is marred by individualism and isolationism entirely inappropriate to the development of a competitive edge for localities.[2] Because tourism is difficult to delineate, it has never been able to organise itself as a collective sector. This makes it difficult for 'outsiders' to approach the industry and, vice versa, has also contributed to a lack of political muscle for the industry. The fragmented nature of the tourism system makes the issues of leadership and co-ordination of prime importance but, simultaneously, extremely problematic. There are numerous tensions and difficulties with trying to lead or co-ordinate such a diverse and fragmented industry.

The small-scale nature of most tourism and recreation businesses, furthermore, has several influences on the organisation of the tourism system. Most businesses, especially the very small ones, express a lack of involvement and interest in the wider organisation of tourism in their locality, an attitude sometimes leading to extreme frustration on the part of those trying to co-ordinate the tourism system. This has been blamed on the industry's lack of vision, its insufficient long-term strategic planning, its inability to look beyond its own direct business interests and a persistent view of other businesses as competitors. On the other hand, the problem with the large national and international tourism businesses is that these generally contribute very little to a locality's tourism system, apart from the direct business and customers they generate. They can be relatively detached from the local tourism system and are more rooted in national and international structures. A further problem associated with this general lack of involvement is the fact that the industry has grown accustomed to being supported by governmental organisations. Recently, however, the organisations involved in tourism have begun to realise the value of synergy and the need to pull together for the collective good. Tourism businesses seem to be getting more professional and more outward-oriented, resulting in an increased number of partnerships. All in all it can be concluded that the specific culture of tourism, although an advantage in some circumstances, seems to hamper an effective organisation of the tourism system.

## 'Inevitability'

The third set of factors that shapes the state and structure of the tourism system is the influence of 'coincidence'. Often, the development of the organisational structure, the direction it takes or the barriers that constrain improvement are beyond anybody's control. Some outcomes seem to be 'inevitable' and influenced by a certain amount of 'chance'. These uncontrollable circumstances impede getting closer to an ideal organisational model of tourism and the research upon which this paper is based showed that many people simply reconciled to this situation. One of these uncontrollable circumstances was found to be the influence of history on the present-day organisational structure of tourism. Certain structures have evolved over time and although they might today seem far from ideal, they nevertheless work well because people have learned to work within or around them. Another uncontrollable circumstance is the influence of chance factors, probably influenced by the 'human' element, so to speak, in all these organisational structures. In some cases an ideal model comes about because the right people were in the right place at the right time. The opposite can also happen when partnerships fail to materialise because of personalities that do not get on.

## The current state of flux of tourism and governance

The fields of tourism and governance are currently experiencing a great deal of change caused by a number of internal and external pressures. It is not surprising then that the organisational state and structure of the tourism system is in a state of flux. The field of governance has undergone several processes of change over the last decade and this not only applies to theoretical debates on the subject but also to the practice of governing. These changes have affected all territorial levels of governance, from the global down to the local. Issues such as participation, accountability, democracy, sustainability and modernisation are at the centre of current debates on government and governance. The research for this paper has shown that most governmental and semi-governmental organisations feel that they are under some sort of pressure to adapt their organisational structure and culture to changing circumstances. Most local authorities in the case studies had just completed a process of reorganisation, were in the middle of it or were planning a restructuring for the near future. Organisations such as the Dutch Chambers of Commerce were reviewing their regional and sub-regional structures. Developments like the creation of Regional Development Agencies in England must be seem in the same context. Sub-regional as well as regional co-operation and partnerships between public and private sector organisations appear to be gaining importance. Tourism in its various guises -as an academic disciple, as an activity and as an industry- is also currently experiencing a range of changes and pressures. Over the last few decades the tourism system has become more diverse and complex, necessitating a more effective and co-ordinated organisation of the tourism sector. The amateurism of the smaller tourism businesses can hamper co-operation efforts and the sector needs to become more professional and less fragmented. Tourism is a relatively young sector that needs to emancipate itself in order to be taken seriously in political debates. Several changed aspects on the demand-side of the tourism system have, furthermore, increased the importance of the governance of urban tourism. The growth in short breaks, the increase in the number of holidays taken each year and the increased popularity of urban destinations and heritage tourism provides a growing potential market for cities. This means at the same time that all cities face increasingly sophisticated competition from other destinations nationally and overseas, which are becoming more easily accessible and being offered at competitive prices.

It can be concluded that the fields of governance and of tourism are both experiencing a great deal of change at the moment. This has an influence on and is reflected in the current state of flux of the organisation of the tourism system. In England as well as the Netherlands, national government was at the time of conducting the research in the processes of reviewing the national support structures for tourism, with similar debates taking place at both sides of the Channel. The domestic tourist boards (English Tourist Board and Stichting Toerisme en Recreatie AVN) were seen to be causing duplication of activities and wastage of resources. Both governments wanted to give more responsibilities to the overseas tourist boards (British Tourist Authority and Nederlands Bureau voor Toerisme) and the regional tourist boards. In addition, the organisational boundaries of regional tourist boards in the Netherlands, and to a lesser extent also in England, were undergoing a process of review. There is a move in tourism towards more co-operation with sub-regional and regional partners but many think this move is not happening quickly enough. Too often other localities and businesses are still seen as competitors. It would seem that it is more the national and regional structures that are being adapted and that the local organisation of tourism is perhaps slow in picking up on this trend, although this is improving. Compared to the pace of developments in fields like technology and consumer demands, institutional change can be very slow which means that mismatch or institutional failure becomes a possibility.

# Conclusion

Not all of the above four elements exert the same amount of influence on the organisation of tourism but what they have in common is a certain 'uncontrollability'. It would thus be tempting to conclude that it is unfeasible to want to improve the organisation of tourism. With the intrinsic characteristics of the tourism industry and certain uncontrollable circumstances having such a large influence on its organisational structure, it could be argued that attempts at improving the structure are desperate and futile. The complex nature of tourism means that tourism planning is not a rational activity. This does, however, by no means imply that the organisation of tourism cannot be improved or that localities should not have ambitions towards achieving this. What it does mean is that any realistic strategy to adapt the organisational structure of the tourism system should take into account the four factors identified here and try to work with and around these, or as one of the interviewees in the case studies phrased it:

> *If that's the way the organisation is, the way the industry is organised then you take it with those benefits, disadvantages and wastage. But to try and introduce a degree of uniformity would destroy the very nature of the product.*

# Towards an analytical framework for the governance of urban tourism: The concept of institutional thickness

The previous sections have deconstructed the organisational structure of the tourism system to its origins in order to determine what the influences are on its nature and its development. To be able to make recommendations on how to improve the organisational structure and culture of the tourism system, an analytical framework is needed against which we can 'measure' and compare the organisational capacity of tourism systems. Using Amin and Thrift's concept of institutional thickness[3] as an analytical framework enables us to bridge the theoretical and empirical parts of the research. The following sections conceptualise the relationship between institutional thickness and tourism development. The underlying aim is to establish whether it is possible for a locality to be successful in tourism without an institutionally thick tourism system or, vice versa, whether there are localities that are institutionally thick but not very successful in tourism. We would assume that a successful tourism destination requires more than the presence of a range of interesting attractions and that the organisational structure and culture of its tourism system exert a great amount of influence, either positive or negative, on this success. Amin and Thrift's concept of institutional thickness has been adapted to fit the specific parameters of this research. The institutional thickness of a tourism system can be defined by a combination of six characteristics. The following six sections describe each element and analyse their relevance and contribution to a successful tourism system.

## Collective representation

No tourism system can be effectively organised if it does not have a collective representation by a multiplicity of organisations and institutions. This is, first of all, instigated by the diverse nature of tourism activities, of the tourism industry, and of tourism's impacts. There are numerous participants in the tourism policy system, some of who are directly involved and part of the tourism industry, others who are more indirectly involved and part of a wider tourism community. As Elliott (1997) correctly observes 'the world of tourism management is extremely complex and the various principles and issues all intermingle and affect one another.[4] This implies that no single organisation or group can effectively deal with tourism on its own. Secondly, the necessity of a collective representation in the tourism system is also reflected in the changes to the general institutional landscape, reflecting the politics of partnerships and networks. The drawing in of actors and organisations from across the community to perform participatory management is a central aspect of governance. The national and local institutional terrain is now occupied by an increasingly differentiated range of agencies involved in policy formulation and delivery.[5] All parties interested in or affected by tourism within a particular market or locality, known as stakeholders, should collectively manage the tourism system.

## Inter-institutional interaction and synergy

Having a plethora of various kinds of organisations on different geographical levels is meaningless if these organisations do not co-operate and communicate. All these organisations with their various objectives are interrelated and dependent upon one another to a greater or lesser degree. The test of a good manager, as Elliott (1997, 11) writes, is to be able to understand this complexity, operate effectively and efficiently within the system, reconcile or balance conflicting objectives and so achieve certain aims. In the recent tourism literature, more and more researchers have argued the need for increased collaboration in the planning process (Bramwell and Sharman 1999; Elliott 1997; Jamal and Getz 1995; Sautter and Leisen 1999). The most basic argument presented in this literature is the need to more actively involve all persons affected by or interested in tourism policies. Achieving congruency across and between all tourism stakeholders should be encouraged, thus increasing the likelihood of collaboration and compromise in the planning and implementation process.[6] Although the research for this paper has shown that most stakeholders acknowledge the importance of co-operation, in practice creating partnerships and linkages is easier said than done. People will only take part in a partnership if they are convinced the process and it outcomes will benefit them and their organisation, or at least if the advantages outweigh the disadvantages.

## Flexibility and openness

The third element contributing to the institutional thickness of a tourism system is flexibility and openness. This applies to several aspects of the co-operation process. First of all, while it is important for the various partners to be able to retain their own identity they should at the same time be flexible enough to be willing to make compromises. That is, of course, the crux of partnerships. Secondly, networks should be flexible and 'open' so as to include formal as well as informal structures, long-term as well as ad hoc activities and permanent as well as temporary members. A network of partnerships is a fluid structure in a continuous process of creation. There are several reasons to explain this need for some degree of flexibility. First of all, the organisation of any tourism system needs to be flexible because of the nature of the tourism sector. Tourism is a dynamic, fragmented and diverse industry and if it wants to involve all stakeholders then a fixed structure is inadequate. Secondly, the organisation of a tourism system needs to be flexible because of the way governance works these days. Traditional, fixed structures have been replaced with more flexible, outward-oriented networks. Organisational cultures have come closer together, thereby greatly increasing the potential for more openness and co-operation. A lot of activities are now undertaken on an ad hoc, project basis and partners are sought as and when necessary. This means, amongst other things, that there is no longer a universal division of roles. Instead, each organisation plays various roles in various situations. Governmental budget cuts have furthermore meant that many co-operative structures were abolished and replaced by temporary partnerships. Many organisations -not just tourism businesses- are also becoming more entrepreneurial and commercial in the way they execute activities and are increasingly focused on outputs and benefits, a trend which further contributes to the popularity of ad hoc activities. It is, however, important to note that there are limits to this flexibility and openness. Too much of it and a network can become unstructured and incomprehensible. It also carries with it a risk of duplication of activities.

## Co-ordination

A fourth and very important element constituting the institutional thickness of a locality's tourism system is co-ordination. Every partnership or network needs some form of leadership to co-ordinate activities and responsibilities. Who or what can best provide this leadership depends on the nature of the partnership. The organisation of networks cannot be based on hierarchical relations. Its structure is neither 'top-down' nor 'bottom-up'. Consequently, leadership and co-ordination are problematic issues in governance and even more so in tourism because of the complex and fragmented nature of the industry and the wider tourism system. These problems are exacerbated by the current confusion on roles and responsibilities amongst policy makers caused by the constant state of change urban governance is in. Each organisation has to find a new role for itself in this network of partnerships and then adjust its culture and structure to it. A majority of interviewees in the research - on the local, regional as well as the national level- observed a lack of leadership for tourism. One of the problems is that none of the present organisations in their current format have the ability to perform this leadership and co-ordination role. Most city councils feel that they, in their new role as enablers and as partners, should no longer provide the sole leadership in a locality. The TIC (in England) or VVV (in the Netherlands) have not got the expertise or resources to lead the tourism system, despite the fact that they are the only organisation involved in tourism on a full-time basis. The Chamber of Commerce represents all economic sectors and is therefore not in a position to provide leadership for the tourism industry either. The increase in ad hoc and temporary partnerships has not made things easier for the tourism industry who are having to get used to dealing with a greater number of constantly changing collectives. The establishment of a co-ordinating body might obviate this problem.

## Identification with a common objective

The fifth element contributing to the institutional thickness of a locality's tourism system is identification with a common objective. Ideally, participation in partnerships should lead to a collective representation of normally sectional and individual interests. The various institutions in a network must have the same goal in mind to be able to co-operate effectively. The objective of a partnership can vary depending on its nature and type. It can be, for example, developmental, promotional, strategic, co-ordinating or representational. Different organisations can have opposite objectives but also mutual ones. It is a challenge to make sure that all stakeholders focus on the latter. This objective must be sharply defined and supported by all participants so that each can assess its individual contribution to this common goal. Alignment and consensus in stakeholder orientations is an important element in the success of a partnership. It is also of vital importance to communicate this vision to other partnerships and interested parties. Despite the fact that each partnership can have a different role within the tourism system, it is of great importance that all these partnerships share one overarching objective: they must pursue what is best for the city and acknowledge the contribution that tourism can make to this.

## The limits of institutional thickness

Localities should be aware of the risk that the organisational network of the tourism system can become overcrowded and unwieldy. The concept of institutional thickness should not be misinterpreted. It is not simply a matter of 'the more (thicker) the better'. A network which is institutionally too thick is not beneficial to an effective organisation because it is too rigid and inflexible. This goes for the tourism system but also for urban governance in general. There are limits too what is workable and manageable. The problem is that it is virtually impossible to define these limits or set rules for it, since it depends very much on contextual factors. Also, in some cases it might be more a matter of the wrong kind of organisations or a lack of linkages between them instead of simply too many organisations. When new partnerships are put in place they should overcome fragmentation, not create even more confusion. Unwieldy tourism systems carry with them a risk of duplication and can make co-ordination extremely difficult. There are certain fields within tourism which are more 'overcrowded' than others, for example promotion.

## Conclusion: The importance of horizontal and vertical linkages in the tourism system

We have seen that the culture and structure of governance in a city as well as its culture of tourism shape the organisational structure of each tourism system and therefore produce a different structure in each locality. Localities must therefore not make the mistake to assume that the presence of all of the above six factors of institutional thickness will guarantee a perfect and successful organisation of their tourism system. The particular mix of ingredients will depend on the specific contextual factors in the locality. Thus, as Buxton *et al.* (1998, 6) note, institutions are no mere reflection of market forces, but are shaped in specific periods and may function rather better in some contexts than others. Institutional thickness does not represent an ideal model of urban governance to be copied in every detail. The ideal organisational structure of the tourism system will be different in every locality. Furthermore, the pursuit of elusive ideal organisational models should not be the objective of any locality's tourism strategies. It is important that structures work in a particular context and setting.

Without going into the details of institutional differences, the significance and influence of contextual factors on the tourism system -whether that be on the local, regional or national level- has been one of the main findings of this research. The same organisation can have a different role in England or in the Netherlands. The main points of difference in this respect are between English and Dutch local authorities, Chambers of Commerce and Tourism Information Centres. In contrast to English Chambers of Commerce, membership of a Dutch Chamber is compulsory for all businesses. Dutch Chambers therefore -theoretically- represent the whole private sector in a locality. This could explain why their role in tourism is more elaborate than that of their English counterparts. Dutch Chambers have a well-established mediating role between the private and public sector and are also involved in policy making for tourism. Another point England and the Netherlands differ on is the role of the Tourism Information Centre. English TICs are mostly responsible for the provision of information on tourism and leisure activities and facilities. Dutch VVVs have, beside this role, also an important responsibility in promoting the city's assets and developing tourism 'products'. This is reflected in the fact that English TICs are part of the public sector and Dutch VVVs, while receiving some governmental funding, are part of the private sector. The role of English local authorities in tourism is somewhat more pronounced than that of Dutch local authorities. This could possibly be explained by the fact that certain activities and services of English local authorities are in the Netherlands the (shared) responsibility of the VVV and/or the Chamber of Commerce. This does not, however, mean that Dutch local authorities do not acknowledge the importance of tourism.

Despite these differences, the interviewees in England and the Netherlands had remarkably similar views on how to improve the present structure and culture of the tourism system. The research has made clear that there is an urgent need in most localities to create an umbrella organisation for tourism.[7] This co-ordinating body should be a partnership of all partnerships and should unite the interests of all tourism stakeholders. This co-ordinating body could be just one person or a more extended organisation but, whatever the form of this body, it is important that it is seen to be neutral and not attached to any existing organisation, as noted by most interviewees. One should be cautious, however, that this body does not become simply another partnership. In some localities more co-ordination will mean establishing new organisations. In others it will mean decreasing the number of existing organisations. In all cases it is vital for the success of such a body that its power and role is endorsed and acknowledged by all stakeholders. However, differences in organisational cultures and tensions between partners can hamper a smooth co-operation process. In addition, the fact that more and more partners are being involved in the planning and implementation of tourism has in some cases led to confusion on roles and responsibilities. Despite these difficulties, there are clear advantages to be had from working in partnerships. Co-operation produces additionally and can thus improve the quality of the collective tourism 'product' because organisations complement each other's activities. Co-operation also makes it easier to portray a collective identity for a locality. Moreover, differences in organisational cultures can be an advantage since a multiplicity of opinions and cultures in a partnership presents a stimulating environment to reach creative and innovative solutions. Partnerships can also improve understanding between organisations with different cultures. The increased co-operation between the public and the private sector, for example, has meant that the two have come closer together and now have a better appreciation of each other's procedures and ways of working. Co-operation between different sectors and between localities in the tourism system is, furthermore, a necessity because of the fragmented and diverse nature of the tourism industry and because of the increasingly competitive and global market.

In summary, it can be concluded that a successful tourism destination requires more than the presence of a range of interesting attractions. The institutional thickness and the culture of governance in a locality are of equal importance in explaining a city's success in tourism. There is growing acknowledgment that poor inter-organisational communication and co-ordination lead to a duplication of effort, to activities that overlap and conflict and to fragmented decision-making. The majority of tourism stakeholders in both the public and private sector are increasingly aware of their dependence upon each other and the importance of partnership and exchange. In most cities horizontal co-operation within the tourism system is not a problem with several sectoral representative organisations in place. This is, however, only a starting point on the way to creating vertical linkages between these partners and to creating 'umbrella' organisations. Although this is proving very hard to do in practice, it is of vital importance if localities aspire to be successful in tourism. To best serve the needs of visitors and tourists alike, 'all columns in the tourism industry should be eliminated', according to a Dutch newspaper article.[8] The article goes on to argue that the ultimate modern tourist attraction does not make a standard product. The product will look different every time and only exists at the point of consumption. The customer decides what the product will be. Hence, the tourism sector should focus more on markets and themes rather than on their own products and geographical boundaries, based on the argument that tourists are looking for a holiday experience rather than a particular destination.[9] A modern tourism industry needs a modern organisational structure and culture with horizontal and, more importantly, vertical linkages between the various stakeholders. In the long run a badly organised tourism system can have detrimental effects on a locality's success in tourism, especially in a time when issues of partnership and sustainability are high on the political agenda.

## Endnotes

1.  This paper is based on evidence collected through a comparative study of Dutch and English governance structures for tourism. Six medium-sized cities with a varying degree of success in tourism have been selected for a close examination and analysis of their tourism systems. The English case studies were Oxford, Bristol and Shrewsbury and these have been compared with the Dutch cities of Delft, Tilburg and Zwolle. The research was mainly based on semi-structured interviews with key stakeholders in the cities' tourism systems complemented with a study of secondary resources.

2.  Tourism Research Group (1996), *South West Tourist Industry. Competitiveness Report* Exeter: University of Exeter, p. 11.

3.  Amin A and Thrift N (1994), 'Living in the Global' in A Amin and N Thrift (eds.) *Globalisation, Institutions and Regional Development in Europe* Oxford: Oxford University Press, p. 1-22; Amin A and Thrift N (1995) 'Globalisation, Institutional 'Thickness' and the Local Economy' in P Healey *et al.* (eds.) *Managing Cities: The New Urban Context* Chichester: Wiley, p. 91-108. Amin and Thrift (1995, 106), writing about the economic vitality of localities in the light of globalisation, define institutional thickness as 'the capacity of places to develop, consolidate and transmit structures of representation, interaction and innovation'.

4.    Elliott J (1997), Tourism. Politics and public Sector Management London: Routledge, p. 11.

5.    Jones M (1999), New Institutional Spaces. TECs and the Remaking of Economic Governance London: Jessica Kingsley Publishers, p. 36.

6.    Sautter E and B Leisen (1999), 'Managing Stakeholders. A Tourism Planning Model' Annals of Tourism Research 26 (2): 318.

7.    The specific structure, culture and remit of this organisation will depend on local circumstances, local ambitions and local needs.

8.    Rutten, C. (1999), 'Brabant Niet Presenteren als een Plat Cliché' Brabants Dagblad 24 April.

9.    Ashworth and Tunbridge (1990, 263-264), note that, while the characteristic geographical 'package' is the nodal city-centred region, there is an increasing tendency to develop regional packages in which several (usually small) cities form an integral but less central part of what amounts to a uniform regional identity. They do, however, also go on to argue that the selling of distinct identities of European regions as a commodified 'couleur locale' is as old as tourism itself.

# References

Amin, A. and Thrift, N. (1994), 'Living in the Global' in A. Amin, and N. Thrift, (eds.) *Globalisation, Institutions and Regional Development in Europe* Oxford University Press, Oxford, pp. 1-22.

Amin, A. and Thrift, N. (1995), 'Globalisation, Institutional 'Thickness' and the Local Economy' in P. Healey *et al.* (eds.) *Managing Cities: The New Urban Context* Wiley, Chichester, pp. 91-108.

Ashworth, G. and Tunbridge, J. (1990), *The Tourist-Historic City* Belhaven Press, London.

Bramwell, B. and Sharman, A. (1999), 'Collaboration in Local Tourism Policymaking' *Annals of Tourism Research*, 26 (2), pp. 392-415.

Buxton, T., Chapman, P. and Temple, P. (eds.) (1998), *Britain's Economic Performance* Routledge, London.

Elliott, J. (1997), Tourism. Politics and public Sector Management Routledge, London.

Harvey, D. (1989), 'From Managerialism to Entrepreneurialism: the Transformation in Urban Governance in Late Capitalism' *Geografiska Annaler*, 71B, 1, pp. 3-17.

Healey, P. *et al.* (eds.) (1995), *Managing Cities. The New Urban Context* Wiley, Chichester.

Jamal, T. and Getz, D. (1995), 'Collaboration Theory and Community Tourism Planning' *Annals of Tourism Research* 22 (1): 186-204.

Jones, M. (1999), *New Institutional Spaces. TECs and the Remaking of Economic Governance* Jessica Kingsley Publishers, London.

Leach, S., Stewart, J. and Walsh, K. (1994), *The Changing Organisation and Management of Local Government* Macmillan, London.

Rutten, C. (1999), 'Brabant Niet Presenteren als een Plat Cliché' *Brabants Dagblad* 24 April.

Sautter, E. and B, Leisen. (1999), 'Managing Stakeholders. A Tourism Planning Model' *Annals of Tourism Research* 26 (2): 312-328.

Stewart, M. and Stoker, G. (1995), *Local Government in the 1990s* Macmillan, London.

Tourism Research Group, (1996), *South West Tourist Industry. Competitiveness Report* University of Exeter, Exeter.

# Urban tourism and environmental sustainability – taking an integrated approach

*Walter Jamieson*

Asian Institute of Technology, Thailand

*Pallavi Mandke*

Asian Institute of Technology, Thailand

## Introduction

With 44.5% of the world's urban population, Asia and the Pacific contains some of the world's fastest growing cities, reflecting the fact that it also contains most of the nations with the highest economic growth rates since 1980 (UNCHS/HABITAT, 1996). By the year 2015 the population of the cities in Asia and the Pacific is expected to increase by 20% and a total of over 50% of each country's population will be residing in the cities. In the face of this rapid demographic growth in the cities and the deteriorating living and environmental conditions most cities are not prepared to absorb the growth. To add to this burden, cities like Bangkok through promotion of tourism add a floating population of 7 million every year and are targeting for more in the coming years. Promotion of tourism for economic growth is high on the national agenda of the countries in Asia, with Thailand declaring the years 1998 – 99 as 'Amazing Thailand years', Cambodia declaring 1999 as the 'Visit Cambodia' year and Lao and Vietnam following the same path. In 1998 Asia received 62 million visitors, of which 29.5 million visitors went to South East Asia (PATA, 1998). Table 1 shows the growth in visitor arrivals to South East Asia.

**Table 1    Visitor Arrivals to South East Asia**

| Country | 1994 | 1995 | 1996 | 1997 | 1998 |
|---------|------|------|------|------|------|
| Brunei | - | - | - | - | 964,080 |
| Cambodia | 176,555 | 219,680 | 260,489 | 218,843 | 186,333 |
| Indonesia | 4,006,312 | 4,324,229 | 5,034,472 | 4,431,450 | 4,606,416 |
| Lao PDR | 146,155 | 346,460 | 403,000 | 463,200 | 500,200 |
| Malaysia | 7,197,229 | 7,468,749 | 7,138,452 | 6,210,921 | 5,550,748 |
| Philippines | 1,573,821 | 1,760,163 | 2,050,117 | 2,222,523 | 2,149,357 |
| Singapore | 6,898,951 | 7,137,255 | 7,298,592 | 7,197,871 | 6,242,153 |
| Thailand | 6,166,496 | 6,923,384 | 7,603,702 | 7,293,957 | 7,842,760 |
| Vietnam | 940,707 | 1,358,182 | 1,607,155 | 1,719,918 | 1,520,128 |
| TOTAL | 27,106,226 | 29,538,102 | 31,395,979 | 29,758,683 | 29,562,175 |

*Source:* PATA, 1998

# The need for strategic planning for sustainable tourism development

For many Asian cities and in fact, countries, tourism development provides much-needed employment and foreign exchange earnings. The increased wealth generated by tourism can also be directed towards the improvement of various aspects of the urban environment. There are also the significant social, economic, cultural and ecological negative impacts that result from poorly planned and managed tourism development.

It is clear from the challenge described above that the significant issues facing Asian cities when combined with the need to develop tourism as both a positive and negative force requires sound strategic planning and management. Otherwise cities and towns are not going to be in a position to economically benefit from tourism and achieve sustainable development.

There is increasing awareness that sustainable tourism development is necessary for all stakeholders whether they are community members, members of the tourism industry or those concerned with improving the environment and seeking to conserve natural and cultural environmental features.

There is increasing evidence that an integrated approach to tourism planning and management is now required to achieve sustainable tourism. Urban planning and urban management and planning for tourism purposes have rarely been seen as allied fields. Where there has been planning for tourism it is often a separate activity from the more traditional areas of urban policy analysis and making. It is only relatively recently that there is a growing recognition of the importance of combining the needs of traditional urban management (transportation, land use planning, marketing offices, economic development, fire and safety etc) with the need to plan for tourism.

There are important reasons to ensure a sound relationship between urban planning and management on one hand and strategic tourism destination management. The tourists are demanding safe and clean tourism destinations. They also put a high value on urban design, ease of movement and demand satisfaction from the attractions and hospitality facilities provided within urban environments. Sustainable management of such issues as solid waste, clean water, air emissions and air quality, and environmental protection must be achieved. In order to accomplish these objectives, all disciplines must work together in developing important solutions.

Specific example of new approaches that are required to ensure sustainable development include:

- The creation of economic instruments that provide incentives for environmental improvement and protection while ensuring that poverty conditions are alleviated.

- The development of management and organisational structures to allow innovative technologies to be used in both the destinations themselves as well as hospitality facilities (e.g. solar and wind energy, recycling grey water, clean production techniques).

- The design of tourism planning and management processes that take into account social, economic, environmental and cultural factors.

The model of destination management presented below provides an indication of the range of factors that have to be considered in managing destinations. This paper will concentrate on selected aspects of the overall management process.

**Figure 1    Total Tourism Destination Management**

# Tourism Destination Management

| Product Marketing & Development | Destination Planning | Organizational & Management Structures | Destination & Site Operations |
|---|---|---|---|

**Product Marketing & Development**
- **Marketing:**
  Research
  Development of a Marketing Strategy
  Development of a Promotion Strategy
- **Product Development:**
  Product Design
  Site Planing
  Route Planning
  Conservation Strategies
  EMS for Facilities
  Financing
  Interpretation
- **Training of Public & Private Sector Staff**

**Destination Planning**
- Destination Analysis
- Policy Development
- Transportation Planning
- Land Use & Physical Planning
- Urban Environmental Management Strategies
- Determination of Carrying Capacity
- Impact Assessment
- Training of Public & Private Sector Staff

**Organizational & Management Structures**
- Development of Leadership & Management Capacities
- Management of Stakeholder Participation
- Design of Organizational Structures
- Creation of Partnerships
- Training of Public & Private Sector Staff

**Destination & Site Operations**
- **Environmental Management:**
  Waste
  Water
  Sewage
  Air Quality
- **Disaster Planning::**
  Natural Disasters
  Fire
- Heritage Resource Conservation
- Site/Attraction Management
- Security
- Training of Public & Private Sector Staff

# An integrated approach to planning and management for better tourism and better environment

There are 2 major components of an integrated planning and management process: multi - stakeholder approach and multi - disciplinary approaches. The multi – stakeholder approach will detail who should be involved in the planning process and what individual tasks should be while the multi – disciplinary approach will discuss the use of various tools and streams of knowledge for sustainable tourism. There are a number of tools that help to integrate the 2 approaches and they include Environmental Impact Assessment (EIA), Cumulative Effects Assessment (CEA), Environmental Management Systems (EMS), Public Participation, etc. These approaches will be illustrated by the research and demonstrations carried out by the Training and Technology Transfer Program (TTTP) of the Canadian Universities Consortium Urban Environmental Management Project (CUC UEM) using these various management tools.

## Environmental management systems

For sustainable development of popular destinations with a large number of hotels and guesthouses it becomes important to implement environmental management systems (EMS) in the hotels. The most common issue in the implementation of EMS is the willingness of all categories of hotels to adopt a holistic system. In a research study carried out by one of the authors in Goa, India it was observed that the lower category or smaller hotels had a low willingness to adopt environmental practices. It was clear that without a combined effort of the various stakeholders it was not feasible to implement an environmental management program given that each of the stakeholders played an important role in applying checks and balances in the implementation of an environmental management program. Table 2 lists all the stakeholders and their roles in developing and implementing an environmental management program in Goa.

The involvement of the various categories of stakeholders from the government institutions, private sector, people's groups and media also demonstrate the need for inter-disciplinarity and multi-disciplinarity in implementing EMS in hotels. Technical experts, planners, social scientists, managers in the field of water, waste, energy, etc. are required to interact and operate collectively for a common goal. People's groups, media and the regulatory authorities can help to control and regulate each other's behavior for environmental sustainability.

The following table lists the stakeholders in 4 categories namely government institutions, private sector, people's groups and media, shows their level of importance in implementing environmental management systems in hotels and makes a comment on their existing role and justifies the level of importance of the stakeholder.

**Table 2    Role of the Stakeholders in Implementing Environmental Management Programs in Goa**

| Stakeholders | Potential Importance | Comments |
|---|---|---|
| **Government Institutions** | | |
| Goa State Pollution Control Board (PCB) | 5 | Has no role in setting standards and monitoring the environment of hotels as they do in all other industries. Has a very high importance if necessary standard regulations are to be established. |
| Department of Town and Country Planning (DTCP) | 4 | Poor implementation of the CZR: all 3 beachside hotels in the sample had violated the CZR. DTCP is a highly important regulatory body for construction activities and, therefore, the organisation must improve its implementation of the CZR. |
| Panjim Municipal Council (PMC) | 4 | The PMC is the prime body responsible for handling waste in the city, and majority of the hotels give their waste to the PMC. There are some problems in the way the waste is managed by the PMC. PMC's role is important in improving the city's waste management system. |
| **Government Institutions** | | |
| Department of Tourism | 5 | Environment is low on the agenda of this department and it does not consider managing hotels as a part of its responsibilities. But as hotels are the backbone of the tourism industry, and as the department registers and classifies hotels and markets them through various publications, it is considered a potentially very important body to promote environmental management in hotels. |

| PWD | 4 | PWD has no conservation program, but would be effective if they limited the consumption of water by hotels. |
|---|---|---|
| Goa State Electricity Board | 4 | Has no conservation program, but would be effective if they limited the consumption of water by hotels. |
| **Private Bodies** | | |
| Private Contractors for waste collection | 3 | They do what is expected of them |
| Chartered Travel Agents | 2 | They lay conditions primarily for better hygienic conditions not so much for the environment. Although they can help bring about change it is difficult to regulate as they operate in the free market. |
| Travel and Tourism Association of Goa | 4 | A forum of hotels that could be used positively to make hotel management aware and conscious of the environmental issues. |
| Institute of Hotel Management, Goa | 2 | Most of the young professionals take formal training from this institute in Goa hence it would be effective to introduce formal environmental training as part of the institute's curriculum. |
| Suppliers of Bio-degradable products | 3 | Most of the suppliers are in Mumbai and rarely cater to Goa, but as they could play an important role in changing the trends in the hotels it is necessary to establish links with them. |
| **People/Groups** | | |
| Chartered Tourists | 4 | Act as powerful pressure groups and demand environmentally-friendly behaviour from hotels. |
| Indian Tourists | 2 | Indian tourists are not at all environmentally conscious. |
| JGF (Jagrut Goenkaranchi Fouz) | 4 | They are an active people's group ready to handle issues that would involve them as an important pressure group over hotels to implement environmental management programs. However, they need to be directed to take up the issue of hotels. |
| Goa Foundation | 4 | They file petitions against offences committed by hotels and have designed and piloted a Green Hotels' Program of their own. They could be encouraged to create an incentive based labelling program for hotels such as the Green Leaf Program. |
| Local Community | 3 | The local community is not motivated and is poorly organised to act as a pressure group over the hotels. But if well organised with the help of JGF the community can be activated to push the hotels to implement environmental management programs. |
| Hotel Staff | 4 | The hotel staff is not environmentally conscious as the management does not think it necessary to invest in the floating staff. But as the staff is the implementing hand of the environmental practices they are potentially very important. |
| Hotel Management | 5 | They are partially aware and are partially implementing environmental practices, but to attain effective management there is a need to improve the role of the management, and as it all begins with their commitment to the cause they are the most important stakeholders. |
| **Media** | | |
| Newspapers | 5 | The local newspapers have been vigilant about the environmental pollution caused by the hotels. As such, media portrayal of the hotel is a very effective tool to make hotels environmentally conscious. |

*(Source*: Mandke Pallavi, 1999)
Key: Very important - 5   Fairly important – 4   Neutral – 3   Not so important – 2
Not at all important - 1

The stakeholder involvement is also combined with an exchange between the stakeholders in this case between the hotels and the other stakeholders. The following figure shows the exchange between the hotels and the stakeholders in the case of Goa. It is when the expectations from this exchange are fulfilled all the stakeholders perform their roles that implementing environmental management programs in hotels is possible.

**Figure 2    Exchange between Stakeholders and the Hotels**

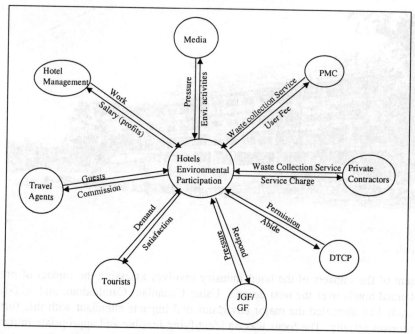

The project's experience in Hua Hin, Thailand reiterates the same, where TTTP with the help of the Thailand Environmental Institute is implementing cleaner production in hotels. After training the hotel management and the staff in the various cleaner production techniques the project is now shifting its focus from the hotels to a macro level. In this phase the project will work with various stakeholders to create favorable conditions for the hotels to implement environmental management programs and in turn contribute to make the destination environmentally sustainable.

## Cumulative effects assessment

The TTTP has entered into a Memorandum of Understanding with the Ministry of Environment in Cambodia to work co-operatively on assessing cumulative effects of the growing hotel industry in Siem Reap. Siem Reap, a community seven kms from the famous Angkor temples, caters to the hospitality needs of the tourists that visit Angkor. Cambodian environment and tourism officials have identified a range of environmental issues that face the Siem Reap community as it further develops its tourism potential. Issues of sanitation, sewage, availability of clean water, and the quality of the river are only some of the issues facing both the community and the national government. There is recognition of the importance of effectively dealing with these issues in order to protect the welfare and health of local inhabitants. There is also a strong recognition of the potentially negative impacts which poor environmental management will have on the success of Siem Reap as a tourism destination. International experience has demonstrated that issues of sanitation and environmental quality are important determinants in ensuring the success of a tourism destination.

**Photo 1    Hotels as large as 150 rooms are being constructed in a town without a sewerage system**

The assessment of the impacts of the hotel industry involves assessing the impact of present as well as planned hotels over the next decade. Using Canadian, Cambodian, and AIT-based experts the study has identified the major environmental impacts attendant with this form of hotel based tourism activity. The focus was on identifying feasible and appropriate mitigative measures for the community that will provide a basis for decision-making and future actions. Together, the assessment and identified measures will also assist the community in their efforts to secure international funding for the implementation of specific actions (e.g., design and construction of an appropriate sewerage system). There is recognition that there are a number of other actors and dimensions in helping to plan and manage the community. The Project is attempting to interact with as many stakeholders as possible.

This project has been used as an example to illustrate the various aspects that can be covered under UEM and how tools like EIA or CEA can be used to draw environmentally sustainable solutions.

## Public participation in developing a tourism plan

The development of a tourism plan in Klong Khwang, Thailand by the CUC UEM Project is yet another example of urban environmental management and tourism. This project was driven by the larger concern for growing international interest in small community tourism that has made the task of maintaining cultural and environmental integrity in fragile communities a critical development and management issue. Klong Khwang was used as a demonstration site to understand community based tourism destination management. This community was identified by the Tourism Authority of Thailand (TAT) as a community with tourism potential given such attractions such as Thailand's oldest stone reclining Buddha, an archeological site of an ancient city and an intact traditional community form.

**Photo 2    Thailand's oldest stone reclining Buddha at Klong Khwang**

TTTP has assisted Klong Khwang in its tourism development process specifically by helping to strengthen the strategic planning skills of local officials. TTTP encouraged the consideration of issues such as carrying capacity, social and environmental impacts, and marketing. At the community level, the Project has promoted community participation in key project activities to reinforce the community's role as stakeholder in the decision-making process. This process involved an interesting mix of dialogue and action, including a full-scale experimental group tour. Further, at both government and community levels, the concept of Klong Khwang forming part of a destination "circuit" with Korat and Phimai has again been emphasised as a development option. As a tourism destination, Klong Khwang is still in its formative stages. However, as this development moves forward, efforts are being made to help the community achieve its tourism objectives without compromising the principles of environmental sustainability, cultural integrity and community participation.

The Tourism Working Group of APEC has recognised this effort as a good example of sustainable tourism.

Another example of TTTP's people's participation and stakeholder involvement is its tourism development project in Phimai, Thailand. This Project is involved in tourism destination management and tourism development planning. While there are a number of demonstration initiatives in several Southeast Asian countries, we will describe two initiatives that illustrate this aspect of our work. A destination management plan is being developed in Phimai in Thailand with an Angkor-period temple, annual festivals, historic Banyan tree, museum, restaurants and hotels, Phimai attracts thousands of visitors annually.

**Photo 3    A view of the Phimai archaeological site at present**

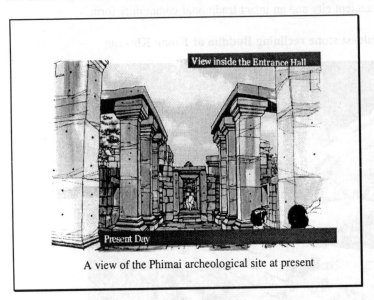

A view of the Phimai archeological site at present

In an effort to improve Phimai's established position as a cultural tourism destination, the Regional Office of the Fine Arts Department and the TTTP are focusing on specific project objectives, including:

- improved interpretation and preservation strategies for the historical site,

- enhanced commercial street experiences to support additional economic activity,

- the development of museum options to increase visitation rates,

- dealing with the problems of traffic circulation and congestion around the sanctuary site,

- finding suitable parking that does not have negative impacts on surrounding land uses

**Photo 4    Interpretation of the Phimai site as it might have been 1000 years ago**

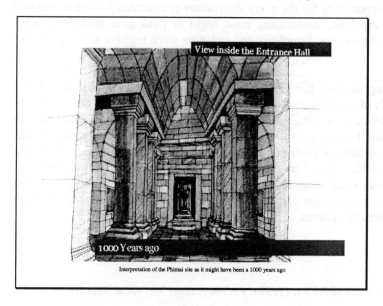

Interpretation of the Phimai site as it might have been a 1000 years ago

The nature of the issues in Phimai demand that a concerted and united community effort is required to achieve the tourism development objectives identified by the regional office. While a full-fledged exercise in community participation involving all interest groups is beyond the scope of the TTTP demonstration, we have been able to assist in identifying feasible strategies to strengthen Phimai's economic and tourism development and management efforts. Through information sessions, illustrations of possible new design features in various key locations in Phimai, and interpretative options using computer technology, the TTTP will provide the Regional Office with a foundation for community dialogue and sustainable development. Furthermore, the notion of Phimai forming part of a destination "circuit" with Korat and Klong Khwang in the North East of Thailand has been identified as a development option.

For more information on CUC UEM projects, visit the web site http://www.cuc.ait.ac.th

# Conclusion

The clear relationship between good quality urban environments and successful tourism in cities makes it imperative that issues of pollution, congestion, clean water, well-designed environments etc. are dealt with. Carrying out this type of work in a rapidly growing urban area is most difficult especially when combined with the economic issues facing most Asian cities. The examples presented above are used to illustrate the importance of using a range of tools and approaches in making sustainable urban destination management happen. Certainly one of the most important dimensions of managing urban destinations is in the need to take into account the needs and concerns of a wide range of stakeholders. Without the support of and successful participation of the stakeholders it is highly unlikely that the dual aims of economic development and urban environmental improvement will occur.

It is equally evident that unless a range of issues and concerns are dealt with in an integrated way there is little or no opportunity for the many dimensions of community to be considered and improved. At the very least, destinations must begin to think in a multidisciplinary fashion. It is only when the various disciplines and concerns work together that we can see any level of success.

Finally, the extensive range of tools that are available must be creatively utilised in order to provide the desired levels of scientific and technical information. Having said all of this, the authors recognise the difficulty of achieving the goal of sustainable urban tourism but see this as the target that must be constantly aimed for if sustainability is to be achieved. The authors recognise the importance of continued research and documentation of successful case studies if we are to better understand the mechanisms that can contribute to sustainability. The authors and their colleagues continue to work in these areas with a stress on urban finance, organisation and management and the design of regulatory and voluntary systems for environmental management systems.

# References

Pacific Asia Travel Association (PATA), (1998), PATA Annual Statistical Report.

United Nations Centre for Human Settlements (HABITAT), (UNCHS/HABITAT) (1996), An Urbanising World, Oxford University Press, Oxford, UK.

# Revitalisation of urban heritage - or the commodification of tradition?

## Basil Ahmed Kamel

University of California, USA

## Abstract

The production of urban space and its surrounding architecture was long perceived as an outcome of social and cultural forces that create, produce and shape the habitual patterns of life. Scholars, like Graburn, Harvey and others argue that most reconstructions of heritage and tradition focus on the social, conceptual and behavioural recollections that shaped the urban landscape. In doing so, these reproductions conflict with urban reality that is nowadays detached from place and is formed only to rely on its essence. Heritage and tradition here become the means to the production of architecture and the urban space rather than the end.

This paper focuses on understanding the process by which architecture and urban space is produced as means to preserve and construct tradition and heritage. It questions the purpose, outcome and use of these built landscapes. The premise is that these built landscapes are an outcome of other processes, those that are more in touch with urban reality and the worldwide mechanisms of production and consumption. Within these processes, the body of heritage and tradition - and by that I mean the beliefs, conceptual themes and productive systems on the one hand, and the resources, indigenous architecture, arts and crafts on the other - are being systematically dismantled, appropriated and transformed to accommodate new settings.

The paper focuses on a specific case study in Egypt, a country of rich heritage and tradition that has been influenced by both global and local forces of change and transformation. The challenge of livelihood pauses an enormous pressure on the processes and mechanisms of social and cultural habitual patterns. This is reflected dramatically on the built landscapes and how people deal with their new environs. The conflict is manifested in areas of touristic developments along the coasts of the Red Sea. The paper highlights how the natives and tourists interact within the reproduced context in an attempt to answer the question: Is it the revitalisation of urban heritage or the commodification of tradition?

# From Hassan Fathy to Michael Graves: Concepts and envisions

When Hassan Fathy looked to the Nubian indigenous architecture in Egypt for inspiration, his intent was to seek solutions for the crisis in architecture and the urban environment of the time. To him, the growing alienation resulting from "modern" architecture was to be only reversed by re-rooting one's self in tradition and the vernacular. The architecture he produced was one that 'he thought' would tune itself to the evolution of time linking the divine to the knowledge of mankind.

Space to Fathy was an outcome of a common language. To comprehend it, live it, and appreciate it, one has to be part of it and it has to be part of one's self. This blend and intimacy were his vision of an architecture that is by the people and for the people. But slowly as the experiments became reality, Fathy himself realised that the vernacular is too far and tradition is sometimes way too deep (Figures 1 and 2).

Figures 1 & 2: Hassan Fathy's Al Gourna and Michael Graves' El Gouna: Although miles apart in space and time, yet linked by a challenge to tradition and modernity.
**Source: Architectural Digest 1999 & Steele 1988**

The reuse of traditional architecture and urban settings has been and will always be a controversial issue in a world of changing economy and global technological advancements. How, why, for what purpose, in what context, etc. are but a few questions. What adds to the complexity of these issues is the competition to cross local markets to a global arena of different values, structures, interests and pace. The Sawiris brothers, owners of Orascom Investment Company, challenged these issues - unintentionally - while developing their new touristic city of El Gouna at the Red Sea in Egypt. The outcome is a glitzy city, a new Fantasy Land in the Middle East with the works of local and international architects (Figure 3). The works of Michael Graves draws from the lines of thought of Fathy's ideologies manifested in Ramy Al Dahan and Soheir Farid's work in the initial development of the city (Figures 4 and 5). The process reflects the unveiling of how, when, for what purpose, and, in what context tradition can survive.

Figure 3: A collage of styles, symbols and meanings created by Michael Graves to intrigue a unique experience to the user. A combination of the Nubian vernacular and Pharaonic Monumentalism established this dialogue. **Source: Architectural Digest 1999.**

Figures 4 & 5: The design of Kafr El Gouna represented the architecture of Hassan Fathi in recreating the dwellings of Nubia and Upper **Egypt. Source: By Author**

# Egypt: A growing conflict between old and new

A decade ago, tourism in Egypt was controlled by a handful few. With a strict control over the economy the private sector for decades had little opportunity to interfere in the market of tourism. In the mid eighties, the statist, socialist Egypt of the old has changed to become the very model (as noted by the International Monetary Fund and the World Bank) of a modern emerging market challenging its way out of the stronghold of central planning. The private sector now controls almost 80% of the Egyptian Economy (*The Economist*, 1999).

The physical changes in the urban scene of Egypt have been dramatic. The once empty Mediterranean shoreline has become a solid block of wall-to-wall summer homes with private beaches and marinas. The Red Sea coast and Sinai have also been transformed to a touristic enchanting landscape, and in areas, not much different than the fantasy of the new Las Vegas where the recreation of heritage sites became means of place promotion.

To many developers, the choice of the architecture of the place was a dilemma. The aim was to create a place of uniqueness that would represent to the tourist the comfort of his home as well as the enthusiasm of the place. To architects, the issues were more complex.

The reliance on the deliberate cultural anonymity or alternatively, the deliberate western hegemony of high modernism, or the traditional forms, symbols, representations and meanings of local architecture was always a dilemma. As the architecture seeks its unique expression, architects capitalising on traditional and vernacular architecture questioned which specific local tradition to elevate into a building, and which symbol - or group of symbols - can be the most represented in the modern state. The reason for this confusion was simply because there is great uncertainty about what is still alive from tradition within the different categories of locals, consumers and the state. Architects who attempt to make the social and cultural preferences get caught in the paradox of the modern universal civilisation, the contemporary sub-cultures within the country and the traditional indigenous or vernacular representations. The question thus becomes, which is the one to represent? The outcome to this process of establishing authenticity is often a glibly masking and decoration of modern buildings from an incoherent variety of historical and regional contexts.

When the question becomes: Is there common ground? One can then seek to find an answer. Is it possible to represent the diversity of cultural groups, the influence of the globalisation and modernity, the effect of the left indigenous vocabulary, and the values, symbols, representations of the past, of tradition? If there is a turn towards the process of architecture rather than its outcome, there may be some cues to how to resolve this paradox. The process of producing architecture through history was a collective communal process that represents its value systems, its enthusiasm and prosperity. Whether this process was done explicitly through participatory approaches (mostly in the creation of the dwellings and the urban settings) or done implicitly by individuals that were part of the culture the outcome was an architecture comprehended, shared and experienced without conceptual and behavioural conflict.

## Tradition, the vernacular and the indigenous: What is really left?

It is important to the argument to shed some light on some conceptual themes related to the use of the terms tradition, vernacular and indigenous in architecture and space production. The term tradition in architectural practice in my opinion cannot be defined irrelevant to context and in particular to communities. Tradition is both a process and an outcome. The practices, performances, and patterns of behaviour within a group of people based upon common values, needs and ideas lead to the formulation of a common expression, accepted and comprehended by all, that is, the community. In that sense tradition is an outcome of a collective process that involves a communal group or groups of people.

The term "tradition"[1] has been widely and differently used by many scholars, writers and researchers in several disciplines to give a variety of meanings, depending on the stated arguments and the personal interpretations. Amos Rapoport indicates that there can be different kinds of traditions as he notes that: "Since anything can become a tradition by being transmitted over time, tradition is a very general concept potentially applicable to many domains: lifestyles, behaviours, institutions, law, art, philosophy, built environments, . . . and so on. It follows that different mechanisms of transmission may be used, although all involve people."(Rapoport, 1989). Any tradition can thus be defined as a handed down logically integrated, functional, sense-making whole that represents a collection of customs, rules, patterns of behaviour and habits that form a shared value system.

But all traditions are constantly changing; no culture can be described as static. Parts of a tradition even change at different times and degrees, consequently, perfect integration and perfect fit are impossible. Values seem to change more slowly than other aspects of tradition. Although this reluctance to change in the face of rapid technological advances often induces serious stresses, this essential conservatism of values serve as a brake on uncontrolled change, usually slowing the process to the point where a society can absorb new elements without threatening its basic structure and unifying core. Unlike transformation, which usually cuts tradition, change in any society can occur and is accommodated by those phases and aspects in tradition that are affected by it. Unfortunately this was not always the case, not because progress and technology destroy continuity, but it is the method of adoption and implementation that cuts and transforms societies segregating them from their traditions.

Tradition makes possible the largely instinctive interaction between individuals that is a prerequisite to social life. Through the language, life patterns, expressions of forms, and other symbols, it provides for the communication and understanding that is essential to the ongoing activities of daily living. It supplies people with cues that enable them to understand and anticipate the behaviour of others and to know how to respond to it. In that sense two line of thoughts are detected: the first concludes that any process of development or change should start within people, so as to guarantee a continuation of tradition, and a successful interaction between the society and this developmental process. Imposing change and development as a process starting outside the community does not necessarily lead to an understanding and a participation of the society to ensure its success. Second comes tradition as an expression, an outcome, whether vernacular, spontaneous, indigenous or simply traditional. When talking about a physical expression of tradition we are hence referring to an architecture that reveals certain values based on collective ideologies and practices.

Before engaging in any further discussions let me first put the terms vernacular, spontaneous and indigenous in context. As the definition of the term in linguistics suggests vernacular means "native, of one's own native country, and not of foreign origin or learned formation."[2] It is also explained as "(that) which is spoken or written naturally at a particular period."[3] The use of the word with reference to architecture normally refers to an indigenous type of building, but which is thought to be of considerable value. This view deliberately considers vernacular architecture as a physical expression with a symbolic reference to uniqueness and importance as well as an outcome of local materials and practices which is not anonymously the case. As Amos Rapoport explains he classified vernacular as part of folk tradition: "The folk tradition, on the one hand, is the direct . . . translation into physical form of a culture, its needs and values - as well as the desires, dreams, and passions . . . it is . . . the "ideal" environment of a people expressed in buildings and settlements . . . .. The folk tradition is much more closely related to the culture of the majority and life as it is really lived." (Rapoport, 1969).

This statement represents a wide perspective of the vernacular that I would not advocate. Although vernacular architecture usually deals with correct formalisations and expressions yet it is difficult to describe this translation of a culture as the ideal environment, I would have rather used the term appropriate instead of ideal because it does not deny this vernacular outcome to grow adapt and even change. As Norberg-Schulz puts it, vernacular architecture matches the "Genius Loci" of place (Nurberg-Schulz, 1980).[4] It expresses the inner identity of people in models that are constantly being adjusted and reshaped.

The term vernacular as perceived by architects and planners further induces two aspects that need questioning. The first is the idea that vernacular architecture is an outcome of the users without qualified architects or builders and constructed without using graphic tools. In many cases and in different parts of the world evidence showed that this statement is not totally true for there is at least an organised system, a process with technical input that is not necessarily impute by architects beyond the vernacular outcome. The second is the idea that vernacular architecture developed entirely from local resources and inputs. In reality, many of these architectural expressions were subject to external influences. Builders and architects - who were the residents themselves, who pioneered this building process, did not hesitate to combine and reintroduce "modern aspects of these times" as a response to progressive ideas or modern comfort. This is were the term indigenous architecture should be introduced to differentiate between architectural outcomes based totally on local materials and concepts, and a vernacular architecture that is produced by natives but has components of other cultural contexts or foreign materials.

It is important to accept the passing away of traditional environments and the evolution of new expressions or modified ones as a normal and healthy process by which societies regenerate themselves. Tradition simply does not die but takes different forms (AlSayyad et al, 1989). These changing forms of traditional expressions in the near past existed primarily in rural areas. One can argue that this is no longer the case as the overwhelming majority of urban poor in developing countries live in new forms of settlements within cities that can be looked upon as a mix between the modern and elements of tradition. AlSayyad explains that: "Behind those structures are traditional modes of existence, traditional lifestyles, traditional practices and traditional economies. In some ways these are the closest thing we have today to traditional vernacular." (AlSayyad et al, 1989). Although the expression is modernised, yet beyond it remains a traditional process that needs to be unveiled, a collective system that preserves traditional values hidden within people. No matter how we as architects and/or planners try, the only means to unveil this process is to become part of it.

## Space production and place promotion

One common way to pursue design that responds to diverse cultures, the state, and tradition was through the common request that architects and designers should make concerted efforts to study the politics, the traditions and the cultures of the country they were asked to symbolise. Both in concept and in practice this notion usually failed because the complexity is overwhelming. The history is full of meanings and values that are hidden within, not easy to comprehend even by insiders, and furthermore the pressures of politics, economy and personal egos are too great to offer enough time and resources for this in-depth study. What really happened that in most cases the architect or designer looked towards "kitsch" to identify and confront assumptions and biases by virtue of personal background and preferences. Accordingly, architects -- except for a few attempts -- have been unable to bridge the problem of using both history and our contemporary context as fixed images, a static, unchanging entity rather than as a dynamic evolving process. Hence, "history in this

sense is codified into a series of inspiring icons to be readily recycled in current design."
(Richardson, 1989). In the same complexity, architects see the present as a slice in context.
No references are made to cross cultural, or diverse life patterns that co-exist in the world of
today in the city, in the urban space and even within the same dwelling unit. This focus
creates an architecture of narrow understanding and level of appreciation; furthermore it is
transformed from being a normative product accompanying culture to an artistic
representation of a concept, idea, or sub-culture. The architecture does not reflect the
experience of the community but becomes an exhibit that sometimes requires a title to
explain its experience.

The idea that there is a direct relationship between "culture" and the "built form" deserves
critical attention. There is a disciplinary conceptual separation that we talk about that
identifies this relationship. I do not argue the concept but I would like to redefine the
relationship in terms of both the context of the term culture and the context of the built
forms. In the traditional systems of producing built form the notion of this conceptual
separation did not exist. On the contrary, in the work of architects today cultural
considerations are normally absent and if available they are applied to a project to fit it in a
specific context or to fit a certain group of people whether users or clients. In that sense,
cultural contexts are not essential or intrinsic to the architectural practice. Culture hence
becomes a domain separable from the principles of modern form production. Europeans by
mid nineteenth century had come to view the person as set apart from the physical world as
one who controls it. This ideology had its applicability during the colonial periods, where
this distinction was an outcome of the ignorance of the processes of evolution and interaction
culture and representation from both sides, the coloniser and the colonised, in other words,
the traditional and the modern. In the contemporary architecture, the idea of linking separate
spheres of culture and built form as means to produce a more rooted architecture that relates
to 'local identity' and 'authenticity' can be mistaken. In fact, it may be a major stumbling
block to identify an architecture that ties the contemporary cultural diverse contexts of today,
simply because it is only comprehended and read by those who create these fictitious links
within there personal analogies and biases.

Richardson (1989) suggests that nineteenth-century definitions of culture are to blame for the
neglect of place in disciplinary studies like geography and anthropology. He also emphasises
the conceptual separation of place and culture as part of the distinction between geography
and anthropology. Some of the most influential studies of the relationship between culture
and built form have approached the former through the latter (e.g. Rapoport 1969, Glassie
1975, Bourdieu 1977, and Vale 1992.), that is they used vernacular architecture, objects,
spaces and zones to determine the social practice. The analysis here starts with material
forms as means of getting at the other tangible (or less tangible) habits and beliefs that
defines and orders the built form. Roderick Lawrence's (1987) work on the study of
contemporary urban communities is important as he introduces a perspective that treats "the
effective and spatial characteristics" of urban settings as complementary to the processes that
determined the needs, requirements, and means for implementation: "people and built
environments are linked in an active and reactive sense" (Lawrence 1987). Hence, it is
virtuous to agree that tradition makes possible the largely instinctive interaction between
individuals that is a prerequisite to social life. Through the language, life patterns,
expressions of forms, and other symbols, it provides for the communication and
understanding that is essential to the ongoing activities of daily living. It supplies people with

cues that enable them to understand and anticipate the behaviour of others and to know how to respond to it.

If we, as architects, planners and professionals, consider what we treasure in tradition is that collective process of making and consuming -- the commonness and not the uniqueness that reinforces the collectivity -- we ought to understand that beyond these expressions is a collective process, a communal system of common meanings that are attributed to its forms (Abu Lughod, 1992). Accordingly, the architectural outcome becomes a reflection of one's self, an invaluable mirror of the context and the setting, a revival of the divine models of the past, and a journey of thought into the future.

## Fathy's architecture becomes fantasy land

The development of Kafr El-Gouna presents a true example of the conflicts and issues raised above. In 1989, Orascom (an Egyptian construction corporation) established a sister company, Orascom Projects and Tourist Developments to develop 500 hectares of purchased land 22 Kilometres north of Hurghada, the fast developing touristic town at the Red Sea. The aim was to capitalise on the climate, clear waters and coral reefs of the Red Sea to create a large-scale resort project. As a driving force in marketing strategy and within a highly competitive market where supply is fast exceeding demand, the new village and resorts had to display a uniquely exotic attraction not only in services, but in its image and experience (World Architecture 1999).

"Samih Sawiris, chairman of Orascom, envisaged a fully independent resort town with hotels, villas and shopping boutiques; as well as a school, a hospital, small factories and other support facilities . . . designed around a series of linked [semi]-artificial lagoons sprawling around Kafr El Gouna to resemble a traditional fishing village" (World Architecture 1999). Although nothing is really left to be indigenous about the village in terms of its setting, yet the essence of traditional life patterns is lively recognised. Kafr El-Gouna, the village, was designed by Ramy Al Dahan and Soheir Farid in a joint venture with Ahmed Hamdi to represent an authentic Nubian architecture derived from the aesthetics of Hassan Fathy. The village was to host the natives, resort employees and staff members so as to recreate a traditional living working community (Figures 6 and 7).

Figure 6 & 7: The village of El Gouna represents a recreation of Nubian living working community in our modern times. **Source: By Author**

"There have been structural and cost complications with the design . . . and Orascom had to hire extra-skilled workers to build the vaults and domes that were required by the design, let alone the brick wall bearing" noted Hani Ayed in an interview for World Architecture magazine (World Architecture, 1999). This led to establishing a group of workers well trained for this vernacular type of architecture, a treasure that Michael Graves capitalised upon in his design of the Miramar resort later developed. The design of the village attempted to arrange the houses and support facilities along a group of winding alleys with subtle tones of pastel colours. Walking within creates an experience of the vernacular, an image that was printed in one's mind through the writings and architecture of Fathy and others (Figure 8). It is vivid that this recreation is a fantasy to both the indigenous population and the tourists. The environment introduced by such architecture was so powerful in creating the uniqueness of the village that the idea of limiting housing to workers and natives became unrealistic. The units and small size apartments were partially utilised in the investment scheme of the Gourna. Worthy of notice is that only a few of the natives of the village were able to live in these houses not only because of their cost but also due to their alien architecture.

Figure 8: The architecture of Hassan Fathy. **Source:Steele, 1988**

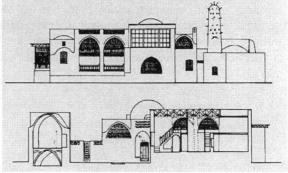

These issues were realised by Michael Graves in his design for the Miramar Sheraton. He neither wanted to build a resort that is too modern that would not capture the authenticity and the fantasy of the traditional, nor did he want to build a replica of Fathy's work as it was already there. He did what he does best; experiment with the foliage of a group of elements, colours, ideas and landscapes to create the fantasy (Figures 9 and 10). The fantasy was not only meant to be for the tourists, but for the natives and the indigenous as well.

Within a collaboration with Ramy Al Dahan and Soheir Farid, Michael Graves based his scheme on a basic collage of geometric elements and colours in different scales and situations put together to create a series of dialogues between the user and the used, the building and the context, the past, the present and the future.

*"The client wanted my take on it. He wanted to see what I would do with those materials, that place, that labour force."* (Schmertz, 1999)

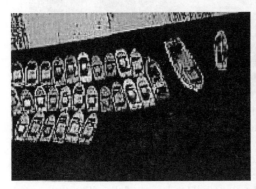

Figures 9 & 10:  The play of colors was not unique to fishing villages in the Red Sea.
**Source: Rossi, 1990.**

Michael Graves was intrigued by the skill and rapidity with which the handmade brick walls, domes and vaults were erected. He realised that the speed and economy of the process "would facilitate and enhance what he does best - invent a playful and endlessly varied aesthetic full of references to the past. For the Miramar, this was to be Egypt's Nubian vernacular combined with Pharaonic monumentalism."(Schmertz, 1999). Except for the cylindrical columns that carry reinforced concrete beams for large spans, everything was constructed quickly and inexpensively of brick by the local skilled labour (Figures 11, 12 and 13).

Figures 11, 12 & 13: For the Miramar, this was to be Egypt's Nubian vernacular combined with a style representing Pharaonic monumentalism. **Source: Architectural Digest, 1999**

Walking between the clusters of the resort is but an experience through time and space. It is a wild, intriguing recreation of the past in the context of the modern (Figure 14). Michael Graves' flexibility in combining the essence and originality of the place, his thoughts and beliefs about colour, collage and style, and, the notion of the modern created a successful vocabulary to transform El Gouna to a place of pleasure, authenticity, fantasy and delight a perfect scene for tourism.

Figure 14: Walking between the clusters of the resort is but an experience through time and space. It is a wild, intriguing recreation of the past in the context of the modern.
**Source: Architectural Digest, 1999**

The experience is wildly different than that of the neighbouring Hurghada resorts. There, the architecture of the place is an outcome of very individualistic trials by local and foreign architects that aim to provide for modern services and leisure facilities. What is missing is the feeling of authenticity and fantasy that is becoming core to the whole notion of touristic architecture and place promotion.

What is interesting though is the ability of this new trend in touristic architecture to recreate the social liveliness of traditional places. This is done through a delicate awareness and response by the produced architecture to the need for livelihood by the natives and the realisation of their abilities to adapt to and adopt certain tourism oriented behavioural patterns. At El Gouna, a flow of small business and labour moved from Hurghada to relocate and/or work at El Gouna. The natives were aware that the recreation of a traditional social life within the newly designed development is key to the success of tourism. The interaction between the natives and tourists goes beyond the buying and selling, or preparing for trips and excursions to a more complex social interaction to experience the habitual behaviours. This notion is becoming part of the touristic package that is seen promoted in advertisements for El Gouna.

## Concluding remarks: Is it the revitalisation of urban heritage or the commodification of tradition?

The experience of Kafr El Gouna is but one example in a long series of attempts by architects and urban designers to respond to the demands of the present with an eye on the richness, mystery and fantasy drawn from the past. Here, the architects did not claim that they were creating an architecture that reflects tradition in its social and spatial forms. They simply capitalised on the essence of the tradition through a complex reading of elements in the vocabulary that resembles only thoughts, ideas and perceptions. The collage of these elements to produce the built form became the wild card for touristic attraction. The experience is not much different from passing by the waterways of Venice or the winding streets of ancient cities or the domes of Fathy's traditional architecture. To the foreigner it is but a recreation that goes beyond the reality of spatial forms to the essence of space with all its mix between the imaginary and the real. This type of architecture steps beyond real space to cross to a virtual space recreated in the minds and spirits of the users.

The premise that these new types of global, yet context specific architectures are detrimental to the cultural values, qualities and meanings of the architecture of place is mistaken especially when dealing with projects that aim to create that fantasy. The problem occurs when a recreation of different contextual architecture in places that are irrelevant come to be. Ironically, several other architects in El Gouna produced an architecture that replicates styles of different contexts, the design of the Movenpick Hotel by Wimberley Allison and Goo based on a Mediterranean style is but one example.

Tourism is becoming an industry of extreme powers that aim to deal with a virtual recreation of diverse experiences to be lived through by the users. Architecture is becoming a strong tool in this recreation. The notions of tradition, as well as the elements of modernity (or post modernity to conform with the literature of time) have often been diluted down to a set of diagrams and formulae whose fixed nature negates the necessity to look at these elements and components as a dynamic and evolving condition that steps beyond the mere representations. The treatment of the past present and future in a layered and hierarchic system defies the architecture from stepping into a virtual space that can cross through time. The bringing together of these elements, concepts, and meanings produce endless variations of thought and experiences that are crucial to successful touristic marketing.

## Endnotes

1.  In Germanic and Latin languages the term 'tradition' is defined in both the Oxford and Webster dictionaries as the process of handing down or handing over, derived from the Latin word *tradit* ('tradere' - the past participle): to hand over or to deliver. In the Near and Middle Eastern peninsula the synonym to the word tradition is not well defined. There are a number of terms that convey a similar meaning from the Arabic and Farsi languages: *taqlid* and *mohaka* both conveying the meaning of copying, imitating and adopting ideas, *rewaya* having the primary meaning of transmitting, relating, and story telling. There are other terms that are used to give a similar meaning such as *adat* (customs and habits) and *taqalid* coming from the word *taqlid* previously stated. The term *hadatha* is more likely to give the meaning of transferring and relating by word of mouth

2.  See the Concise Oxford Dictionary, Fifth Edition.

3.  See Webster's Third International Dictionary.

4.  The term is a poetic expression indicating that architecture brings into presence the immediate meanings of the local earth and sky.

# References

Abu-Lughod, J. (1992), Disappearing Dichotomies: First World - Third World; Traditional - Modern. *TDSR* Vol. 111, No. 11.

Bourdieu, P. (1977), *Outline of a Theory of Practice*, Cambridge University Press, Cambridge.

Durkee, A. N. (1987), Tradition and Technology. In *Muslim Education Quarterly,* Vol.4, No. 3, Spring Issue, The Islamic Academy, Cambridge.

The Economist (1999), A Survey of Egypt: Old and New. In, *The Economist*, March 20th-26th.

Lawrence, R. J. (1987), *Housing, Dwellings and Homes: Design, Theory, Research and Practice*, John Wiley, Chichester, England.

Nasr, S. H. (1973), Commentary. In Ardalan, Nader and Bakhtiar, Laleh; *The Sense Of Unity,* The University of Chicago Press, U.S.A., London.

Norberg-Shulz, C. (1980), Genius Loci: *Towards a New Phenomenology of Architecture*, Rizzolli Publications, New York.

Rapoport, A. (1969), *House Form and Culture*, Prentice, New Jersey.

Rapoport, A. (1989), On The Attributes of "Tradition", in *Dwellings, Settlements and Tradition, Cross-Cultural Perspectives,* (Ed) Bourdier, Jean-Paul and AlSayyad, Nezar; University Press of America and IASTE, Lanham, U.S.A

Richardson, M. (1989), Place and Culture. In John A. Agnew and James S. Duncan (eds.), *The Power of Place*, Unwind Hymn, Boston.

Rodenbeck, M. and Rossi, Guido (1991), *Egypt From the Air*. Thames and Hudson, Ltd., Great Britain.

Schmertz, M. (1999), Egyptian Mirage: Michael Graves' Sheraton Miramar Rises on the Red Sea. In *Architectural Digest*, January, The Conde Nast Publications Inc., New York.

Shils, E. (1981), *Tradition,* University of Chicago Press, Chicago, U.S.A.

Steele, J. (1988), *Hassan Fathy*. Academy Editions, Great Britain.

Vale, L. (1992), Designing National Identity: Post Colonial Capitols as Inter-cultural Dilemas. In AlSayyad et al (eds), *Forms of Dominance*, Avebury: Great Britain.

World Architecture (1999), "Country Focus: Egypt. Issue Number 75, April.

# The city breaks option

*Atanas Kazakov*

Sofia St Kilment Ohridski University, Bulgaria

## Introduction

At the start of the 21st Century the tourism industry is one of the fastest growing industries in the world. The efforts of the specialists working in this area are concentrated in satisfying more and more customers with about 661 million expected arrivals in the year 2000. Something else, they try to exceed their expectations. This will increase the profit from the industry. The only way for it is to offer new forms of tourism, to find and interpret new attractions in new destinations, as well as some older but forgotten ones. The common trends for increase of free time and income, as well as the desire of people to have more than two holidays per year are just a few of the reasons which lead to the popularity of the so called city breaks tours.

They are short/usually one to three days duration/ tours in a particular city, or around it in the near surroundings. The most suitable types of transport are by airplane and by car. The main characteristics of these packages are:

- Travel in groups or individually – It depends on the tourist demand.

- program full with visits to cultural, historical, archaeological, natural objects, concerts, cultural events, attractions, and entertainment facilities in the city and in the near vicinity

- Possibilities for shopping

This is a special tourist product, which could be determined as special interest travel. The tourists have higher requirements with respect to the quality of the product, tourist resources, transport and tourist infrastructure, and the level of services. They are intelligent, open-minded cosmopolites. The price that they pay for these products is usually also higher. It includes:

- Return flight

- Transfer airport – hotel - airport

- Accommodation

- Meals when they are included in the price

- Services from a local tourist agent

- Guided city tour with a visit of the most famous places

- Entrance fees

The vertical integration is the reason the biggest airline companies to offer city breaks all over the world. They own big Tour Operator companies, Travel Agents, and Hotel chains, which gives to them the opportunity to sell the most attractive city destinations.

The question is, could Bulgaria be included in the list of tourist destinations offering this product and at what price?

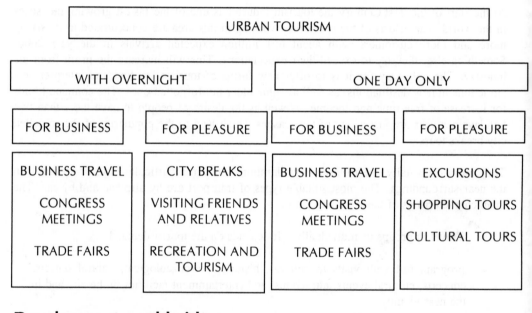

## Development worldwide

What is the reason to speak about city breaks? Why are they so popular today?

The first answer possible is consistency. In just a few days we are in a position to reveal the traditions, the culture and the history of a country. There is no mistake. Cities represent all these elements as a mirror. They were, are, and will be centres where the life is turned on constantly. With every single touch to the cities, we reveal local people, who actually leave them as a heritage to the world. People stand behind the scene, and even hundreds of years later a tourist could find their souls in the cities. They create the atmosphere of the city, and the main reasons why to visit it. *The atmosphere* is the element, which give to London, Amsterdam, Athens, Berlin, Paris, Istanbul, Vienna, and etc. possibility to be included in the brochures for city breaks. These are cities for which we could say that when we see them we have seen the country. They are like labels of the their development, sign and guarantee for quality of the product.

As we know the *history of the world* has been written in Europe. This is the main reason why cities in Europe have started to offer this tourist product. Here is involved also another factor - *transport accessibility* The second step was to include cities from the Atlantic coast of North America or near to it, like Boston, New York, Washington, Chicago, Montreal, and Toronto in the brochures. The final step till nowadays was to include cities from North Africa, like Marrakech, and Cairo and Jerusalem in Asia. There is another clear element that facilitates the development of city breaks, and it is *the tourist market*. Still more than 50% of tourist arrivals are towards Europe. This continent is also the main generic region of tourists. The cities which act as their destinations are whether in the continent, or next to it. This makes their location also a very important factor for the development of the city breaks.

# Resources     *Cities*

The destinations that offer this kind of tourist product usually have the following resources:

- Contrast of the culture and the way of life - As they are more different, as the city is more interesting for the tourists and visitors. The level of their preservation is also very important for the tourists. We travel because of the difference between us. If we could not find evidence for it we count that the journey has failed.

- Information and communication technologies - without them we could not speak of any interaction between the supply, and the demand.

- Traditions - There are such cities that attract visitors since many years, all over the year, every year. Every day is different there even for the local citizens. The tourists find a new city each time they go there - a very attracting reason to travel.     *HK lack of*

- Well known theatre, or opera scenes worldwide, as well as famous art galleries - The tourists for city breaks are people with specific interests, and a concert with Lucciano Pavaroti in Milan, could attract millions of people.

- Preserved old part of the city - this element is unique on one hand, and on the other it is very interesting how local people today incorporate it in their life.

- Live atmosphere - The spirit and the harmony in the city form this element which we could not feel from the postcards. Only the tourists know what it means to be in Munich during the October Beer Festival, walking on Champ's Elise in Paris, or dining out in the old part of Plovdiv.

- Architectural uniqueness - The architecture is a result of historical development. Preserved history means wisdom. Is it not the search of wisdom one of our main reasons to travel? The complexity of local history, culture, architecture and the way of life are essential, and very important when we choose a city destination.

- Well known scientific or cultural institutions worldwide - A few tourists visit these places in a city, but they act as a very strong attraction.

- Well known industry enterprises - "Renault", "Toyota", "Sony", and "Philips" are trademarks acknowledged all over the world. Places of the real production, processes, technologies, attract not only specialists. This is the place to say that the tourist program for the city break packages must be very well balanced. It should include different parts of the whole called city. And maybe this is the right place to say that "city break" does not mean visit of the central part of the city only. It could include also resources that are out of the city but still connected to it, and are situated not far from it.

- Well known religious places worldwide - It is recommended in such cases to have an accent on the specific theme.

- Festivals or trade fairs - Cities that are hosts to such events give excellent all year round opportunities for city breaks themes. These places are most suitable for cultural and business relationships.

# Factors for the development of city breaks

- Fashion trends – This is one of the most effective factors when speaking for the demand side of the industry. Usually the biggest Tour Operator companies determine them. This means that the bigger the profit for them, the more likely for destinations to be included in their offer. It is the often change of this factor that makes the diversity of the tourism supply side at any moment.

- Syndrome of identification – This is the feeling that everybody has when going to a place which attracts him or her. The tourist does not have any difficulties to identify himself or herself with the local people, culture, or way of living. Usually the syndrome is active when the tourist visits a cosmopolite city like London, or New York, where many different cultures are mixed together. It is very important that the local people accept also this situation.

- Advertising - Each city that has resources for the development of city breaks, and the factors are in its favour needs advertising. There is no other way to go on the tourism stage. Living in an information society we could not rely on the good will of the tourists. Without information, and advertising nobody would go to a WonderLand.

- Level of services – This is one of the most important factors. If the tourist is surrounded by stony faces, if there is no smile, if the personnel is not ready to help, if there is not customer care, then the destination could be lost forever. This is a factor that easy could lead to identification with the destination.

- Uniqueness of the resources – Here we count everything that makes the city different and easy to remember for the tourists. The mix of culture, architecture, history, atmosphere and parks could outline the city. We could always find something new in such cities.

- Diversity of the supply – There is no way for the tourist in an interesting city to be bored. In the tourism industry we have the so-called segmentation process. It is better for a tourist enterprise to offer services for particular kind of tourists. We could not satisfy all of them.

In the city is a little bit different. It must be ready to attract more than just a few segments. This means there should be places of interest for as many people as possible.

- Exotic – This means an unknown place, or a place far from the place of origin. As we said the regions for city breaks are closely situated. But they are so many that always there will be a place we have not visited.

- Economic stability – Without it there could not be a tourism supply, or at least not a quality type of supply. This factor together with the political stability determines the development not only of city breaks, but also the development of the tourism itself.

- Cleanliness – It is obligatory for all tourist facilities. It should be the philosophy of the industry as a whole. Nobody would travel to, or have respect for, a dirty city.

- Interpretation of the tourist resources – The possibility easy to understand them is very important. First they should have information about the resources in and around the city, and their exact location. Second they should be explained to visitors in their own language. The explanation must be compared with another famous resources from the place of origin of the tourists. This will facilitate the process of identification with the destination. Tourist brochures and leaflets are very important for the interpretation, but we should not forget also the interpreters, specialists who will reveal the universe of natural beauty, and heritage of the city destination.

- Situation close to natural resources – Cities situated near to the sea, the mountains, or a natural phenomenon are interesting for visitors. They attract them first as scenery, which surrounds the city, and second as a tourist resource.

- Famous chains of high quality hotel chains – The tourists who travel to city destinations use a better class of hotels, with plenty of services offered. In most cases this are hotels from worldwide hotel chains like Hilton International, Sheraton, Savoy, etc.

- Excellent transport infrastructure and organisation of the transport – The transport infrastructure must be on a very high level because of at least two reasons:

- The traffic difficulties because of the visitor's pressure. Visitors should not cause changes to the normal way of life.

- The access to the city destination must be excellent.

If a city without airport is to be offered for city break destination, the road system must be in an excellent condition. This is something which has not been made till today, because the tourists stay for a limited period of time, but there is a chance also for this kind of destinations.

- Lack of diseases in the region of the city destination

- Well-organised health system in the destination – In case of injury or disease tourists could count on the system. This creates also a good image for the destination.

# Problems

The development of tourism is always connected with a threat for the environment. During the city breaks the tourists are concentrated on a very limited area. This creates problems like pollution of the environment, no matter whether it is noise, garbage, air, water pollution, or something else. The higher level of social problems like crime, and prostitution is also evident.

We could even say that the normal way of life of local people is disturbed. There are traffic jams, and higher price level, something that is very well known among the tourists.

The tourist resources could be easily destroyed from the visitors, in a way that we could not speak about sustainability of the tourism development.

## Resources for city break in Bulgaria

Bulgaria is a small country situated in South Eastern Europe. It has cities from different epochs – ancient, medieval, contemporary. They are situated near to the capital – Sofia, and other suitable airports – Plovdiv, Varna, and Bourgas. There is no point in Bulgaria, which could not be reached within 6 to 10 hours' drive. This is a very interesting option for us, because the essence of the city break could be extended. We could offer city breaks packages which have two cities in one package, or city and sea break, or city and mountain break, or city, mountain and monastery break. The cultural, architectural, and spiritual heritage of Bulgaria gives opportunities for a richer product. There are numerous possibilities for different city break packages. It all depends on our customers. Their interests make their choice tailor-made, and of course unique.

## References

Staedte Tourismus (1991), *Eine Planungs- und Orientierungshilfe fuer klein- und mittelstaedte*, ADAC, Muenchen.

# Developing rural tourism in remote areas - are networks a solution?

*Raija Komppula*

North Karelia Polytechnic, Finland

## Introduction: Rural tourism as a part of the Finnish tourism industry

Finland is well known as a nature tourism destination. The most significant strengths of Finland are the low degree of pollution, large number of forests and lakes, wilderness, reasonable accessibility, snow and lots of activities to offer. According to travel statistics nature is the most notable attraction for foreign tourists (Finnish Tourist Board 1999).

Forests, waterways and local culture are emphasised when marketing and developing tourism in rural regions (Maaseutumatkailun teemaryhmä 1996), which cover 99 percent of Finland's area (Silvennoinen et. al.1997). According to Borg (1997), rural tourism is defined as tourism which takes place outside of densely populated communities and tourist centres. It is often considered small-sized and connected to farm industry and outdoor activities, offering the guests individual service (Borg 1997).

Although Finland is known as a nature tourism destination, the tourism industry focuses on densely populated southern provinces, where nature is not the main attraction. (Statistics of Finland 1999). The major part of registered overnights especially by foreigners is for business travel and directed to towns in Southern-Finland. Leisure tourism has bigger significance elsewhere in Finland, but the volumes are still small. Demand is low and enterprises have not grown bigger than micro-sized enterprises.

Half of the hotel units employ less than 30 persons, 35 percent less than five employees. Other kinds of accommodation establishments are micro-sized (less than five employees) with average turnover about 500 000 FIM. These enterprises are active only seasonally (Harju-Autti1998).

Three quarters of the 3600 rural tourism enterprises had originally been farms. Most of the tourism companies in rural regions are part-time enterprises. Tourism is the main source of income only for 15 percent of the rural tourism enterprises in Finland. Capacities of rural tourism enterprises are small (the average number of beds is 11 per company). One third of the companies offer accommodation and organised activity services, another one third offers only accommodation and the rest offers other combinations (Maaseutupolitiikan yhteistyöryhmä, 1997).

Most of the companies, which offer different kinds of activity services are located in the countryside. Over 60 percent of these, about 400 companies, were founded in the 1990s. The number of companies specialised in nature- and adventure-excursions, fishing services etc. has been significally increasing since 1993. Almost a quarter of these enterprises do not have full-time personnel, 44 percent have less than two employees (Aalto et.al 1999).

Most important partners for these activity service companies are hotels, other activity service companies and local tourism organisations. 71 percent of the companies have participated in marketing or development projects, which most often are more or less financed by regional funds supported by the European Union. Common opinion among the entrepreneurs is that the projects are not long enough, continuity is not well considered, and the results are quite poor. More than the half of the activity service companies (61%)consider co-operation between the tourism companies very important and only four percent consider them unnecessary (Aalto et.al. 1999).

## Regional tourism industry – an issue-based network

The tourism industry in a region can be seen as a network of actors who operate in different sectors of business in order to produce the total tourism product of the region. In regional tourism businesses a network can be defined as a group of independently owned and managed firms and other interests that agree to co-operate in order to achieve some common goals, because each partner's individual success is tied to the success of the overall network. Nets are defined as local concentrations of a network. Thus nets are considered as parts of a wider network. In everyday talk these terms are often used interchangeably.

The local and regional development programs in tourism are often organised in the form of projects partly funded by public authorities and the European Union. The projects are based on an issue, which may be, for example, product development, local development or marketing. The actors in the project may also form an issue-based net or a network, where the actors share a common vision of the issue as identified and activities are based on co-operative relationships (Brito 1997). These nets and networks are not meant to be life-long but to exist for a certain time-span and purpose. Some are often of a short term nature, others may function for several years. After the project the net or the network should continue without external support.

Our approach is based on the assumption that in the tourism industry network co-operation between private companies as well as with public actors is necessary and inevitable (see e.g. Boedlender et al. 1991, Laws 1995, Middleton 1989, Pearce 1992). The success of a network also requires the commitment to co-operate with the other actors involved. The level of commitment to the issue-based nets and networks differs between the actors. Brito (1997) argues that in issue-based networks, a small subset of interested actors are leading the collective action process and the bulk membership may be made up of a mass of passive actors not directly committed to the collective effort though supporting it for future possible benefits.

The purpose of this paper is to discuss the commitment to a net and/or a network. We focus on company's behaviour and exclude the public sector actors as well as the local residents.

We will firstly make a short literature review on the concept of commitment and then introduce results of a case study about three different issue based nets in a tourism network in a region in Finland.

We have been collecting the data by interviewing entrepreneurs and analysing documents. An important source of information is action research-based: the author has been the Head of the Board of the region N Tourist Service, which has made access to industry information much easier.

## Commitment to a network - literature review

In this research a company's commitment to the network is defined as the company's willingness and ability to accept the goals of the network and to make efforts (Anderson - Weitz 1992, Dwyer et al 1987, Nummela 1996 ) in order to participate in implementing the goals with a long term orientation (Ganesan 1994, Moorman et al. 1992, Shamdasani - Seth 1995).

The development of commitment is a gradual process (e.g. Anderson - Weitz 1992, Sharma 1993, Wilson - Mummaleni 1986) and during the development of the relationship the commitment tends to strengthen ( Dwyer et al. 1987, Hyvönen 1992, Young - Denize 1995). A company's commitment to a network is a process that ties the company to the network and relationships within it. The maintaining factor in this relationship is co-operation, and commitment is a series of ongoing small decisions about investment of time, money or other resources in the relationship.

The first step in committing oneself to a network is the perception of the need for co-operation ( Anderson et al. 1997), which may cause the desire to invest in that co-operation. Expectations of the future co-operation (Anderson - Weitz 1992, Dwyer et al. 1987, Håkansson- Snehota 1995), experience of the partners involved (Komppula 1996, Håkansson- Snehota 1995), prior experience of co-operations (Komppula 1996, Håkansson-Snehota 1995), perceptions of the other partners' commitment (Anderson - Weitz 1992), available information about the potential partner (Komppula 1996), the quality and existence of available alternatives (Nummela 1996), company's relative market position (Komppula 1996, Nummela 1996) as well as expectations of future outcomes of the co-operation (Komppula 1996) that may affect actor's desire to invest resources in the co-operation.

Commitment can be divided into attitudinal and behavioural commitment (e.g. Denize - Young 1996, Cullen - Johnson 1995, Halinen 1994, Hyvönen 1992, Komppula 1996). Attitudinal focus is characterised by factors relating to the belief in the network's goals and values, willingness to extend effort for the network and the desire to remain in the network. (Williams - Hazer 1986). Behavioural commitment is realised in the concrete behaviour through which the partners become committed and can be measured with concrete actions as well as material and non-material investments.

The degree of investments in the co-operation may be determined by the actor's satisfaction with previous outcomes of the relationship (Nummela 1996) or other relationships of same kind (Komppula 1996). The investments are also related to the company's ability to invest resources in the co-operation. But an investment is not in itself a commitment (Andersson et al. 1997), it is an indicator of commitment. The size of the company and the relative position in the market as well as the position of the life cycle of the company determine the company's ability to invest in the co-operation (Komppula 1996). The outcomes of these relationships are evaluated in comparison to the expected and achieved rewards as well as the costs incurred (Nummela 1996).

Gundlach et al (1995) suggest the temporal dimension as the third component of commitment referring to the long term orientation of the commitment. Continuity decisions are closely related to the overall level of satisfaction or dissatisfaction with the ongoing co-operation. Satisfaction is a result of the evaluation of the expected and experienced outcomes of this co-operation (Shamdasani - Sheth 1995). In general, development of commitment is largely a function of the perceived benefits (satisfaction and economic performance) of the relationship (Cullen - Johnson 1995, Möller - Wilson 1995, Wilson - Mummaleni 1986). Satisfaction leads to further investments, strengthens the trust towards the network and leads to continuing co-operation. Dissatisfaction may lead to mistrust and a desire to leave the network.

Attitudinal and behavioural commitment are strongly interrelated. The more co-operatively the partners behave the more positive their attitudes towards co-operation tend to be (Nummela 1996). The first two phases of the network commitment process (i.e. the need for co-operation and desire to invest) represent the attitudinal character of commitment. In the early phases of the co-operation commitment is mostly attitudinal but behavioural commitment develops over time (Nummela 1996).

Trust plays an important role in the development of commitment. Moorman et. al (1993) define trust as a willingness to rely on an exchange partner in whom one has confidence. Considerable researchers view trust as a belief, confidence or expectation about an exchange partner's trustworthiness that results from the partner's expertise, reliability or intentionality. Collaborative history between the actors (Andersson et. al 1997) as well as competence (Shamdasani - Seth 1995) and expertise (Moorman et al 1993) are suggested as an important foundation of trust.

According to our earlier results the relation of trust and commitment is somewhat different in dyadic and network relationships (Komppula 1996). One may co-operate with a partner for years in a network although he does not fully trust the other. Both partners may also be committed to a dyadic relationship because e.g. there may be no other alternatives. The effect of mistrust may be reduced by decreasing future transaction costs or by contractual schemes e.g. by prepayments or other sanctions. It may be discussed if a "force" has anything to do with commitment which seems to be considered as a positive concept. On the other hand even written contracts will not necessarily protect companies from opportunistic behaviour, such as withholding or distorting information (Hunt- Morgan 1994).

Thus, trust is not a necessary condition for co-operative actions to occur (Mayer et. al 1995, Young and Wilkinson 1989) because co-operation will not necessarily put a party at risk whereas trust implies a willingness to take risks. But the perceived outcome of the co-operative actions will determine whether the relationship continues to be based on trust or if the trust is turned into mistrust which may lead to a relationship influenced by power, relative dependence and conflict (Andersson et. al 1997).

Nevertheless, trust is a necessary condition for longitudinal network commitment which only makes sense if the future of the actor's relationship with other partys or the network is of importance. Commitment also has a more distinct priority dimension: in a lot of situations it is not enough to know that the other party is trustworthy but also that the other will actively support the partner, to reciprocate. The commitment is a result of actions and counteractions between the parties involved (Håkansson - Snehota 1995).

We also agree with several authors who suggest that the lack of commitment is one of the most significant reasons for dissatisfaction in interpartner co-operation (Jonninen 1995, Komppula 1996, Murto-Koivisto - Vesalainen 1995, Shamdasani - Seth 1995 etc.) especially in multipartner collaborations. In successful network co-operation both trust and commitment are the key elements.

# The cases

## The V-villages

The V-villages tourism project began in 1994 when a couple of the local small entrepreneurs decided to make a development plan for the small family enterprises with the objective of developing a village-tourism product, which could give more income for all the entrepreneurs and guarantee the survival of the villages in the future.

The co-operation was motivated by Mr R who moved back to the villages after living twenty years in town. Very quickly the development project was the common issue for the whole area. Most of the entrepreneurs were involved, including non-tourism companies. The first goals of the project were to develop village tourism packaged products, develop the quality of the total offer and to develop a more professional business environment. Social contacts were very important, meetings were informal and, as they said, the "being" and doing together" atmosphere was important.

Mr R was the natural leader for the network and he took the responsibility to oversee the development of new forms of activities and development projects. In order to fulfil the legal regulations concerning the marketing and sales of packaged tours, a co-operative company was founded. All 13 entrepreneurs participated in the marketing activities. Public funding was of course an important incentive to participate in the network. Problems began to occur after two-three years.

In spite of the varying level of interest in co-operative action the network co-operation is still going on, after five years of project activities. The latest development project aims to the year 2001 and all the 13 original entrepreneurs are still involved.

## Case 2: The fishing tourism project M

The Fishing tourism project M began in 1994 when the project leader was doing a research and mapping project relating to the stock of fish in the region N lakes and rivers. During the course of that work he discussed with several entrepreneurs who had previously tried to develop fishing tourism alone without any support from the regional tourism marketing authorities.

This was the antecedent for the three year fishing tourism project M, which officially began in 1996. The objective of the project was to develop a network of fishing tourism centres in region N. The project was funded by the ministry of agriculture, the European Union and by the companies involved.

The project leader first collected information about the lakes and established where definite opportunities for fishing existed, and then contacted the companies operating in the area. The objective was to develop one centre at the time and then increase the amount of the centres up to six or seven. The idea of the project was that these local fishing centres would be the centre points of local nets. The centre would serve as a starting point for fishing trips. These centres also have information about the other centres in the region. The number of the companies in the project has increased to about 60 at the present time.

The overall goals of the project were explained to each company when they were asked to consider joining the project. The project leader selected the core companies. The companies have to pay an annual fee for which they receive consultancy, certain marketing operations and training services. For marketing and educational tours they must, however, pay extra fees. One incentive for joining the network is the financial support available for investments, which is available for all the companies in the network.

Most of the core companies in the project are very committed to the goals of the network. The commitment is measured by their activities and participation in training, educational tours to other fishing tourism areas of Finland, and by their marketing activities. The companies feel that the project leader is working for them and that the regular meetings with other companies are very important. Most of the companies did not know each other before the project but now the social exchange between the members of the network is significant.

## Case 3: The MF, network of nature programme services and professional wilderness guides

MF is a network of seven small family enterprises and a group of wilderness guides. The importance of MF is not equally felt by the member companies: most of the companies get only a small part of their income from MF productions, whereas some of the guides are dependent on the network.

MF have developed tourism operations in harmony with nature and according to unique local traditions and culture. Their products include activities like white-water rafting, canoeing, fishing, hiking, husky safaris, snowmobile safaris, snowshoe hiking and Icelandic horse riding tours. The most important perceived values within the network are responsibility towards nature conservation, sustainability and a respect for the local traditions. Warm hearted customer service and hospitality is a core value.

Initially these companies were not very enthusiastic about sustainable tourism ideals. Quite quickly however, they learned that this was the trend especially as incoming foreign tourists and leisure users had an increasing awareness and respect about the sustainable tourism ideals.

The product development phase lasted about two years and by 1995 Ms P had a ready concept of sustainable nature based activities which she gave the name MF. The formation of the network took two more years although all of this time numerous activities were implemented in the name and spirit of MF. Most of the companies were implementing the activities following the advice of Ms P but there was not any in-depth discussion about the values. The key companies were still working as they had done before their product was sold under the brand of MF. The MF activities were for most of the companies only a minor part of their turnover. The guides had in fact internalised the values of MF much better than the companies had.

The main motive for the companies to participate in the MF network was that they expected to gain more customers through the activities of the tourist service and the marketing of the brand as a whole. The product development and brand building took several years and the companies were expecting significant outcomes on the sales side. The brand became famous in Finland and the companies were waiting for paying customers.

In practice, all the monetary exchanges concerning the visitor groups were processed through the tourist service which was the responsible agency. The companies were in practice its subcontractors. The fact that the network was actually operating under the governance of the municipal tourist service caused many problems.

During 1997-1999 MF was organised as a public funded development project. One of the part time guides was invited to work as the co-ordinator of the project. The objectives were to extend marketing operations and continue brand building. One of the project goals was to build a criteria list for MF products and entrepreneurs, together with some kind of written rules of how to produce tourism products in a MF "spirit".

Before the development project MF was a loose co-operative arrangement run by a strong leader, Ms P. Co-operation and exchange between the guides was active but there were no regular meetings for the whole group of entrepreneurs. Links were mostly dyadic between an entrepreneur and Ms P and co-operative activities concentrated in the operative production of MF products. Discussions about the companies' needs and expectations about the network were rare. The companies' commitment to MF can be described as fairly low at the beginning of the development project. Most of the companies had not invested in the product development themselves, but trusted Ms P's ability to organise activities, guides and the needed equipments for MF operations.

Because the strong leader Ms P was no longer running the network, the members were unaware about the original goals of MF. One factor which lowered the commitment to the network was the mistrust some companies felt towards the new co-ordinator: the lack of written strategies and rules and goals gave the co-ordinator the opportunity to "adapt" the rules which meant that there occurred sometimes confusing situations.

## Discussion

The case V-villages is an example of a network which was originated from the network members' own initiatives. There was no external push, but the people who knew each other began to plan activities in order to achieve common goals. The active and informal social exchange made the co-operation in the beginning "fun". There were regular meetings and a trusting atmosphere. The goals and values of the network were mutually set. The attitudinal commitment was strong in the beginning during the first two phases of the development process. A crucial role was played by a strong and active leader, although there were a couple of other active members, too. The behavioural commitment to the network was measured by the companies' participation in meetings, voluntary work projects and other activities.

A very important determinant for the high level of commitment to the V-Villages network was the founding of the co-operative company, which made the funding, shares of outcome and inputs clear. It also gave the network the independency from external actors. In V-Villages case the problems with commitment were quickly solved through discussion.

The fishing project M is an example of a successful externally led network where the companies of the network were committed to the goals of the network and participated actively training and development activities. The main reason for the high level of commitment was that need for the development project was strongly perceived among the companies: goals and values were discussed and there was a consensus about the working procedure. The project leader co-ordinated and implemented activities, collected the information and took care of information flows. He had also been the activator of the local co-operation.

The atmosphere in the common meetings was open, the companies were not forced to any given procedures but the development of every fishing centre could happen on their own terms. The only problem was that the network grew too large: the project leader had insufficient time to visit all 60 companies as often as in the beginning and it was difficult to find the time for network meetings which, however, were seen as the most important means of co-operation. The need for formalising the local nets and finding them appropriate leaders was the next step in order to sustain the commitment to the network.

The last case, MF, is an example of a network which is developed from subcontractor relations into a network where co-operation between the members was the process whereby programme services packages would be produced. The network members could not impact the values of the network or the choice of other members, the network was instead, built by one person, based on a product-need.

One problem with this network was the existence of two groups of actors, wilderness guides and companies. The attitudinal commitment of the guides was high, they were building the network with Ms P. The companies which were accepted were not attitudinally committed. Their only motive was the benefit they could get from the network, but they were ready to leave it if they got the same benefit from something else. The maintaining factor was the strong leader.

In this latter case the development of commitment was very slow, because the first two phases of the process (perception of the need for co-operation and desire to invest in co-operation) were almost lacking: the companies were asked to join the network in circumstances where the benefit of being a member of the network were perceivable. For the company it was a question of undertaking transactions which were implemented by a certain MF procedure with a perceivable outcome. Some of the companies internalised the values of MF during this time, which made the attitudinal commitment possible.

All the respondents were of the opinion that in rural areas the success of tourism is dependent on the actors' willingness and ability to co-operate. During the interviews with the network leaders and members the question of the need of a functioning regional tourism network and a network strategy was also discussed. All the respondents considered the regional co-operation important and inevitable, too. They wanted some kind of co-ordination for all the local and issue-based nets and networks as well as for development projects. The most common opinion was that the regional federation or the regional tourist service should take the responsibility for co-ordinating these nets and networks.

# Conclusions

In an issue-based net and network the member companies' commitment to the network is crucial in terms of the continuation of the co-operation. If the companies are committed to the idea of the network and the co-operation is not dependent on an external push or a leader there is then, a strong chance of success. The method of formalising the net seems to be of as much importance as well as written rules or values eventually formalised.

Company's commitment to a network is not a part or a result of a process, but occurs simultaneously during the process developing element, which begins from a need to co-operate and demands evidence of the results and benefits of the co-operative actions. The need can be based on actor's values and goals, which are similar to the values and goals of the network, or the need is based on the perception of the benefits of co-operation.

Actor's commitment can be divided into two types: commitment to networking and commitment to the "issue" (values and goals of the network). In both types of commitment the behavioural and attitudinal dimension are perceived.

Attitudinal commitment to the issue means actor's willingness to invest in activities concerning the implementation of the goals of the net within the company's own actions. If an actor's attitudinal relation towards co-operation (attitudinal commitment to co-operation) is positive, then it can be assumed that a willingness to invest in common activities is high. Behavioural commitment refers mainly to an actor's capability to invest in its own action and /or in co-operation. The capability is dependent on actors' willingness to invest but also on company's material and immaterial resources.

Company's willingness to invest is influenced by the characteristics of the company and in small enterprises especially by the characteristics of the entrepreneur. Goals of the network and the information available before and during the network activities as well as the company's dependence on tourism income are another group of factors affecting the tourism company's willingness to invest in the issue or in the co-operation in network context.

We agree with several authors by saying that the development of commitment is largely a function of the perceived benefits of the network (Cullen -Johnson 1995, Moller-Wilson 1995, Wilson - Mummaleni 1986). A network may function without special or successful outcomes for a long time if the members trust that some benefits will accrue in the future. Attitudinal commitment declines very quickly however, if the company feels that there is nothing going on within the network. If there is no attitudinal commitment to the network the readiness to leave the network after the first problems is high.

# References

Aalto, K., Laiho, M., Talonen, H. (1999), *Matkailun ohjelmapalveluyritysten myynti- ja informaatiokanavat. Loppuraportti 31.8.1999.* Tampereen yliopiston Liiketaloustieteellisen tutkimuskeskuksen julkaisuja 9. Tampere.

Anderson, E., Weitz, B. (1992), The use of Pledges to build and sustain Commitment in the Distribution Channels. *Journal of Marketing Research*, Vol. 29, No.1, pp. 18-34.

Andersson, U., Johanson, M., Silver, L. (1997), The Role of Trust, Commitment and Cupertino in Business Relationships, in Mazet Florence, Salle Robert and Jean-Paul Valla (eds.) *Interaction, Relationships and Network in Business Markets. Proceedings of 13th IMP Conference, Lyon, France Work in Progress Papers,* Volume 2. pp. 9-23.

Boedlender, J., Jefferson, A., Jenkins, C., Lickorish, (1991), *Developing Tourism Destinations. Policies and Perspectives.* Longman, Hong Kong.

Borg, P. (1997), Maaseutumatkailun suuri tuleminen. *Maaseudun uusi aika.* 1/97.

Brito, C. (1997), Issue-Based Nets: a Methodological Approach to the Sampling Issue in Industrial Networks Research. in Mazet Florence, Salle Robert and Jean-Paul Valla (eds.) *Interaction, Relationships and Network in Business Markets. Proceedings of 13th IMP Conference, Lyon, France. Competitive Papers.* pp 87-110.

Cullen, J. B., Johnson, J. L. (1995), Japanese and local partner commitment to IJVs: Psychological consequences of outcomes and investments in the IJV relationship, *Journal of International Business Studies,* Vol. 26, No.1, pp.91-115.

Denize, S., Young, L. (1996), Measuring Commitment in Business Service Relationships, in Seth, Jagdish N. - Söllner, Albrecht (eds.), *Development, Management and Governance of Relationships, Proceedings of The International Conference on Relationship Marketing,* March 29-31, 1996, Berlin. pp. 169-174.

Dwyer, F. R., - Schurr, P. H., Oh, S. (1987),Developing Buyer-Seller Relationships, *Journal of Marketing,* Vol. 51, No. 2, pp. 11-27.

Finnish Tourist Board (1999), *Rajahaastattelututkimus, osa 3, Ulkomaalaiset matkailijat Suomessa vuonna 1998*. MEK A:103.

Ganesan, S. (1994), Determinants of Long Term Orientation in Buyer-Seller Relationships, *Journal of Marketing*, Vol. 58, No. 2, 1-19.

Go, F. M., Milne, D., Whittles, L. J. R. (1992), Communities as Destinations: A Market in Taxonomy for the Effective Implementation of the Tourism Action Plan. *Journal of Travel Research*, Spring 1992, pp. 31-37.

Gray, B. (1985), Conditions facilitating Interorganisational Collaboration. *Human Relations* No. 38, pp. 911-936.

Gundlach, G. T., Achrol, R. S., Mentzer, J. T. (1995), The Structure of Commitment in Exchange, *Journal of Marketing* Vol. 59 (January 1995), s. 78-92.

Gunn, C. A.(1993), *Tourism Planning. Basics, Concepts, Cases*. Third edition. Taylor and Francis, Washington.

Halinen, A.(1994), *Exchange Relationships in Professional Services. A Study of Relationship Development in the Advertising Sector*. Publications of The Turku School of Economics and Business Administration, Series A-6:1994, Turku.

Harju-Autti, A. (1998), *Toimialaraportti Majoitustoiminta*. KTM Toimiala-infomedia. 1998-2. Helsinki.

Heath, E., Wall, G. (1992), *Marketing Tourism Destinations. A Strategic Planning Approach*. John Wiley and Sons. Inc. Canada.

Hernesniemi, H., Lammi, M., Yla-Anttila, P. (1995), *Kansallinen kilpailukyky ja teollinen tulevaisuus*. The Research Institute of the Finnish Economy. Taloustieto Oy. Helsinki.

Hunt, S. D., Morgan, R. M. (1994), Relationship Marketing in the Era of Network Competition, *Marketing Management* Vol. 3, No 1, pp.19-28.

Hyvonen S. (1992*), Channel Member Commitment. An Investigation of Finnish Wholesaler-Retailer Dyads,* Publications of The Helsinki School of Economics and Business Administration, Series Working Papers W-4:1992, Helsinki.

Hakansson, H., Snehota, I. (eds.) (1995), *Developing Relationships in Business Networks*. Routledge. London.

Jamal, T. B., Getz, D. (1995), Collaboration Theory and Community Tourism Planning. *Annals of Tourism Research*, Vol.22, No 1, pp.186-206.

Jarillo, J. C., Stevenson, H. H. (1991), Co-operative Strategies - The Payoffs and Pitfalls. *Long Range Planning*, 1991: Vol. 24, No 1, pp.64-70.

Jonninen, P. (1995), *Yrittajien yhteistyoasenteet ja verkostoituminen.* Publications of the Helsinki Research Institute for Business Administration, Series B 118, Helsinki.

Komppula, R.(1996), *Matkailuyritysten horisontaalinen yhteistyo ja yhteistyon esteet - case Lieksa.* Publications of the Turku School of Economics and Business Administration, Series D-1:1996.

Komppula, R., Haahti, A., Saari, M.(1997), Patterns of Collaboration in Formation of Regional Tourism Strategy, in Mazet Florence, Salle Robert and Jean-Paul Valla (eds.) *Interaction, Relationships and Network in Business Markets. Proceedings of 13th IMP Conference*, Lyon, France Work in Progress Papers, Volume 1. pp. 333-354.

Komppula, R.(1997), Pohjois-Karjalan matkailustrategian synty ja yritysten valmius sitoutua strategiaan. Lieksan oppimiskeskuksen julkaisusarja A:3.

Komppula, R. (1998), Factors affecting SME's commitment to a issue-based network - Case North Karelia Tourism Strategy. *Proceedings of Conference on Growth and Job Creation in SME;s.* Mikkeli January 7-9.'98. Helsinki School of Economics and Business Administration. Mikkeli. pp. 474-497.

Laws, E. (1995), Tourist Destination Management. Issues, analysis and policies, Routledge, London.

Maaseutumatkailun teemaryhmä (1996), *Suomen maaseutumatkailun kehittäminen.* Suuntaviivat vuoteen 2005. 26.2.1996.

Maaseutupolitiikan yhteistyöryhmä (1997), *Maaseutumatkailun kapasiteettiselvitys.*

Mayer, R., Davis, J., Schoorman, D. (1995), An Integrative Model of Organisational Trust. *Academy of Management Review*, Vol. 20, No. 3, pp. 709-734.

Middleton, V. (1989), Tourist product. in: Witt, Stephen F. and Moutinho, Luiz, pp.573-573. *Tourism Marketing and Management Handbook.* Prentice Hall: Englewood Cliffs, N J. 573-576.

Moorman, C. - Deshpande, R. - Zaltman, G. (1993), Factors Affecting Trust in Market Research Relationships. *Journal of Marketing* Vol. 57, January 1993, pp. 81-101.

Moorman, C., Zaltman, G., Deshpande, R. (1992), Relationships Between Providers and users of Market Research: The Dynamics of Trust Within and Between Organisations. *Journal of Marketing Research* Vol. XXIX August, pp. 314-328.

Morgan, R. M., Hunt, S. D. (1994), The Commitment - Trust Theory of Relationship Marketing. *Journal of Marketing*, 1994: Vol. 58, (July 1994), pp. 20-38.

Moutinho, L. (1990), Strategies for Tourism Destination Development: An Investigation of the Role of Small Business. in: Ashworth, G., Goodall, B. (eds.), *Marketing Tourism Places.* New York , London: Routledge.

Murto-Koivisto, E., Vesalainen, J. (1995), *PKT-yritysyhteistyon kehittyminen ja tuloksellisuus. Seurantatutkimus yhdeksasta yhteistyoryhmasta.* Research Reports of the Ministry of Trade and Industry, No. 105/1995, Helsinki.

Nummela, N. (1996), Commitment to a Network: Analysing A Case, *Proceedings of the 12th International Conference on Industrial Marketing and Purchasing in Karlsruhe* 1996, 1037-1072.

Oliver, C. (1990), Determinants of Interorganisational Relationships: Integration and Future Directions. *Academy of Management Review*, 1990: Vol. 15, No. 2, pp.241-265.

Palmer, A., Bejou, D. (1995), Tourism Destination Marketing Alliances. *Annals of Tourism Research,* Vol. 22, No 3, pp. 616-629.

Pearce, D. (1992), *Tourist Organisations,* Longman Group Ltd, Hong Kong.

Pohjois-Karjalan liitto - Suomen Matkailun Kehitys Oy (1996*), Pohjois-Karjalan matkailufakta 1994.* Suomen Matkailun kehitys Oy, Matkailun koulutus- ja tutkimuskeskus. MKTK:n julkaisuja C: 9 1996. Savonlinna 1995.

Selin, S., Chavez, D. (1995), Developing an evolutionary Tourism Partnership Model. *Annals of Tourism Research*, Vol.22, No. 4, pp. 844-856.

Shamdasani, P. N., Sheth, J. N. (1995), An experimental approach to investigating satisfaction and continuity in marketing alliances, *European Journal of Marketing*, Vol. 29 No.4, 6-23.

Sharma, D. D. (1993), Commitment in and Evolution of the Strategic Alliances. *Paper presented at the 9th IMP Conference, Bath, September 1993.*

Silvennoinen H., Tahvanainen, L., Tyrväinen, L. (1997), *Matkailu, maaseutu ja ympäristö: matkailun nykytila ja tulevaisuuden näkymät suomessa ja Pohjois-Karjalassa.* Joensuun yliopiston metsätieteellinen tiedekunta, Tiedonantoja 57.

Smith, S. L. J. (1995), *Tourism Analysis. Handbook.* 2nd edition. Longman Group Ltd, London.

Statistics Finland (1999), *Tourism Statistics. Transport and Tourism.* Tilastokeskus:Helsinki.

Williams, L. J., Hazer, J. T. (1986), Antecedents and Consequences of Satisfaction and Commitment in Turnover Models: A Reanalysis Using Latent Variable Structural Equation Methods. *Journal of Applied Psychology* 1986, Vol. 71, No. 2, 219-231.

Wilson, D. T., Mummaleni, V. (1986), Bonding and Commitment in Buyer-Seller Relationships: A preliminary Conceptualisation. *Industrial Marketing and Purchasing*, Vol. 1, No. 3, pp.44-58.

Young, L. C., Denize, S. (1995), A Concept of Commitment: Alternative Views of relational Continuity in Business Service Relationships. *Journal of Business and Industrial Marketing*, Vol. 10 No. 5, pp. 47-62.

# Problems in developing tourism entrepreneurship in a rural region: A case study

*Hilkka Lassila*

Pohjois Savo Polytechnic, Finland

## Abstract

The aim of this study is to evaluate entrepreneurial potential and their attitudes for tourism entrepreneurship in a rural area. The paper introduces findings of one case study, where the target group is tourism entrepreneurs in a rural region. The region of this case is situated in the middle of Finland and it belongs to the EU's Objective 5b -programme. Tourism has been selected as one of the key points of future development of this region. The tourist products of this region are based on beauty and originality of nature. The source of income has changed quite quickly from agriculture to services.

The research material was collected by telephone survey (n = 99). The entrepreneurs qualified attitudes against entrepeneurship, developing their business, training, co-operation and networking. The collection of data was done during summer 1999. Earlier a case study was done which dealt with constructing a new regional tourism organisation and co-operation in this region. The research was conducted in 1997-1998.

The paper introduces the findings of this case study. This paper tries to explain problems which have influenced the development of rural tourism in this region and what could or should be done in the future to improve success of tourism of the region. Due to the EU's Objective One -programme there will be large number of financial resources available in the beginning of the millennium. These resources could be addressed to develop tourism business.

## Introduction

Although the tourism industry is one of the most significant industries, there cannot be found many international studies of SMEs (Shaw and Williams 1990 and 1994; Page, Forer and Lawton 1999). Most of the SMEs are small or medium sized enterprises (Shaw and Williams

1994). Some of the small enterprises' research has been made in the context of tourism in rural regions (e.g. Getz and Page 1997).

Tourism is almost entirely based on the supply of tourism in rural regions in Finland and especially in Eastern Finland. Even if there are some local ski resorts (e.g. Tahko and Koli), which also have hotel capacity, the production of program services and a notable part of accommodation services depend on the supply of small family enterprises' services.

It is easy to become an entrepreneur in tourism in rural region. 72 percent of the tourism entrepreneurs – total number of 3600 - had originally been farmers (Rural Politics' Theme Group 1997). Rural tourism entrepreneurs haven't had much experience from the field and its business. This knowledge is often based on entrepreneurs' own interests or on interpretation of clients' experiences (Morrison, Rimmington and Williams 1999).

Tourism in rural regions is the main industry for only 15 percent of tourism entrepreneurs in Finland. However, there are more than 15 percent full-time rural tourism entrepreneurs only in North-Savo, in Eastern Finland (Rural Politics' Co-operative Group 1997). Part-time entrepreneurship causes several problems to the development of the industry. Accommodation capacities of private entrepreneurs are limited (average 11 beds per company) and desire and ability to participate in the collective marketing procedures are insignificant. There is no pressure to increase the capacity and marketing. On the other hand, the planning of activity is reactive. And the activity is not planned on the basis of the changes in a turbulent environment (Rural Politics' Theme Group 1997, Komppula 1996, 1997, 1998, 1999; Lassila and Komppula 1999). The rural entrepreneurs are on average more satisfied in the location of their enterprise (Curran, J. and Storey, D. 1993) than entrepreneurs in urban regions.

Tourism is one of the main focuses both in the strategy of Finland in 2000 (The Ministry of Trade and Industry 1996) and in the development strategy of Nort-Savo (the Regional Council of North-Savo 1996). Tourism is one the fastest growing industrial fields in the world and both individual travelling and active holidaymaking - especially focusing in nature and culture - are believed to grow further globally. Inbound tourism, particularly tourism in rural regions, is focused on pure nature and local products. So it cannot be seen as mass tourism. Tourism in rural areas seems to be an opportunity for remote regions facing structural changes. Therefore, the significance of travelling in the rural regions and the chances of developing the rural tourism entrepreneurship should be strengthened.

The traditional rural tourism field needs new supporting industries. Rural tourism in North-Savo has an excellent basis: pure nature, good location and unique climate. It can be said that tourism could be developed as a productive industry for the rural areas in the future: the services could be preserved and the movement of population could be decreased. Future goals are a viable countryside, a good place to live and work.

## Countryside and tourism in rural regions

Countryside is located outside a densely populated community, which can be subgrouped: countryside near cities (urban-rural fringe), central countryside and remote countryside (rural hinterland) (Ministry of Trade and Industry 1997; Bryant 1982). The character and level of these areas varies. The criteria of countryside must be defined in each case individually, because for example the discrimination made on the basis of the densely populated community's population varies in each location. Traditionally typical characteristics for rural regions include small populations and no large urban centre, long distances from big towns and a dominant farming industry. However the situation is changing, especially in regions nearby towns. Rural regions are also defined regions where the population has paid jobs in towns and where the farming industry is almost disappeared. Although there is no European wide, mutual understanding on the definition of countryside.

Tourism in rural regions is defined in many ways. Davidson (1992, 140-141) concludes rural regions as "the definition of tourism in rural areas covers the tourism activities which have been organised and hosted by local people. These tourism activities are based on natural and man-made environmental strengths." Borg (1997) defines tourism in rural regions as "tourism which occurs not in densely populated communities and travelling centres, but in rural areas, and which often is small-sized, focused to individual service and related both to agriculture and forestry and to outdoor recreation".

According to the Rural Tourism's Theme Group, tourism in rural regions is called entrepreneurship, which is based on natural preconditions and resources of countryside - nature, landscape, culture, human, family- and small, rural tourism entrepreneurship (Ministry of Trade and Industry 1997).

Agriculture and forestry is often conceived to be part of tourism in rural regions. Because of the structural changes in countryside, tourism has replaced farming as a source of livelihood. Nowadays, there cannot be often found agriculture and farming, which is associated with tourism enterprises in rural regions. There are enterprises of farming tourism, where the tourism product's attraction is based on existing or redundant agriculture and farming.

In other words tourism in rural regions is tourism which is based on the natural preconditions and resources of the countryside. Tourism in rural regions exploits the space of rural settlement, pure nature and know-how and culture of local people as an industry. All the forms of tourism in rural regions - services of accommodation, restaurants, and other activities - have the local carrying capacities. Principals of the enduring development should be observed in rural tourism. Tourism in the countryside has developed from the earlier cottage renting and farm accommodation to versatile, modern and family-oriented tourism entrepreneurship.

Tourism in rural regions is concentrated on teamwork between areas, people and products. The region without a population cannot offer friendliness and the region without a tourism product cannot fulfil the expectations of a customer. It also must be noticed that rural tourism excludes travelling in unoccupied, untouched deserts, where attractions are based on the "wild" nature. The cultural environment, created by a human, is missing in deserts too. Rural tourism does not also include tourism in bigger town centres and travelling and health destinations in rustic areas.

The OECD (1994) has published a list of terms, which refer to tourism and enterprises in rural regions. These terms exist in this research, in its operational environment and its target groups:

- sparsley populated areas with under 10 000 inhabitants,

- natural environment,

- existing outdoor activities,

- individual activities,

- weak infrastructure,

- locally owned and small enterprises,

- part-time tourism entrepreneurs,

- entrepreneurs partly engaged to agriculture and forestry,

- employees live close to their workplace,

- business is strongly affected by seasons,

- personal relationship with strangers,

- unskilled management,

- local atmosphere.

# Rural tourism in the region of North-Savo

It is hard to find regional and up-to-date information about rural tourism enterprises. According to the Central Statistical Office the target groups of statistics of accommodation are tourism enterprises, which offer over ten rooms/cottages. This statistic does not cover private cottage renting. The Ministry of Trade and Industry's branch report "Maaseutumatkailu" (i.e. "Tourism in rural regions") offers nation-wide information about the structure, development, products and marketing of rural tourism. The Theme Group of Rural Tourism made a study of capacity (n=127) in 1997. The following results were found in enterprises in North-Savo (nation-wide average in brackets):

- the average year of foundation was 1985 (1984),

- 20% of respondents were fulltime rural tourism entrepreneurs (15%),

- 68% of respondents owned a farm,

- about 2/3 of respondents were open through year,

# The survey

The tourism strategy of North-Savo has two goals: firstly to develop high-quality travelling products, which are based on natural attractions, and secondly to increase the number of tourists more rapidly than the average for Finland. Procedures are for instance the strengthening of tourism knowledge and the product development of tourism. These recorded actions also support the directives of program 1 of North-Savo. The planning of the development procedures and efficient utilisation of resources requires preclarification, which includes information about entrepreneurs, bases of corporations and attitudes.

The research material was collected by phone interviews using the structured form in June 1999. The target group was tourism entrepreneurs chosen from the area of North-Savo, which belongs to the Regional Development Program-5B of the European Union. This target group includes the following counties: Iisalmi, Karttula, Keitele, Kiuruvesi, Lapinlahti, Leppävirta, Maaninka, Pielavesi, Rautalampi, Sonkajärvi, Suonenjoki, Tervo, Varkaus, Varpaisjärvi, Vehmersalmi, Vesanto and Vieremä.

In this research the rural regions include densely populated communities with under 10 000 inhabitants. Enterprises situated in Iisalmi (population 16 418) and Varkaus (population 19 825) were not taken into account. Tourism entrepreneurs were classified as entrepreneurs whose products were directed towards travellers and the meaning of tourism as an income formation was quite significant (about 25 - 30%). The amount of income formation was based on the entrepreneur's own announcement. Both entrepreneurs, who did part-time, small tourism activity and entrepreneurs whose products were basically directed to local people, were not qualified for the target group.

The interview consists of enterprises based on private entrepreneurship and owned by an entrepreneur or his/her family. The interview did not include community owned enterprises. Questions concerning entrepreneurs were directed towards the person, who was perceived as the primary entrepreneur by the family.

Respondents' addresses were collected from the post register of the tourism industry of the Regional Council of North-Savo (updated in autumn 1998). Addresses were checked from the persons who worked with tourism livelihoods in counties or in districts. The total size of the target group was 109 entrepreneurs, of which 99 were interviewed. Seven entrepreneurs were not reached -it is possible, that they were not qualified to the target group. Three entrepreneurs did not want to participate in the interview.

The purpose of the study was to find answers to the following aspects from the target group:

- the types of enterprises and their development,

- the age and educational background of entrepreneurs,

- entrepreneurs' attitudes towards development of business, co-operation and training.

# The results

37,4 percent of the target group announced to be full-time tourism entrepreneurs, which is clearly higher than the nation-wide average in 1996. Most of the part-time tourism enterprises (67%) were small-sized and 30 percent of the total family income came from tourism.

72 percent of the enterprises were open all year, that also exceeds the nation-wide average. Almost half of the entrepreneurs (45,5%) had more than one type of tourism livelihood services to offer. 6,1% of the entrepreneurs were practising only restaurant services, 21,2%, only accommodation and 7% only programme services. Total accommodation capacity varied between the different types of accommodation forms and several enterprises had various forms of accommodations available. Over one third (35%) of the enterprises offering accommodation had focused on cottage renting.

77,8% of the enterprises were situated in scattered settlements outside densely populated communities. The research done by the Ministry of Trade and Industry, supports the opinion that most of the countryside tourism enterprises (88%) are situated in the actual countryside. The research also shows that there are less tourism enterprises in the peripheral areas of towns and densely populated communities (The Ministry of Trade and Industry 1997).

The target group's business is very young. Most of the enterprises (71,4%) were founded in the 90s and over half of the enterprises in 1995 or after. Tourism has clearly risen as one of the most significant countryside livelihoods in the 90s. All of the respondents were family businesses. Business was run either alone or together with family members (57,7%) and outside labour force was used either regularly or only seasonally in 42,3 percent of the enterprises. More than half (53,5%) of the respondents has agreed delivering services via outside sales organisation.

The entrepreneur's personal qualities were also observed. The average age of the tourism entrepreneur in rural regions was 50 years (40,4% of the respondents). Against the general assumptions, the number of entrepreneurs at the age of under 30 years was almost the same as the number of entrepreneurs of the age of over 61 years.

The level of education had arisen along the new entrepreneurs' generation. 14% of respondents had only gone to elementary school and only 11% of the respondents had graduated from university/college. The fields of vocational education differed: agriculture and forestry 32%, commercial 17%, accommodation and restaurant services 12% and other fields total 39%.

# Future aspects and plans

Interviewed entrepreneurs had a strong belief in the future. The future is seen as very or quite positive by 92 percent of the respondents. And about 70 percent of the entrepreneurs aimed at developing and/or expanding its business in the near future. Six of the respondents planned to quit and/or downsize the tourism business in rural regions. According to entrepreneurs the development of business is concentrated in all aspects of tourism.

Co-operation and networking between enterprises is considered important for successful small businesses. The entrepreneurs had positive attitudes towards co-operation between enterprises: 63,6 percent of the respondents had participated in some kind of co-operation (other than sales) for the last years and 34,3 percent of them announced that there were no problems to co-operate. Some problems occurred in 29,3 percent of the respondents. None of the co-operatively working entrepreneurs found any more problems. The main problem was that the level of participation varied between co-operative enterprises. The second problem was that the co-operative enterprises did not know each other well enough. For the third problem the respondents mentioned the lack of resources.

When asked why the entrepreneurs did not participate in co-operation, the most important reason was shortage of time. It was also the main reason for half of the entrepreneurs, who did not attend co-operation. Secondly was the absence of suitable co-partners and thirdly the entrepreneurs did not see any reason for co-operation.

Over half of the interviewed countryside tourism entrepreneurs (57,6%) had participated in advanced training of their fields during the last three years. The reason, why some of the entrepreneurs (23,2%) could not take part was shortage of time. Five entrepreneurs were not interested in advanced training. Only two entrepreneurs pronounced that suitable training was not available. It can be seen that the supply of education is versatile and sufficient.

If there would be suitable education available, the entrepreneurs would invest money in the following way (FIM/person/education):

- 32,1% under 500 FIM     (under 85 euros),

- 27,4%: 500 - 1 000 FIM   (85 - 170 euros),

- 19%: 1000 - 1 500 FIM   (170 - 254 euros),

- 21,4%: over 1 500 FIM    (over 254 euros).

The need for education differed between the subjects of education. Previously, entrepreneurs required marketing and sales education, but also product development and languages were popular.

The form of education was also part of the research. Most of the entrepreneurs (50,6%) supported multiple education, which included both normal education, distance education and individual consulting. 59 percent of the entrepreneurs were willing to educate themselves for a maximum two days per month and only 3,6 percent were willing to spend over a week per month for normal education. The total duration of education should not last over one year (78% of respondents).

In the last part of the research statements and entrepreneurs' opinions about co-operation, education and the future aspects of tourism entrepreneurship were compared. Entrepreneurs evaluated statements by points at the scale from one to five. Number one meant that entrepreneurs totally disagreed and number five was for total agreement. The results can be seen as indicative, but it must be noted that the statements can be misunderstood in the phone interview.

## The mean/the standard deviation

| The Statement | Mean | S.D. |
|---|---|---|
| The continuous development of the tourism product is important in our enterprise. | 4,44 | 0,87 |
| Co-operation and networking is important between enterprises in rural regions. | 4,32 | 0,93 |
| The meaning of tourism livelihood is very significant in the countryside of North-Savo in the future. | 4,18 | 0,92 |
| I would like to study, but I do not have time as an entrepreneur. | 3,70 | 1,35 |
| The problem of co-operation is that the level of the commitment differs | 3,52 | 1,15 |
| The marketing of our services via networks (e.g. Internet) is crucially important for our business at the moment or in the future. | 3,48 | 1,15 |
| I would like to participate in different projects of co-operation. | 3,31 | 1,13 |
| It is important for the foundation of the co-operation that the partners know each other earlier. | 3,30 | 1,32 |
| It takes too much time to achieve concrete results in co-operation between enterprises. | 3,30 | 1,16 |
| My biggest problem in the tourism business is marketing. | 3,21 | 1,24 |
| I would like to study and participate in different educational projects, but the proper education is not available. | 2,59 | 1,19 |

## Conclusions

The future prospects for tourism in rural regions are bright. Rural tourism as a product seems to be very suitable for a family-oriented consumer, who respects environmental aspects and nature.

Although tourism is increasing and rural tourism has growing markets, tourism as an industry cannot save the countryside alone. Not all people want to carry on tourism business in the countryside, neither is everyone capable as an entrepreneur of producing services. Furthermore, the structural features, especially the location, must be advantageous for business. Most of the local entrepreneurs practice tourism in rural regions as a part-time livelihood. Therefore significant resources are not invested in a tourism livelihood.

Networks and networking have recently been increasingly popular in discussing linkages between the small business owners and the wider environment. It is reasonable to expect that small business owners in rural areas would more actively network than owners in urban areas. Among other things, Curran et al. (1993) has stated in several studies that if they (i.e. small business owners) do business more within local than the urban areas, networking should be easier. Alternatively, they may be a more insular, because of the low density of population which means there are fewer outsiders to connect with in relation to specific, sectoral issues. For example, Meyer-Krahmer (1985) found a higher percentage of "no outward orientedness" in firms located in rural regions and a stronger preference for internal problem solving.

Many researchers have indicated that co-operation and networking is one of the success factors in business. Co-operation done in their own village is a natural form of co-operation for rural tourism entrepreneurs. People of a village can set a common goal to create village of countryside tourism. In order to reach the goal, they have to gather all the ideas of services and developing those ideas into a product. The core of this kind of village is various services of accommodation and restaurants, which are supported by attached and program services. Surely the sight of the town or a cultural product can be the attraction. This is the way that entrepreneurs from different levels and capabilities could participate in developing the village as much as they have resources.

According to the earlier study (Lassila and Komppula 1999) entrepreneurs experienced satisfactory co-operation inside the village, when the co-operation had the best opportunities to succeed. Until now sales had been the problem, which can be solved with increasing automatic data processing and netshopping. Village tourism is the main concept for producing services and organising co-operation. The village tourism utilises all the local resources, from different fields' entrepreneurs, various producers of groceries, artisans to tourism entrepreneurs. Networks produce the services by using different relationships of acquisition. Successful village tourism expects that networking entrepreneurs have a common goal, readiness of expectation and the quality idea of tourism product, which guides the acts of all people.

Regeneration is a challenge for many family enterprises. According to Koiranen (1999) commitment of the family enterprise's manager is based often to emotional reasons and independence and traditions are overemphasised. However the fast changes in economy require the continuous follow-up of time and the ability to change. According to research by Smallbone et al. (1993) the best survivors of the SME sector were enterprises which adapted their business to correspond to the variable market situations.

This research is primarily a survey for further research, in which my aim is to solve both commitment to entrepreneurship and to the concept of success among tourism entrepreneurs in rural regions. The commitment had been classified as emotional or effectual commitment, loyalty or normative commitment, calculating commitment for economical reasons or commitment to projects during a certain time in the context of family entrepreneurship (Hjorth and Koiranen 1995). In my opinion the form of commitment influences the way that the entrepreneur sees the success as a entrepreneur and what is the motivation of entrepreneurship. One of the most important factors, which affects the success of family enterprise is the motivation of the owner manager (Neubauer F. and Lank A.G. 1998). According to my observations, part of the entrepreneurs are emotionally committed to entrepreneurship (landscape of the childhood, legacy etc.) and success is not limited by economical goals. Entrepreneurship gives a possibility to live in ones own environment and the eligible development of business is not the primary purpose.

The development of the entrepreneur influences the success of rural tourism enterprise. The evaluation of people should be observed from the point of view of cognitive (knowledge, skills), affective (emotion) and conative (will) (Koiranen and Ruohotie 1999). According to research, the cognitive level of entrepreneurs was good and entrepreneurs wanted to educate themselves in this target group. The problem was mainly the variable level of education, education of suitable forms and contents are available for entrepreneurs today. The problems for the developing entrepreneurs have are situated at the levels of effectual and conative.

For the last few years, there have been economic resources for developing tourism in the area with the Objective 5-program of the European Union. In many cases the development projects have not achieved permanent results and the work of development is unfinished. Reasons lie behind the versatile level and wideness of different development projects and the undevelopment of procedures. Of course there are also projects which have achieved good-quality and permanent results.

In the near future there will be more assets to spend on both the development of tourism in rural regions, other countryside industries and other economical activities in the support area of the European Union. It can be said that there are more assets at the moment than ever before or there will be in the future. This might mean that both financial and mental resources must be concentrated to focus on the targets of capable and desirous of development. The number of permanent workplaces and profitable businesses namely an industry, which will be capable to independently assume responsibility for its own development in the future.

# References

Borg, P. (1997), Maaseutumatkailun suuri tuleminen? Maaseudun uusi aika 1:pp. 9-15.

Bryant, C. R., Russwurm, L. H. and McLellan, A. G. (1982), *The City's Countryside*, Harlow, Longman.

Curran, J. and Storey, D. (1993), *The Location of Small and Medium Enterprises: Are there urban-rural differences* in Curran, J. and Storey D. (ed.) Small firms in Urban and Rural Locations, Routledge Small Business Series, London: Routledge.

Davidson, Rob. (1992), *Tourism in Europe*. London: Longman.

Getz, D. and Page, S. J. (Eds.) (1997), *The Business of Rural Tourism: International Perspectives*. London: International Thomson Publishing.

Hjorth, D and Koiranen, M. (1994), in Haahti A. J. *Growth through Networks, recent Research in European Entrepreneurship* – RENT VIII Conference Proceedings, University of Tampere, School of Business Administration, Series C: Conference Proceedings and Occasional Papers 4, Tampere.

Koiranen, M. (1998), Perheyrittäminen. Huomioita suku- ja perheyrittämisestä. Konetuumat Oy, Tampere.

Koiranen, M. and Ruohotie, P. (1999), *The Developmental challenges in the Co-operation and Training and Working Life*, Edita Oy, Edita.

Komppula, R. (1996), Matkailuyritysten horisontaalinen yhteistyö ja yhteistyön esteet - Case Lieksa. Publications of the Turku School of Economics and Business Administration, Series D1:1996.

Komppula, R.(1997), Pohjois-Karjalan matkailustrategian synty ja yritysten valmius sitoutua strategiaan. Lieksan oppimiskeskuksen julkaisusarja A:3.

Komppula, R. (1998), *Factors affecting SME's commitment to an issue-based network - Case North Karelia Tourism Strategy* in Proceedings of Conference on Growth and Job Creation in SME;s. Mikkeli January 7-9.98. Helsinki School of Economics and Business Administration. Mikkeli, 474-497.

Komppula, R. (1999), *Tourism Company's commitment to co-operative networks in 1999 European Conference*, Travel and Tourism Research Association, Conference Papers. Dublin Tourism Research Centre.

KTM (1996), Suomen matkailustrategia vuoteen 2000. Kauppa- ja teollisuusministeriön julkaisuja, Helsinki

KTM Maaseutumatkailun toimialaraportti (1997). KTM Työvoima- ja elinkeinokeskus, Helsinki

Lassila, H. and Komppula, R. (1999), *Constructing a New Regional Tourism Or*ganisation – A Case Study in McLoghlin, D. and Horan C. (ed.), Proceedings of The 15th Annual IMP Conference, University College, Dublin.

Maaseutumatkailun kapasiteettiselvitys (1997), Maaseutumatkailun teemaryhmä, Savonlinna.

Mayer-Krahmer, F. (1985). *Innovation Behaviour and Regional Indigenous Potential*, Regional Studies, 19, 523-34.

Morrison, A., Rimmington, M. and Williams, C. (1999), *Entrepreneurship in the Hospitality, Tourism and Leisure Industries*. Bath: Butterworth-Heinemann.

Neubauer, F. and Lank, A. G. (1998), *The Family Business. Its Governance for Sustainability*. Basingstoke: Macmillan.

OECD (1994), *Tourism Policy and International Tourism in OECD Countries: 1991-1992*. Special Feature Tourism Strategies and Rural Development: Organisation for Economic Co-operation and Development. Paris.

Page, S. J. , Forer, P. and Lawton, G. R. (1999), *Small Business Development and Tourism: Terra incognita?*. Tourism Management 20 (1999), 435-459.

Pohjois-Savon liitto. Pohjois-Savon matkailustrategia, (1996), (unpublished).

Shaw, G. and Williams, A. (1990), *Tourism, Economic Development and the Role of Entrepreneurial Activity* in Cooper C. (ed.) Progress in Tourism, Recreation and Hospitality Management (Vol. 2). Chichester: Wiley.

Shaw, G. and Williams, A. (1994), *Critical Issues in Tourism: A geographical perspective*, Oxford, Blackwell.

Smallbone D., North, D. and Leigh R. (1993), *The Growth and Survival of Mature Manufacturing SMEs in the 1980s: an Urban-Rural Comparison* in Curran, J. and Storey D. (ed.) Small firms in Urban and Rural Locations, Routledge Small Business Series, London Routledge.

# A role for a services marketing approach to tourism product development

*Gillian Lyons*

University of Wolverhampton, UK

## Introduction

New product and service development generally has been highlighted as a key research requirement by the Marketing Science Institute together with Houston (1998) and Ingram (1998). Wright and Charlett (1995) highlight the need to improve the marketing process in order to eliminate both the high failure rate of new products and difficulties with diffusion and adoption. Whilst this is clearly important for tangible products it is even more crucial for a small market town or rural destination to ensure that the product offering does not fail. Regardless of any man-made attraction which may be incorporated, it is its own product and does not therefore have a range of backup resources and raw materials from which to construct new offerings. Neither does it have the facility to hide failure behind new names, badgings and packaging. The Heart of England Tourist Board (HOTB) (1998) has issued strategic guidelines for new product development which include a market led and innovative approach.

Although there is a wealth of literature relating to consumer behaviour, place marketing and other aspects of tourism, there is rather less relating to destination product/service development. Much could be termed "functional" as opposed to "procedural," and generally relates to the exploitation of "given" attractions to specific segments, rather than the process of developing a product or service which is "new". Quality improvements to a specific aspect of the service offer and the difficulties of an integrated approach to an intangible heterogeneous phenomenon also receive attention. From a destination perspective, the nature of the resource base together with public sector involvement tends to emphasise spatial planning models, using what might be termed as a production approach rather than a market led needs base from which ideas are generated.

## Rural tourism and product development

The received image of the rural tourist is of one who enjoys landscape, nature, wild life and natural and built heritage. Such resources are inherently fragile, therefore product development must take account of sustainability, a concept which recognises that heritage in all forms must be preserved for future generations; environmental and quality of life safeguards need to be embedded in product development. Research into tourism impacts by the Rural Development Commission (1996) indicated that tourism benefits were not well understood by the communities under study, with recommendations for a bottom up approach to planning and development (1997).

This paper draws on a range of literature and an exploratory qualitative study focusing on a small market town in rural Middle England, desirous of economic regeneration in order to offset local agricultural decline. The aim of the study was to identify issues pertinent to the product development process, and to evaluate the potential use of services marketing frameworks as a tool in this context.

# Tourism models and frameworks in product/service development

## A look at some of the literature

Much of the marketing, and indeed other, literature directly related to tourism exhibits a distinct lack of dedicated models and frameworks, a point reinforced by Hall and Jenkins (1995) who bemoan the paucity of clearly defined frameworks, analytical and theoretical, along with relevant illustrative case studies. In the more general context of product development, Gordon (1996) suggests the lack of formal ongoing frameworks for the generation and screening of new ideas. Deficiency in dedicated tools of analysis stems partly from the perceived unsuitability of accepted service or manufacturing frameworks, some of which having been criticised in their own right by authors such as Chase (1981). This observation referred to service systems having their basis in manufacturing methodologies, leading to an over- emphasis with physical aspects of service design and delivery, whilst taking little account of pyscho-social dynamics. The viewpoint is countered by Middleton (1998) who, whilst writing in relation to the concept of sustainable tourism, advocates component creation and propounds the use of a manufacturing principle for small organisations. This approach has potential for standardisation of quality, but the problem still remains with regard to mechanisms for the base definition of core and peripheral products. Authors such as Bramwell (1993) and Clarke (1995) indicate the issue of tourism development as being a marketing management problem with a paucity of research (Page and Getz, 1997).

Cowell (1998) points to the overall neglect of new service product development as emanating from a narrow view of the skill base, limited resources and the lack of innovation found in public sector organisations. Kosters (1988) refers to the passive role of government at all levels, interested solely in promotion, ignoring innovation, whilst Pessenier (1966) highlights issues of capability which may be potential rather than actual. It is reasonable to assume that the nature and level of marketing skills within local government is variable; within the scope of the study, promotion based activities were dominant.

Many authors adopt the classic marketing approach of idea generation, forwards. Seaton and Bennett (1996) admit the benefits of product research and testing, but refer to the impossibility of this framework in the tourism arena. Only rarely, is it possible to shape a product from the first principles, being constrained by geographic and physical limitations. The same authors refer to concepts of Adoption and Diffusion theory (Rogers 1962) and Trickle Down theory (Robertson 1971), where tourism development starts with a small elitist product, but claim operational and evaluation difficulties render both methods unacceptable.

Roberto (1987) advocates Problem Detection Analysis utilising an open question followed by a list of concerns - a form of Gap Analysis. He is of the opinion that the successful undertaking of this gives a product advantage by uncovering major needs. In the case of rural tourism however, such analysis cannot be focused solely on the market need alone due to the close interplay of the actors. The needs approach is also mentioned by Woodruff (1995) and Cooper (1998), who utilises a benefits led service encounter framework with the emphasis on benefit identification as a base, relating primarily to the tourism consumer. Community perceptions or product roles are unclear.

# Product development

## The tourism offer

The scope of tourism has grown along with participation, in tandem with participant levels of experience, confidence and sophistication; this, coupled with increased access, disillusionment with both popular offerings and lifestyles, indicates a need, which in turn provides opportunities for increased tourist independence linked to product diversity. Complexity arises from diverse wants and expectations, but also from intangibility, tourist involvement and the number of variables included in the tourism experience, which are outside the control of a single organisation.

Even though tourism service failure produces adverse publicity, there is a tendency to focus upon tourism products as physical attractions frequently involving quite frenetic activity in the process of enjoyment. The expression "been there, done that, got the tee-shirt" sums up a popular view of the tourism product as progression up or down a list of "approved" destinations and attractions, rather than an holistic service experience. Differing psycho-social traits and motivations of tourists across their life-stages are not well understood. As a consequence, a school of thought exists which indicates that no mass attraction = zero tourism. Where this viewpoint is embedded in a culturally closed environment, there is little appreciation of differing tourist types and forms of tourism offer, the potential environmental and revenue implications, and the roles of and benefits for other stakeholders within the host community.

## Innovation

Innovation stems from information, creativity and an entrepreneurial outlook. Herbig, Golden and Dunphy (1994) refer to the ability to apply capital to existing resources in order to create a new product; Cooper (1998) supports an innovative application to an existing process and product portfolio. Since tourism development usually starts with (local) government, not historically noted for marketing and entrepreneurial activities, there is a need for external support in the absence of comprehensive, easily understood product development frameworks.

Successful development depends on how closely consumer needs are fulfilled and the match to perceptions and aspirations. In the case of tourism, equally important measures relate to the extent to which revenue is generated for the producer, the degree of sustainability, and the tangible and cultural benefits for the host community; the latter aspects are frequently contingent upon the former. Conversely, the work of Doxey (1975), Ap (1992), Wheeler (1995) indicates that host attitudes and reactions will impact on the experience of the tourist in a number of ways, not least by the welcome extended. This will be affected by perceived benefits over costs, together with an appreciation of ways in which such benefits accrue. A benefits led approach should not relate solely to the tourist; some degree of knowledge and mutual understanding of motivation and inter-relationships is paramount. Frameworks which foster some commonality of culture and respect between host, provider and visitor are being recognised as desirable tools.

There is an increased need for innovative solutions to what are fundamentally regeneration problems on the one hand and issues of sustainability on the other, in order to address destination development, decline or competitive saturation. Product development is a broad and complex issue and in tourism requires increased applications of research energy and expertise.

## Response to change

Economic regeneration is a driver for new tourism development, often soliciting and attracting large amounts of external investment, consequential loss of control and frequently resulting in a changed identity. The pursuit of revenue streams as the common objective, based solely on success elsewhere is often employed. Whilst this is acceptable and/or desirable in certain cases, it is inappropriate in others. Priorities of investors linked to market positioning, based on forecasts of market growth in similar situations elsewhere, dictate the product portfolio.

There is a recognition that organisations should be more attuned to customer needs (Morash, Droge and Vickery, 1997), responsive to changing requirements by the provision of core and augmented services. This necessitates being closer to the consumer and the market, with timely information, and the knowledge and ability to use and interpret such information with regard to development and modification of products. Tourism is a dynamic market - Bramwell (1993) indicates the greater affluence, education, quality requirements and spending of rural tourists, whilst Mathur, Sherman and Schiffman (1998) provide an attitude and lifestyle distinction between the elderly mature and the ageing post war tourist. Service providers must assess how such demographic changes influence the market place and to what extent invention or innovation can best serve these and other markets. It is perhaps pertinent to remind ourselves that in both the growing mature market, for a fair proportion of the mid twenty to thirty plus age group, tourism is no longer a novelty or a luxury, but a necessary part of every day living. Increasing disposable income, more leisure time and experience breed a discerning and demanding consumer who requires a choice of products to match both life-stage and whim.

# The nature of the product

## Difficulties of definition

Difficulty in defining and shaping a product stems partly from a lack of homogeneity. The aggregation of service elements, the bundles of characteristics, and the physical elements of place are differently interpreted and experienced by both providers and recipients within a wide variety of variables. Segmentation and profiling are valuable tools in minimising incompatibilities, but it is the quality of the exercise, the underpinning foundations and an holistic matching/prioritising process which determines success. Andreassin and Lindestad (1998) make reference to the expectations of quality, together with the perception of the quality/value link citing the signalling role of corporate image, where it is difficult to evaluate service attributes. Image has a both negative and positive of implications in tourism product development- being capable of both factual and mythical interpretation., but can only act as a provocateur of interest. The tourist or visitor has no way, except perhaps by way of received recommendation, of being able to evaluate or compare the experience until s/he has experienced it. Even then, due to the changing interplay of the actors, an identical repeat experience is not guaranteed.

Proctor (1996) and Theobald (1998) highlight the need for quality and service excellence and the literature shows that in this respect, tourists are becoming more demanding. The nature of the tourism experience precludes a singularly precise definition of the term "quality" due to difficulties of standardisation. Even a common base philosophy of fitness for purpose and exceeding expectations, brings us full circle to the requirement of a developmental framework for identifying pertinent core and peripheral products in which to embed the elusiveness of quality.

## The role of image

The destination or product image aids decision-making, but is only truly reflective of a quality experience if the reality - the product/service on offer - matches the perception. Work by Ryan (1991) makes reference to the ability of the tourist to adapt to realities together with the nature of the critical encounter that shaped the reality. It is this, he opines which creates the link between tourism and marketing. The dynamic nature of the sector however, dictates that that the link with marketing occurs or should occur at a far earlier stage - that of product development. Whilst he goes on to state, quite rightly, that the tourism service performance has by its nature, inherent problems of control and standardisation, it could be argued that rather than the advocated *application* of marketing processes to specific characteristics of the tourism industry, the marketing discipline should *define and shape* the characteristics and attributes of the tourism offer. Notwithstanding, the majority of tourism development results from top down rather than bottom up planning processes.

Seaton (1994) asks questions in respect of what the product is, what it is thought to be, and how it is represented. These categories relate to physical characteristics, image and image representation - images formed by experience, recommendation, education etc. and images promulgated by promotion. To this could be added physical regeneration, authenticity and dramaturgy.

Cooper (1994) refers to the use of image as a product development tool; Shostack (1977) is of the opinion that image is a method of differentiating the product and presenting it to the target market. A theory postulated by Firat, Dholakia and Venkatesh (1995) and Firat, Schultz and Clifford (1997) opens up the concept that images should not represent the product, rather that products should be constructed around images, a reflection of post-modern marketing strategies of consumer empowerment in the construction and representation of experiences which enhances self image. Cova (1997) in his work on "communitas" in services marketing touches on this with his view that individuals seek to build an identity through the purchase of services There is a tension however, relating to the nature of experiences pinned to self image as opposed to those which relate to self actualisation. Deeper analysis begs the question as to whether indeed, in the latter case, products as such can be constructed at all.

## Self actualisation

The term self-actualisation implies a consciously undertaken participative stance in the tourism process.

Crompton (1979) makes reference to pyscho-sociological motivations coupled with a need to re-balance the equilibrium, whilst Bloch (1981) refers to interest, arousal and emotion which may be aroused by products. Growth in the Living Museums sector suggests growth in both history and nostalgia as tourism foci. There is an increasing body of evidence that independent self-seeking and achievement is being used as both an escape from modern day pressures and as a re-affirmation of self - worth in a world where people are increasingly judged by material accoutrements. The work of Seaton (1994) makes reference to " the pursuit of the other" - the solicitation of an experience which contrast with everyday lifestyles. This lifestyle - induced experiential motivation is perhaps the touchstone of marketing based, as opposed to production oriented, product development, especially in rural tourism. It is important to recognise that in this age of information and education, there is declining tolerance for commercial activities which operate at the expense, in all interpretations, of the indigenous population.

## Two-sided self-actualisation audit

Self-identity, actualisation and quality of reward, cut both ways. Therefore, if marketing is interpreted as the profitable delivery of products which satisfy consumer needs and wants, a range of location specific issues require evaluation, such as:

- *Who* are the tourists?

- What do the relevant parties to supply *think* that they want?

- What are the *core and peripheral* attributes of the tourist experience?

- Is what they want easily available?

- Is the *community* willing to supply what they want?

The term "profitability" has a more complex interpretation when applied to the amalgam of elements provided by a range of stakeholders, with critical implications for sustainability, harmony, retention of identity and control, dictating that the following should also be explored:

- Does anyone want what we already have?

- What is the existing/potential volume and value?

- Is this capable of being exploited and managed without destruction of the essence - of the product, of the community?

- What are the costs and benefits?

- Is there compatibility of stakeholder objectives?

- Is there capability for service supply?

It is necessary for the long-term strategic viewpoint to be adopted, in order to construct compatible tourism.

# A services marketing approach

## Tools of analysis

Otto and Brent Ritchie (1996) confirm that there is no model which encapsulates the service experience in tourism, neither does a satisfactory product development framework exist.

Most services marketing frameworks of analysis and development relate to specific organisational elements of the service encounter and are used to enhance both quality and value of a previously identified product or product range. One method, *Service Blueprinting*, utilises the idea of convergent and divergent scripts to employ a two-sided approach to service development (Hoffman and Bateson 1997). The authors' assertion is that service blueprints are capable of being used in the new product development process. They refer to issues of complexity (the number of elements in service provision) and divergence (extent of personal interpretation) and whilst their work relates to specific service provision - restaurants, florists - extending the scope of the above elements has a tourism development potential. There is little evidence that similar models are used in tourism development, although the authors cite cases from the hospitality arena. Use of this method helps in accounting for issues of complexity, and facilitates positioning strategies. The embedded concept of script analysis lends itself as a tool with which to determine whether or not local perception of an appropriate tourism offering accords with the requirements of potential or indeed, actual but previously unidentified, tourists.

## The role of physical attributes

The importance of the physical perspective in the tourism experience, acknowledged by Heart of England Tourist Board (HOTB, 1998) is implicit in the concept of Servicescapes (Bitner 1992). This relates to the impact of the built, as opposed to natural, environment; the essence of the research alleges that "approach" or avoidance" behaviours, demonstrated by tendencies to stay and explore, or to visit and leave, are triggered by the physical environment. Bitner discusses the effect upon the interpersonal interactions of provider/beneficiary, with regard to the representation of social norms, conventions and expectations. Interpretation of the latter aspect highlights a need to determine the criteria by which a tourist categorises information and communication as being a facilitative tool or a product feature.

Otto and Brent Ritchie (1996) refer a to the "psychological environment" and to the "subjective personal experience and feelings experienced by consumers". The built environment can provoke feelings of safety, excitement or danger, and the ambience should clearly relate to the ethos.

Lovelock (1983) refers to the customers entering the service factory stating that satisfaction will be influenced by the interaction with personnel, facilities, the options and flexibility which the service offers and the characteristics of other customers. This author acknowledges that the consumer experiences not only the core product, but other aspects of the system, and that these also have a place in the total product or service. The community and employees are part of the whole experience and their roles are more likely to contribute to a successful product if they are recognised and included at the outset.

Perhaps the most composite product-environment model is the *Servuction* model (Eiglier and Langeard et al, 1981) as outlined in Hoffman and Bateson (1997) and which was employed by Warnaby and Davies (1997) in their study of cities as shopping destinations. In its pure form it relates to the service firm, its processes and its operating environment. It acknowledges the dynamic nature of consumer expectations, the complex interaction of the components, and the strategies of pro-activity or reaction to change. The system postulates four components of a service experience: the *inanimate environment* (that which the system represents). In the case of tourism, this may include elements such as shops, scenery, *personnel - service* (direct involvement. such as tour guides) and *contact* (indirect involvement such as public car park attendants); *other customers* (who impact upon the service experience) and the *invisible organisation* (the facilitating process and systems). The model demonstrates that consumers are a fundamental part of the service development *process* but the literature demonstrates that they are also at the heart of the *product*.

# The research and the product perception

## Background

The study set out to identify stakeholder perceptions, knowledge of, attitude towards and ideas for, tourism product development in a small market town, which was deemed to have virtually no tourism activity. As an exploratory study, there was no pre-conceived hypothesis, rather the intention to uncover issues needing further examination. It was anticipated that at some stage in the research process, pointers towards the construction of a development framework might emerge.

In-depth interviews, focus groups, open questionnaires were amongst a range of data gathering tools employed.

A resume of some of the issues identified is contained hereafter.

## The analysis

The first stage data analysis identified the following:-

- A general consensus prevailed within the sample in that the town was not thought to attract tourists.

- There was little accord between supply side stakeholders as to the desirability of tourism as an economic regenerator, primarily due to preconceived notions of tourist inclinations and behaviour.

- The town was deemed to be unable to supply any attraction for future tourism given the current resource status, and furthermore could not compete with regional honeypot sites.

- Private sector investment would be required in order to redress the above, primarily for the provision of a purpose built physical attraction. This would dilute control.

- There was an admitted lack of expertise with regard to tourism product/service development.

- The responsibility and skills in this respect were considered to lie elsewhere, both in the public and private sector.

## The second stage analysis

The second stage involved an identification of tourist activity and the product constituents which comprised the experience. This was undertaken using a number of sources, among them contacting signatories in a visitors book, open ended qualitative statement sheets left in hotel bedrooms, and random approaches in cafes and other public places.

Data indicated the presence of both overnight and day visitors, the former international and domestic, both groups comprising a mix of leisure and business motives. The leisure visitors were predominantly AB, silver segment, falling into two broad categories - self-actualising exploration and hedonistic relaxation. The first were aligned to the international set, the latter to domestic day visitors. There was a commonality of product requirement with variants appropriate to the prime motivation.

A grounded analysis yielded two distinct leisure tourist typologies accessing a product portfolio which was thought not to exist, being:

> *Questors* - mature, AB, independent, self actualising activities, non invasive tourists - high spenders with a penchant for involvement in everyday local culture and special interest tourism; and

> *Shires* - mature ABC1, traditional values and pastimes, comfort, good food, "good" (expensive) classic clothes, relaxation indulgent, enjoyed small local festivals and events.

The groups had different orientations - passive versus active, independent versus group active, but were synergistic in age, social class, values and the non-invasive and high spending traits.

The essence of the experience was the absence of a constructed form of tourist entertainment, and freedom to explore both surroundings and self. The service encounter, which included local cultural interaction in addition to high levels of service, was paramount. A core element was the authenticity of the physical environment and service offering, reflecting the ambience and culture of nostalgic experience, self-actualising discovery and relaxation. The tourists displayed none of the characteristics which alarmed residents; their traits indicated that increased revenue from a portfolio of sympathetic, sustainable tourism was possible. In this respect the outcome concords with Ashworth and Voogd (1994), highlighting potential mismatches in perceptions of product constituents.

The data, together with that from the other stakeholder sets was subsequently fed into a form of script mapping, thence to a three dimensional Product Perception Gap analysis encompassing the views of the tourists, residents and service providers.

A further filtering exercise, which included public sector constraint data, was undertaken via a framework euphemistically entitled a Preliminary Product Pointer. This stage of analysis highlighted problem areas, which when taken into consideration, provided a base raft of knowledge from which to both identify current product attributes and commence a bounded idea generation exercise.

The use of script mapping yielded a number of issues relating both to product and process. In relation to overt design and development of the product offering, it became clear that characteristics embedded in the service marketing frameworks previously identified, were not only pertinent to discrete service encounters but could be instrumental in the design and development of tourism products. Aspects of the *Servuction and Servicescape* models were particularly evident; on the supply side, little appreciation of the importance of aesthetic and intangible service elements indicated discrepant perceptions by the service factory with regard to core and peripheral benefits.

Desired product characteristics and attributes did not accord with the perceptions of the host community or the public sector, being far less intrusive, requiring small amounts of *enhancement* rather than *investment* capital. The needs of a *"policy defined"* target market are not necessarily concomitant with those of an *under-researched existing* market, potentially resulting in the missing of opportunities accruing from product differentiation.

Whilst more generally used in the environment of the firm, script analysis has potential as a development tool in a destination whose product encompasses an amalgam of service encounters. An expanded version of Product Perception Gap analysis would provide a more finely tuned facility for "unbundling" the product. It has a number of applications - demonstrating differences in objectives; that tourism need not be invasive; that service levels are paramount; that limited capital to an existing resource set can provide acceptable products. The Preliminary Product Pointer focuses attention on the detail of that which is currently being enjoyed as tourism, and allows the evaluation of synergistic developments.

# Conclusion

The critical difference, embedded in the use of service marketing frameworks as product development tools, relates to the *holistic* nature of the appraisal. Additional to the core categories, the approach provides investigative and decision-making techniques which incorporate a range of aspects such as needs, benefits, situational and gap analysis, image, perceptions and capabilities. Philosophical and practical departures are highlighted with regard to the nature of product development. There is a clear role for such "organisation" based tools within the multiple stakeholder integrated yet independent, arena of tourism development and provision.

The research revealed that reactions based solely upon pre-defined "objective based" competitive development for the "average regional tourist" could in fact, destroy the embryo product, at the same time incurring higher costs, host antipathy, and less than optimum economic benefit.

Whilst the focus of study was exploratory, but primarily attuned to new product identification and development, important issues relating to the *process* by which such development is successfully implemented were also highlighted. Issues of capability, responsibility, control and communication, the existence of deficiencies which, unattended, would manifest more crucially with a higher volume of tourism. Such knowledge, pinned to discrete products, enables strategic decisions to be taken with regard to the appropriate up-scaling of destination resources and has a part to play in assisting in minimisation of both co-producer and consumer risks.

It seems to be the case that the process elements of product development is at least as problematic as the initial product definition. Perhaps further research into services marketing applications to tourism will provide an insight as to the most appropriate tools with which to over come the stumbling blocks.

## A final thought

Rural tourism and market towns are a special case by virtue of culture, resources, expertise and sustainability, generally though to attract a particular type of visitor or tourist.

The outcome of this study provides another dimension to that of the current issues with regard to commodification, image and place product marketing within rural tourism. The product as experienced was raw, locally unrecognised and therefore not promoted, with a consequential lack of imagery and mythical embellishments.

This confirms the absence of a singular mythical image of rurality, but by making the distinction between the pursuit of self actualisation versus the pursuit of self image, it raises the question as to the nature of the circumstances and mechanisms whereby resources are used in the promotion of place as the product, as opposed place as a product facilitator.

# References

Andreassin, T. W. and Lindestad, B. (1998), Customer Loyalty and Complex Services, The Impact of corporate image on quality, customer satisfaction and loyalty for customers with varying degrees of service expertise, *International Journal of Service Industry Management* Vol 9 Issue 1 1998.

Ap. J. (1992), Residents perceptions on tourism impacts, *Annals of Tourism Research* vol.19 no. 4 1992 pp 665-9,0.

Ashworth G. J and Voogd, H. (1994), Marketing and place promotion, in Gold J. R and Ward, S.V. (eds) *Place promotion, the use of publicity and marketing to sell towns and regions*. John Wiley and Son, Chichester.

Bateson, J. E. G. (1992), *Managing Services Marketing*, 2nd ed, The Dryden Press, Fort Worth Texas.

Bateson, J. E. G. (1995), *Managing Services Marketing*, The Dryden Press, Fort Worth. Texas.

Bitner, M. J. (1992), "Servicescapes: the impact of physical surroundings on customers and employees", *Journal of Marketing* No 56 April pp57-71.

Bloch, P. H. (1981), Involvement beyond the purchase process: conceptual issues and empirical investigation" in Mitchell, A. (ed), *Advances in Consumer Research*, Vol 9 Association for Consumer Research, Ann Arbor, MI pp413-417.

Bramwell, B. (1993), *Tourism Strategies and Rural Development*. Paris, OECD Books.

Chase, R. B. (1981), Customer contact approach to service: Theoretical bases and practical extensions. USA, *Operations Research* 29 (4).

Clarke, J. (1995), The effective marketing of small scale tourism enterprises through national structures; lessons from a two-way comparative study of farm tourist accommodation in the UK. *Journal of Location Marketing* 1 2 pp 79 - 86.

Cooper, J. R. A. (1998), Multidimensional approach to the adoption of innovation, *Management Decision*, Vol 36 Issue 8.

Cooper, C. (1994), The destination image: an update, in Seaton. A. V. (ed), *Tourism, the state of the art*, Chichester, Wiley.

Cova, B. (1997), Community and Consumption. Towards a definition of the "linking value" of product or services, *European Journal of Marketing* Vol. 31 Issue 3,4.

Cowell, D. (1989), *The Marketing Of Services*, Oxford, Heinneman Professional Publishing.

Crompton, J. L. (1979), Motivations for pleasure vacations, *Annals of Tourism Research*, 6, Vol 24.

Doxey, G. V. (1975), in Murphy, P. E. (1985), *Tourism a community approach*. London, Routledge.

Firat, A. F., and Dholakia, N. and Venkatesh, A. (1995), Post modernity, the age of marketing, *International Journal of Research in Marketing* no 10 pp227-49.

Firat, A. and Shultz 1., Clifford J. (1997), From segmentation to fragmentation Markets and marketing strategy in the post modern era, *European Journal of Marketing* Vol 31 Issue 3,4.

Gordon, G. (1996), "New Product Development practices in consumer versus business product organisations", *Journal of Consumer Marketing* Vol 13 No 2 pp 34-47.

Hall, C. M. and Jenkins, J. (1995), *Tourism and Public Policy*, London, Routledge.

Herbig, P., Golden, J. E. and Dunphy, S. (1994), The Relationship of Structure to Entrepreneurial and Innovative Success, *Marketing Intelligence and Planning* Vol 12 Issue 9.

Hoffman, K. D. and Bateson J. E. F. (1997), *Essentials of Services Marketing*, Dryden Press, Harcourt Brace. USA.

Ingram, H. .(1996), Clusters and gaps in hospitality and tourism academic research, *International Journal of Contemporary Hospitality Management* 8 (7).

Kosters, M. J. Changing tourism requires a different management approach in Goodall, B. and Ashworth, G. (eds), (1988), *Marketing in the tourism industry: the promotion of destination regions*, Beckenham, Croom Helm Ltd.

Lovelock, C. H. (1983), Classifying services to gain strategic marketing insights, Journal of Marketing summer 9–20 1983.

Lovelock, C. H. (1991), *Services Marketing, text, cases and readings*. New Jersey, Prentice Hall International.

Lovelock, C. H. (1992), *Managing Services*, New Jersey, Prentice-Hall International.

Lue, C. M. Crompton J. l. and Fesenmaier, J. R. (1993), Conceptualisation of multi destination pleasure trips, *Annals of Tourism Research*, 20 (2): 289–301.

Mathur, A. Sherman E., Schiffman, Leon G, (1998), Opportunities for marketing travel services to the new-age elderly, *The Journal of Services Marketing* Vol 12 Issue 4.

Middleton, V. C., Hawkins R. J. (1998*), Sustainable tourism - a marketing perspective*, Oxford, Butterworth Heinemann.

Morash, E. A., Droge, C., Vickery, S. (1997), Boundary spanning interfaces between logistics, production, marketing and new product development, International *Journal of Physical Distribution and logistics management* 27 (5/6).

Otto, J. E. and Brent R. J. R. (1996), The Service Experience in Tourism. *Tourism Management* ,Vol.17 No 3 pp 165–174.

Page, S. and Getz, D. (1997), (eds), T*he Business of Rural Tourism - International Perspectives,* London. Thompson Business Research.

Pessenier, E. A. (1966), *New Product design - an analytical approach*, McGraw Hill Book Co.

Proctor, T. (1996), *Marketing Management, integrating theory and practice*, London, International Thompson Business Press.

Rogers, E. M. (1962), *Diffusion of Innovation*, New York, The Free Press.

Robertson, T. (1971), *Communication and Innovative Behaviour*, New York, Holt, Ringhart and Winston.

Roberto, E. L. (1987), *Applied Market Research Metro Manila: Ateneo de Manila* University Press.

Ryan, C. ( 1991b), "Tourism Marketing – a symbiotic relationship", *Tourism Management*, June pp101–11.

Seaton. A. V.(ed) *Tourism, the state of the art*, Chichester, Wiley.

Seaton, A. V. and Bennett, G. (1996), *Marketing Tourism Products: Concepts, Issues and Cases*, Oxford, International Thompson.

Shostack, G. L. Breaking free from product marketing, *Journal of Marketing* 41 April 73-80 1977.

Theobald, W. F. (1998), *Global Tourism*, 2nd edition, Oxford, Butterworth-Heinneman.

Warnaby, G and Davies, B. J. (1997), Commentary: Cities as service factories? Using the servuction system for marketing cities as shopping destinations, *International Journal of Retail and Distribution Management*, Vol 25 Issue 6.

Wheeler, M. (1995), Tourism Marketing Ethics: an introduction, *International Marketing Review* Vol 12 Issue 4.

Woodruff, H. (1995), *Services Marketing*, London, Pitman Publishing.

Wright, Malcolm, and Charlett, Don, (1995) , New Product Diffusion Models in Marketing: An Assessment of Two Approaches, *Marketing Bulletin*, 1995,6, 32-41.

## Other sources

Marketing Science Institute http://192.138.193.9?crim/msi.htm.

Heart of England Tourist Board (1998), Visitor Focus - Growing Prosperity in the Heart of England 1998 – 2003.

Rural Development Commission (1997), The Impact of Tourism on Rural Settlements.

# The tourist maze: People and urban space

## Martine C Middleton

University of Central Lancashire, UK

## Introduction

Cities world-wide, are set to absorb unprecedented levels of tourism growth. In 1995 international tourist arrivals were 563 million and are predicted to reach 1.6 billion by the year 2020 (WTO). Debate needs to shift from *why* tourists visit places, to what they actually *do* when they are there.

The paper commences by acknowledging the growing numbers of tourists attracted to urban destinations. The economic rationale of tourism policy encourages social interaction between residents and incoming visitors sharing the same environment. The urban fabric of cities provides a platform upon which social and cultural diversity may be displayed. However, fuelled by economic impetus cities are becoming increasingly homogenous. The continuous extension of the built environment succeeds in enhancing the provision of things to do – but what about things to see?

The paper argues that cities are in danger of (over)emphasising function, at the expense of the form of the surrounding environment. Cities have shifted away from centres of production to become foci of consumption (Zukin, 1992). The form of the built environment is being identified by commercial dominance creating an abundance of enclosed spatial zones i.e. shopping malls, leisure centres, man-made attractions. Culler notes that (1981:128) tourist 'attractions' offer an elaborately contrived indirect experience, an artificial product to be consumed in the very places where the real thing is free as air. The management of visitors is directed towards the active utilisation of space evaluated by the frequency, capacity, cost and quantity of use. Tourist cities compliment this by addressing the appropriateness of physical provision to social use. As we enter the Millennium throughout Europe and beyond, the unified aim is to provide and maintain a *quality* environment. Cities have a vision for the future combining the needs and wants of their users with public and private strategic development (Middleton, 1999).

Urban conurbations have changing economic frameworks, increased social diversity and encroaching physical uniformity. The success of cities need not solely be expressed in terms of value and volume e.g. number of tourists and level of expenditure. This 'conveyer-belt' approach to management is linked to the temporary presence of the individual tourists. It needs to be superseded by the collective appraisal of tourism as a dynamic and competitive industry. One that is increasingly economically developed yet socially determined. Quality environments combine the active (things to do) with the passive (things to see) to create the overall (total) tourist experience. The paper seeks to recognise the positive economic and social perspectives of tourism and presents the need for tempered physical control and development. This balance should be re-addressed by spatial development within the built environment. The use of open, public space has been undervalued by its static and complacent nature, its' lack of economic return and understated ownership. The paper argues that the utilisation of free and open space dilutes tourist traffic, celebrates cultural disparity and diversity and more importantly, has the ability to appeal and pervade the total tourist experience reminiscent of the stay. This composite approach is beneficial to tourists and residents, planners and practitioners and alleviates growing demand upon a physical finite resource. The work culminates in advocating positive policy-making as an integral element to the urban sustainability of the future.

## Urban places

> *"Big city, Bright lights"* the lure to the tourist.

As we enter the millennium, one acknowledged accomplishment has been the constant increase in the level of social and economic mobility throughout the world. This century has come to a close with over half of the worlds population living in urban areas (Clark, 1996). Cities from the developing world have emerged to represent some of the largest urban populations of the century. Such a widespread trend reiterates the global character of urbanisation as a predominant issue. Ultimately this last decade has witnessed an increasing amount of competition between international cities within Europe and the rest of the world.

Urban areas have embarked upon strategic initiatives that have altered their physical landscape and what they have to offer. The trend of spatial restructuring has resulted in a myriad of physical, economic and social changes being induced within long established, traditional city centres. The creation of global metropolitan cultures is a predominant aspect of urban change that has attracted significant attention (Featherstone, 1990; Zukin, 1992; Bianchini, 1998). Many metropolitan cultures have produced a series of identifiable traits that are common to all places. The preference towards post-modern architecture has become a prevalent feature in major cities influencing a greater degree of similarity in superficial appearance. As cities continue to assume a role of increasing uniformity, the homogeneity of built areas inevitably becomes standardised (Relph, 1987). City planners and providers have endeavoured to consistently extend the provision of man-made facilities and amenities in an effort to meet increases in consumer demand. The spatial restructuring of urban places has provided the opportunity to converge a more diverse range of social use whilst increasing economic benefits. It is the proportion of finite urban space that has determined the quantity of indoor, multi-use space being predominantly dedicated to commercial and leisure orientated activities. The concept of locating goods and services *'under one roof'* is far from new yet is a trend that should be viewed with caution. It is the increasing physical size and scale of modern leisure provision that has gained such unprecedented momentum. These urban landmarks have become the new successful attractions that now dominate the urban landscape. People of all ages are drawn in their multitudes to these 'megamalls'. These are centres of consumption dedicated to active participation on a wide collective basis over extended periods of time. The service economy continually seeks to extend provision over physical space and amount of time to achieve resource optimisation. The achievement of 'consumer citizenship' (Bianchi, 1988) is illustrated by the need for materialistic acquisition. This form of demand reflects the *ability* to participate more than the unfulfilled *want*. In some ways, this demonstrated use of buying power appears to validate the success of the overall visit. It could be said that this assertion epitomises the closing momentum of the last decade of the century. From economic solidarity and greater social disparity; the 'haves 'and 'have nots'. It is issues and implications that emerge from such trends that instigate further debate.

The World Tourism Organisation has predicted that cities are set to absorb unprecedented levels of tourism growth throughout the world (1999). The majority of this increase in tourist activity will require further acquisition of urban development specifically dedicated to extending the levels of service provision. Cities continue to grow in physical size in an attempt to accommodate the scope of social demands from tourists, excursionists and residents alike. The promise of a plethora of things to both see and do, serves to entice an increasing number into new and unfamiliar environments (Page, 1995). However today, urban environments are reflecting a sense of the familiar as they assume common commercial provision. A predominant amount of newly acquired urban space has been allocated or reclaimed, to future retail development throughout the country. The predominant stakeholders in consumer goods and services represent international brand names that cater for the universal marketplace.

Cities represent areas dedicated to economic sustainability that have become to some extent, self-sufficient. The sophisticated level of expansive superstructure of the city attracts the non-resident into its confines. However, the city collectively attracts people by its omnipotent amalgam of social and economic complexity that sets cities apart from other tourist destinations. The intensity of city life is ranked with the size, density and heterogeneity of those who participate within it. It is this eclectic mix that most often encompasses the uniqueness of change and cultural commodification (Featherstone, 1990). The enveloping physical environment is brought to life and commonly addressed in humanistic terms; being 'alive' - 'heart' of the city, 'upbeat', pulsating in resonance as individuals interpret experience into meaning.

## Consuming the city

The visual consumption of the city is an ongoing experience that is enriched by the level of choice and depth of experience. The mobility and chosen activities of tourists remain of paramount importance in evaluating the overall tourist experience. Indeed, what visitors choose *not* to do needs to be of equal importance to the planners and providers of tourism services. Shaw and Williams (1994) recognise that both the production and consumption of tourism are important approaches to the analysis of tourism since; production is the method by which a complex of businesses and industries are involved in the supply of tourism services and products, and how they are delivered to consumers; and consumption, is how, where, why and when the tourist actually consumes tourism services and products (Page, 1995).

**Figure 1    Urban Tourism consolidation**

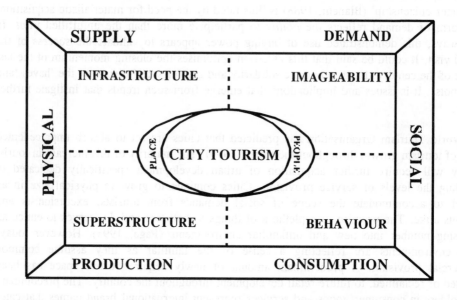

The above figure illustrates the synergy between the physical and social dimensions and the application of the economic premise of supply and demand. The central point indicates the phenomenon of urban tourism. Tourism within the post-industrial city is embedded within the lower left-hand corner dependent upon the physical, heightened superstructure. Different levels of physical, economic or social attributes determine the emphasis of centrifuge.

The intangible attributes of expectation and the seeking of new experiences have traditionally underpinned the majority of tourist activity. The ability to observe and experience first hand has sustained the movements typified by the 'flaneur' as he wanders and witnesses new sights. Here it is argued that this premise, derived from a social perspective has changed (Middleton, 1999). This has undergone a shift in emphasis away from the intrinsic, passive appreciation of a new unfamiliar environment. The pace of society has become faster. It has been superseded by a more active, extrinsic interaction with the visitor becoming a part of the new surroundings. Visitors are not content with voyeuristic experience but actively pursue social interaction and economic exchange. In doing so, people are confronted by a 'maze' of built and enclosed space - a labyrinth of shops, centres and man-made attractions designed and presented to entice. This environment may be interesting by its juxtaposition of landscape and buildings. Indeed, Urry refers to a de-differentiation between tourism *per se* and some social practices e.g. shopping. This distinction produces a 'colonised' tourist gaze which can have considerable implications for the quality of the environment where other social activities occur (Urry, 1995:190).

Current urban processes have adopted this 'colonised' approach to spatial development. The trend for out-of-town shopping has produced extensive retail and consumer provision enclosed under one roof. Such centres are becoming commonplace throughout the U.K as they each emerge bigger and better than the one before. The proliferation of built and enclosed environments serves to cocoon the people inside from the external surroundings. The world of the artificial and surreal is presented waiting to be explored and experienced. The atmosphere is pervaded by the use of created sights, synthetic smells and specially selected forms of music. The use of subliminal sounds and visual associations serve to entice the visitor into a world of commercial lifestyling and psychographic manipulation (Pettican, 1999).

This clinically created approach to service sector delivery serves to reinforce the sense of the notion of insiders and outsiders (Relph, 1987). Being inside the centre provides the safety of a known, secure environment. The visitor is comforted by the presence of the uniformed guards, electronic tagging and use of CCTV. More importantly, the centre has succeeded in bringing together those sharing a common purpose whilst excluding those who do not. One distinct social trait is the increasing desire for human safety and security having a profound effect upon urban environments. This affects all types of individual decisions from where, why and when to visit a place. Conditions must be conducive within spatial urban forms for the activity to materialise. The vacating of one's own space to occupy that of another, has had the process of transition made more familiar, safe and secure.

However, by facilitating social transition the standardisation of the experience is becoming sanitised. Featherstone (1990) asserts that the everyday life of big cities is becoming aestheticisd. In acclaiming the aesthetic potential of mass culture and the aestheticised perceptions of people, visitors are encouraged to participate the complex sign play of symbolism throughout the built environment and urban fabric of the city. The sight of new visual landscapes giving rise to the tourist 'gaze' has been superseded by the site of a built network of enclosed streets and precincts. This labyrinth of warren produced space appears familiar in its commercial name, yet disorientating in its physical setting. The tourist is presented with a maze upon which to decipher anticipation and meaning. This overtly spatially defined activity shapes the practice in which we participate, it is an enigma within itself.

Urry (1990) offers a multi-level interpretation of the 'tourist gaze'. It represents the plural mix of socially organised ways of seeing what is highly prevalent and powerful in contemporary society. It is the scope of these tourist 'gazes' that constitute a series of combined ways of seeing and explaining the world. They have important historical, economic, social, cultural and visual ramifications. As patterns of tourism activity change, so does the 'tourist gaze' alter: they are significantly connected to the wider cultural changes of postmodernity that are becoming more universalised. Furthermore, Urry states that the activity of gazing in tourism in the contemporary world is becoming increasingly difficult to distinguish from other social practices typically those of leisure, sport and shopping.

The proliferation of postmodern architecture has facilitated the preferred practice of the 'post-tourist'. Such terminology was cited by Feifer (1985) who recognised some visitors as revelling in the inauthentic, the artificial. The more complex and multiple the experience, the more pleasure the post-tourist derives. Historically the urban landscape of the city has offered a series of distinct sights unique to the place itself. Whilst many of these sites remain intact they have been overshadowed by a number of new, imposing sites that wait to be visited.

## Spatial forms

As cities undergo economic transition, physical changes are justified to meet the needs of emergent demand. The exodus away from central locations has created a vacuum within which an improved balanced provision maintains the opportunity to emerge. The same phenomenon occurred in preceding years in the United States of America. Abandoned, derelict buildings became occupied and adapted to new forms of use. A process of 'gentrification' introduced a greater social presence within changing spaces and their existing economy. The U.K has witnessed parallel developments within the restructuring of post-industrial cities. Namely, by creating phased zones that encompass a mix of retail, commercial and residential space to fulfil a physical, economic and socially defined rationale.

The creation and restructuring of space within the confines of the city can be seen as either 'open'(outdoor) or 'closed'(indoor) in nature. This raises several pervasive issues that permeate throughout modern society. Namely;

- ratio of space between the two                                SPATIAL DEVELOPMENT

- accessibility and carrying capacity                          SUSTAINABILITY

- size and scale of facilities and amenities                   PROVISION

- division of ownership between the public and          CONTROL
  private sectors.

  *(Middleton, 1999)*

Underpinning each of these interrelated elements is the maintenance of efficient and effective resource management that aims to provide a quality environment.

The diversification of space has extended the social use of people and place into an efficient night-time economy (Bianchini, 1998). The integration of shopping as a specific recreational activity has been differentiated further. Household necessities such as groceries remain locally accessible and are identified as necessary, routine tasks. Travelling to expansive shopping malls acquires value by the amount of time spent to arrive, and the impressive allocation of purpose built space. This recreational pursuit is dedicated to *personal purchases* denoting ones own preference, choice and use. The ability to control and enhance the surrounding environment has been a key theme to consumerism since the 1950s. The use of purpose built arenas has increased in number, size and level of provision. The need to extend the amount of enclosed space for social use has continued to dominate the urban landscape of the UK. Landmark shopping centre developments in the UK feature:

1956    The Bull Ring Centre, Birmingham, opened as the first enclosed shopping centre.

1976    The Arndale Centre, Manchester, first town shopping centre scheme with over 1 million sq.ft.

1976    Brent Cross, Hendon, North London, first free standing centre to be built.

1983    Retail park development becomes significant; first year over 250,000 sq.ft. opened.

1986    The Metro Centre, Gateshead, first free standing regional centre of over 1 million sq.ft.

1989    Fosse Park, Leicester, first of the hybrid shopping centres with both bulky goods and high street traders.

1993    Clarks Village, Street, Somerset, first purpose built factory outlet shopping centre.

1996    Brookfield Retail Park, Cheshunt, first out of town retail park to be occupied exclusively by high street tenants

1998    The Trafford Centre, Manchester. The largest retail and leisure centre with high technology.

*(The Oxford Institute of Retail Management 1999)*

Moreover, the UK has over 1,300 shopping centres culminating in the largest total of shopping centres in any country outside of North America. The addition of numerous outlets has had a reactionary effect upon the remainder of the regional setting. These major retail centres are superseding the traditional city centre in place identity and use. Falk (1998) argues that the revival of town and city centres is necessary if towns are not to become 'like a doughnut with the hole in the middle.' In an effort to combat this, city centres are actively developing evening economies and central population levels in metropolitan cities are rising e.g. Manchester. Visitor surveys conducted in towns and cities seek to ascertain the reason for visiting. The Association of Town Centre Management (ATCM) have identified shopping as the main specific motivation behind 75 per cent of all visits to those places surveyed. The places designated as wholly tourist destinations, the result was still 55-65 per cent of trips primarily for shopping.

The 'retail revolution' has dramatically altered the heart of many UK cities. The British retail movement has experienced three waves of decentralisation (Schiller, 1986, 1994). The first wave occurred during the 1970s as supermarkets moved away from central locations to facilitate space for more durable forms of shopping. The second waves created a plethora of retail parks throughout the country. In the period 1987-90, 50% of all shopping floor-space opened was on retail parks. These have grown in size from under 1 million square feet in 1990 to commanding in excess of 25 million by the close of 1990. The third wave has seen further out-of-town migration of many major retail providers of goods and services. The process of decentralisation has manifested beyond the accepted 'three waves of out of town retailing' (Schiller, 1986) to encompass the further two of regional shopping centres and factory outlets (Tomalin, 1998). Tourism appears to be sanctioned by not *what* you buy, but *where* you choose to buy it. Changing government policy during the 1990's has curtailed some decentralisation of trading centre retail development in response to social implications

Large-scale developments have a direct impact upon the shopping and leisure patterns of people within the UK. As the frequency, capacity and mixed use within these centres increases a reactionary effect occurs elsewhere. This phenomenon occurred previously when cities were solely centres of production and people moved to the outskirts to live and commute into work. This imbalance between economic and social determinants recognised the need of dual-use developments. Cities need to co-ordinate strategic planning throughout the urban destination to meet economic viability and sustain social interaction whilst serving the needs over time.

The significance of strategic location is focal to successful city development. The management of urban spaces reflects elements of a functional, social, spatial, contextual and visual nature (DoE/ATCM, 1997). The success of such a design policy can be facilitated by the increased ease of accessibility, movement and scope of consumer choice. Additional facilities, enhanced environmental quality and sense of safety/security are stated goals. This explicit criteria is well met by the out of town shopping development. Its strategic location is served with extensive road networks. Large areas of commercial space have been designed to accommodate the increasing needs of both provider and consumer. The man-made environment remains prescriptive in temperature and capacity thereby regulating a degree of quality within the environment. However, it is by latter element of public safety that indoor provision benefits. Shopping malls project a sense of safety with the presence of corporate security guards scattered throughout the retail complex. Visitors are united in purpose and location within a common indoor enclosure. In excluding 'others' they empower themselves. This provides a feeling of social well-being and economic worth .

## Spatial functions

In simple terms, tourists travel to cities to experience what 'there is to see and do'. It is the provision of these services that constitute the tourist experience. Jansen-Verbeke (1986) constructed an effective approach to evaluating urban tourism. The framework addresses the area as a leisure product comprising of groups of primary, secondary and additional elements. Primary elements are defined as either an activity place incorporating the main tourist attractions or leisure setting including the physical and socio-cultural characteristics of the city. Secondary elements consist of the support facilities which tourists consume throughout their visit. Additional elements relate to tourist infrastructure supporting the visit; accessibility, parking and information services. The model indicates how the different elements of urban tourism interact and represent the city as a leisure product.

**Table 1    The elements of tourism (based on *Jansen-Verbeke, 1986*)**

| Activity Place | Leisure Setting |
|---|---|
| **Cultural Facilities** | **Physical Characteristics** |
| *Theatres | *Historical street patterns |
| *Concert halls | *Interesting buildings |
| *Cinemas | *Ancient monuments and statues |
| *Exhibitions | *Ecclesiastical buildings |
| *Museums and art galleries | *Parks and green areas |
| **Sports Facilities** | *Water, canals and river fronts |
| *indoor and outdoor | *Harbours |
| **Amusement Facilities** | **Socio-Cultural Features** |
| *Casinos | *Liveliness of the place |
| *Bingo Halls | *language |
| *Nightclubs | *Local customs and costumes |
| *Organised events | *folklore |
| *Festivities | *Friendliness |
|  | *Security |
| **Secondary Elements** | **Additional Elements** |
| *Hotel and catering facilities | *Accessibility and parking facilities |
| *Shopping facilities | *tourist facilities: information offices, signposts, guides, maps |
| *Markets | and leaflets, etc. |

Jansen-Verbeke (1988) states that tourists consume a 'bundle of products' from those on offer within the city. Research into tourism activity often evaluates the success of the policy and its practice, solely by economic determinants. Tourists are provided with an increasing selection of things to do during their stay. The continued provision of tourist superstructure forces change within the built environment. The continued sophistication of the discerning tourist needs to be addressed as an influence upon urban design, not as a major determinant.

From the framework tourists may select one or more of these products during the stay. Jansen-Verbeke (1988) explores the concept of inner city tourism system and addresses the relationship between the product, tourist and promoter. It would appear that shopping has transcended from a secondary element, to a primary determining motive for visit. This transition has been facilitated by all of the three parties in the relationship. The product is the centre itself; the providers are the organisations within the centre and the 'urban' tourist is increasingly affluent, mobile and consumer driven. It has been questioned whether cities are becoming solely service factories and if they should be marketed as shopping destinations in their own right (Wharnaby and Davies, 1997)

The marketing of destinations involves formulating and projecting the desired image of the city. Place-imagery involves the meeting of the product and consumer via the marketing process. City marketing can be spatially described as

> *"a process whereby urban activities are as closely as possible related to the demands of targeted customers so as to maximise the efficient social and economic functioning of the area concerned in accordance with whatever goals have been established"* (Ashworth and Voogd, 1990)

The importance of location is often justified by the amount of consumer spending within a developed, capitalist economy. The assessment and monitoring of consumer expenditure is an essential element to aligning supply and demand within a capitalist economy.

**Table 2    Spending value: £bn.**

| Consumer spending | 1997 | 1998 | 1999 | 2000 | 2001 | 2002 |
|---|---|---|---|---|---|---|
| Reading | 5.62 | 5.80 | 5.95 | 6.09 | 6.22 | 6.35 |
| Home entertainment | 14.21 | 14.83 | 15.27 | 15.83 | 16.49 | 17.09 |
| House and garden | 10.37 | 11.18 | 11.64 | 12.17 | 12.79 | 13.41 |
| Hobbies and pastimes | 6.96 | 7.37 | 7.58 | 7.81 | 8.07 | 8.34 |
| *In the home* | *37.17* | *39.19* | *40.44* | *41.91* | *43.57* | *45.19* |
| Eating out | 27.82 | 29.26 | 31.58 | 33.28 | 35.15 | 37.20 |
| Alcoholic drink | 28.63 | 30.15 | 32.02 | 33.72 | 34.99 | 35.89 |
| Eating and drinking | 56.45 | 60.11 | 63.60 | 67.00 | 70.14 | 73.09 |
| Local entertainment | 3.45 | 3.69 | 3.90 | 4.11 | 4.32 | 4.54 |
| Gambling | 6.15 | 6.38 | 6.58 | 6.80 | 7.03 | 7.23 |
| Active sport | 5.18 | 5.53 | 5.77 | 6.03 | 6.32 | 6.61 |
| Neighbourhood leisure | 14.78 | 15.60 | 16.26 | 16.94 | 17.67 | 18.39 |
| Sightseeing | 0.80 | 0.86 | 0.92 | 0.97 | 1.03 | 1.09 |
| Holidays in the UK. | 8.03 | 8.62 | 9.00 | 9.34 | 9.72 | 10.07 |
| Holidays overseas | 17.42 | 19.27 | 20.63 | 22.16 | 23.60 | 24.92 |
| Holidays and tourism | 26.25 | 28.75 | 30.54 | 32.48 | 34.35 | 36.08 |
| **AWAY FROM HOME** | **97.48** | **104.45** | **110.40** | **116.42** | **122.16** | *127.56* |
| **ALL LEISURE** | **134.65** | **143.64** | **150.84** | **158.33** | **165.73** | 172.75 |

(*Source:* Chris Gratton, Leisure Forecasts 1998-2002, The Leisure Industries Research Centre.)

The table above predicts leisure spending until the year 2002.

Comparisons may be made between in the 'home' and 'away from home' expenditure whereby the split is moving towards a one quarter/three quarters ratio (Gratton, 1998).

The location of consumer sites within the city conurbation remains of paramount importance. It is underpinned by the attributes of accessibility, attractiveness and amenities. These elements combine to facilitate the success of service sector provision to the widest possible audience. Actual and potential customer markets may evaluate the significance of commercial location. Cities themselves provide an immediate residential consumer market whilst acting as a magnet to many outside of its confines. Over eighty per cent of the 58 million of the British population are urban dwellers. The increasing amount of leisure time and discretionary income enables the greater movement of people. In addition to this, eighty per cent of the population live within a 15 minute drive of at least two shopping centres, the high street and the town centre (Bianchini et al, 1988). The retail revolution is transforming and determining the shape of our cities. Improved transport systems increase frequency, reduce travelling time and aim to be cost effective within city management schemes. The composite framework of the city consists of physical systems designed to meet the needs of those they serve; transport, housing, commerce and leisure. It is the changing use of leisure time that is creating a diversified approach into focused consumerism. This may threaten the motive i.e. shopping, to travel unless the experience is enhanced in another way. The 'Disneyfication' of the artificial, man-made environment needs to be supplemented by the 'distinctive' and specialised recognition of social diversification. Manchester has succeeded in capitalising on the 'pink pound' and a healthy evening economy to maintain an identifiable social perspective to urban change. There exists a shift from the homogenous market of mass consumption to a more individualistic, heterogeneous evolvement to extended service provision.

## Shopping as a preferred activity

The theory of centrality and the process of transition within cities may be approached by economic or social determinants. The emphasis is changing away from production to greater levels of consumption (Zukin, 1982; 1992). The total value of all the shopping centres in the UK is now estimated at a new record of over £21 billion (Investment Property Databank, 2000). The Visiting, Friends and Relatives (VFR) market segment remains a substantial sector of the domestic tourism market. In the North West of England over half of the accommodation used during 1998 fell into this sector. Domestic tourists spent £970 mn. in the region alone with a further £423 being spent by overseas visitors (NWTB, 1999). Manchester is the dominant retail centre in the North West with over 790,000 people regularly shopping in the city centre (Shaw, 1999). Manchester is a post-industrial city and the landscape has altered to reflect a changing economy. Unlike many other cities Manchester has never possessed a residential sector within the city centre. It is through recent initiatives that people are being encouraged to habit in space where they both live and work. This is an integral element to achieving a viable evening economy within land that encompasses planned diversity. Zukin advocates the relevance of 'clustering' production units in relation to both customers and suppliers and states;

> "..consumption units are increasingly spread out, diffused, standardised and reproduced. Decentralisation reduces the power of consumption spaces: it requires conscious action to restore their specific meaning" (1992:201).

Deriving social meaning from urban places can be induced or deduced from the immediate environment. Open spaces within cities allow the passive appreciation of a mixed ambience unique to that locality. It remains as individual perception to how one sees the world. Alternatively, indoor spaces appeal to the collective approach to society providing a series of prescribed meanings from the man-made surroundings. The significance of changing image has affected the city of Manchester in the U.K. The city has recently undergone an extensive period of physical and economic transition. However, it is from the emerging social outlook that the city has emerged successful.

## Manchester - a metropolitan, post-industrial city

Greater Manchester consists of a total of 10 local authorities forming a metropolitan basis representing the capital of the North-West of England. It possess an annual disposable income of £43bn and GDP of £50bn. The shopping and entertainment provision of Manchester city centre have 11 million people living within 50 miles (80 kilometres) and a claimed 60% of the UK population living within a two hour drive (Townroe, 1998).

Manchester has a strong industrial past that is reflected in its economic basis and architectural façade. It is undoubtedly a city in the process of economic, physical and social transition. The urban landscape has undertaken major financial investment and reconstruction. This is especially evident within retail and office locations whereby city policy actively integrates housing and entertainment into one overall scheme. Redevelopment that followed the 1996 IRA bomb commercially affected the service provision and image of the city. A financial injection of over £500 million has now been invested to revitalise the city centre.

The retail industry in Manchester has radically been re-presented since late 1997. An increase of 1.5 million square feet of retail and leisure space has been added to the city, reinforcing the city's position as the prime major retail centre outside of London. The city is experiencing insatiable demand from retailers and investors. (Bailey, 1998). Out of town shopping is altering the nature of the city by alleviating retail congestion and releasing previously established space to be redeveloped to meet todays needs. Environmental awareness amongst planning practitioners and discerning consumers alike has encouraged an 'open/outdoor' development of service sector provision. It aims to add to the ambience, character and geniality of the area whilst diluting demand over physical space and time. Manchester is a prime example of facilitating out of town shopping supporting the new regional development of The Trafford Centre. Public policy has always practised the 'cubist' theory of value and volume within older retail centres. Increase floor space and build upwards to increase the volume and optimise the value of the retail environment.

At the close of 1998 The Trafford Centre in Manchester opened offering 1.5 million square feet of retail space, 20-screen multiplex, an indoor sports complex and hotel. The cost of such physical development amounted to over £600 million and is designed to last more than 150 years. The centre commands a larger catchment population than any other regional shopping centre with 5.3 million people living in under 45 minutes drive time. Visitor figures are set at over 30 million per year and rising. The approach to the centre is dominated by a huge luminous dome that is larger than that of St. Pauls cathedral and is circled by Botticelli babies with musical flutes. The diversity of the centre compares with the novelty of the enclosed setting. The development includes six themed restaurants from different world destinations. It offers the decking of an ocean liner accompanied with attractively lit pool. Above this is a painted ceiling resembling the 'sky' which changes in 20 minutes from dawn to day to night. It is the scale of the artificiality of the surroundings that transfers the role of the observer into the function of the participant.

The Trafford Centre has already begun to dominate the actual city skyline. Tourists flocked to the centre in the initial months and trade remains buoyant. Mobility around such a large venue is assisted by electronic vehicles and buggies for children. The centre provides a high security presence utilising over 320 CCTV cameras throughout the site. By the time the Commonwealth Games takes place in 2002 the city centre will have added net retail floor space virtually equivalent to the size of the Trafford Centre (Royle, 1999)

Manchester faces a dilemma. It wants to be a 'new' city whilst maintaining its proud industrial heritage. Undoubtedly new city development has the upper hand. It is a city that is often compared to its provincial rivals. Numerous British cities that are post-industrial in nature have experienced a renaissance. Ageing factories, a declining economy and redundant landscape have been transformed due to city authority initiatives, architectural design and sense of civic pride. In central Manchester, identifiable changes to the street scene have emerged fuelled by the impetus of achieving a 24-hour living city. Cafes and bars continue to open across the city centre responding to the growing needs of both residents and incoming visitors. Recent developments include Deansgate Locks (50,000 sq.ft) of retail and leisure and the newly opened Marks and Spencer's store representing their largest in the world. Continuous enhancement of the accessibility to the city and mobility around it has been met by extending the airport. However, it is the adoption of a modern tram system, Metrolink that has connected the south and east of the city to many of the recent leisure attractions i.e. Sportcity, M.E.N Arena.

Urban design remains a complex issue within city development. Modern day urban design aims to incorporate a composite amalgam of economic development and social provision. People are encouraged to walk more to offset traffic congestion with the introduction of pedestrian areas. Zoning, waterfront rejuvenation, mixed-use developments combining commerce and residential use has improved many of the post industrial cities e.g. Manchester, Liverpool. The public parts of cities are participatory environments and deserve specific recognition.

## Conclusion

The paper has argued that the increasing number, and size, of indoor shopping centres threaten the physical maintenance and social use of outdoor city space. The consistent rise in consumer activity acts as a catalyst away from the city and into these major shopping centres that are dedicated to retail development. The out-of-town trend of service location proportions new values and priorities related by economic participation. This process should not be allowed to lessen the status of outdoor space but enhance its appreciation by comparison. The professionally designed maze of arcades and walkways serve to compliment the tourist urban experience. It is not a replacement for the genuine article. Successful urban policies need to maintain and encourage a balanced provision of public and private space for social use. There are many valid reasons why built space continues to be the predominant form of preferred provision. Increasing commercial privatisation, ease of accessibility, the extended consumer choice and evident competition.

The power of convenience, safety and security will remain a driving force within today's consumer market. However, let us not underestimate the value of open space. It should not be negated by its passive, subliminal nature but celebrated as distinct in its own right. The retention of public space is complementary to the physical, economic and social impacts of tourism. Tourists dedicate their quality leisure time towards specific places and activities. The importance of perception, expectation and experience of the tourist within the tourism destination area is prone to magnification. The power of tourism continues to escalate in economic growth globally. Cities are economic focal points that recognise the tangible benefits of tourism. The process needs to be tempered by urban management strategy.

Mullins (1991:326) states that cities become tourist destinations because of their ability to provide fun, pleasure, relaxation and recreation as opposed to fulfilling basic needs. He states; *"That such large cities should be built for this reason - and built for visitors - is most unusual in the history of western urbanisation"*. This is a phenomena that is rapidly being turned around and cities are becoming increasingly prone to commodification for external enticement as opposed to internal explication. Culler notes that (1981:128) tourist 'attractions' offer an elaborately contrived indirect experience, an artificial product to be consumed in the very places where the real thing as free as air."

The aesthetic interpretation of environmental awareness is assuming a greater precedence amongst designers. Long term economic viability is more easily achieved when practised as part of the equation combined with physical attractiveness and social acceptance encompass change. The architectural landscaping of the built environment is an all-embracing framework that needs to meet the demands of those who live and work within it. The appropriateness of the physical dimension is judged by people it serves. The urban environment is multi-functional in use segregated into spatial zones by planners and practitioners. Sustainable development aims to maintain positive resources for the use of future generations. Achieving environmental awareness and quality has become a uniform goal throughout Britain. The 'people-place' synergy is a long-term strategy that embodies change with economic viability and social cohesion.

# References

Ashworth, G. J., and Voogd, H. (1990), *Selling the City*, Belhaven: London.

Association of Town Centre Management, (1994), The Effectiveness of Town Centre Management – Research Study, ATCM, London.

Bailey, Stuart B. (1998), Regional Survey of Greater Manchester, Retail, *Property Week*, May 8.

Bianchini, F., Fisher, M., Montgomery, J., Worpole, K. (1988), *City Centres, City Cultures*, Centre for Local and Economic Strategies, Manchester.

Clark, D. (1996), *Urban World/Global City*, Routledge: London.

Culler, J (1981), Semiotics of Tourism, *American Journal of Semiotics*, Vol.1. pp.127-40.

Department of Environment/Association of Town Centre Management (1997), *Managing Urban Spaces in Town Centres: A Good Practice Guide*. London: HMSO.

Falk, N. (1998), Resourcing the revival of town and city centres, *Journal of the Built Environment*, Vol.24 No.1 pp:6-15.

Featherstone, M. (1990), Perspectives on Consumer Culture, *Sociology*, Vol. 24, pp.5-22.

Feifer, M. (1985), *Going Places*, London: Macmillan.

Gratton, C. (1998), A Sure Bet, *Tourism Management*, Vol.18, No.4.

Jansen - Verbeke, M. (1986), Inner city tourism, resources and promoters, *Annals of Tourism Research*,13, 79-100.

Jansen Vebeke, (1989), Inner cities and urban tourism in the Netherlands,: new challenges for local authorities, P. Bramham, I. Henry, H. Mommas and H. van der Poel. (eds) *Leisure and Urban Processes: critical studies of Leisure Policy in Western European Cities*.

Middleton, M. C. (1999), Cities: resident readers and others, *Critical Textwork: An Introduction to Varieties of Discourse and Analysis*. I. Parker (editor). Open University Press: Buckingham pp117 - 128.

Middleton, M. C. (1999), The Tourist Trap: the increased enclosure of urban space, *Tourism Education and Industry Symposium Conference Proceedings,* School of Tourism and Services Management, Jyvaskyla Polytechnic, FINLAND. pp. 338 - 354.

Montgomery, J. (Ed.) (1995), Urban vitality and The Culture of Cities, *Planning Practice and Research,* Vol. 10, pt. 2, pp.101-19.

Mullins, P. (1991), Tourism Urbanisation, *International Journal of Urban and Regional Research*, 15, No.3, pp 326-42.

Page, S. (1995), *Urban Tourism*, London: Routledge.

Pettican, A.(1999), Shopping and the shaping of identities, *The City*, Number 7.

Royle, D. (1999), Comment, Regional Survey Greater Manchester, *Property Week*, 14/5/99.

Shaw, A. (1999), Market Review, James Lang Wootten.

Shaw, G., and Williams, A. M. (1994), *Critical Issues in Toutism: A Geographical Perspective*, Oxford: Blackwell.

Shilling, R. (1994), Vitality and Viability: Challenge to the Town Centre, *International Journal of Retail and Distribution Management*, Vol.22 No.6 pp.46-50.

Tomalin, C. (1998), Urban Space in Town Centres: a route to success?, *Journal of the Built Environment*, Vol.24 No.1 pp31-41.

Townroe, P. (1998), United in the cause of new investment, *Property Week,* May 8.

Urry, J. (1990), *The Tourist Gaze*, London: Sage Publications.

Urry, J.(1995), *Consuming Places*, London: Routledge.

Wharnaby, G., and Davis, B. J. (1997), Cities as service factories? Using the servuction system for marketing cities as shopping destinations, *International Journal of Retail and Distribution Management*. Vol.25, No. 6 pp.204-210.

Zukin, S. (1992), Postmodern Urban Landscapes : Mapping Culture and Power, in Lash, S. and Friedman, J. (eds), *Modernity and Power*, Blackwell, Oxford.

# Exploring issues of space and sexuality in Manchester's gay village

## Annette Pritchard, Diane Sedgley and Nigel J Morgan

University of Wales Institute, UK

## Abstract

This paper explores issues of gay leisure space and place and investigates the attitudes of commercial operators in Manchester's gay village to the degaying of the quarter. It begins by discussing the factors responsible for the emergence of Manchester's gay village in the 1980s and then, using in-depth interviews with those now working in the village's bars, clubs and restaurants, it investigates attitudes to the way the village has developed and evolved. It emerges that reactions to the integration of gays and straights in the village are mixed - with some welcoming it and others seeing it as a backward step which could ultimately erase the unique gay space of the area. The paper also highlights the absence of clearly defined lesbian spaces within the village and explores some of the reasons for this, concluding by suggesting some future research questions.

## Introduction

Initially, this paper investigates the factors responsible for the emergence of Manchester's gay village, focusing in particular on the role of the gay community as well as the role of the city council in this process. The paper then moves on to consider how the village has changed and evolved over time, highlighting the degaying process which has occurred there. It attempts to consider the factors contributing to and the significance of the degaying process within the village and in this respect develops previous work by Pritchard *et al* (2000) on the extent to which homosexuality in general is 'being "normalised" and subsumed into some heterosexual norm.' Whilst a number of writers have commented on the degaying process within the gay village, there has been little attempt to explore the views of those who manage and use the gay leisure space which the village provides - the focus of the second part of this paper. First, however, the paper contextualises the field research by discussing the earlier development of the Manchester village.

# The emergence of Manchester's gay village

Since the 1980s Manchester City Council (MCC) has been actively trying to transform the city's image from one associated with industrial decline and urban decay to one of dynamism and vision. The aim has been to position Manchester as a 'European regional capital', an 'international city of outstanding commercial, cultural and creative potential' (Marketing Manchester, 1998). The council's 'Manchester City Guide' (1998-99), describes it as 'the liveliest of cities' and 'an outward looking European city'. Indeed the city has seen a number of major projects come to fruition in the last few years, including the Bridgewater Hall, NYNEX arena, National Stadium, Lowry Centre, Convention Centre, and the second airport runway, as well as the city's successful bid to host the Commonwealth Games. In addition, as part of the city's regeneration programme, MCC has also presided over and encouraged the development of a number of unique city quarters - Chinatown, the Millennium quarter, Castlefield, the Northern quarter and the area which is the focus of this paper - the gay and lesbian village.

## The village's beginnings

As long ago as the 1950s, there were a number of gay pubs and clubs scattered around Manchester where homosexuals could meet anonymously and with the passing of the 1967 Sexual Offences Act, an increasing number of venues opened up, particularly around the vicinity of 'the village'. However it was not until the mid-1980s that the gay village, with its unique identity emerged and gradually developed into 'one of the queerest pieces of real estate Europe has to offer' (Lesbian and Gay Guide to Greater Manchester). Today the village comprises nine clubs and 20 bars, as well as a number of shops, hairdressers and restaurants. Many of these newer venues are fronted by large windows and convey a sense of openness and accessibility, a far cry from the early gay venues that, by necessity, were hidden. As Binnie (1995:195) comments, 'in these new venues, gay men are not hidden behind closed doors. Straight passers-by can look in and observe gay men' thus, meeting the demands of a new generation 'who are more "out" than their predecessors - an increasingly confident generation of lesbians and gay men whose sense of pride means they want to be visible and not ignored.'

The area's location, like many other gay quarters, is close to a transport terminal (Chorlton Street bus and coach station) and, until the recent 'gentrification' of the area, was a 'red light' district, described by Finnegan (1997:9) as 'a seedy, barren urban wasteland where few "respectable" visitors dared tread'. However, the gradual gentrification process which has accompanied the development of the village, now means that unlike many gay areas, the village has managed to throw off an 'urban tradition in which "forbidden sexualities" are only to be pursued in seedy and sordid surroundings' (Taylor, Evans and Fraser 1996:185). Various explanations have been put forward to explain why gay areas such as the village emerge within urban areas and many of these place particular emphasis on the prior existence of a sizeable gay community. As Hindle (1994:8) notes: 'Whether or not any sort of gay community comes into existence at all is determined by the number of gay people in the area and urban areas with their larger populations will have larger gay numbers.' Manchester is also a significant university city and Whittle (1994:33) has suggested that the higher education institutions offered many young lesbians and gays a legitimate opportunity to leave home and come to the city. 'They were in turn to provide the clientele and consumers for the development of a gay social life within the city.' It has also been suggested that the shift from manufacturing to service industries may have contributed to the village's development by attracting a 'high proportion of gay people not only to work, but also to live in these areas' (Hindle 1994:23).

However, whilst these explanations may well have resonance, in themselves they are insufficient to explain how Manchester, 'a city like many in the North dominated culturally, by powerful social myths regarding the power of heterosexual men...' (Taylor, Evans and Fraser 1996:180), should have seen the emergence of the UK's first gay quarter. The development of such a distinctive gay space is also significant given the political context of the 1980s. This was a decade when the 'demonization of homosexuality played a crucial role in the legitimation of the Thatcherite attack on local government autonomy' and 'a time in which homophobic attitudes and practises increased dramatically in Britain' (Smith 1994:17). In fact, the village in part, represented a rebellion against such Thatcherite, right-wing philosophies and was also a reaction to 'a huge homophobic policing campaign' staged by Manchester's then Chief Constable - James Anderton (Skeggs 1999:218).

## Manchester city council's support for the village

Taylor *et al* (1996:196) have already explored Manchester's culture of 'toleration' and 'celebration' towards minority cultures - as evidenced by Chinatown, Prestwich (an area of concentrated Jewish settlement) and Wilmslow Road (with a sizeable Indian community). They suggest that Manchester's size means it is 'large enough to include numerous minority cultures, while small enough to retain a friendly atmosphere' (Taylor *et al* 1996:72). They also acknowledge the role gay people themselves have played in the development of the village, describing it as 'the product of the initiative and energy of individuals and groups within the gay and lesbian "community" in Manchester reappropriating the city centre area of warehouses and canals' (Taylor *et al* 1996:186). It also seems likely that the MCC's positive attitude to the village, particularly since the election of a 'left-wing' Labour council in 1981, was crucial to the village's development. Indeed, the council positively welcomed the village's development which contributed to its twin commitments of equality of opportunity and the economic regeneration of the city. The gentrification of the quarter and the development of a distinctive gay space has made a valuable contribution to the generation of both tourist revenue and employment opportunities. Indeed, MCC (1998) 'recognises that the Village is not only an essential social space for lesbians and gay men. It is also a unique and vibrant part of the city centre, attracting visitors, spending power and jobs to the City.'

The council's support for the village can be seen in a number of ways – it 'has made sure that it regularly has a visible and supportive profile in the Village, aware that its support sends a powerful message against homophobia' (Manchester City Council's Support for the Lesbian and Gay Village 1998). MCC's contributions to infrastructural improvements have also been important, repaving and pedestrianising Canal Street, improving the lighting of the area and providing grants for building restoration. It has also used its regulatory role to improve services offered by bars such as a scheme to ensure door staff are licensed, encouraging no glass policies on the streets, encouraging bars to clean their frontages and enforcing a ban on unsightly advertising material. The council has also built partnerships with other agencies to increase the safety of the village. In particular, it actively works with the police through the Greater Manchester Lesbian and Gay Policing Initiative to improve safety and support the anti-hate crime initiative which encourages lesbians and gay men to report homophobic crimes. The council has also played a crucial role in the development of the annual Mardi Gras festival that now attracts 150,000 visitors to the City each year.

The council's extensive role in the development of the village may reflect the greater tolerance within society of gays and lesbians who 'are being embraced by the mainstream with a vigour which makes homophobia look dated and passé' (Aitkenhead 1997:24). Supporting the village maybe MCC's way of indicating to the outside world that 'its internal economic, social, cultural, political and sexual geographies have changed dramatically...' (Hindle 1994:16). It may also be, however, that MCC's willingness to accommodate the gay village is merely an indication of its desire to control gay and lesbian behaviour. Whittle (1994:30) feels that gays can be seen to have gained a gay 'safe' space in return for being a 'contributor to the State's interests through your social and sexual habits (which of course follow the State directed guidelines on safe sex) and your economic means (which as a gay person... contribute towards the gentrification of otherwise run down and unattractive inner-city).'

## Evidence of a degaying of the village

It could be argued that the greater acceptance of homosexuality in society is merely a way of undermining the integrity of gay and lesbian communities, contributing to their 'degaying' – diluting and eroding gay spaces and identities. Through acceptance, gay space looses its uniqueness and 'opportunities to challenge the prevailing masculine orthodoxy and to create different ontologies are limited...' so that eventually the subculture ceases to be subcultural and the normalisation denies the significance of sexuality in a world defined by heterosexuality (Pritchard *et al.* 2000). In the case of Manchester, this raises the question of whether the development of the gay village came from '... gay people to cater for gay peoples' needs or was it a developmental, commercial and policing ploy 'to keep lesbians and gay men in a separate, easily surveillance, easily exploited, easily commercialised and easily sanitised environment?' (Whittle 1994:31).

The inevitability of degaying is that the area becomes more accessible and attractive to heterosexuals, who are then seen to be attempting to reclaim previously gay spaces (Whittle 1994, Valentine 1996, Pritchard *et al.* 1998). This seems an issue of some concern in Manchester because, as the village has developed into 'one of the city's most lively and trendy areas' with its 'stylish waterside café bars, pubs and restaurants' (Manchester City Guide) it has attracted an increasing number of straight visitors, including many women 'who want to relax in a hassle-free, peaceful and friendly environment' as well as 'gangs of "straight" young men who come to gawp, poke fun, abuse and bring violence and trouble' (Finnegan 1997). Concerns have emerged that the village, once an area where gay sexuality could be affirmed, is becoming just another stylish part of the city. There is some feeling is that the village has become a 'victim of its own success' (Finnegan 1997) and questions have even been raised in local newspapers over whether it should become 'the San Francisco of Europe - with a world famous reputation as a welcoming, fun-filled refuge for gays and lesbians? Or should it bow to mounting commercial pressures and become a mainstream city centre attraction for straight visitors? The Gay Village or just The Village? (Manchester Evening News, 1/12/97).

As early as 1996, Taylor, Evans and Fraser (1996:187), interpreted the development of 'a cottage' in a disused warehouse to the south of the village, as an indication that the degaying process had already begun and that some gays were starting to feel excluded from the area, saying that 'the co-presence of this hidden sexual economy alongside the Village itself is an important gloss on the Village's own self confident descriptions.' Certainly, its shift towards a mixed clientele and the consequent degaying process appears to be now well advanced (Pritchard *et al.* 1998) and has, to a large extent, been accelerated by the commercial sector. Indeed, some would contend that the gay businesses themselves have played a crucial role in the degaying of the village. As Binnie (1995:87) argues:

> *whilst it is important to struggle for and celebrate, the ever greater choices of safe spaces - venues where gay men can be ourselves, become ourselves - we must remain ever sanguine and cynical about the role played by pink businesses in gay life. Pink businesses after all, do operate as businesses, rather than charities.*

Rather than regarding the village as an example of a very crude form of social control whereby MCC sought to control and define gay life by regulation and incorporation, the village can perhaps be more appropriately seen as a product of late-modern capitalism and commercialism. It is the commercial sector which has driven the evolution of the gay village, dictating the formation of '... a market place in which queer people are now seen as cultural consumers, just another tribe amidst and like all other cultural consumers' (Whittle 1994:37). Some of the village bars explicitly mention that they are targeting a 'mixed' clientele. One describes itself as 'a more *mixed* venue, with chilled sounds and a casual crowd during the week, getting busier, louder and *straighter* at the weekends.' Another promotes itself as catering for 'a predominantly hetero crowd' its gay friendly ambience making it 'a *bit* of a homo hangout too' (Lesbian and Gay guide to Greater Manchester 1998 italics added).

## Study methodology

Given the challenges involved in researching the village's commercial operators' views on the potentially sensitive issue of its degaying, this study adopted an exploratory, qualitative approach. As Priest (1996:106) argues:

> *When the goal is to understand the "insider's" perspective, a quantitative design is just not the way to go. You can't write effective questions for a survey without a better understanding of the worldview of those you want to study.*

Qualitative, exploratory approaches are concerned to investigate meanings which 'reside in social practice, and not just in the heads of individuals' (Dey 1993:11) and here, in-depth interviews were used to explore issues of sexuality, degaying and space in the village. Seale (1998: 205) has described interviews as offering the researcher the opportunity to gain 'more authentic' and 'less exploitative' accounts of experience than is offered by other methodologies. As with all research techniques, there was concern over the number of interviews which should be undertaken. There are no definitive guidelines, although Churchill (1995) suggests that qualitative research should be continually reviewed as it is being conducted, if additional interviews do not add further insights, then the field work should cease. Here, seven interviews (lasting up to an hour) were conducted with commercial operators (two of whom managed bars owned by large breweries, two were night-club owners, and the others were a pub tenant, a bar owner and a restaurant owner).

## Results and discussion

A number of themes emerged from the interviews, particularly centring on integration and alienation and thus the (re)negotiation of space within the village. Given that these interviews were conducted with commercial operators, it is only to be expected that commercial concerns figure largely. Having said this, the research complements earlier work which discusses the use of gay leisure space and the significance of sexuality in contemporary society (Pritchard *et al.* 1998, 2000).

### Integration - commerce, tolerance or uneasy 'policing'?

'Integration' in terms of both heterosexual and homosexual use of space was broadly welcomed by the interviewees because of the commercial opportunities it offered. The priority for the managers and owners of the large and (to a lesser extent) the small-scale venues in this research was predominantly commercial success. Concurrent with that was a realisation that the gay market alone would not guarantee commercial viability given the increased competition in the ever expanding village. It was no longer viable for many businesses to simply target the gay market: as one manager of a large brewery-owned pub commented, 'There are too many businesses round here to say we want just one sort of clientele.' Another manager of a large chain pub explained that targeting a mixed market was more than a commercial decision - '... on the street now there are perhaps 20–25 bars so I don't believe every single bar down here could operate [with gay customers alone]. It's also not very good for business being a hundred percent gay because, gays are so faddy. As soon as the next new bar opens, they just move.'

Other bar operators were conscious that, although economic survival meant having to appeal to a mixed clientele, there was a definite fear of alienating their gay clientele by encouraging a heterosexual colonisation of gay spaces. For example in one bar, the pub tenant found that: 'Maybe two to three years ago, the village was becoming popular with straight people, and the [name of pub], which had always been regarded as a gay bar, was being swallowed up by the integration process, with the straights coming in... just to see the sort of side-show. Our regular gay customers no longer felt comfortable in here.' By contrast, some interviewees saw integration as 'healthy', indicating the acceptability and 'normality' of homosexuality. One bar manager advocated openness, saying:

> *I think it's healthy to share because you are educating people that we're not perverted freaks but that we're completely normal. We do the same things as everybody else does but we sleep with the same sex... It's nice to invite people into your environment and say look, we have a good time, if you want to come along and have a good time with us, you're welcome.*

Integration was not seen as having a particularly heavy price and for these participants, the village is a place where they can be themselves, be open about their sexuality and at the same time be safe. As one pub manager from a large brewery remarked:

> *I think it's a trendy, cultural part of Manchester where gays are a hundred percent accepted. Whereas you would never be a hundred percent accepted on Deansgate... the attitude... compared to here, is so much different... I think people who come to Canal Street know that they might see two guys kissing and know that they might see guys walk up and down the street holding hands or whatever - they know what to expect here.*

However, conceivably increased heterosexual utilisation of the village is not particularly reliable evidence for societal acceptance. Most bars operate screening policies and encourage selective heterosexual usage, many having 'hosts' on the door who establish a person's attitude, in some cases not just towards homosexuality but to minority groups in general. 'We actually have a host who works on this door ... I want good, friendly people in here... if we get bad vibes from anyone, they're just moved to one side. I want a really attitude-free bar down here. I don't want any discrimination against colour, race or sexuality.' Another bar manager commented on the preferred customer base by saying 'Our policy in this venue is "nice" people, no idiots. We don't want gangs of people, gay or straights, just "nice" people, and so far we've got away with it. We do okay.' This desire to influence and select clientele with an appropriately tolerant attitude was not restricted to heterosexuals. One manager argued that tolerance should be towards all, including the attitude of homosexuals towards straights. 'I think just so long as people's attitudes are right. If a black guy walked in the bar and all these white guys started calling him nigger, that's just as wrong as if a straight person walks in here and is called by gays. I think that people who should be down in the village are people who can accept everyone else's lifestyle.'

Thus, whilst entry to commercial gay space may depend on attitudes towards homosexuality (and minority groups) rather than sexual preferences, what results is a selective and partial form of integration that cannot legitimately be used as evidence for a wider social acceptance. Hence while stickers on some bar windows read 'integration not segregation,' blackboards placed outside others reflect the tension by announcing 'this is a gay place, respect it.' Some bars have responded to the challenge of managing gay and straight interactions by introducing segregated areas. 'As owners... we wanted to maintain the gayness of the bar, so we now actually have a policy where straight people are asked to come upstairs and it's more or less exclusively gay downstairs, predominantly male' said one pub tenant.

There is strong evidence to suggest that the impetus for the degaying process is being generated from within the village, born out of desire to become more mainstream, more accepted and even more 'normal'. At times, it seemed more important to tolerate heterosexual behaviour in the quarter than to tolerate particularly overt gays whose sexuality is more challenging. One participant said: 'I see just as much disrespect to straights as to gays. Basically if a big bunch of Queens see a heterosexual couple snog they [the couple] get slagged down for it here, which is wrong.' There appears to be a broad range of reasons defending the inclusion of straights into the village and the consequential intolerance of certain gays. In some cases 'gay rights activists' face mounting resentment because of their perceived intolerance of straights. 'I feel that you get all the gay rights activists that want equal opportunities for everyone and they want the age of consent lowered but, when straights come down to their streets, it's "get out."' 'There are also a lot of guys and girls who are like the lads next door... who sleep with their own sex who want to come out to bars and have really good food and a really good atmosphere and not have all that camp thing shoved down their faces.'

Not surprisingly, given the contested nature and ongoing negotiation of space, whereas the interviewees above saw the village's growth, and particularly the move towards mixed venues as positive, there were equally as many who felt that the integration had led to a loss of identity and to the creation of a less welcoming and less safe environment. Challenging the belief that it was possible to 'screen' clientele, one owner of a small restaurant felt that the village had become:

> *a general drinking area... getting rougher so that it's not a gay or straight issue.*
> *The larger bars have no control on the nature of their clientele and they are*
> *letting anyone in to fill them. It's attracting a more down-market element so that*
> *the operations have a more 'batten down the hatches' mentality... It's all right*
> *integrating and being welcoming to the whole of society but... it's counter-*
> *productive because it's just made it bloody rough.*

There was particular criticism of the effects of the Mardi Gras, with some interviewees saying that it has been responsible for opening the floodgates to large volumes of people, irrespective of their sexuality and created vulnerability and insecurity in what was hitherto a relatively 'safe' gay environment. The same restaurant owner commented:

> *It just attracts everyone, people with carrier bags full of cans. What the hell is it*
> *all about? The council is making it open to everyone, but by doing that it's just*
> *putting other people off. A lot of my regular clientele said 'we're going away for*
> *the weekend, we're not coming here.' I absolutely hate it... I door staffed ...*
> *[and] decided whether to let people in or not. We were like a little oasis.*

Although the festival was clearly identified as instrumental in creating a less secure, more mainstream environment, significantly it was the big breweries who were regarded as most culpable. A night club owner felt that 'The pink pound has been exploited in the village – the gay village is not now run by gay people for gay people, but by the big breweries.' In these interviews it was pink businesses that were seen as being loyal to the original character and ethos of the area. A bar owner commented that 'The privately owned places are trying to keep to a gay policy because they are gay owned. It's the big breweries who are not really bothered, they want the money in the till, whether it's gay, straight or whatever.' As a result, these (often small scale) pink businesses are seen as uninterested in profit and as purists with the interests of the village as their priority.

## A call for new gay-only territory

The ongoing commercialisation of gay space and the subsequent emphasis on profit by the breweries has led to a situation where 'There aren't a lot of traditional gay bars left in the village, it has got commercial. It's not even known as the gay village now, the 'gay' has been dropped' said one bar owner. Consequently, it was felt that many gay venues were being forced to retreat further into the village, distancing themselves from Canal Street. 'Canal Street was gay at first. Now that's gone straight and I think people are moving over this way now. There's us, the Rembrandt, Thomson Arms, Cruz. I think it will move from Canal Street round the car park round here, to Bloom Street' said a bar manager of a large brewery chain. It could be argued from this that the degaying process which is so clearly evident is not merely leading to the erosion of gay space, but also to its translocation. This suggests that those searching for the unique and exclusive aspects of gay life will move on as it becomes impossible for them to accept the inevitable consequences and compromises associated with development. Their increasing alienation and disillusionment may be viewed as a stimulus for the quest for new territory.

Others have sought to develop alternative strategies for regaining safe, gay space through the introduction of membership schemes. 'I think what's going to happen longer term round here, certain bars will decide its members only - the rest will be like the Wild West. They'll be tightly controlled, smaller venues because there's so much rubbish around, piling up in minibuses at either end of the street to do a pub crawl' said a restaurant owner. Hence an owner of one of the newer nighclubs stated 'We opened in June '98 as a gay-only venue. We have a membership system where you have to sign a card saying you're gay... It means it's a safe venue and a gay space for gay people. We've claimed back a part of the village. None of this "integrate not segregate".'

There was also a feeling that the breweries' 'trendy' bars and upmarket restaurants had, in particular, alienated and excluded older, less affluent gays who do not fit into the 'trendy set'. Indeed, research done by Taylor, Evans and Fraser (1996:189) on the village, found that 'the priority placed on the idea of "a scene" directed at younger, high spending gay consumers was ... a form of discrimination.' Discrimination also seemed to exist towards those who did not fit into the category of 'normal' homosexuals. Thus, although the 'escape from the ghetto' may be welcomed by some as a 'confirmation of equality' 'the new tolerance only applies those who are "virtually normal", not to those who offer society more "problematic" versions of lesbian and gay identity' (Pritchard *et al*, 2000). Instead they have become second class citizens, even excluded from their own community.

## The experience of lesbians in the village

For lesbians, the concept of degaying and the loss of gay space within the village, is a difficult one because, like many other gay areas, the village had no unique lesbian space until December 1998 when Vanilla opened. This lack of permanent lesbian venues within the village, reflects Skegg's (1999:216) contention that the village is a predominantly male space because: 'Gay men have a greater volume of and access to different forms of legitimate capital which can be spatialized, unlike most lesbians.' As a result, lesbians' experience of the village is very different from that of gay men. 'Gay men in this village, whatever they are into, they can find. If they want to go clubbing in Paradise all weekend they can. If they want to stand in the bar in the Rembrandt and just chat, if they want to go to Chains which is S&M they can do that, whereas women haven't had that choice.'

Indeed, venue owners in the village thought that lesbians had less disposable income but also felt that the shortage of venues was related to the fact that lesbians were less overt than many men about their sexuality. 'I think gay men have got more money than gay women, you also find more gay men dancing on stages to camp music than gay women. They're all exhibitionists basically. They all want to be noticed but you find a lot of gay women don't want to be noticed.' Another explanation for lesbians' lack of influence within the village and the absence of lesbian venues seen in these interviews was the perception that women tended to be on the scene for a shorter time than men. 'A lot of women come onto the scene to find a partner and, once they've found a partner, they go off it again. So, they might be a customer of yours for six months regularly on a Friday and Saturday but, as soon as they've found their new playmate, you'll not see them again.'

The absence of lesbian space has obviously constrained the ways in which women have been able to use the village, restricting their choices of venue to those that are 'Second rate, once a month or once a week in not the most luxurious club or bar. Lesbians haven't really been catered for.' Lesbians have been less targeted by the marketing campaigns than gay men and they have not attached themselves to particular venues 'they've just gone out to a club and they just had meals somewhere or other ... there has never actually been one bar that all the girls go to. No bar had a lesbian identity' until the development of Vanilla. The owner of this venue was keen to stress that the absence of lesbian venues should not be interpreted as women not wanting them. 'If you know anything about the women's scene, which we obviously do, then you're aware that there's also a lot of professional women out there that want their own space... I've worked on the gay scene for a long time, worked in the café/bar restaurant scene for the last 12 years and I'm a gay woman myself, and I'm sick of not being catered for.'

Since Vanilla has opened, it is not only proving to be a commercial success but the owner has had much positive feedback from clients who 'tell us every Saturday night that they wanted a venue like this. People shaking my hand because I've taken the risk.' In an interesting development, gay men are now frequenting Vanilla as a sanctuary from the mixed environment of the rest of the village. 'Men are welcome as guests and, a lot of men feel very safe in here because, what we've created is a gay environment. It's obviously not attracting straight men and they feel quite safe.' However, the difficulty now confronting Vanilla is that, because of the demand and since it is the only lesbian bar, it has to try and cater for all market segments within the lesbian market:

> *We've got to cater for such diverse categories of women because, this is the only one. Really we could do with five different types of Vanillas – for all different age groups or for whatever they are into. When it gets to 9.00 p.m. on a Friday night and we have to turn into a really lively city centre bar, the older ladies, who want to go on chatting and drinking their coffees and brandies, start to leave. It's unfortunate... but the bar is full of younger women who want to get pissed, it's very awkward.*

## Conclusion

It is evident from this examination of the evolution of Manchester's gay village that it is contested space, characterised by conflict and accommodation, whether easy or uneasy. That the space has changed dramatically with the recent influx of big businesses seems incontestable and the drive for profit to sustain these businesses has been a significant factor in the attempts to attract more (and diverse) markets to the village. Participants in this study also recognised, however, the inherent tensions and dangers which an influx of heterosexual customers can pose to the integrity of gay space, thereby destroying that safety and uniqueness which provided the initial attraction. Whilst 'integration' was supported as a means of promoting greater social acceptance, it was also apparent that this integration had to be 'policed' to screen out less tolerant people and could even serve to discriminate against less 'acceptable' versions of homosexuality.

Perhaps the most significant finding of the research concerns the role of lesbians within the gay village. Women have only achieved a recognisably unique space very recently, a venue which is now attracting gay men - a development which may threaten this lesbian space in the future. Rothenberg (1995: 168) cites a number of reasons for the lack of influence of lesbians in the city – income discrepancies, the importance placed by lesbians on relationships rather than territory and space and the fact that men 'do not face the same sorts of daily oppressions as women.' The issue of women's use of public leisure space is one which deserves much more examination in tourism studies since marginalisation is configured in diverse and intersecting ways - sexuality, gender, race and social class combine to create layers of oppression (Pritchard and Morgan 2000). The problems of developing female spaces are by no means unique to lesbians - witness the small number of female only clubs in the UK by contrast to male only establishments. In fact, this must be seen in the context of a society where public space has been traditionally characterised as male space and today, women's use of space continues to be policed by, amongst others, themselves in order to protect themselves. In terms of gay and lesbian spaces, future research could usefully explore not only lesbians' relations and negotiations with gay men, but also their encounters with heterosexual women and men in gay and straight places.

# References

Aitkenhead, D. (1997), 'The queen is dead', *The Modern Review* November: 23-26.

Anon. (1998), 'Debate: Mardi Gras. Is It Good for Manchester?' *Manchester Evening News,* 31 August.

Anon. (1998), 'What we Thought of Mardi Gras', *Manchester Evening News*, 4 September.

Anon. (1997), 'How You Voted On: Mardi Gras', *Manchester Evening News*, 16 August.

Binnie, J. (1995), 'Trading Places: consumption, sexuality and the production of queer space' 182-199 in Bell, D. and Valentine, G. (eds.) *Mapping Desire: geographies of sexualities*, Routledge.

Churchill, G. A. (1995), *Marketing Research: Methodological Foundations,* The Dryden Press, Orlando, USA.

Dey, I. (1993), *Qualitative Data Analysis,* Routledge, London.

Finnegan, M. (1997), 'The Village That's Paying the Price of Success', *Manchester Evening News*, December 1, 9.

Hindle, P. (1994), 'Gay Communities and Gay Space in the City' 7-25, in Whittle S (ed.) *The Margins of the City: gay men's urban lives*, Arena.

Lesbian and Gay Guide to Greater Manchester, Healthy Gay Manchester 1998.

Manchester City Council (1998), *Manchester City Council's Support for the Lesbian and Gay Village*.

Marketing Manchester (1998), *Marketing Manchester, an introductory profile*.

Manchester City Guide for Visitors 1998-99, Marketing and Visitor Services, Manchester City Council.

Priest, S. H. (1996), *Doing Media Research: An Introduction*, Sage, London.

Pritchard, A. and Morgan, N. J. (2000), 'Constructing Tourism Landscapes. Gender, Sexuality and Space.' *Tourism Geographies*, 2 (1) in press.

Pritchard, A., Morgan, N., Sedgley, D., Khan, E., Jenkins, A. (2000), 'Sexuality and Holiday Choices: Conversations with Gay and Lesbian Tourists', *Leisure Studies*, forthcoming.

Pritchard, A. Morgan, N. J. Sedgley, D. Jenkins, A. (1998), 'Reaching out to the gay tourist: opportunities and threats in an emerging market segment', *Tourism Management* 19 (3) 273-282.

Rothenberg, T. (1995),'And She Told Two Friends' lesbians creating urban social space 164-169 in Bell, D. and Valentine, G. (eds.) *Mapping Desire: geographies of sexualities,* Routledge.

Seale, C. (1998), 'Qualitative Interviewing', 202-16 in Seale C. (ed.) *Researching Society and Culture*, Sage, London.

Skeggs, B. (1999), 'Matter out of place: visibilities and sexualities in leisure spaces', *Leisure Studies* 18 (3): 213-232.

Smith, A. M. (1994), *New Right Discourse on Race and Sexuality, Britain 1968-1990,* Cambridge University Press.

Taylor, I., Evans, K. and Fraser, P., (1996*), A Tale of Two Cities: global change, local feeling and everyday life in the North of England. A study of Manchester and Sheffield,* Routledge.

Valentine, G. (1996), '(Re)negotiating the Heterosexual Street', 146-55 in Duncan N., (ed.) *Bodyspace. Destabilizing geographies of gender and sexuality*, Routledge, London.

Whittle, S. (1994), Consuming Differences: The Collaboration of the Gay Body with the Cultural State 27-41 in Whittle S. (ed.) *The Margins of the City: gay men's urban lives,* Arena.

# An examination of networking and collaboration amongst rural tourism providers: The case for relationship marketing

**Gunjan Saxena**

Staffordshire University, UK

## Abstract

Much attention has been devoted in recent years to the concept of tourism partnerships and the need for tourism businesses to co-operate in order to be competitive. The paper examines the application of the theory of relationship marketing, in the rural tourism context to build partnerships, and develop a conceptual framework which facilitates the move towards a more humanistic and relationship-based model of resource management. Tourism comprises of businesses engaged in transportation, accommodation, food, beverages, attractions and events, as well as marketing and distribution network to deliver services to a dispersed and complex market. Pressures to survive in an increasingly competitive environment with limited capital readily make alliances and networks vital to gain a competitive advantage. It is therefore stressed that tourism providers can network their capabilities to reduce risks and enhance opportunities through mutual co-operation and inter-dependence to gain and sustain competitive advantage.

## Introduction

The paper focuses on marketing alliances which can be defined as purposive strategic relationships between independent businesses or firms who share compatible goals, strive for mutual benefit, and acknowledge a high level of mutual interdependence, formed primarily to gain competitive advantage in the marketplace (Bleeke and Ernst, 1991; Powell, 1990). They can afford an organisation access to new technologies or markets; the ability to provide a wider range of products/ services, economies of scale in joint research and or production, access to complementary skills and sharing of risks (Powell, 1987). Much attention has been focused in recent years on marketing alliances, defined in terms of synergistic or symbiotic relationships between two or more independent entities (Adler, 1966; Varadarajan and Rajaratnam, 1986) that is, an alliance of resources designed to increase the market potential of all entities involved. Partnerships and destination alliances assume significance with the growth in tourism, and as a destination's assets and resources, such as its infrastructure and recreational facilities are increasingly being shared by its inhabitants, visitors, public and private stakeholders (Jamal and Getz, 1995). Thus, as tourism development takes on the characteristics of a public and social good, whose benefits may be shared by the numerous stakeholders in the local destination, joint decision making and collaboration amongst them, becomes crucial (Reed, 1997; Jamal and Getz, 1995; Jordan, 1989). Parvatiyar and Sheth (1994) regard relationships as an orientation that seeks to develop close interactions with selected suppliers and competitors for value creation through co-operation and collaborative efforts. Such co-operative and collaborative efforts produce long-term relationships and mutual synergy for the co-operating parties. Inherent in co-operation and collaboration, and (social) exchange as constituents of relationship is the idea of reciprocity and symmetry (Bagozzi, 1995). From reciprocity, it follows that relational benefits to all parties involved are to be discussed (Berry, 1995) and that without symmetry of this benefit, relationships will not emerge or will deteriorate. From its long chain of distribution system to its fragmented supply components, the tourism field is, by its very nature, dependent upon inter-relationships to achieve organisational and regional goals (Selin and Beason, 1991). Thus, these inter-dependencies that underlie interactions amongst tourism providers in the public, private and voluntary sector become an important research area.

In the context of tourism, the need for a dialogue group, a consultative forum and an environment policy review group has been stressed to achieve quality tourism by the EC Fifth Action programme (1993) at the European level. In UK, general government policy recognises the economic and social significance of tourism and recreation as well as the need to regulate and facilitate their development through strategic guidance and co-operation of a wide range of organisations (PPG 17; PPG 21). Further, the UK Sustainable Development Strategy (1994) is committed to set up a forum or round table to bring together representations of the main sectors or groups and creation of a Citizens' Environment Initiative. It recognises the key part to be played by individuals as green consumers, voluntary bodies, local authorities, and others (Sustainable Development: The UK Strategy, 1994), and enlist their support and commitment over the coming years. Concern for sustainability has become the organising concept, central to the management of tourism growth. This has resulted in a changing perspective away from the short term to the long term, which in turn has seen the adoption of a strategic approach to both markets and destination planning/management. There is a clear need to highlight the link between the adoption of sustainable tourism principles and the disciplined, longer-term perspective provided by the strategic planning of both destinations and markets. Thus, the environment concerns validate pooling resources for producing and promoting sustainable tourism destination product, not only for long term habitat preservation, but also to ensure that any tourism development is integrated with the area's overall economic objectives (Getz and Jamal, 1994). Relationship marketing is suggested as a possible approach, for joint management of tourism growth, in accordance with the concept of sustainable development, that stresses environmental limit or carrying capacity.

This paper advocates that the concepts and methods of relationship marketing offer a potentially useful framework for understanding, explaining and managing networks and collaborations. Broadly, however, the key concepts, processes and elements in relationship marketing, central to understanding, networking and inter-organisational collaboration amongst rural tourism providers include (Payne, 1995; Bagozzi, 1979; Berry, 1991; Gronroos, 1990a; Gummesson, 1987; Webster, 1990):

- The relational exchange as opposed to transactional exchange which means identifying, establishing, maintaining, enhancing, and when necessary terminating social relationships amongst providers formed as a result of business transactions.

- Emphasis on trust and commitment that reinforce social relationships formed as a result of ongoing business interactions amongst partners.

- Shift of emphasis from products and firms to people, organisations, and social processes. The emphasis is on the social and associational nature of marketing and businesses in general.

- Interactivity, which implies exchange of information between partners based on honesty and open communication.

- Emphasis on exchange and mutual fulfilment of promises. The promises are of an economic nature concerning exchange of goods, services that lead to social contacts and future commitments.

It is these key elements of relationship marketing that are suggested to build or possibly to redefine relationships between key tourism stakeholders, with a major focus on marketing alliances, to achieve policy goals and processes of sustainable tourism within the rural tourism destination like the Peak National Park. Marketing in the rural tourism context, is more of a process which secures the objectives of conservation, recreation and access for public benefit in both public and privately owned land (Countryside Commission, 1981b). It is about reaching particular kinds of visitors who may be most suited to the special needs and conditions of the local environment and economy, and projecting certain messages to them which influence how they feel about a place. The aim of this paper is therefore to demonstrate what could be achieved by joint working and co-operation through the use of marketing practices embodied in the approach of relationship marketing. The central focus of the discussion which follows is the dynamics of the relationship marketing which can be used to achieve proactive ties between tourism providers in the public, private and the voluntary sector.

# Relationship marketing

The term relationship marketing emphasises variables and processes such as trust, commitment, social norms, and so on-exactly the same set of variables characterising network relationships. The key structural issue in relationship marketing stems from its raison d'etre: exchanging resources to provide mutual benefits and thus achieve mutual goals. Relationship marketing draws its ideas from the streams of research which are the Nordic School of Service (Gronroos and Gummesson, 1985; Berry and Parasuraman, 1993), which examines management and marketing from a service perspective, and the IMP Group (Hakansson, 1982; Hakansson and Snehota, 1995), which takes a network and interaction approach to understanding business practice. A common denominator of these two schools of thought is that marketing is more a management issue than a function, and that managing marketing normally must be built upon relationships, not on transactions alone. Building and managing relationships has become a philosophical cornerstone of both the Nordic School of Service and the IMP Group since the late 1970s. Within North America, the development of relationship marketing can be traced to the work of Theodore Levitt and Barbara Bund Jackson at the Harvard Business School in Industrial Markets, and Len Barry and his colleagues at the Texas AandM University in service markets. Though it was first coined by Berry (1983) in the United States, relationship marketing as a term was not commonly used until the latter part of the 1980s. Comprehensively, however, it can be defined as the process of identifying and establishing, maintaining and enhancing, and when necessary also terminating relationships with customers and other stakeholders, at a profit so that the objectives of all parties involved are met, and that this is done by a mutual exchange and fulfilment of promises (Gronroos, 1990; 1997). Sheth and Parvatiyar (1994) state that relationship marketing is the understanding, explanation and management of the on-going collaborative business relationship between suppliers whereas Gummesson (1995) defines it as a marketing approach based on relationships, interactions, and networks. In more general terms, Gronroos (1996) defines relationship oriented approach to marketing as a phenomenon related to the relationships between a firm and its environment. It points out that marketing includes all necessary efforts required to prepare an organisation for activities needed to manage the interfaces with its environment. Markets are, of course, of several kinds: customers, distributors, suppliers, networks of co-operating partners. The relationship philosophy relies on co-operation and a trusting relationship with other stakeholders and network partners. Relationships entail communication content (information), exchange content (goods and services), and normative content (mutual expectations). Complex networks of personal relationships provide the linkages between aspiring entrepreneurs, market opportunities, and resources. Within these networks, there are strong ties and weak ties (Granovetter, 1973). Strong ties are often familial or friendship relationships, whereas weak ties are more likely to be solely business or customer contacts. When an entrepreneur's most immediate social ties are strong, information flows quickly, and each person tends to know what the other knows. However, fresh information on new ideas and business opportunities tends to come from separate clusters that are connected to the primary social network by weak ties. Through these weak ties, an entrepreneur can gain information and control benefits that can lead to sustainable competitive advantage (Burt, 1992).

While the approach has been widely used in the corporate sector, the potential application of this emerging body of knowledge for managing the complex and dynamic tourism domain has not been clearly addressed. Hence, there is a need to examine its application to create partnerships with a recognition that tourism plays an important role in revitalising rural communities and economies, historically dependent on natural resource-based commodities. There are three key mechanisms inherent in the approach to achieve effective resource management, which differentiate it from the conventional marketing. First, it provides a framework, which focuses on strategic decisions concerning collaboration between providers. Second, it recognises variables like trust, commitment, mutual understanding and reciprocity that encourage and stimulate entrepreneurial and innovative thinking towards partnership building (e.g., Anderson and Narus,1990; Day and Klein, 1987;Dwyer, Schurr and Oh, 1987; Frazier, Spekman and O'Neal, 1988; Salmond and Spekman, 1986). Third, it engenders an organisational values system and strategies conducive to partnerships. It is appropriate in the sustainable tourism context because it recognises the importance of partnerships between suppliers, which affect the broad framework of tourism provision in a national park setting where resource conservation is the primary aim. With the rise in tourist attractions in urban areas, tourism businesses in rural areas can effectively withstand growing competition by increasingly engaging in relationship marketing activities and by partnering with other suppliers and businesses, including competitors. It is important to note that relationships amongst businesses are built upon trust and mutuality, glued together by bonds, which are social and economic and based on mutual exchange of resources. Partners get to know each other through these bonds, and thereby come to know what the interacting partner is capable of doing. Thus, as an alternative perspective relationship marketing may require that basic marketing structures are reshaped to incorporate variables like commitment, trust, co-operation, mutual goals, interdependence, structural bonds and social bonds as the answer to intense competition is not rivalry but co-operation (Wilson, 1995). Gronroos (1999) contends that relationship marketing is more than the synonym used for developing alliances, and networks, or as part of marketing communications only. It requires a totally new approach to some of the fundamental thoughts in marketing. It can be used to address the personal dimension of the relationships amongst tourism providers in the rural sector.

## A conceptual model

How can relationships amongst rural tourism businesses be conceptualised? The existence of long-term relationships is not self-explaining. This is why it is important to inquire into the reasons for establishing relationships and the factors that influence their development, sustainability, and specific form. While the formation of partnering relationships is often viewed as a panacea for businesses, the prescription to form an alliance to gain competitive advantage overlooks the fact that many strategic partnerships do not succeed. Thus any model of partnerships needs to incorporate factors that are associated with their success. It is important to recognise that in any partnership there exists a set of process-related constructs that help guide the flow of information between partners, manage the depth and breadth of interaction, and capture the complex and dynamic interchange between partners. This process is characterised by five general phases (Scanzoni, 1979). The first phase in this relationship cycle is called awareness and refers to the recognition of feasible partners with whom resources and expertise can be exchanged. There is no formal or informal interaction between the parties. They only try to position themselves in the best possible way for possible future interactions. After awareness comes exploration, which is the search and trial phase in relational exchange. In this phase potential exchange partners first consider obligations, benefits, burdens and, the possibility of exchange. The third phase is called expansion, which refers to the continual increase in benefits obtained by exchange partners leading to their gradual interdependence. The main distinction between this phase and the previous phase of exploration is that now the partners trust each other to a greater extent and are satisfied with the relationship, which leads to increased interactions and risk taking. If relationships develop then commitment is formed between two business partners. Commitment is the most desirable aspect of relationships and refers to an implicit and explicit pledge of relational continuity between exchange partners (Dwyer et. al., 1987). Commitment is established on the basis of two assumptions. The first is that partners provide relatively high levels of inputs to the association. The second assumption pertains to durability, i.e., the common belief of effectiveness of future exchange, also referred to as continuation. The final process of the relationship development is dissolution where the partners privately evaluate their dissatisfaction with the other party, concluding that the costs of continuing outweigh the disadvantages of the relationship. It should be emphasised that of these five phases, the fourth phase of commitment should play a central role in the development of a model that highlights the notion of relational exchanges in marketing alliances.

**Figure 1    Conceptual Model of Antecedents to Partnership Building and Success Indicators**

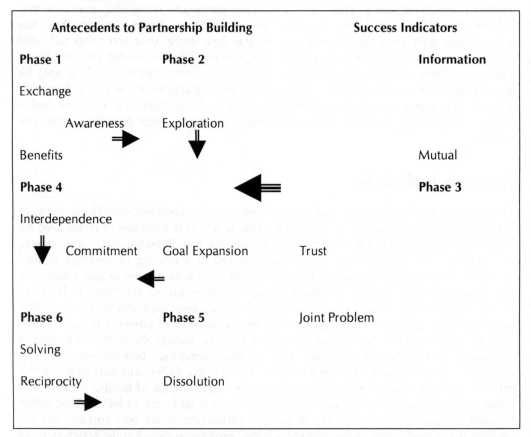

It is hypothesised that the above mentioned phases can provide a context to examine the degree to which the principles of relationship marketing, are incorporated in the existing tourism marketing alliances or partnerships in the Peak District National Park. Within a broad framework of relationship marketing, the research related to inter-relationships or inter-dependencies between key tourism stakeholders is likely to range across a number of levels and units of analysis depending upon the particular question addressed. In the context of examining inter-relationships between different tourism organisations, research investigations are likely to focus on an organisation's relations with other organisations. Differences and similarities between the organisations are examined to better understand how the organisations interrelate. From the network perspective, the emphasis is on specifying the nature of the relationship between two or more organisations. Here, needs and interests are not defined in terms of a single organisation, but in terms of inter-dependencies among tourism stakeholders affected by some issue. Existing networks in the study area should provide a context to examine the use and current application of the principles of relationship marketing in marketing alliances between key tourism stakeholders. It is important to recognise that the long-term character of relationships is defined and shaped by a larger institutional framework where the glue that binds the entire network together is an elaborate pattern of interdependence and reciprocity (Achrol, 1997).

## Existing rural tourism partnerships

The existing rural tourism partnerships have had considerable success in co-ordinating marketing activity within their areas and focusing this onto sensitive themes and images. But they are categorised by partnerships between the public, private and voluntary sector rather than business to business partnerships. For example, the Dartmoor Area Tourism Initiative brought together the local authorities, National Park and the local tourism association to co-ordinate their marketing for the greater Dartmoor area, one aim being to spread visitor pressure outside the park. The Settle and Carlisle Railway Development Company created a marketing group of all authorities along the railway line. Establishing joint activity like this is an important way of extending the reach of the project and ensuring that sensitive marketing continues after the project has finished. Rural tourism partnerships have helped to create a new identity for destination areas, and to project a green image, appropriate to the area's environment. This is well demonstrated by the Tarka Project, adopted in 1989 by Devon County Council to take forward an integrated strategy promoting conservation, recreation and tourism in the area. Project Explore is an initiative between local interests and agencies aimed at encouraging the development of green tourism in South-East Cornwall. It was a joint venture between Caradon District Council, and the South Cornwall Heritage Coast Service, aimed to promote and develop tourism based on the character of the area. The Devon and Cornwall Rail Partnership has seen the forging of partnerships between Devon County Council, Cornwall County Council, Rural Development Commission, Regional Development Commission, Regional Railways, Countryside Commission, University of Plymouth and the Cornwall Tourist Development Action Programme (first year only). Purbeck Heritage Committee is a partnership of local agencies and interests set up to co-ordinate a strategy for protecting the character and environment of Purbeck and promoting sustainable development. The Dartmoor Area Tourism Initiative attracted ten sponsors contributing to the core budget, comprising regional and national tourist boards, Countryside Commission, district and county councils, Dartmoor Tourist Association and Duchy of Cornwall. The Peak Tourism Partnership is a national pilot project, bringing together national agencies and local interests, to explore new approaches to managing visitors and tourism in the Peak District National Park. The North Pennines Tourism Partnership is a project developed to market rural tourism in a remote upland area, based on and maintaining its intrinsic qualities. The partnership objectives are concerned with strengthening rural tourism by improving image and marketing, quality and standards at existing attractions and accommodation, seeking modest development appropriate to the environment, promoting informal countryside activities, rural arts and crafts, and conserving the character and appearance of the landscape, towns and villages. Agencies successfully show that economic development through tourism can be compatible with landscape designation. Partnership between South Somerset District Council and Countryside Commission (now Countryside Agency) illustrates an attempt to sensitively promote rural tourism, attracting visitors who care about the environment, rather than trying to change visitors' attitudes. These partnerships highlight where the policies and activities of the key stakeholders interrelate, and identify opportunities for collaboration and integration over a range of topics to bring about mutual benefits. Also, the social ties between partners, vested interests, strong sense of community and personal attachment to the resource also play an important role in these alliances. It is important to note here that though existing networks play an important role in these partnerships, the business-to-business collaboration and networking has not been adequately addressed.

## Management implications and conclusions

Management implications of using the approach of relationship marketing strategies are far reaching. It requires the key tourism stakeholders to look beyond their immediate concerns, to take a broader perspective and develop stronger cross-functional capabilities, leading to much closer relationships between suppliers, internal staff, customers and other relevant markets. However, the best strategy for the area, may depend on what type of stakeholders it is serving and on where in its lifecycle the tourism situation exists. Rural areas as tourist destinations are dynamic: they evolve and change over time. This is due to changes in the preferences and needs of visitors, the gradual deterioration and possible replacement of the original natural and cultural attractions which were responsible for the initial popularity of the area (Butler, 1980). It is suggested by authors that research examining tourism partnerships is needed at both the network and organisational level of analysis (Selin and Chavez, 1995). It is aimed to achieve the same to an extent using the principles and concepts of relationship marketing.

This paper is, therefore, intended as a signpost to scholars interested in collaborative processes in the tourism field. Additionally, with respect to external validity, some of the lessons learned in the environmentally sensitive, tourism destination of the Peak District National Park where the research currently focuses about marketing alliances might be applicable to similar destination settings. It is hoped that some of the basic principles and concepts of relationship marketing used in addressing tourism partnerships issues, can possibly provide a conceptual framework for future interpretive case studies and longitudinal research designs, needed to capture the complexity of collaborative processes in the tourism field. The most immediate practical benefit of any further research in the field, however, would be to guide the development of new collaborative tourism destination marketing alliances at the regional, national, and global level, within the tourism framework in the rural settings. The added dimension to the partnerships is that the partners are competitors as well, which creates interesting challenges (i.e., anti-trust implications) about sharing information and trust. Also, the task of marketing is not so much to identify potential markets when applied in the sustainable tourism context as to educate the consumer about sustainability and sensitive tourism practices, which makes the traditional marketing approach inappropriate.

# References

Achrol, Ravi S. (1997), Changes in the Theory of Interorganisational Relations in Marketing: Toward a Network Paradigm. *Journal of the Academy of Marketing Science*. Vol. 25. No. 1. pp. 56-71.

Adler, Lee. (1966), Symbiotic Marketing. *Harvard Business Review*. Vol. 44 (November-December). pp. 59-71.

Anderson, J. C. and J. A. Narus. (1990), A Model of Distributor Firm and Manufacturer Firm Working Partnerships. *Journal of Marketing*. Vol. 54. No. 1. pp. 42-58.

Bagozzi, Richard P. (1979), *'Toward a Formal Theory of Marketing Exchanges.'* In Ferell, O. C., Brown, and C. W. Lamb (eds.) Chicago, American Marketing Association. pp. 431-447.

Bagozzi, R. P. (1995), Reflections on Relationship Marketing in Consumer Markets. *Journal of the Academy of Marketing Science*. Vol. 23. pp. 272-277.

Berry, Leonard L. and A. Parasuraman. (1991), *Marketing Services. Competing Through Quality*. The Free Press, A Division of Macmillan Inc. N.Y.

Berry, L. L. (1995), Relationship Marketing of Services-Growing Interest, Emerging Perspectives. *Journal of the Academy of Marketing Science*. Vol. 23. pp.236-245.

Bleeke, J. and D. Ernst. (1991), The way to win in cross-border alliances. *Harvard Business Review*. Pp. 127-135.

Blois, K. J. (1996), Relationship Marketing in Organisational Markets: When is it Appropriate? *Journal of Marketing Management*. Vol. 12. pp. 161-173.

Brodie, Roderick J., Nicole E. Coviello, Richard W. Brookes and Victoria Little. (1997), Towards a Paradigm Shift in Marketing? An Examination of Current Marketing Practices. *Journal of Marketing Management*. Vol. 13. pp. 383-406.

Butler, R. (1980), The Concept of a Tourism Area Cycle, *Canadian Geographer*. Vol. 24. pp. 5-12.

Butler, Richard. (1992), Alternative Tourism: The Thin Edge of the Wedge. In Smith, Valene L. and William R. Eadington. 1994. *Tourism Alternatives*. John Wiley and Sons, Sussex, England.

Butler, Richard, C. Michael Hall and Johan Jenkins. (1998), *Tourism and Recreation in Rural Areas*. John Wiley and Sons, Chichester.

Christopher, Martin, Adrian Payne and David Ballantyne. (1991), *Relationship Marketing. Bringing Quality, Customer Service and Marketing together*. Butterworth-Heinemann Ltd., Oxford.

Copulsky, J. R. and M .J. Wolf. (1990), Relationship Marketing: Positioning for the Future. *Journal of Business Strategy*. Vol. 11. No. 4. pp. 16-20.

Dwyer, F. Robert, Paul H. Schurr, and Sejo Oh. (1987), Developing Buyer – Seller Relationships. *Journal of Marketing*. Vol. 51(April). pp. 11-27.

Edwards, Ron Prof. Chair. (1990), *A Vision For National Parks*. The Evidence of the Council for National Parks to the National Parks Review Panel. Shelton Street, London.

Getz, Donald and Tazim B. Jamal. (1994), The Environment –Community Symbiosis: A Case for Collaborative Tourism Planning. *Journal of Sustainable Tourism*. Vol. 2. No. 3.

Gray, B. (1985), *Conditions Facilitating Interorganisational Collaboration*. Human Relations 38: 911-936.

Gronroos, C. (1990b), *Service Management and Marketing and Managing the Moments of Truth in Service Competition*. Lexington Books, Lexington.

Gummesson, E. (1995), Relationsmarknadsfoering: Fraan 4P till 30R. Liber-Hermods, Malmo. In Brodie, Roderick J., Nicole E. Coviello, Richard W. Brookes and Victoria Little. 1997. Towards a Paradigm Shift in Marketing? An Examination of Current Marketing Practices. *Journal of Marketing Management*. Vol. 13. pp. 383-406.

Gray, Tim S.(Ed.) (1995), *UK Environmental Policy in the 1990s*. MacMillan Press Ltd.,London.

Gronroos, Christian. (1990), 'The Marketing Strategy Continuum: Toward A Marketing Concept for the 1990s.' Swedish School of Economics and Business Administration Working Papers.

Gronroos, Christian. (1990a), 'Marketing Redefined.' *Management Decision*. Vol. 28. 8. pp. 5-9.

Gummesson, E. (1987), 'The New Marketing- developing long term interactive relationships'. Long Range Planning. Vol. 20. No. 4. pp. 10-20.

Hakansson, Hakan. (ed.).(1982), *International Marketing and Purchasing of Industrial Goods*. Wiley, New York.

Hakansson, Hakan and Snehota, Ivan. (1995), *Developing Relationships in Business Networks*. Routledge, London.

Jamal, Tazim B. and Donald Getz. (1995), Collaboration Theory and Community Tourism Planning. *Annals of Tourism Research*. Vol. 22. No. 1. pp. 186-204. Elsevier Science Limited, USA.

Kotler, P. (1992), Marketing's New Paradigm: What's really happening out there? *Planning Review*. Vol. 20. No. 5. pp. 50-52.

Laarman, J. G. and H. M. Gresgen. (1996), Pricing Policy in Nature Based Tourism. *Tourism Management*. 17: 247-254.

Lehtinen, U. (1995), *Shifting the Paradigm? Our Present State of Ignorance*. 3rd international colloquium in Relationship Marketing. Monash University, Australia.

Levine, S. and P. E. White. (1961), Exchange as a Conceptual Framework for the Study of Inter-organisational Relationships. *Administrative Science Quarterly*. Vol. 5. No. 4. pp. 583-601.

Levitt, Theodore. (1983), *The Marketing Imagination*. The Free Press, New York.

Lowe, P. and Flynn, A. (1989), Environmental Politics and Policy in the 1980s in J. Mohan (ed.) *The Political Geography of Contemporary Brita*in. Macmillian Press, London, UK.

McKenna, Regis. (1991), 'Marketing is Everything'. *Harvard Business Review* (January/February), 65-79.

McKercher, B. (1993), The Unrecognised Threat to tourism. Can tourism survive 'sustainability'? *Tourism Management* , 14(2), 131-6.

Moorman, Christine, Gerald Zaltman and Rohit Deshpande. (1992), 'Relationships between Providers and Users of Market Research: The Dynamics of Trust Within and Between Organisations.' *Journal of Marketing Research*. Vol. 24. August. pp. 314- 328.

Morgan, R. M. and S. D. Hunt. (1994), The Commitment –Trust Theory of Relationship Marketing. *Journal of Marketing*. Vol. 58. No. 3. pp. 20-38.

Magrath, A. J. and K. G. Hardy. (1994), Building Customer Partnerships. *Business Horizons*. Vol. Vol. 37. No. 1. pp. 24-28.

Morgan, R. M. and S. D. Hunt. (1994), The Commitment –Trust Theory of Relationship Marketing. *Journal of Marketing*. Vol. 58. No. 3. pp. 20-38.

Murphy, P. E. (1985), *Tourism: A Community Approach*. Meuthen, New York.

Orams, M .B. (1995), Towards a more Desirable form of Ecotourism. *Tourism Management* 16: 3-8.

Parvatiyar, A., and Sheth, J. (1994), *Paradigm Shift in Marketing Theory and Approach: The Emergence of Relationship Marketing. In Relationship Marketing: Theory, Methods, and Applications*. Section I, Session 2.1, J. Sheth and A. Parvatiyar (eds.). 1994. Centre for Relationship Marketing. Emory University, Atlanta. GA.

Payne, Adrian. (1991), *Relationship Marketing: A Broadened View of Marketing*. pp. 31. Cranfield Management Series.

Payne, Adrian (Ed.). (1995*), Advances in Relationship Marketing. Cranfield School of Management*. Kogan Page Ltd., London.

Pearce, P. L. (1993), Fundamentals of Tourist Motivation. *In Tourism Research –Critiques and Challenges*. D. G. Pearce and R. W. Butler. (Eds.) pp.113-134. London: Routledge.

Peterson, Robert A. (1995), Relationship Marketing and the Consumer. *Journal of the Academy of Marketing Science*. Vol. 23 (Fall). pp. 278-281.

Powell, W. (1990), Neither Market nor Hierarchy. Research in Organisational Behaviour. pp. 295-336.

Powell, Walter, W. (1987). "Hybrid Organisational Arrangements: New Form or Transitional Development". *California Management Review*, 30(1), pp. 67-87.

Reed, Maurice. (1997), Power Relations and Community Based Tourism Planning. *Annals of Tourism Research*. Vol. 24. No. 3. pp. 566-591. Elsevier Science Limited.

Reid, L. (1987), Recreation and Tourism Workshops. In *Proceedings of the Symposium on Tourism and Recreation: a Growing Partnership*. pp. 41-57. Sagamore Publishing, Ashville NC.

Schatz, C., L. H. McAvoy, and D. W. Lime. (1990), Co-operation in Resource Management Planning: Evaluating a Model Process for Promoting Partnerships between Resource Managers and Private Sector providers. Proceedings of Leisure Research Symposium. National Recreation and Park Association, Alexandra, V.A.

Selin, Steven and Kim Beason. (1991), Inter-organisational Relations in Tourism. *Annals of Tourism Research*. Vol. 18. pp. 639-652. Pergamon Press plc and J. Jafari.

Selin, Steve and Debbie Chavez. (1995), Developing an Evolutionary Tourism Partnership Model. *Annals of Tourism Research*. Vol. 22. No. 4. Pp. 844-856. Elsevier Science Limited, U.S.A.

Selin, S. and Myers, N. (1995), Correlates of partnership effectiveness: The Coalition for unified recreation in the Eastern Sierra. *Journal of Park and Recreation Administration*. Vol. 13. No. 4. pp. 38-47.

Sheth, J. N. (1995), *Searching for a Definition of Relationship Marketing. 3rd International Colloquium in Relationship Marketing*. Monash University, Melbourne University, Australia.

Spekman, Robert E. and Kirti Sawhney. (1990), Toward a Conceptual Understanding of the Antecedents of Strategic Alliances. *Marketing Science Institute*. Report No. 90-114.

Sustainable Development. The UK Strategy. (1994), Cm 2426. *The Summary Report*.

Webster, C. (1990), 'Towards the Measurement of the Marketing Culture of a Service Firm'. *Journal of Business Research*. Vol. 21. pp. 345-362.

Wilson, David T. (1995), An Integrated Model of Buyer-Seller Relationships. *Journal of the Academy of Marketing Science*. Vol. 23. pp. 335-345.

# Surviving the millennium experience: The future of urban regeneration in Greenwich

## *Melanie K Smith and Karen A Smith*

University of Greenwich, London, UK

*"Greenwich has become a globally recognised model for regeneration, regeneration for which the Dome has been a catalyst and is helping to bring prosperity to one of the poorest parts of London and to the UK as a whole."*
(Lord Falconer, 1999:1)

## Introduction

This paper will analyse the extent to which the decision to base the Millennium Dome Exhibition in the London Borough of Greenwich (LBG) has contributed to urban regeneration in the local area. Despite the controversy surrounding the construction of this temporary structure, it will be argued that the potential long-term economic and social benefits will more than compensate for the cost of its construction.

Greenwich is one of the most deprived boroughs in the country, but the Millennium Dome has acted as a catalyst for many of the environmental, economic and social changes that have been taking place in recent years. The paper will consider the Dome as an example of a flagship cultural mega-event which has provided the stimulus for other developments in the local area. Many of the regeneration projects within Greenwich Borough focus on environmental improvements, the development of new cultural and tourist attractions and facilities, and the creation of employment prospects for local people. It is hoped that the urban regeneration process in Greenwich will serve a dual purpose in encouraging and retaining more visitors, as well as improving the quality of life and standard of living for local people. The extent to which a permanent legacy is created for the Borough may depend on the future fate of the Millennium Dome as a cultural attraction. However, this paper will attempt to demonstrate that, irrespective of the Dome's future, its presence has made a considerable contribution to the enhancement of the local area.

# The role of flagship initiatives in the urban regeneration process

*"Urban regeneration is a composite concept, encompassing economic, environmental, social, cultural, symbolic and political dimensions."* (Bianchini, 1993a:211)

The urban regeneration process is a complex one, and the motivations for embarking on large-scale regeneration projects are varied. They may form part of the Government's agenda for the economic or cultural regeneration of former industrial cities that have fallen into decline; the enhancement of external image may be viewed as a means of attracting inward investment and tourism; or projects may be a way of initiating wider environmental improvements and infrastructure developments. A key factor in all of these motivations is that initial funding will have a cumulative effect, acting as a catalyst for further inward investment and the development of other initiatives.

Major urban regeneration projects often include flagship projects which act as the figurehead and focus for the wider development programme. Bianchini (1993b:16) cites examples of European cities such as Glasgow, Liverpool, Barcelona, Frankfurt, and Montpellier which have all used cultural flagships as "powerful symbols of urban renaissance" to enhance their image and to attract tourists.

One of the most commonly adopted tools in flagship projects is a special event; these can be categorised according to their size and scale: ranging from local, major, and hallmark events to mega-events at the largest scale (McDonnell *et al*, 1999). Mega-events are those that are so large they affect whole economies and attract worldwide coverage in the global media: "...by way of their size or significance, [mega-events] are those that yield extraordinarily high levels of tourism, media coverage, prestige, or economic impact for the host community or destination" (Getz, 1997:6). The majority of the prominent and reported mega-events are those associated with sport, for example, the Olympics or the Football World Cup, and those associated with business and trade, such as World Fairs and Expositions. By their sheer scale, these events will all aim to attract tourists as well as local, regional, national or even international markets. However, ominously, McDonnell *et al* (1999:22) warn that: "...the larger the event and the higher its profile, the greater the potential for things to go wrong, generating negative impacts". Essex and Chalkley (1998:187) also point out the huge expense associated with the hosting of mega-events such as the Olympic Games and the legacy of debt that inevitably follows, stressing the importance of a regeneration imperative: "....the costs involved in staging the Games are now so high that host cities can often only justify the expenditure when it is seen as leading to a major programme of regeneration and improvement".

Events, by their very definition, are of a temporary nature, however many leave a permanent legacy in the form of large physical structures such as stadiums and exhibition halls, but also in associated developments. In this way flagship mega events can be used as catalysts for urban renewal, and for the creation of new or expanded infrastructure (McDonnell *et al*, 1999). This can include increased provision for tourism such as hotels and other facilities, along with improved road and public transport links. As stated by Hall (1992:69): "The hosting of mega-events is often deliberately exploited in an attempt to 'rejuvenate' or develop urban areas through the construction and development of new infrastructure...road and rail networks, airports, sewage and housing". Hall (1992) also identifies the importance of the level of public financial involvement, the political effects, the construction of facilities, and the impact on both the economic and, significantly, the *social* fabric of the host community. As noted by Evans (1996), the social impacts of mega-events tend to be under-researched and under-valued compared to the economic and tourism dimensions.

## The Millennium Dome as an example of a flagship mega-event

The Millennium Dome is the flagship in the redevelopment of a derelict brownfield site in south east London: the Greenwich Peninsula. Although the Dome is being promoted as the 'must-see' tourist attraction of the millennium year, as noted by Stevens (2000), the most commonly used definitions of 'visitor attractions' (for example, BTA), would exclude the Millennium Dome since it is not a permanently established destination, and it is only accessible, at present, on a pre-booked basis. It may therefore be better to consider the Dome as a time-limited 'mega event', although in response to criticisms of wastefulness (Smith and Jenner, 1998), the building's structure will become a more permanent legacy.

Public and media reaction to the Dome has been largely sceptical, but it should be noted that the public reaction to flagship initiatives in Britain has always been less than favourable. As stated by Simon Jenkins (Member of the Millennium Commission): "...the history of these exhibitions [...] is the history of cynical preamble. They are hated, loathed and despised in advance, but as soon as they are open, they are great, seminal cultural events. It is always thus..." (quoted in Carling and Seely, 1998:8). However, during and since its construction, the Dome has received a great deal of negative press:

> *"Most major building projects provoke debate and controversy, but the construction of few buildings in modern times has attracted as much scrutiny and hostility as the Millennium Dome in Greenwich."* (Irvine, 1999:2)

# The Millennium Dome as a catalyst for the regeneration of Greenwich

*The following section provides an overview of the Millennium Dome's history and rationale for its construction on the formerly derelict Greenwich Peninsula, part of the London Borough of Greenwich.*

## A borough in need of regeneration?

The London Borough of Greenwich (LBG) suffers from considerable social and economic deprivation, including high unemployment and low levels of education. In 1991, LBG was ranked the 14th most deprived borough in the country against 13 deprivation measures (OPCS, 1993). LBG's unemployment rate in Spring 1997 was 13%, compared to 9.1% for London and 7.1% for the UK. It was also estimated that the number of people who claim Income Support was around 23% (ONS, 1998). Although recent statistics suggest a marked improvement (for example, Greenwich Council estimated in March 2000 that the unemployment rate in Greenwich was 8% compared to the London average of 6.6%), there are clear disparities between certain wards within the Borough. For example, there are pockets of wealth in Blackheath and the centre of historic Greenwich, but areas such as East Greenwich, Woolwich, Plumstead, Deptford and Thamesmead are still suffering from severe deprivation.

The contrast between wards within the Borough has arguably always been marked. For example, Jennings (1999:105) refers to "...the constant relationship between well-to-do, elegant Greenwich and the gritty hard-working real world around it". Even Greenwich town itself is somewhat divided in its fortunes, and there has always been a stark contrast between historic Maritime Greenwich, and the run-down areas that surround it, especially East Greenwich. As stated by Irvine (1999:13) "Greenwich was, and to a large extent still is, a town of two halves. The splendour of the magnificent buildings created by Wren and others, the riverside walk and trendy restaurants mask the considerable poverty and deprivation which exists on the numerous rundown council housing estates, often located in the same roads as highly-expensive properties". However, with the regeneration of the Peninsula and other areas of East Greenwich, it is hoped that some of these economic disparities may be addressed. Many of the developments focus on the creation of a long-term legacy for the Borough, so the results may not be imminent, but the transformation of a contaminated wasteland to host an international mega-event and cultural flagship is definitely a promising start!

## From dereliction to dome

It was only in 1995 that the Millennium Commission began the work of selecting a site for their proposed millennium celebrations. The final choice was between extending the existing site at Birmingham's National Exhibition Centre, or the redevelopment of a 294 acre derelict brownfield site at Greenwich. The decision went in favour of Greenwich on the basis of the connection with Greenwich Mean Time; the belief that London would be able to attract bigger international coverage and visitors; and "...because it had the potential for a spectacular development which would at the same time regenerate a deprived area" (Smith and Jenner, 1998:86). There was a clear political influence in the decision to use the millennium festival as a catalyst for the rejuvenation of this declined area: as stated by Greenwich MP Nick Raynsford: "Picking Greenwich had enormous advantages. There was a huge regeneration potential for a very depressed part of London in an area of serious industrial decline and high unemployment" (quoted in Irvine, 1999:48).

The idea of the Dome as a way of celebrating the Millennium was a legacy from the Conservative administration and on taking office in 1997, Tony Blair's New Labour government was initially sceptical about the cost of the scheme, the use of public money, and the overall value of the project. The final decision to go ahead with the construction of the Dome appeared to be partly influenced by the views of the Chairman of the British Tourist Authority, David Quamby, and Robert Ayling, the (then) Chairman of British Airways, a sponsor of the Dome. This implies that the potential to attract tourists to the Dome was viewed as a major consideration in its construction.

The Greenwich Peninsula site is located in the north of the Borough, bordering the Thames, and was used over the last century primarily as a gasworks, but had lain derelict and contaminated for the past decade or so. The area was purchased by English Partnerships (a Government sponsored regeneration agency) in February 1997 from British Gas, and the principal aim was to decontaminate the area and regenerate the infrastructure of the site in preparation for the Millennium Dome exhibition in the year 2000. Although English Partnerships prepared the site for the Millennium Experience, the site itself was leased to the New Millennium Experience Company (NMEC) until June 2001, when it reverts back to English Partnerships. There is an option for the NMEC to extend the lease by a further twelve months, subject to paying commercial rental. This may well become likely if the decision is made to keep the Dome open after the year 2000 in a bid to increase visitor numbers, which have so far failed to meet the projected targets (Guardian, 2000). It should be noted that this will be a controversial decision given that the advertising of the Dome has stressed the importance of visiting the Dome during the year 2000, with the slogan '*One amazing day, one year only*'.

The original plan for the Dome had specified private sector leadership, however a distinct lack of interest from the private sector led to public sector management through the NMEC, a Limited company of which the government is the sole shareholder. The total budget of the Millennium Exhibition was £758 million: private sector involvement is through sponsorship, £150 million in total, with other funding (£194 million) coming from commercial revenue (ticket sales, merchandising and licensing), £449 million from the National Lottery through the Millennium Commission, and £15 million from disposal proceeds. However, one of the many controversies surrounding the Dome has been funding, and as recently as January 2000 the government had to provide further resources through the lottery in the form of a £60 million loan.

Unfortunately, the Dome has thus far failed to meet its targets in terms of visitor numbers since it opened in January 2000. The sacking of NMEC's Chief Executive Jennie Page in March 2000 was controversial, and the future of the Dome under the new Chief Executive Pierre-Yves Gerbeau remains to be seen. Gerbeau's previous position as part of the team credited with turning around the fortunes of the ailing EuroDisney and relaunching it as the more successful Disneyland Paris led to initial fears in the press of the possible 'Disneyfication' of the site.

## The future of the Millennium Dome site

The Government was initially criticised by, amongst others, the Select Committee for the Dome, for lacking strategic vision in its consideration of the long-term use of the Dome site. In response to this concern, a statement was issued by Peter Mandelson (then Minister Without Portfolio who was initially responsible for the project, along with the Secretary of State) in December 1997, which referred to 'a number of valuable legacies' that could already be identified, including improvements to public transport, Thames River Services, roads and pedestrian walkways on the Peninsula, and the construction of the Millennium Village. He also referred to a range of possible long-term uses for the Dome itself. In 1999, Lord Falconer, who took over responsibility for the Dome after Mandelson's resignation, talked about the future of the Dome and stressed that the government were open-minded about the possibilities for the site, but were considering the importance of a long-term legacy.

The government's objectives for the future of the Dome include: financial consideration, commercial and environmental sustainability, regeneration, innovation, cultural significance, and transport (Branson, 1999). Initially, up to 65 companies and organisations made bids to take over the Dome, in February 2000 these were narrowed to a shortlist of six:

- City of the Future – a technology theme park.

- Dome Europe – a high technology business and retail destination.

- Greenwich Media World – a mixed-use leisure and business destination focused on media and communications.

- International Merchandise and Cultural Centre – a huge goods, services and tourism bazaar.

- Legacy plc – an industrial campus for work, leisure and retail.

- Sports Dome 2001 – a multiple sports facility.

A further shortlisting will reduce the number again and a final decision is due in late summer.

## Measuring the impacts of the Millennium Dome

The measurement of both the positive and negative impacts of the Dome will be crucial to the evaluation of its long-term success. The Dome Minister Lord Falconer recently commissioned a report entitled *The Impact of the Dome: A New Report*. This report will primarily analyse the Dome's economic impacts, such as the amount of private sector investment in local projects, employment creation, and the increase in foreign tourist expenditure in the local and national economy. It will also emphasise the Dome's role in promoting training and education, its impact on infrastructural and transport developments in London, and the strengthening of social cohesion through community action (Falconer, 1999). In 1999, the NMEC, LBG, and English Partnerships also commissioned the UK Research Partnerships to produce an economic impact study of the Dome, the first stage of which focused on the number of construction works generated for the whole Peninsula. The next stage of the study will run from spring to autumn 2000, and will focus on the tourism generated by the Dome and the impact that this will have on Greenwich and the Borough as a whole, including employment creation and other long-term social benefits (English Partnerships, 2000).

## Regeneration initiatives in Greenwich

The importance of a borough-wide strategy for Greenwich is obviously a key concern for LBG who are keen to extend the benefits of regeneration beyond the Dome site in an attempt to address the wider social and economic inequalities. The Mayor of Greenwich, John Fahy, is quoted as stating that:

*"What we need to do is to publicise more clearly the overall strategy, that the council is not engaged in simply improving the peninsula. Equally, if we are going to protect all of our town centres, we have to create an environment in which we reduce significantly unemployment levels, provide new opportunities for all."* (Barton, 2000:13)

In terms of regeneration, a number of significant developments have been taking place in recent years within the LBG which aim to enhance the physical environment, to boost the local economy, and to generate social and cultural benefits for local communities. This includes the reclamation and re-development of derelict land, infrastructural improvements, residential and waterfront developments, internal and external image enhancement, tourism and cultural development, and employment creation for local people.

## Gentrification and 'property-led' regeneration

Researchers in the field of urban regeneration often warn of the dangers of 'property-led' regeneration initiatives. For example, Zukin (1988) points out some of the problems of regeneration in the United States in the 1970s, and the displacement of lower-income residents because of residential developments and rising property prices. Bianchini (1993a:202) refers to examples of cities such as Frankfurt that have developed 'cultural districts' which "...[have] generated gentrification, displaced local residents and facilities, and increased land values, rents, and the local cost of living, as measured - for example - by the prices charged by local shops". 'Gentrification' is indeed a concept for which many urban regeneration projects have been criticised in recent years. As stated by Keith and Rogers (1991:24) "Gentrification benefits selectively, takes away with one hand as it gives with another, bestowing respectability at a cost of displacement. The inner city is transformed, but for whom?"

On the north bank of the Thames, directly opposite Greenwich Peninsula and the Dome is Docklands; the initial redevelopment of this area in the 1980s has been heavily criticised for the lack of benefits that fed down to the local communities in East London. Whilst it is difficult to measure the 'trickle-down' effects of regeneration, particularly the more indirect benefits, Colenutt (1991:34) states that in the view of the area's local authorities, residents of the East End are getting "...little more than crumbs from Docklands. On occasions larger pieces fall from the table, but given the vast size of the investment cake, the East End has got very little". The high levels of unemployment and homelessness did not appear to be addressed by the regeneration process in this area, and the contrast between rich and poor seems to be as marked as ever: "Canary Wharf represents a city in which trade is now digital, not water-borne. Dickensian terraced houses, the bijou properties of the beneficiaries of the computer age, stand side by side with estates in which the Borough's less fortunate wait hopefully for the jobs to return" (LBG, 1999:18). Parallels can be drawn with its near-neighbour, the Greenwich Peninsula: the lessons from Docklands must include recognition of the importance of community involvement and benefits such as developing new residential complexes for local people and the creation of jobs in an area of such high unemployment.

## Urban regeneration and local community developments

It is now accepted that for regeneration schemes to succeed, local communities must benefit: "Measures to improve the competitiveness of the local economy must take account of the existing economic, social and environmental context. Where jobs are to be created or housing improved, it should be clear that the existing population will be the main beneficiaries" (Community Development Foundation, 1995:11). For example, much of the regeneration of UK cities which characterised the 1980s was managed through Urban Development Corporations (UDC); a House of Commons Employment Committee 1988 report concluded that "UDCs cannot be regarded as a success if buildings and land are regenerated but the local community are by-passed and do not benefit from regeneration" (Para 89). Bianchini (1993a:212) also stressed the importance of local community interests in urban regeneration initiatives "…an explicit commitment to revitalise the cultural, social and political life of local residents should precede and sustain the formulation of physical and economic regeneration strategies".

The lessons of the past on the importance of community involvement have at least appeared to be incorporated into policy documents and strategies although future appraisal will be needed to judge how effective these are in the long-term. For example, the *Integrated Regeneration Strategy for the London Borough of Greenwich*, produced in 1994 by Victor Hausner Associates, focused on both "…the economic development of the Borough, and the improvement of social, community and quality of life conditions" (Victor and Hausner, 1994:13), see table 1.

**Table 1    Main Themes Identified in the LBG Integrated Regeneration Strategy**

| Economic | Social, Community and Quality of Life |
|---|---|
| Tourism | Housing |
| Development sites | Community action |
| Transport | The environment |
| Industry | Transport and access |
| Economic potential within the community | Healthcare |
| Small business and entrepreneurs | Crime |
|  | Training and education |

*Source*: Victor and Hausner (1994:13)

As part of this community strategy, the Greenwich Sustainable Millennium Network was established in 1995; it focuses on community involvement in the development and regeneration of the local area. Local concerns have been addressed, such as inequality, lack of employment creation, the poor integration of the local transport infrastructure, pollution, and the potentially negative impacts of tourism.

In September 1996, as part of a Single Regeneration Budget (SRB) bid, Greenwich Council vowed "...to secure the necessary resources to ensure that the Millennium will make a lasting contribution to the long-term regeneration of the area and its communities" (LBG, 1996:1) and identified a series of objectives for regeneration:

- The creation of new infrastructure;

- A substantial growth in local employment and business capacity;

- The renewal and replacement of housing stock;

- The redevelopment of derelict sites;

- Sustainable improvements to the environment; and

- The active participation and empowerment of its local communities.

A number of initiatives have already been developed over the past few years which aim to protect community interests, to benefit the local communities, to create employment, to develop education and training schemes, and to encourage local entrepreneurship. Greenwich Borough Council has helped to establish education and training schemes for local people, especially the young and the unemployed in deprived areas, such as the Greenwich 'Meeters and Greeters' and tour guiding schemes which are being run in conjunction with local colleges. The development of tourism in the Borough should also help to create employment in the hospitality, leisure and retail sectors, as emphasised in the *Skills for the Millennium in Thames Gateway* programme, funded by Round 3 of the SRB (Thomas *et al*, 1998). NMEC has committed £1 million for training, employment and skills-development for local people and local business. In addition to the initial construction jobs, 2000 staff have been recruited to work at the Dome, and a further 3000 in the associated catering, security and maintenance companies (NMEC, 1999). However, this should only be the first stage of the employment generation process, as stated by Deputy Leader of Greenwich Borough Council, Councillor Bob Harris "...in the Borough, we expect as many as 25,000 jobs to be created in the coming seven years. And a major improvement in transport and other infrastructure will help to ensure that these benefits spread across Greenwich and beyond" (quoted in Sumner, 2000:25).

One example of this wider borough-wide strategy is Greenwich Council's bid for £5.75 million SRB funding in partnership with Bexley Council and Thamesmead Town, for projects in Abbey Wood and Thamesmead. *Take Another Look at Abbey Wood and Thamesmead* is a programme of projects totalling £18.6m to address social exclusion, help people to access employment, engage young people and promote community development across the area. Elsewhere in the Borough Greenwich Development Agency, Woolwich Development Agency and Creekside Partnership are now well into their regeneration programmes, with total funds (SRB, private sector and other matching) amounting to well over £200m (Thames Gateway London Partnership, 1998).

It is difficult to measure the success of many of these initiatives in terms of their level of community involvement or benefit. Although this discussion has identified various elements of impact, for example, number of jobs created, a comprehensive evaluation projects is required to fully assess the regeneration programme. For example, a local resident in a recent letter to the Council's own newspaper, *Greenwich Time*, made the plea "We really hope the regeneration of Woolwich and Greenwich will give local people more employment, training and housing opportunities" (2000:6).

## Residential developments

One of the ways in which local communities stand to benefit from the regeneration process is through the creation of improved housing and residential developments. The problems of the past in terms of property-led regeneration of areas such as Docklands have been discussed above and attempts have been made to incorporate the lessons learned from such experiences. The regeneration of the Greenwich Peninsula incorporates two main residential developments: the Millennium Village and the Meridian Quarter. The development of the 32 acre mixed-used Millennium Village stems from the Government's policy of developing brownfield sites in urban areas. It aims to set new standards of environmental quality and energy efficiency, and 1,400 mixed tenure homes are planned. However, the project has already run into problems; the original architects, Hunt Thompson Associates (HTA), eventually parted company with the Greenwich Millennium Village consortium in June 1999, after conflicts over the proposed nature of the development. There appeared to be concern on the part of the architects that the original idea of creating a 'social mix' and the integration of private and social housing was to be watered-down (Grigsby, 1999). It was originally estimated that 20 per cent of the Millennium Village would offer 'affordable housing' (DETR, 1999). This figure is already arguably too low if the local communities are to become the main beneficiaries, but this may also raise the question 'affordable for whom?': an advertisement on page 32 of the same local newspaper, *The Wharf*, advertises the Millennium Village properties as 'luxury apartments overlooking a lake and a park', quoting prices that would not be affordable for the average teacher or nurse, let alone the poorest sectors of the local communities. The residential complex includes other features such as a yacht club, which suggests that the gentrification of East Greenwich may not be too far away!

On another part of the Peninsula, on land adjacent to the Dome itself, Quintain property company are planning another mixed-use scheme, to be known as the Meridian Quarter. The project has received the backing of Greenwich Council, and must aim to complement plans for the Millennium Village and the future use of the Dome site. Architect Terry Farrell plans to make the Meridian Quarter "the centrepiece of urban renaissance", and Quintain director Nicholas Shattock believes the scheme "can become a flagship example of the principles of urban renaissance. The opportunity exists to create a new quarter which will balance the development on the Peninsula, maximise the potential for the Dome and provide employment" (quoted in Branson, 2000:16). He cites examples of potential employment creation in the craft and creative industries, commercial, retail, leisure, tourism, marina, hotel and conference facilities.

Other residential projects in the Borough include a new urban village at Gallions Reach, being developed by Thamesmead Town, which will provide 1,500 much needed homes.

Housing Estates in Charlton have received an £18 million boost from the Government's Estate Renewal Challenge Find, which will go towards a £35 million programme of repairs, improvements and the redevelopment of 1280 homes (Thames Gateway London Partnership, 1998).

## Transport infrastructure

Transport has also been a key element in the redevelopment of Greenwich Peninsula. The Blackwall Tunnel Approach Road cuts the East Greenwich site in two providing excellent, if congested, road access. However, public transport access to the area had long been regarded as poor. Central to the government's plans for the site was the extension of the Jubilee Tube line which, after much delay, finally opened in time for the millennium celebrations and links the site to central and east London. NMEC have adopted a strict sustainable transport policy for the Dome: the only parking available is for disabled visitors. Promotional literature, including the booking form itself, present a range of ways to get to the Dome, including tube, mainline train, bus, boat from Greenwich or Westminster, pre-booked coach, or shuttle bus transfer from one of four park-and-ride sites around London. In an effort to enforce this strategy, a two-mile controlled parking zone surrounds the Dome to south and will be in place throughout 2000. Plans for the zone initially raised concerns from local residents, however the early signs are that the envisaged problems, for example a loss of business in local shopping areas, have not been significant. Indeed, local shops are more likely to suffer from lost trade due to the inclusion in the peninsula redevelopment of large retail units, including an 'eco-friendly' Sainsburys.

## Regeneration projects across Greenwich Borough

It is important to note that the Greenwich Peninsula is not the only regeneration project within LBG's area. The most prominent of these other projects is The Greenwich Waterfront Partnership. This covers an area is made up of approximately 1012 ha of the LBG and includes about 11km of the south bank of the River Thames, with almost half the area lying in Thamesmead town, and also including the Peninsula site (Bailey *et al*, 1995). The Waterfront Strategy was launched in 1991, and the Greenwich Waterfront Development Partnership was set up as an equal partnership of Council, business and community representatives. This provides the framework for support to developers and investors and has provided the context for pump-priming Government funding. The priority is for physical regeneration, extending seven miles from Deptford to Thamesmead, which is over 1000 acres of development land. New homes, schools, workplaces, open spaces are being created from previously derelict sites in Deptford, West and East Greenwich, Woolwich and Thamesmead: "Flagship development sites are being transformed into vibrant new communities" (Thames Gateway, 1998:1).

On the western edge of LBG, on its border with Lewisham Council, the Greenwich Reach East Project aims to develop 400,000 sq ft of currently derelict and partly contaminated land into a mixed retail and leisure development. Together with residential areas, this project includes a hotel, a major cruise liner terminal, river boardwalk, car parking and related coach, bus and taxi parking and servicing, riverside pedestrian footpath and cycleway including bridge over Deptford Creek, together with associated highway works, works to river walls and landscaping. The proposed hotel will offer much needed accommodation in Greenwich and will provide approximately 130 beds. It is hoped that the scheme will create 1,500 permanent full-time and part-time jobs, as well as creating spin off benefits in the local economy, which will lead to further job creation. The cruise line terminal also has the potential of dramatically increasing visitor numbers to historic Greenwich.

# The role of tourism and culture in the regeneration process

It is clear from the above discussion, that the potential of the Dome to attract tourists was a key factor in the rationale for its construction, and plays a major role in the impacts of the development.

## The role of tourism in the redevelopment of Greenwich

NMEC's target for the Dome is 12 million visitors, and although early figures fell far short of the goal, this is hardly surprising given the seasonal nature of tourism in London and the 'millennium hangover' in terms of interest and personal finances! More recently audiences have picked up and the first capacity day was reached during the February half-term school holidays, emphasising the role of the Dome as a family activity.

If achieved, the predicted increase in tourism as a result of the Millennium Dome Exhibition during the year 2000 should provide a means of creating further economic, social and cultural benefits for the local environment and community. Although Greenwich has traditionally attracted a day-trip market (D'Alessandro, 1997), it is hoped that the development of more accommodation, catering, retail and entertainment facilities in the local area should help to encourage longer-staying, higher-spending visitors, hence increasing the economic benefits of tourism. The image of Greenwich as a tourism destination has been enhanced significantly by the international publicity surrounding the Dome. As stated by Lord Falconer (1999:1) "By creating jobs, supporting British industry and boosting tourism, the Dome has already justified its very existence and is establishing its own legacy".

The English Tourism Board estimated that the direct additional impact of the Dome on receipts from overseas tourism could be as much as £300 to £500 million, and an extra one million bednights from overnight domestic visitors to London (ETB, 1999). Although this was based on the original visitor target number of 12 million (BTA, 1999), this still constitutes a considerable contribution to the country's economy. Unfortunately, the accommodation provision in Greenwich itself is limited, therefore the local economy may not benefit as much as it could from overnight stays and visitor expenditure. However, employment creation, the development of new housing, and cultural and leisure provision appear to be key priorities in the Government's agenda for the regeneration of the local area. The benefits of regeneration for the local community should always be high on the political agenda when developing flagship events. A number of cultural projects, such as arts festivals and special events have been planned as part of the Cultural Regeneration Strategy and Greenwich Cultural Plan for the Millennium, many of which are focusing on the needs of local communities, as well as aiming to provide a positive image and to create a lasting legacy for the local area.

## The cultural regeneration strategy

*"......apart from the global spotlight, how will the year 2000 be different for the residents of Greenwich? How will a pensioner in Plumstead, a shopper in Eltham, a factory worker in Thamesmead and a family in East Greenwich want to mark the passing of the Millennium year? How can the people of Greenwich celebrate the year 2000 in ways which are relevant to their lives and their communities, and what will make them more proud to be in Greenwich than anywhere else?"* (Dix, 1999:1)

Section 106 of the planning gain agreement for the building of the Dome created a fund of £300,000 for local cultural activities, which was subsequently matched with a further £300,000 from the LBG (London Arts Board, 1999). This money forms the core of the cultural regeneration fund for Greenwich, and the implementation of the Greenwich Cultural Plan for 1998, and the Millennium Festival for the People of the London Borough of Greenwich 2000. The aims of these initiatives are to celebrate the diversity of the local communities and their culture, and to create a lasting legacy in terms of cultural provision, internal and external image enhancement, and the development of cultural pride. Many of the attractions are likely be popular with tourists and visitors from outside the local area, as a number of festivals, carnivals, and special events are planned for the year 2000 and beyond.

## A boost for heritage

World Heritage Site designation of historic Maritime Greenwich in 1997 has clearly boosted the profile of Greenwich as a cultural destination (Smith, 2000). Other heritage sites in the Borough are also hoping to attract visitors in order to benefit from increased expenditure in the local economy and image enhancement. English Partnerships are promoting development of the Royal Arsenal Site in Woolwich. This is another mixed-use brownfield development incorporating residential, leisure, small businesses and light industry, and it aims to revitalise the Woolwich town centre and the surrounding area (Grigsby, 2000). The relocation of the historic Royal Artillery Museum to the Arsenal has also been boosted by £5 million Lottery funding. It is hoped that visitors may be encouraged to visit the site whilst they are in the local area, or visiting historic Greenwich.

In Charlton, the Council is spending £400,000 on the upgrading of Charlton House over the next three years, and Greenwich Development Agency is assisting shopkeepers to improve their properties, and to increase the attractiveness of the area for shoppers and visitors. Eltham is also being promoted as a desirable place to live, as well as being a potential tourist attraction (Gillham, 2000), in particular Eltham Palace, recently refurbished by English Heritage.

# The future of urban regeneration in Greenwich

The long-term aim of the *Greenwich Council Performance Plan for Regeneration and Planning* is "To provide new opportunities to improve the prosperity and environment of Greenwich, and the social well-being and quality of life of its residents" (Greenwich Time,

2000:8-9). Table 2 provides a summary of the Council's aims for the next five years with regard to regeneration.

**Table 2    Greenwich Borough's Regeneration Objectives 2000-2004**

| **Greenwich Performance Plan 2000**<br>**Regeneration and Planning: Key Tasks 2000-4** |
| --- |
| Continue the Borough's regeneration, realising benefits for the whole borough from investments now occurring in the Greenwich Waterfront.<br><br>Borough-wide planning of regeneration and development strategies including:<br><br>• Co-ordination of the Community Plan covering the economic, social and environmental well-being of the area over the next 15-20 years<br><br>• The integrated transport strategy to ensure good quality public transport<br><br>• The economic development strategy to secure a better economic future<br><br>• The unitary development plan guiding building and land development<br><br>• A property management plan for the Council<br><br>• Continue housing renewal through redevelopment and improvement of priority residential areas<br><br>• Enhance the quality of the borough's environment and control development<br><br>• Improve the management of the borough's highways |

*Source*: Greenwich Time, 16 March 2000, LBG

One of the principal aims of the Performance Plan is to create new opportunities for strategic and economic development through the co-ordination of cultural and tourism development. Clearly, the Dome itself as a cultural attraction will contribute to the cultural regeneration process and tourism development in the local area, but the extent to which tourism can be used as a long-term regeneration tool will ultimately depend upon the nature of the future attraction on the Peninsula. Although visitors will still no doubt be motivated to visit historic Greenwich, it is this more run-down and deprived area of Greenwich that could benefit the most from visitor expenditure and an enhanced image. The replacement of the Millennium Exhibition with a tourism or leisure attraction would be highly beneficial for the long-term economic regeneration of this area. The temporary boost in employment for local people that has been created as a result of the Dome's construction and operation will hopefully be sustained, although the number and nature of the jobs provided will be highly dependent on the future use of the Dome site.

In conclusion, it can be seen that the Dome has much in common with other mega-events and international cultural flagship initiatives. It is of a temporary nature (albeit of longer duration than the average sporting event or Expo), and it is a high cost, high risk project which has consequently attracted a certain degree of public and media hostility. Despite the controversies surrounding the project, it is clear from the analysis of these regeneration initiatives that the long-term contribution of the Dome to the local area has been largely positive. It has had a significant impact on both the local and national economy, especially in terms of tourism development and employment creation; it has contributed to the image enhancement of Greenwich as a tourist destination; and it has acted as a catalyst for widespread urban regeneration. Having survived the Millennium Experience and the year 2000, the London Borough of Greenwich can hopefully look forward to a prosperous future, both as a living and working community, and as a popular tourism destination.

# References

Bailey, N. *et al* (1995), *Partnership Agencies in British Urban Policy*. The Natural and Built Environment, Series 6, UCL Press Ltd, London.

Barton, J. (2000), 'Interview: John Fahy, Greenwich Mayor' *Median Line Magazine*, February, pp.11-13.

Bianchini, F. (1993a), 'Culture, conflict and cities: issues and prospects for the 1990s' in Bianchini, F. and Parkinson, M. (Eds) (1993) *Cultural policy and urban regeneration: The West European experience,* Manchester University Press, Manchester.

Bianchini, F. (1993b), 'Remaking European Cities: the role of cultural policies' in Bianchini, F. and Parkinson, M. (Eds) (1993) *Cultural policy and urban regeneration: The West European experience,* Manchester University Press, Manchester.

Branson, C. (1999), 'After the ball is over' *Meridian Line Magazine*, December, p.20.

Branson, C. (2000), 'Smart ideas for the peninsula' *Meridian Line Magazine*, January, p.16.

Carling, P. and Seely, A. (1998), *The Millennium Dome*. Research Paper 98/32, March 12, House of Commons Library.

Colenutt, B. (1991), 'The London Docklands Development Corporation: Has the community benefited?' in Keith, M. and Rogers, A (Eds) (1991) *Rhetoric and Reality in the Inner City*, Mansell Publishing Ltd, London, pp. 31-41.

Community Development Foundation, (1995), *Guidelines to the Community Involvement of the SRB Challenge Fund*. London Borough of Greenwich, April.

D'Alessandro, R. (1997), *A Leap into the New Millennium, 1997-2002 Greenwich Tourism Strategy Framework: a discussion paper*, London Borough of Greenwich.

Department of the Environment, Transport and the Regions (DETR) (1999), 'Greenwich Millennium Village will set high standards,' *DETR Press Release*, 18 November.

Dix, A. (1999), *Time to Celebrate - A Millennium Festival for the People of the London Borough of Greenwich,* London Borough of Greenwich, Strategic Planning.

English Partnerships (2000), 'Economic Impact Assessment', *Greenwich Peninsula News,* Spring, p. 9.

English Tourist Board (1999), *Impact of the Millennium Experience,* English Tourist Board, London.

Essex, S. and Chalkley, B. (1998), Olympic Games: catalyst of urban change, *Leisure Studies,* 17, pp. 187-206.

Evans, G. (1996), 'The Millennium Festival and Urban Regeneration - planning, politics and the party' in Robinson, M. *et al* (Eds) *Managing Cultural Resources for the Tourist,* Business Education Publishers Ltd, Sunderland, pp. 79-98.

Falconer, C. (1999), 'The Dome does good' says Lord Falconer' *Cabinet Office Press Release.* CAB 301/99.

Getz, D. (1997), *Event Management and Event Tourism,* New York, Cognizant Communication Corp.

Gillham, D. (2000), 'The hidden Eltham' *Meridian Line Magazine,* January, p.32.

Greenwich Council (2000), 'Summary of Greenwich Performance Plan 2000' *Greenwich Time,* March 16, pp. 7-10.

Greenwich Time (2000), 'Letters' *Greenwich Time,* March 16, p.6.

Grigsby, J. (1999) 'Peninsula plans' *Meridian Line Magazine,* December, pp.13-14.

Grigsby, J. (2000), 'Changes at Woolwich Arsenal' *Meridian Line Magazine,* February, pp.18-19.

Guardian (2000), 'Dome chief may seek extra time' *The Guardian,* 13 March [online].

Hall, C. M. (1992), *Hallmark Tourist Events: Impacts, management, planning,* Belhaven Press, London.

House of Commons Employment Committee (1988), *The Employment Effects of the Urban Development Corporations,* Volumes 1 and 2, HMSO, London.

Irvine, A. (1999), *The Battle for the Millennium Dome,* Irvine News Agency, London.

Jennings, C. (1999), *Greenwich: The Place Where Days Begin and End,* Little Brown and Co., London.

Keith, M. and Rogers, A (Eds) (1991), *Rhetoric and Reality in the Inner City*, Mansell Publishing Ltd, London.

London Arts Board (1999), *Arts and the City: Quarterly Newsletter from the London Arts Board,* Winter.

London Borough of Greenwich (1996), *Single Regeneration Budget: The Challenge Fund, Bid Document,* London Borough of Greenwich, September.

London Borough of Greenwich (1999), *Millennium Greenwich,* Pitkin Unichrome Ltd.

McDonnell, I. *et al* (1999), *Festival and Special Event Management*, John Wiley and Sons, Chicester.

New Millennium Experience Company (1999), *Millennium*, March.

Office of National Statistics (1998), *Focus on London 98,* Government Statistical Service, Government Office for London and the London Research Centre, London.

Office of Population Statistics (1993), *1991 Census County Reports, Inner London and Outer London,* OPCS, HMSO: London.

Smith, C. and Jenner, P. (1998), 'The impact of festivals and special events on tourism' *Travel and Tourism Intelligence*, 4, pp.73-91.

Smith, M. (2000), 'Greenwich 2000: Managing Sustainable Tourism in the Shadow of the Dome,' *Tourism 2000: Time for Celebration*, Sheffield, September.

Stevens, T. (2000), 'The future of visitor attractions' *Travel and Tourism Intelligence*, 1, pp.61-84.

Sumner, G. (1999), 'Dome's day draws near' *The Guide Magazine*, December, pp.24-25.

Thames Gateway London Partnership (1998), 'The New Era for Waterfront Development' *TGLP Initiatives Magazine*, Summer [online: http://www.thames. gateway.org.uk]

Thomas, R. *et al* (1999), *Skills for the Millennium: Draft Final Report: A Study of the Tourism, Hospitality and Leisure Sectors*, Leeds Metropolitan University, Leeds.

Victor Hausner Associates (1994), *Greenwich Integrated Strategy: Final Summary Report*, May.

Zukin, S. (1988), *Loft Living - Culture and Capital in Urban Change*, Century Hutchinson, London.

# Tourism, economic development and urban regeneration: A critical evaluation

*John Swarbrooke*

Sheffield Hallam University, UK

## Introduction

In the closing years of the last Millennium, several themes dominated the tourism literature. These themes included sustainable tourism, quality and tourist satisfaction, and the role of tourism in urban regeneration.

Across much of the developed world two phenomena have occurred simultaneously, namely the growth of tourism and the economic decline of many towns and cities that were reliant on traditional industries such as coal and steel production, textiles, and shipbuilding.

It is not surprising therefore, that many policy makers have sought to use tourism to try to bring new prosperity to ailing urban economies.

This phenomenon began in the seaboard cities of the US in the 1970s where the changing nature of trade and shipping was leading to decline in seaports such as Baltimore, Boston, New York and San Francisco. It soon spread to the UK and mainland Europe and then further to countries such as Australia.

Billions of pounds have now been spent trying to use leisure and tourism to regenerate countless towns and cities. In general, there has been a lot of support for these schemes from politicians and entrepreneurs. However, communities have frequently been less enthusiastic.

It has often been difficult to find objective balanced evaluations of the true effects of tourism as an urban regeneration tool.

However, before we go on to evaluate the success or otherwise of tourism as an urban regeneration tool, let us look briefly at the rationale for using tourism in this way.

# Why tourism?

Tourism is perceived to offer a number of benefits for towns and cities, including the following:

(i)   The creation of jobs in significant numbers given that it is a more labour - intensive industry than many manufacturing industries which have become increasingly automated;

(ii)  The injection of external money into the local economy and its circulation around the local economy through the multiplier effect;

(iii) The fact that tourists help ensure the viability, and sometimes stimulate the development, of a wide range of services and facilities which are also enjoyed by local people, ranging from theatres to shops, airports to rail services;

(iv)  The idea that in urban communities which have been badly hit by urban decline, the growth of tourism can enhance local pride. In other words, local people will feel better about their home area when they see that their town or city is viewed as a worthwhile place to visit by tourists;

(v)   The hope that urban tourism can lead to inward investment in other sectors when business people who visit the city as tourists like what they see and decide to invest in the city or re-locate their business there;

(vi)  The view that tourism is less polluting than many traditional manufacturing industries;

(vii) Tourism is seen to be particularly valuable in providing employment for young people, and women wishing to return to the workforce;

(viii) Tourism is perceived to be an industry which can help to find new uses for derelict sites, thus improving the destination's environment;

(ix)  Tourism is seen as a valuable source of tax revenue for national and local government given the fact that tourists pay a lot of taxes, directly and indirectly, including airport taxes, consumer taxes such as VAT, and tourist taxes in some places. This tax income can then be used for the benefit of the local community; and,

(x)   Finally, there is a vague view that, perhaps, tourism is a rather glamorous industry that gives a certain status to a city or town which it would not otherwise enjoy.

As we will see later, there is also a negative side to urban tourism, and even to the points outlined above.

# Tourism: A last resort?

In spite of its perceived benefits, it is interesting to note that in many communities, tourism has been adopted as an urban regeneration tool, almost as a last resort! In many towns and cities it has been almost a strategy of desperation, an approach to be taken when there seems to be little chance of attracting enough other more traditional industries to help regenerate the local economy. Most cities and their populations would probably have preferred to see a renaissance of their traditional industries, rather than the rise of tourism. Or they would have liked to see the arrival of new manufacturing industries rather than the growth of tourism. This fact can lead to cynicism and negative attitudes towards tourism on behalf of many residents.

# A typology of tourism and urban regeneration

Towns and cities have used a variety of methods to try to regenerate their communities, through tourism. Some of them are illustrated in Figure 1.

**Figure 1  A Typology of Tourism and Urban Regeneration**

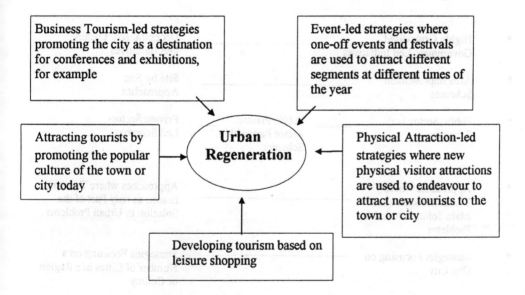

Clearly each of these five categories can have a number of sub-types. Two examples will serve to illustrate this point, as follows:

(i)  Events and festivals can be based on a wide range of themes, but have often been either arts- or sport- related. Edinburgh for instance, has used a city festival to put itself on the tourism map while Sheffield has focused on a sport-related strategy; and,

(ii) Physical attractions can be used as part of an area based approach to rejuvenation, where a critical mass of attractions are used to attract tourists to an area in need of regeneration.

An example of this is the Castlefields area of Manchester in the UK. Alternatively, a single flagship attraction can be used to put a city on the map as a tourist destination, such as the Guggenheim museum in Bilbao.

Clearly, many cities will use a combination of two or three of the approaches outlined in Figure 1.

There are other ways of classifying approaches to the use of tourism as an urban regeneration tool. These are shown in Figure 2.

There are just some of the different ways in which we would classify approaches to the use of tourism as an urban regeneration tool. However, they serve to demonstrate the diversity of approaches that have been or may be adopted.

**Figure 2    Other Approaches to Classifying the Use of Tourism as an Urban Regeneration Tool**

* Highly Centralised,                          Decentralised, Locally
  Government Led Initiatives                    Led Initiatives

* Area Improvement                             Site by Site
  Schemes                                      Approaches

* Public-Sector Led        Public-Private      Private Sector-
  Schemes                  Sector Partnership  Led Schemes
                           Schemes

* Approaches where                             Approaches where Tourism
  Tourism is seen as the                       is seen as only Part of the
  Main Solution to Urban                       Solution to Urban Problems
  Problems

* Strategies Focusing on                       Strategies Focusing on a
  One City                                     Number of Cities in a Region
                                               or County

# The phenomenon of 'cloning' - Baltimore or Barcelona?

Given the potential for very different approaches to tourism and urban regeneration, it is rather surprising that often the approaches taken appear to be very similar from Baltimore to Barcelona, San Francisco to Sydney. This is particularly true in relation to seaports. Here the standard answer appears to be a waterfront development, which will inevitably include, in varying proportions:

- Leisure uses such as museums and galleries, leisure shopping, hotels and restaurants;

- Up-market housing; and,

- Offices.

The leisure uses are usually central to these schemes of which there are now literally hundreds around the world. However the extent of their contribution to urban regeneration is not always clear, as we shall see later.

In inland cities that were formerly dependant on traditional industries, the strategy usually involves one or more museums commemorating these industries. These museums will often be developed in an old building which has some association with the original industry, and these museums tend to have similar elements including themed restaurants and catering.

There is a danger that this uniformity of approach could lead to product standardisation and a loss of local identity for individual towns and cities. This could reduce the long term appeal of these destinations for tourists in the future.

Now it is time for us to begin to explore some key aspects of the relationship between tourism and urban regeneration.

# Key issues in the relationship between tourism and urban regeneration

In this section of the paper, we will explore a number of key issues in the relationship between tourism and urban regeneration. These issues are illustrated in Figure 3.

**Figure 3    Key Issues in the Relationship between Urban Regeneration and Tourism**

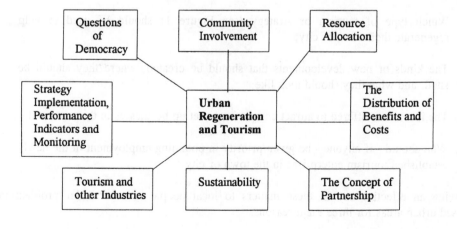

# Questions of democracy

Most uses of tourism as an urban regeneration tool, tend to have been led by the public sector, through central or local government initiatives. While they have been instigated by generally democratically elected bodies, many of these initiatives have been criticised as being undemocratic in the way they have been implemented. In many cases, special agencies have been established to regenerate urban areas, with large budgets and great powers. Often these agencies have been wholly or partly autonomous, with little direct accountability to elected governments on a day-to-day basis.

In many cases they have also had the power to bypass planning controls and 'short-circuit' normal bureaucratic procedures.

Of course, the argument in favour of such an approach is clear. The need for dynamism is often seen to be at odds with the perceived slowness of traditional government departments. Likewise these agencies are thought to be more capable of delivering, stability and consistent policy, than government departments which are subject to short-term political considerations. It is also argued that the new agencies do not have the narrow perspective of individual departments, but can instead take an holistic overview of the urban area.

However, on the other side is the fact that in countries which claim to be democratic, much urban regeneration through tourism has been achieved through largely undemocratic means. This raises ethical issues about the rights of such agencies to exercise power over citizens to, whom they are, at least in theory, wholly or largely answerable. This leads us neatly to the next point, the involvement of the community.

# Community involvement

In most areas where tourism has been used to aid urban regeneration, the community has had little influence over events. Rarely have concerted efforts been made to involve citizens in key decisions such as:

(i) Which type of tourism or strategy (see Figure 1) should be used to help regenerate their town or city;

(ii) The kinds of new developments that should be created, where they should be sited, and what they should look like;

(iii) The incentives offered to attract companies to set up businesses in the area; and,

(iv) Who should - if anyone - be given priority in obtaining employment in the newly established tourism enterprises in the town or city.

Not giving an effective say in these matters to local people is a particular problem in depressed urban areas for three main reasons.

Firstly, it means decisions are taken without the benefit of local expertise which could lead to mistakes. Secondly, it can lead to resentment which may be reflected in a negative attitude towards tourists. Finally, not involving local people in decision-making can further damage their sense of their own worth and further alienate them from the society in which they live. This could be self-defeating because these problems lie at the heart of the difficulties involved in trying to regenerate depressed urban areas.

There is no doubt, as we will see when we look at the UK, that many solutions which are now seen as successful, would probably not have been undertaken if the community had influenced decision-making strategy. However, this does not, surely, justify excluding the very people these projects are supposed to be benefiting.

# Resource allocation

One thing can be said with certainty is that achieving urban regeneration through tourism is a very expensive business. Generally, most of the resources devoted to this purpose come from the public sector in terms of:

(i)   Developing new infrastructure such as roads, airports, and convention centres;

(ii)  Building flagship attractions to act as catalysts for further developments; and,

(iii) Funding training and education to create a labour force that can staff the tourism industry.

Many people voice two major objections to the use of public resources, namely:

- It is morally wrong for poor communities to, in effect, offer subsidies, to wealthy private companies; and,

- That the money invested in tourism could be devoted to more valuable causes. It is often suggested that in depressed urban areas it is the social infrastructure - health, education, and housing - that should be the priority for the allocation of public funds.

It is frequently argued that until health, housing, and education problems are solved or ameliorated, the most disadvantaged local residents can neither contribute to, or fully benefit from, urban regeneration.

However, governments usually argue that they invest resources in tourism in the hope that the economic benefits it brings will provide resources to improve health, education, and housing, for local people.

This sounds sensible but it is not easy to find evidence of this happening in practice, in Europe at least. This brings us nicely to the next issue.

# The distribution of benefits and costs

It is often difficult to reach any conclusion other than that there is not really a fair distribution of benefits and costs in much urban regeneration, particularly from the point of view of the local community.

Private enterprises seem to gain from the incentives they are given by the public sector to locate in an area, while governments can gain some political kudos from what they are perceived to have achieved.

However, local people seem to get a less impressive deal. They fund much of the urban regeneration through their taxes but they see less of the economic benefits than the private enterprises. The jobs that disadvantaged local people may get, though welcome, tend not to be well paid or offer real career prospects.

These regeneration schemes, on the other hand, do bring benefits for tourists. They give them new high-quality destinations for weekend breaks. Perhaps they should be paying more for these breaks to generate more benefits for the local population.

# The concept of partnership

The most fashionable concept in destination management and urban regeneration is the idea of partnership. This usually means bringing together the skills and resources of the public and private sectors. However, often it appears that such partnerships are uneven, with the public sector providing most of the resources and the private sector taking most of the financial benefits. These partnerships, as we have seen, often exclude the people who actually live in the disadvantaged urban areas. Tourists are also not overtly involved in this partnership although their perceived desires are influential in the decision-making process.

# Sustainability

There must be doubts about the long-term sustainability of many tourism-based urban regeneration schemes, for a number of reasons, as follows:

(i)   Many are based on public subsidies. What will happen once these subsidies cease?

(ii)  The schemes tend to be focused on types of tourism which are very popular today such as leisure shopping, interactive museums, and aquariums. Who is to say that these types of attractions will remain popular in the future?

(iii) They are based on the fact that tourism is growing, particularly the short-break market. It is perfectly possible that this growth may not be sustained over time; and,

(iv)  If local people continue to be marginalised in decision-making, there may be a reaction against tourism as a regeneration tool.

If regeneration schemes based on tourism are not sustainable, then many towns and cities may be left with embarrassing, high profile, 'while elephants' that will be difficult to adapt to new uses.

# Tourism and other industries

In many towns and cities, tourism appears to have been thought of in isolation in urban regeneration schemes.

Tourism projects are often separated geographically from other industries because it is perceived that tourism and other industries are not compatible. This is now highly questionable, given the non-polluting, aesthetically pleasing physical appearance of the buildings of the 'new industries' such as information technology.

Also few synergies are explicitly encouraged between tourism and other; potentially complementary industries, again, such as information technology.

There is also an apparent assumption that tourism is either:

- Less attractive than other industries because of its poor reputation on pay and working conditions and its seasonality; and,

- More attractive than other industries because it creates lower levels of pollution than traditional industries.

However, successful, balanced urban communities cannot afford to become over-reliant on any one industry, even tourism. They need to have diversified economies which give appropriate weight to both tourism and other industries.

# Strategy implementation, performance indicators, and monitoring

While we are still better at writing strategies than implementing them, this situation appears to be improving. We are starting to understand that only realistic strategies can be implemented and that implementation requires good organisation, adequate funding, and the involvement of all stakeholders.

However, there is still a tendency for many urban regeneration agencies to see tourism as desirable and to take a rather uncritical view of its benefits.

There is a need to develop more measurable performance indicators and more sophisticated monitoring to ensure that tourism is contributing positively and cost-effectively towards urban regeneration. For example, in every town or city we need to know:

- How much it is costing to attract each tourist?

- How many disadvantaged local people are finding jobs in tourism project? and,

- How the area is performing in relation to other comparable towns or cities?

Regular monitoring needs to take place to see how the implementation of the strategy is progressing. Towns and cities must be prepared to abandon or modify strategies which are failing to achieve satisfactory outcomes, no matter how embarrassing they may be, politically.

We have now briefly considered eight key issues in the relationship between tourism and urban regeneration. Let us try to illustrate some of the points we have made by looking at one particular country, the UK.

# The case of the UK

Tourism has been used as a regeneration tool in the UK for over twenty years.

The UK has based its approach primarily on that used in the USA, but it has been modified for the UK market.

Sometimes the initiatives have been overtly political such as those in Liverpool after the Toxteth riots in 1981. However, in general one must accept that most attempts to use tourism as an urban regeneration tool have been genuine and sincere. Nevertheless, they have also been controversial and are open to criticism, as follows:

1.   Many local authorities have rather uncritically jumped on the bandwagon without understanding the implications, or having a clear idea of the feasibility, of their plans. Often inter-municipality rivalry appears to have driven their actions more than rational decision-making. Many towns have spent money they could not afford on trying - unsuccessfully and unrealistically - to establish themselves as tourist destinations;

2.   The government funded Development Commissions which spent hundreds of millions of pounds transforming the docklands in London and Liverpool, for example, were largely undemocratic and unaccountable to local people. This caused friction with local authorities and prevented the development of partnerships that could have been successful;

3.   Often a short term perspective has been taken. For example, tens of millions of pounds were spent on developing sites for 'Garden Festivals' in the 1980s in Liverpool, Ebbw Vale, Glasgow, Gateshead and Stoke-on-Trent. Sometimes, however, little thought was given to what would be done with these sites after the Garden Festivals were over; and,

4.   Some schemes that were successful in tourism terms appeared to bring few direct benefits for the most disadvantaged local residents. The Albert Dock complex attracts several million visitors a year and has given new life to a formerly

derelict set of very important historic buildings. However, the benefits for the poorest residents of the city are limited by the fact that:

- It is geographically isolated from the greatest areas of deprivation in Liverpool;

- Many of the businesses are run by people from the more affluent areas of Merseyside; and,

- Many of the jobs created have not gone to people from the most disadvantaged sectors of the local community.

Indeed, it could be argued that while the external image of the city has been improved by the Albert Dock, the project has simply led to the gentrification of the Albert Dock area, and indeed the whole South Docks area of the city. This is illustrated graphically by the Tate Gallery of the North. The closure of the Tate and Lyle Sugar Refinery in the area put hundreds of local people out of work, while the opening of the Tate Gallery created few new jobs, but put Liverpool on the map for the London intelligentsia;

5. Where ambitious tourism-based schemes have run into difficulties, there is a danger for the image and credibility of the city as a whole. Leeds, for instance, has been successful in regenerating itself through its growth as a financial centre in particular. However, it has also tried to establish itself as a tourist destination through an attraction-based strategy, led by the Royal Armouries Museum. While this museum offers a high quality experience, its failure to meet its targets for visitor numbers has raised doubts about the prospects of the strategy being fully implemented; and,

6. National Lottery and Millennium Commission funding has in recent years provided large grants for a number of visitor attraction projects that were part of urban regeneration strategies. These projects have tended to be large-scale, imaginative, and highly ambitious in their visitor numbers. It is only the availability of substantial sums of public money that has allowed them to be built. This raises the question of whether they are actually financially viable projects. Many of those opened to date have so far failed to reach their target visitor numbers. This then affects the perceived credibility of the regeneration strategies of the town or city as a whole, and adversely affects its overall image. Many of these projects are also not 'rooted' in the area. There is often little apparent logical reason for them to be in a particular place. This is at odds with the concept of sustainability and the idea of building on local strengths and culture.

Some projects funded under these schemes, while state-of-the-art in terms of technology, are often criticised for being rather cold, technocratic, and lacking in humanity.

They are also often criticised for their high entrance charges. While understandable in financial terms, these high prices tend to exclude the poorest sections of the community, the very people these projects are supposed to be designed to benefit.

Finally, questions have been raised about the opportunity cost of using National Lottery and Millennium Commission money in this way. Many people are asking if the money would not be better spent on reducing class sizes in schools, training schemes, or reducing waiting lists in hospitals. And, the amounts concerned, could achieve a lot if spent elsewhere. Six schemes in Birmingham, Cornwall, Glasgow, Hull, Newcastle, and Portsmouth alone have received around £200 million between them. It would only require a change in the rules to allow lottery funding to be used for education or health instead of visitor attraction projects.

Many UK towns and cities have succeeded in putting themselves on the tourism map, albeit modestly in some cases. Birmingham is now a major international destination for exhibitions and conventions. Hundreds of thousands of people visit places they would otherwise never have gone to because of the building of visitor attractions such as Wigan Pier, the Museum of Photography, Film and TV in Bradford, the National Fishing Heritage Centre in Grimsby, and the Castlefields Quarter in Manchester.

However, the problem has been converting the success of attracting visitors into improvements for the most disadvantaged sectors of the community in these plans.

If we are not careful, the risk is that we will create tourism ghettos in urban areas, oases of leisure and affluence, in deserts of decline and poverty. This form of 'apartheid' could lead, in the future, to resentment of the tourists and tensions between hosts and guests.

# The experience in the USA: Real success or just hype!

Many commentators agree that urban regeneration in general, and the role of tourism in particular, has been most effective in the USA. Certainly, the USA led the way with waterfront developments in cities like New York, San Francisco, Boston, and Baltimore. However, it is still easy to find areas of great poverty and deprivation very close to these developments. Nevertheless, the developments in the USA tend to have at least been commercially successful and taken less public funding than those in the UK. Perhaps, this reflects the different nature of policies and business cultures in the two countries, with the Americans traditionally being less in favour of direct public sector intervention than the British, and having a rather more entrepreneurial risk-taking private sector than the UK. In the end, however, it is still difficult to prove that regeneration through tourism has been any more successful in the USA than in the UK. On the other hand, many US cities do now seem to have a dynamism, for whatever reason, that is lacking in some UK cities.

# Success today but what about tomorrow?

Several cities are widely recognised as success stories in the use of tourism as an urban regeneration tool. Barcelona is one such example. A co-ordinated strategy has seen it become a dynamic, international city with a strong foothold in the European city break market. The city is benefiting from new sports facilities, museums, hotels, restaurants, a major waterfront development, and an impressive airport. While there is still poverty in the city it is a place which has been transformed, at least in part, by tourism. However, this success has brought problems for the city.

Crime has risen dramatically as have property prices and congestion. The growing role of tourism in the economy of the city makes it vulnerable to changes in the tourism market and the growth of competition from other cities such as Bilbao. Tourism and the tourism market are volatile phenomena which are constantly changing. Staying successful requires constant investment to keep ahead of competitors. By embarking on a tourism-led strategy cities are committing themselves to a long-term strategy with no guarantee of success.

# Towards a new approach to tourism and urban regeneration

This paper has been very critical of past and present attempts to use tourism as an urban regeneration tool. To some extent this has been a deliberate reaction to what the author sees as the often too unquestioning acceptance of the idea that tourism is a good thing and a valuable tool in urban regeneration.

However, it is the author's belief that tourism can contribute positively to urban regeneration, but only if it follows certain principles, some of which are outlined below.

1.  The citizens for whom urban regeneration strategies are devised must have a strong say in their development and implementation. There must also be clear lines of accountability between those who devise the strategies, those who pay for them, and those who enjoy or suffer the results of them.

2.  Economic regeneration cannot be divorced from environmental, and particularly social, regeneration. As well as the creation of an attractive, clean environment regeneration requires stable communities, a well trained and educated workforce, people with pride and high self-esteem, safe neighbourhoods, a healthy population, and a growing rather than a declining population. Tourism cannot create these social benefits but it cannot survive for long without them.

3.  Tourism is not a island, it does not exist in isolation. An holistic approach is needed to policy-making which recognises the links between tourism and other economic and social activities. Futuroscope in France is an interesting example of this philosophy where a theme park, a university, and a high tech industry park are neighbours. Industrial tourism, where tourists visit workplaces is another example of this idea.

4. Success means bringing tangible benefits to the most disadvantaged members of the local community. This does not just mean jobs but also other benefits. Tourist taxes could be used to improve local schools and hospitals and tourism organisations could sponsor community development projects. Furthermore, local residents should perhaps enjoy concessionary rates at visitor attractions in the area.

5. Attempts should be made to avoid the 'ghettoisation' of urban tourism. Tourists should be encouraged to leave the tourism oases, such as the waterfront developments, and visit other parts of the city. This would bring both income to these areas as well as raising awareness that there is more to the city than a museum, aquarium, and leisure shopping complex. It would also give the tourist a richer experience. In New York, for example, tours are already offered to the neighbourhoods of the Bronx, Brooklyn, and Harlem. However, we have to be careful that such trips should not be voyeuristic or based on stereotypes. Instead, we should give tourists the chance to meet local people, take part in everyday local events, and visit workplaces.

6. Instead of large-scale prestige projects perhaps we should focus instead upon small-scale projects, growing organically over time, under local managers wherever possible. These smaller projects would give opportunities for local people to develop and use their management skills. And if one of them were to fail, it would not have such great implications in terms of either financial resources or the reputation of the area.

7. There is a need to develop local networks that ensure that as far as possible, the needs of the urban tourism industry are met by local suppliers. This clearly maximises the income generated locally and support local enterprises but it also reduces the leakages of economic benefits from the local economy.

8. Constant objective monitoring is required to ensure that strategies are working satisfactorily. Hype and 'boosterism' must not be confused with reality and allowed to obscure what needs to be done.

9. Finally, there is a need for realism, a need by decision-makers to realise when tourism is not a viable option for a town or city. Some places, it has to be recognised, simply do not have the basic requirements to attract tourists. This could mean that the town or city is:

   • Intrinsically physically unattractive;

   • Lacking in infrastructure;

   • Not perceived as a safe or secure place; and,

   • Not easy to reach by road or rail.

Most of these problems can be overcome in time but usually at great cost and it may well be that the cost will outweigh the potential benefits.

Success also requires effective local government planning, entrepreneurial flair and funding which may or may not be present.

Finally, the urban tourism market is now very competitive. Most towns and cities that have the potential to be successful are already well known. Any town or city trying to enter the market at this relatively late stage will inevitably, therefore, face great competition.

## Tourism and regeneration: The next challenges

The debate around tourism as a regeneration tool has, to date, largely centred upon the issue of industrial and port towns and cities in Western Europe, North America, and Australia. However, in the future this situation may change in the following ways:

1.  An increasing emphasis on tourism and regeneration in the cities of Eastern Europe as they seek to move away from reliance on heavy industry. This has already been seen in cities like Budapest but there is still far more scope for it in countries such as Russia, Bulgaria, Romania and Poland; and,

2.  Changes in agriculture and downward pressure on farm incomes in Western Europe will lead to a growing role for tourism in the regeneration and diversification of rural economies. This is already being seen in countries like France.

In addition we may also see tourism being used to try to improve the quality of life and diversify the urban economy in newly industrialised countries such as South Korea and Taiwan. Here tourism would provide leisure opportunities for local people as well as bringing economic benefits.

The lessons learned from urban areas today may therefore have much wider applications in the future.

At the same time, however conversely the towns that have been built on tourism may themselves be in need of regeneration, notably the coastal resorts of Europe.

Many resorts dating from the 19th Century or the early days of package holiday tourism have been finding it increasingly difficult to compete with newer destinations in Europe and beyond.

In terms of regeneration such resorts have often had two options, namely:

(i)   Following the example of Benidorm which has invested in new attractions and environmental improvements to help it compete better in the modern tourism market;

(ii)  Attempting to reduce reliance on tourism and diversifying the economy by either attracting new industries or becoming commuter or retirement centres.

This choice is likely to face an increasing number of resorts in the years to come, as more and more destinations enter the market and the nature of tourism demand changes.

## Conclusions

This paper, in contrast to much public policy and some academic literature, has offered a highly critical view of the relationship between tourism and urban regeneration. Given the vast amount of public money spent on this link in recent years, the lack of critical evaluation in this field is both surprising and concerning.

The author believes that tourism can play a public role in urban regeneration but only if the issues identified in this paper are successfully resolved.

Otherwise, the danger is that today's tourism-based regeneration projects may become the problem areas of tomorrow. Or alternatively, these projects will become the new ghettos where the disadvantaged stand on the outside looking in on the affluent at play.

# References

Buckley, P. J. and Witt, S. F. (1989), 'Tourism in difficult areas'. *Tourism Management* June. pp. 138-152.

Department of the Environment (1990), *Tourism and the Inner City*. HMSO, London.

Department of the Environment (1990), *An Evaluation of Garden Restaurants*. HMSO, London.

Evans, G. (1996), The Millennium Festival and Urban Regeneration, in Robinson, M. Evans, N. and Callaghan, P. [eds]. *Managing Cultural Resources for the Tourist*. Business Education Publishers. Sunderland.

Hall, C. M. (1994), *Tourism and Politics: Policy, Power, and Place*. John Wiley and Sons. Chichester.

Harrison, L. C. and Husbands, W. (eds). (1996), Practising Responsible Tourism: International Case Studies in *Tourism Planning, Policy and Development*. John Wiley and Sons. New York.

Law, C. M. [ed]. (1996), *Tourism in Major Cities*. Information. Thomson Business Press. London.

Murphy, P. E. [ed]. (1997), *Quality Management in Urban Tourism*. John Wiley and Sons. Chichester.

Page, S. (1995), *Urban Tourism*. Routledge. London.

Swarbrooke, J. (1999), *Sustainable Tourism Management*. CAB International. Wallingford.

Van den Berg, L., Van den Berg, J. and Van der Meer, J. (1995), *Urban Tourism: Performance and Strategies in Eight European Cities*. Avebury. Aldershot.

# A framework for analysing urban tourism

*Duncan Tyler*

South Bank University, UK

## Abstract

The paper brings together a number of urban tourism concepts that so far have been either treated separately or in combination but not as a coherent whole. All, however, interlink to form a framework for analysing the reasons for the rise in urban tourism and the processes that underlie this rise. The concepts are taken from key authors in the field such as Ashworth and Voogd, (1990); Hannigan, (1998); Judd and Fainstein, (1999); Shaw and Jones (1997), Tyler et al, (1998); Tunbridge and Ashworth, (1996), and the urban governance literature of such authors as Valler, (1996) and Stewart and Stoker, (1995).

The framework proposes that the study of urban tourism takes as its central concept the changing form and function of the city. These changes can be seen in relation to four main concepts which form two axes. First, city administrators have had to market their cities in order to seek new inward investment, creating new attractive spaces within the city as part of the process. Taken together with the thesis of the Fantasy City this provides one axis for analysing these changes in form and function. The second axis relates the contestation of space between stakeholders which leads to capacity issues and debates over the nature of tourism development. This gives rise to the need to manage visitors in both historic towns and major cities. The changes in form and function, the relationship between space and management and city marketing and new tourism functions are all affected by their political, economic and social context. Hence issues such as civic leadership, urban policy, formation of partnerships, the enabling authority, changing urban economies and historical dynamics of cities all have a profound impact on how urban tourism is both developed and managed.

The framework is based on analysis of case studies of urban tourism development and management from around the world and can be applied to the development of tourism in cities.

## Introduction

There have been many proposed models to help explain the role of tourism in the modern city. These have included Ashworth and Tunbridge (1990) Tourist Historic City model which traces the changing focus of city function from historic core to more peripheral areas, Ashworth and Voogd, (1990) model on City Marketing, Law's model on regeneration (1992), Shaw, Jones and Ling, (1997) model of contested space in seaports, Pinder, et al, (1989) also on seaports, and Hannigan's, (1998) thesis of the Fantasy City.

All of these models help to explain the role that tourism can play in certain types of cities or in certain situations. Some, such as Law's model were important in their time but the nature of tourism's role in cities has moved on since its conception. Other more encompassing thesis, such as Hannigan's Fantasy City, take little account of the nature of tourism in the historic city, and being based on an analysis of American cities this is understandable, but when linked to other core concepts can help to explain changes in all manner of cities not just the American metropolis.

While writing the concluding chapter of their book (Tyler et al, 1998) Tyler and Guerrier proposed that urban tourism was about the political management of change. In fact, it was about making choices concerning the nature of the changes in city form and function in which tourism had adopted a central role in the late 20th century:

> *"changes may be desirable for some stakeholders and against the interests of others, so inevitably the change process becomes political (p229)."*

However, whilst discussing topics such as the 'aims of urban tourism', 'inclusion, resistance and exclusion', 'scale and pace of change', 'appropriateness of change', 'the politics of change', 'image' and social processes' this did not really amount to the framework which one was searching for.

Twice in the book they quoted Hughes, (1997) who called for researchers in urban tourism to develop 'something approaching a paradigm,' but were not in a position to do this at the time as key material such as Hannigan, (1998) and Judd and Fainstein, (1999) were still to be published.. This paper does not suggest that what is presented here even now provides the over-arching system of thinking that Hughes requests but does try to present a broad ranging framework into which the various models mentioned above an be fitted and used together to try to help explain the role that tourism has adopted in the modern or some may say post-modern city.

## An urban tourism framework

Figure 1 shows the proposed Urban Tourism Framework. This comprises three main elements. The core issue is the change in *City Form and Function* that tourism both helps bring about and is in turn affected by. The underlying concepts that can explain why these changes occur are to do with the contestation of space by urban and tourism stakeholders, the need to manage visitors, the requirement of post-industrial cities to sell themselves on the world inward investment market and the nature and effect of this inward investment by an evermore global entertainment industry. In turn, these concepts are given life by changes in urban governance, including managerial, political and organisational change, within urban areas in the past ten years. These include the rise of partnership arrangements, changes in economic base of many cities, the changing role of city government and the changing nature of urban policy and management regimes. Taken together these issues, concepts and contexts give us a framework for analysing urban tourism and trying to explain its dynamics and effects on all types of cities.

## Figure 1   A Framework for Analysing Urban Tourism

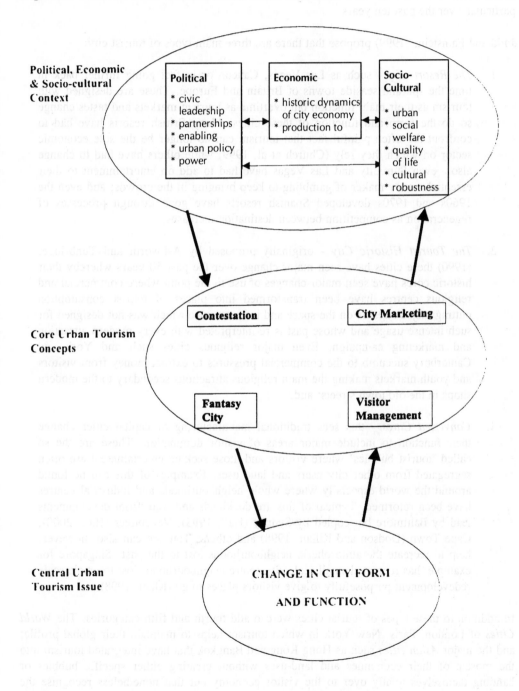

Political, Economic & Socio-cultural Context

**Political**
* civic leadership
* partnerships
* enabling
* urban policy
* power

**Economic**
* historic dynamics of city economy
* production to

**Socio-Cultural**
* urban
* social welfare
* quality of life
* cultural
* robustness

Core Urban Tourism Concepts

Contestation

City Marketing

Fantasy City

Visitor Management

Central Urban Tourism Issue

CHANGE IN CITY FORM AND FUNCTION

# The core issue

The framework tries to be as widely applicable as possible. It takes as its core issue the fact that the rise of tourism has lead to changes the form and function of cities over time, and in particular over the past ten years.

Judd and Fainstein, (1999) propose that there are three main types of tourist city:

1.  *The Resort City* - such as Las Vegas, Cancun or in fact going further back in time the spa and seaside towns of Britain and Europe. These are designed with tourism as their main function but overtime as tourism markets and tastes change so do the form and function of these cities. Many British resorts have had to confront the often painful fact that tourism can no longer be the sole economic sector on which they rely (Church et al, 1999) while others have had to change also - even Sun City and Las Vegas have had to add on entertainment to their essential money maker of gambling to keep bringing in the crowds; and even the 1960s and 1970s developed Spanish resorts have gone through processes of regeneration as competition between destination increases;

2.  *The Tourist Historic City* - originally proposed by Ashworth and Tunbridge, (1990) these cities have seen major change over the past 50 years whereby their historic cores have seen major changes of use to the point where commercial and religious centres have been transformed into places of tourist consumption putting major stresses on the space and infrastructure which was not designed for such intense usage and whose past is re-interpreted with every modern attraction and marketing campaign. Even major religious cities such and York and Canterbury succumb to the commercial pressures to extract money from visitors and youth markets making the main religious attractions secondary to the modern shops in the old town streets; and,

3.  *Converted Cities* - this sees traditional manufacturing or capital cities change their function to include major areas of visitor domination. These are the so called 'tourist bubbles' where visitors and those seeking entertainment are often segregated from other city users and land uses. Examples of this can be found around the world especially where whole neighbourhoods and industrial centres have been reformed. Typical of this are docklands and waterfront developments lead by Baltimore but copied by Sydney (Hall, 1998), Vancouver (Hall, 2000), Cape Town (Dodson and Kilian, 1998) and others. Tourism can also, however, help to recreate the atmospheric neighbourhoods lost to the past. Singapore for example, has recreated small scale city centre neighbourhoods lost to whole scale redevelopment purposefully to give visitors places to go (Khan, 1998).

In addition to these types of tourist cities we can add fourth and fifth categories. The *World Cities* of London, Paris, New York in which tourism helps to maintain their global profile; and the major *Asian cities* such as Hong Kong and Bangkok that have integrated tourism into the mosaic of their economies and land-uses without creating either specific bubbles or handing themselves totally over to the visitor economy but that nonetheless recognise the importance of this sector in maintaining their vitality.

Ashworth (1992) suggested for urban tourism be worth studying as a subject it must have some innate issues at its core. He suggests that this is something to do with the city shaping tourism and tourism in turn shaping the city, and it is worth adding here that this innate interest should be universal across all city types. It is this change in the form and function of the city that is at the centre of this reason to study the subject.

## Core concepts

Although the Core Issue for urban tourism is the 'Change in Form and Function' of the city, there must be some fundamental concepts that underlie and rationalise this change. The Framework, (Fig. 1) suggest that there are four such concepts. These are connected although there are two major axes, these being: the links between the contestation of space and the need for visitor management; and the need to sell the city to inward investors and the thesis of the Fantasy City where pleasure and entertainment become the focus of that investment and city centre activity. Although not exclusive these axes help to explain the two main, often counter-posing, thrusts, namely, the conservation of socio-cultural resources, and the need to maintain the city's diversity and vitality through inward investment. In discussing these axes links will be drawn between the two.

## Contestation of space and visitor management

Contestation is, at its most simple, the clash of views of how space in the city should be used and developed. The identification of space and the relationship of people to it is a socially constructed one, so no two groups of interests share exactly the view of how space could be used, especially when this requires or includes changes in economic usage and the physical shape and land use of city areas (Shaw, Jones and Ling, 1997). Tunbridge (1997) sees the contest based in power struggles largely in terms of the social construction of identity and heritage with complex 'tensions between overall modernisers, tourism provision and sustainable heritage conservation' (Pxvii). The example given by Dodson and Kilian (1998) and Worden (1997) of the struggle over Cape Town's Waterfront development demonstrate this most clearly bringing race, class and social exclusion issues to the fore. In addition, contests may be much more simple such as those of residents feeling crowded out of their own cities by visitors and the infrastructure and facilities put in place for them (Glasson et al, 1995; van der Borg, 1998; Evans, 1998; Olds 1998). Such contests can take many forms including demonstrations, lobbying, the use of the planning participation machinery and occasionally direct action.

It is not to say all urban tourism involves some form of contestation. Cities whose socio-cultural environment is robust may be able to absorb changes brought about by tourism that other more sensitive ones may find difficult to accept, Hughes (1998) gives the example of the strength of the socio-cultural environment of Amsterdam as being one reason why it has become a centre for 'gay' tourism. However, contestation is often a dynamic that is overlooked in the heritage literature and tourism planning literature, possibly because of its political nature being difficult to decipher and research (Hall, 1994).

The corollary of the contestation is to take positive action in order to address the issues that arise. This can be seen in terms of visitor management. This term is used to suggest an ongoing planning process that includes planning before development, taking into account the views of various stakeholders, but also post development management of visitors within the town in order to manage their activities in such a way that does not compromise the interest of other stakeholders. As such visitor management seeks to find an accepted level and type of tourist activity the balances the needs of residents, industry and the environment (ETB Task Force, 1991).

Certain interest groups as such the Historic Towns Forum have been successful in promoting the concept of visitor management, but it is also a concept that is valid in all cities. For instance, the Government Office for London, three London boroughs, and the South Bank Employers Group have co-operated in trying to find a solution through visitor management techniques in getting visitors to explore south of the River Thames away from the congested and noisy Covent Garden area where residents are in conflict with the all-night nature of the new 'cafe-society' that sprang up in the mid late 1990s. Techniques have included creating new attractions and destinations on the south bank, investing in a tourist bus that links to city centre with the new destination, the provision of information, and environmental improvements. In some case more radical steps may be explored, such as Venice's pre-payment scheme whereby visitors are rewarded with discounts and guaranteed entry if they pre-book attractions and restaurant tickets before their departure from home (van der Borg 1998). Such is the growing awareness of the need for visitor management in cities now that such ideas as these, seen as radical not so long ago, are now being discussed in other cities around the world, including London (DCMS, 1999).

However, such contests, and the management techniques applied to overcome them, do not occur in isolation from other main urban tourism concepts. Contestation usually occurs because one stakeholder seeks to change the *status quo*. This change is often driven by Tunbridge's 'modernisers'. Contests can arise between the modernisers, often developers and local politicians, and resident and conservation groups. The latter often either seek to maintain the status quo, or they may be unfavourably disposed to plans to market the city to tourists, whilst the former try to overcome changes in the urban economies that have seen the loss of the manufacturing sector by promoting inward investment in the services industries. Contests particularly arise when the 'modernisation' process is imposed upon a community (Hall, 1994, 1998). This leads to the discussion of the second main conceptual axes of City Marketing and the Fantasy City.

## City marketing and the fantasy city

Ashworth and Voogd's (1990) model sees city marketing as a reaction to economic change - a method of promoting inward investment by marketing, undertaking physical change and image recreation. A major element of this process was to demonstrate to potential investors that your city was a good place to locate because of both business and lifestyle advantages. In creating the image to attract investors often city centres and waterfronts were changed out of all recognition and in some cases local communities were socially and economically excluded from the newly created tourist bubbles (Judd, 1999). City marketing, however, was essentially a boosterist approach to redevelopment (Hall, 2000) believing that all investment was good investment as it created jobs and, therefore, wealth. However, as city marketing became an evermore competitive process it evolved into a more complex movement incorporating public/private partnerships, embracing the consumer driven middle classes and youth markets of city regions and creating not just tourist bubbles but entertainment and cultural quarters in existing city spaces that appealed to those willing or able to spend money on leisure activities, but excluded those who could not. These quarters, therefore, although contributing to the 'saleability' of a city to new investors, often bore little relation to the needs of the poorer elements and geographic areas of cities (e.g. need for low cost housing, better education and training, social welfare support). City marketing had moved on to 'selling the city to the city itself and its region', but only to those who could afford it. City marketing, therefore, links directly into the contestation of space.

Hannigan (1998) in his thesis on the evolution of pleasure and leisure in the American City throughout the 20th Century, links this process directly to the insecurity of the middle classes and the need for the public /private sectors to exploit this section of society in order to remodel city economies. He believes that the Fantasy City provides the safe place in which the middle classes can enjoy their spare time. The city becomes characterised by corporate investment and sponsorship, international brands, predictable themed restaurants and bars, a limited menu of proven attractions (modern arts galleries, IMAX cinemas, aquaria and waterfront developments) and also the privatisation of public space where corporate bodies can guarantee the safety of the middle classes. Everything becomes up for grabs by corporates. Education becomes Edutainment (witness changes to great institutions such as London Zoo, The Natural History Museum and new attractions such the Earth Centre), Shopping becomes Shopertainment, no longer is it enough to buy the goods you need and go home but your stay must be extended, your wallet emptied on peripheral activities, you must be tempted to return to the theatre or cinema in the mall or indeed shop for your entertainment in the Disney and Warner Bros. stores. Eating is transformed from a necessity or a gastronomic experience into a consumer experience, Eatertainment, where the entertainment via theming or sports channels or MTV on multiple screens make food a secondary element of the restaurant.

The Fantasy City appears to be a logical extension of city marketing. Initially attractive but baring up poorly to examination in the face of ideas of contesting space, and indeed not managing visitors but managing out certain unprofitable markets. These sentiments are echoed by Hall (1998) when quoting Huxley's (1991) analysis of the Darling Harbour tourist bubble in Sydney:

> *"The whole concept of the city as 'fun' is redolent with the post-modernist approach to playful spectacle, display and ironical references to other eras. It is the essence of the 'yuppy' lifestyle and yet our cities contain increasing numbers of unemployed, homeless, disadvantaged people: urban infrastructure is inadequate or non-existent at the fringe and outdated and overloaded at the centre. What sort of 'fun' can Merlin [the developer/managers] bring to the city?"*

So whose Fantasy is it? It may be 'fantasy' for the middle classes who can for a short period jump out of their normality into the world of global leisure brands and corporate promises, or, it may be 'fantasy' for the excluded - fantasy in that it can never be experienced only imagined!

However, if the Fantasy City is a logical progression of the city marketing movement has it been inevitable? For this it is necessary to look beyond the physical changes taken place in the city and look at the political and economic environments that have driven the change.

## The political, economic and social context of urban tourism

The development of the late 20th century city has been shaped by the way that cities have been governed and the *changes in city economies from places of production to places of consumption*. This has not been an inevitable process but partly the consequence of the way in which *urban policy* has developed. That is, the decisions taken by politicians in the way that cities should be funded, the structures used to guide their development (e.g. urban development corporations and Single Regeneration Budgets programmes), the knock on effects of central government partisan policies, the limited range of proposals forwarded by development partners and the balance of power between the partners. It is the combination of these factors that Tyler and Guerrier (1998) called the political management of change.

In concluding his paper on Darling Harbour Hall (1998) cites Harvey's (1990) comments on the redeveloped Baltimore Harbour:

> *"The present carnival mask of the Inner Harbour redevelopment conceals the long history of struggle over this space..... The inner city space became a space of conspicuous consumption, celebrating commodities rather than civic values."*

This quote highlights one of the major changes in urban governance over the last 15 years. The old managerialism that characterised public sector urban management has given way to what Stewart and Stoker (1994) describes as the new *'urban entrepreneurialism.'* No longer was civic pride the basis of managing our cities, rather it is about finding new structures to attract private sector entrepreneurs. As public sector resources were squeezed from the 1970s onwards so they lost the capacity and skills to undertake major projects. *Partnership* with the public sector, so favoured by the New Right in the 1980s, was inevitable (Williams, 1995).

Often these changes have been facilitated by central government ideologies. Believing that the public sector had not the skill or culture to take on major redevelopment projects they encouraged, through funding criteria, public / private sector partnerships to be established whereby the public sector became *enabling* rather than executive, providing only the planning and strategic management role and the private sector the vision and the money. Hannigan (1998; 129) characterises these partnerships as being complex:

> *"Of all the alliances to be found in the process of building the Fantasy City [others concerning the packaging of land and financial arrangements], these public private partnerships are the most sensitive and complex. While both parties broadly support a growth orientated strategy, specific goals may differ sharply. Elected officials and public agencies tend to see UEDs [Urban Entertainment Districts] as the most recent brand of magic elixir, providing jobs, tax revenues and perhaps more importantly, a new dynamic image for the community. Cities today cannot rest on their laurels ............ urban managers must find ways to make them safe and secure and to attract tourist dollars."*

> *"Private partners from the entertainment and real estate development industries*
> *share this affinity for safety and security and tourist dollars but their bottom line*
> *is somewhat different. ...............Most of the principal players in UED projects*
> *are more concerned with questions of practicality and profit.... They must*
> *balance what the city wants with what their investors and tenants need in order*
> *to create a financially successful development. "*

Who wins when striking the balance is often a major determinant of what the city finally looks like and of what elements it comprises. Although UEDs in the American form have not really taken hold as such in Europe yet, the principles of partnership arrangements are the same. Although publicly subsidised 'anchor attractions' are still the norm in the UK (The Armadillo in Glasgow, Tate Gallery Extension in London, Royal Armouries Leeds) such projects may not be so prominent in the future as government departments are now questioning the wisdom of projects that need long term public revenue funding - or 'lame duck projects' a two government officials recently described them to me.

We may well see the balance tilt in favour of the private sector partners The implications of this are more middle-class orientated, commercially driven city UEDs rather than cultural quarters.

*Civic leadership* is also important. The strategic vision given by the public sector, the ability to facilitate development and to raise public and governmental support cannot be underestimated as success factors. This is clearly shown by Tyler's (1998) case study of the London Borough of Southwark's attempts to develop a new cultural district in the centre on London. Ashworth and Voogd (1990: 141) also see

> *'leadership producing clearly defined and widely publicly accepted goals.... as a*
> *necessary pre-condition for shaping a collective consciousness and then*
> *projecting it as a positive incentive for new development initiatives whether*
> *financed privately or publicly.'*

Hannigan (1998) and Hall and Jenkins (1995) consider such partnerships to reflect *'new'* *civic values* of the local élites which influence urban redevelopment and planning processes. If the elite values of leaders, developers, investors and urban managers do dominate then contestations of space will become more common place not just during planning processes but also after UEDs, or tourist bubbles, are operational.

# Conclusion

Urban tourism could, by understanding and managing its dynamics contribute to the ongoing development of the city, rather than bring stochastic change which ignores the historical dynamics and context of the city. If it is to help to improve the quality of life of all stakeholders in the city then it should also avoid the problems of being 'solipsistic.' That is it should not ignore the social and welfare issues of the inner city, in the race to create safe middle class entertainment and cultural districts. Given this urban tourism development and management needs to create a new sense of social inclusion that incorporates *all* stakeholders interests into both the partnerships arrangements and the physical structures of the new quarters. Lets hope that the rumours that the London Borough of Southwark's politicians are considering knocking down social housing immediately behind the new Tate Gallery Extension and selling the land off to private developers are not true. If they are true then the strategic vision of a previous council leader who wished to develop the north of the borough to the benefit of its residents and the residents of the poor mid borough will be undone and we shall be on our way to another safe, secure, sanitised cultural quarter which does not address the social welfare problems of the city.

After all urban tourism is the means of overcoming economic and social problems, not the end itself. As Mommaas and van der Poel (1989) observed 'local policy has increasingly sought to stimulate the mixture of economic enterprise, culture and leisure, attempting in this manner to attract the new economic élite to the city', but as Hall (1998) warns 'in focusing on one set of economic and social interests other community interests, particularly those of traditional inner-city residents of lower socio-economic status, are increasingly neglected.'

If a framework such as that given here can help to analyse the dynamics of urban tourism then maybe policy makers can avoid some of the worst excesses of solipsistic stochastic development and we can celebrate the 'ends' of urban tourism development rather than the 'means'.

# References

Ashworth, G. (1992), Is There An Urban Tourism? *Tourism Recreation Research* Vol 1 7 (2) 3 – 8.

Ashworth, G. J. and Tunbridge, J. E. (1990), *The Tourist-Historic City*. London. Belhaven.

Ashworth, G.J. and Voogd, H. (1990) *Selling The City*. London. Belhaven.

Church, A., Ball, C., Bull, R. and Tyler, D. (1999), Tourism's Engagement With Public Policy. Paper presented to the *Royal Geographical Society / Institue of British geographers Limited Life Working Party on Tourism*. Exeter.

Department for Culture Media and Sport (1999), *Tomorrow's Tourism: a growth industry for the new millennium*. London. DCMS.

Dodson, B. and Kilian, D. (1998), From Port to Playground: the redevelopment of the Victoria and Alfred Waterfront, Cape Town. In Tyler, D., Guerrier, Y and Robertson, M. (eds) *Managing Tourism in Cities: policy, process and practice*. Chichester. John Wiley and Sons. 139 – 162.

English Tourist Board Task Force (1991), *Tourism and the Environment. maintaining the balance*. London. ETB.

Evans, K. (1998), Competition For Heritage Space: Cairo's resident / tourist conflict. In Tyler, D., Guerrier, Y. and Robertson, M. (eds)) *Managing Tourism in Cities: policy, process and practice*. Chichester. John Wiley and Sons. 163 – 179.

Glasson, J., Godfrey, K., Goodey, B., Absalom, H. and van der Borg, J. (1995), *Towards Visitor Management: visitor impacts, carrying capacity and management responses in Europe's historic towns and cities*. Aldershot. Avebury.

Hall, C. M. (1994), *Tourism Politics: policy, power and place*. Chichester. John Wiley and Sons.

Hall, C. M. (1998), The Politics of Decision Making and Top Down Planning: Darling Harbour, Sydney. In Tyler, D., Guerrier, Y and Robertson, M. (eds) *Managing Tourism in Cities: policy, process and practice*. Chichester. John Wiley and Sons. 9 – 24.

Hall, C. M. (2000), *Tourism Planning: policy, process and relationships*. London. Prentice Hall.

Hall, C. M. and Jenkins, J. (1995), *Tourism And Public Policy*. London. Routledge.

Hannigan, J. (1998), *Fantasy City: Pleasure and profit in the postmodern metropolis*. London. Routledge.

Hughes, H. (1997), Book Review: Tourism in Major Cities, Law. C. (Ed) *Journal of Vacation Marketing*. 3,2,180.

Harvey, D. (1990), Between Space and Time: reflections on the geographical imagination. *Annals of the American Geographers* 80, 418 – 434.

Hughes, H. (1998), Sexuality, Tourism and Space: the case of gay visitors to Amsterdam. In Tyler, D., Guerrier, Y and Robertson, M. (eds) *Managing Tourism in Cities: policy, process and practice*. Chichester. John Wiley and Sons.

Huxley, M.(1991), Making Cities Fun: darling Harbour and the Immobilisation of the Spectacle In Carroll, P., Donohue, K,. McGovern, M, and McMillen, J. (eds) *Tourism in Australia*. Sydney. Harcourt Brace Jovanovich, 141 –152.

Judd, D. R. and Fainstein, S. S. (eds) (1999), *The Tourist City*. New Haven. Yale University Press.

Khan, H. (1998), the Tourism explosion: policy decisions for Singapore. in Tyler, D., Guerrier, Y and Robertson, M. (eds) *Managing Tourism in Cities: policy, process and practice*. Chichester. John Wiley and Sons.

Law, C. (1992), Urban Tourism and Its Contribution to Economic Regeneration. *Urban Studies* 29, 3/4 599 – 618.

Mommaas, H. and van der Poel, H. (1989), Changes in Economy, Politics and Lifestyles: an essay on the restructuring of urban leisure. In Bramham, P., Henry, I., Mommaas, P. And van der Poel, H. (Eds) *Leisure and Urban Processes critical studies of leisure policy in western European Cities*. London Routledge. 254 – 276.

Olds, K. (1998), Urban Mega Events, Evictions and Housing Rights: the Canadian Case. *Current Issues in Tourism*. 1,1, 2 – 46.

Pinder, D., Hoyle, B. and Husain, S. (1988), Retreat, redundancy and revitalisation: forces, trends and a research agenda, in Hoyle, B. S., Pinder, D. A. and Husain, M. S. (eds.), *Revitalising the Waterfront: International Dimensions of Dockland Redevelopment*, Belhaven, London.

Shaw. B. J., Jones, R. and Ling O. G. (1997), Urban Heritage, Development and Tourism in Southeast Asian Cities: a contestation continuum. In Shaw. B.J. and Jones, R. (eds) (1997) *Contested Urban Heritage: Voices from the Periphery*. Aldershot. Ashgate pp169 – 196.

Shaw. B. J. and Jones, R. (Eds) (1997), *Contested Urban Heritage: Voices from the Periphery*. Aldershot. Ashgate.

Stewart, J. and Stoker, G. (eds) (1995), *Local Government in The 1990s*. Basingstoke. MacMillan.

Tunbridge, J. (1997), Foreward in Shaw. B.J. and Jones, R. (eds) *Contested Urban Heritage: Voices from the Periphery*. Aldershot. Ashgate.

Tyler, D. and Guerrier, Y. (1998), Conclusion: Urban Tourism - the politics and processes of change. In Tyler, D., Guerrier, Y and Robertson, M. (eds) *Managing Tourism in Cities: policy, process and practice*. Chichester. John Wiley and Sons 229 – 238.

Tyler, D., Guerrier, Y. and Robertson, M. (eds) (1998), *Managing Tourism in Cities: policy, process and practice*. Chichester. John Wiley and Sons.

Valler, D. (1996), 'Strategic' Enabling? Cardiff City Council And Local Economic Strategy. *Environment And Planning A* Vol 28 pp 835 –855.

van der Borg, J. (1998), Tourism Management in Venice, Oe How To Deal With Success. In Tyler, D., Guerrier, Y and Robertson, M. (eds)) *Managing Tourism in Cities: policy, process and practice*. Chichester. John Wiley and Sons 125 – 136.

Williams, G. (1995), Local Governance And Urban Prospect: The Potential Of City Pride. *Local Economy* Vol 10 No 2 100 – 107.

Worden, N. (1997), Contesting Heritage in a South African City: Cape Town. In Shaw. B.J. and Jones, R. (Eds) *Contested Urban Heritage: Voices from the Periphery*. Aldershot. Ashgate.

# City tourism - managing place images and creating place brands: The role of mainstream marketing and public relations techniques

*Marit Weber and Julia Tyrrell*

Coventry University, UK

## Introduction

It is now accepted that cities and towns, no matter how industrialised and grimy, are tourism commodities. From Bradford to Barcelona, an uneasy mix of public and private finance is applied to the creation of cities as tourism products. From early beginnings as Economic Development Departments the institutions created to sell the city have become increasingly business-like in their approach, a change in emphasis which is reflected in the introduction of management and marketing terminology. As Stephen Ward[1] points out, in this 'post-Thatcherite, post-Reaganite and post-Communist world...all have begun to show a real awareness of the importance of projecting positive place images and the need to work within a market framework.' Hence the idea of marketing has been embraced by the cities but have the marketers embraced the cities: academic and practicing? An analysis of the literature would certainly indicate that whilst geographers, planners and the newer disciples of Tourism studies are engaged in the debate, marketers remain aloof. Why should this be so? We might argue that the marketing principles are the same, whatever type of product or organisation is involved. Or, do places show such diversity that they cannot be considered as a whole, and are therefore difficult to market, and even more difficult to brand?

So, do the traditional skills of marketing of manufactured brands apply here? Or, is a public relations focus on multiple stakeholders more appropriate? Is a skilled PR operator better than a brand manager at developing an identity for a place, which will differentiate it from other 'brands', will encourage economic development and local pride, will remain faithful to historical roots, as well as satisfying the needs of stakeholders? Hence the growing number of public relations practitioners working in public sector, promotional roles.

Is it possible to develop one clear brand for a town or a city, or is corporate branding more relevant here? Towns and cities offer a 'complex array of features and facilities' (Page[2]), and trying to pull these features together into one corporate identity is made even harder by the nature of a public brand's ownership, and the task of trying to incorporate the demands of different stakeholders.

Places are marketed on different levels and are interconnected. Hence a region may be marketed as many individual attractions and businesses, as town shopping centres, as an area for inward investment, as a tourist destination or as a good place to live. At each level there is a different product with a different image and 'identity', probably a different target market, and a public or private organisation responsible for marketing it.

More problematic, perhaps, is the role of the marketing practitioner in the whole process of the strategic planning and marketing of places. Like other sectors embracing the marketing concept for the first time, those responsible for places still tend to think that strategic decisions are too important for marketers to contribute to.

Drawing on some initial small-scale research in the UK, this exploratory paper will look at the types of marketing practices which are being applied to the marketing of towns and cities and to what effect. What are the characteristics of place marketing, and what implications do these have for those responsible for the marketing of places? To what extent is marketing being carried out by qualified marketing staff, and/or external PR and advertising agencies?

# Research objectives

Our overall interest is in finding out whether marketing, as practised in the commercial world, is happening in those organisations responsible for marketing towns and cities (initially Town Centre Management schemes). Or is the focus on promotion and/or public relations only?

In many cases, such organisations with a broad responsibility for marketing are Town Centre Management (TCM) organisations. We acknowledge that marketing is not their primary role, as the following definition from Guy[3] illustrates. Town Centre Management is 'the process of planning and taking action to improve the vitality and viability of a town or city centre as a whole, involving inputs from both public and private sectors.' For the purposes of this research, they are the most relevant organisations to contact.

The first stage of our research is to investigate the role and status of marketing in Town Centre Management (TCM) organisations in the UK.

- To investigate the extent to which marketing is being practiced in TCM organisations.

- To find out the extent of marketing experience amongst TCM staff.

Follow-up research will be required to look at whether the creation of place brands is an important issue amongst TCMs.

# Theoretical framework

Whilst the idea of selling places was first written about from the 1970's[4], place marketing first received attention in the late 1980's, where places began to be considered as products and a place's users its customers. In marketing terms, the customer purchases a core product, often a tangible product; however, the place product is often many different products, which are usually intangible. It was from this time that Ashworth and Voogd[5] began their work on the development of place marketing as an area of study.

Place marketing is now beginning to receive a bit more attention from researchers. Stephen Ward[6] writing specifically about Selling Places, states that 'there has, until recently, been little work on place advertising and those aspects of place selling where the language has been overtly that of the market. We can see some signs of change, at least in the willingness of public policy researchers to explore such topics.'

Ashworth and Voogd[7] claim that it is difficult to define places as simple products; the place 'product' has an inherent dualism - consisting of the place as a holistic entity, and of the specific services, attributes and facilities that occur within the place', and they advise marketers to be well aware of 'the parallel existence of both meanings, and the practical results that stem from this'.

This complexity is also alluded to by Warnaby and Davies[8] who point out that the main indicators of success or failure of a city are the perceptions of consumers. If this is the case, they state that ' there may well be as many place products as there are perceptions.' For example, just as one person can have a positive image of a city because of its retail mix, another can have a negative opinion of the same place because of its appearance. Thus, it can appear that there are a multitude of products encompassed in the place product. It may be that there is 'a unique product for each and every consumer.'

Ward and Gold suggest that in recent years place promotion has centred around the introduction of new themes which have tended to become familiar and overworked as in the case of the use of retail centres as a draw. Ward states that in re-promoting cities often use an industrial product or landmark to act as a new focal point in their new developments, 'physical relics of the past into sanitised and hyper-real present'. An old industrial item will become the focus for a new leisure project. Cities and towns also adopt the overall strategy of trying to highlight their accumulated heritage and compete for heritage and cultural titles like 'European City of Culture' and 'City of Sport'. Linked to this has been the increased competition to attract prestigious events from the Olympics down.

Marketing is a methodology designed to facilitate the exchange process in ways which are material and demonstrable. The extension of marketing techniques to intangible services has required a certain amount of paradigmatic adjustment, services need to be defined mapped and made tangible in many cases to help marketers control the exchange and monitor its success. With places the amorphous nature of the product combined with the indefinability of success has yet to be conquered. Yet 'the marketing approach offers the nearest thing to a practical expertise for those undertaking place promotion' Gold and Ward (1994).

A danger of the marketing approach is the distilling of the product offering to package it for external consumption. Place, where we live or were born, is a concept which is related to our identities. Simplification can look like stereotyping, a process which is enthusiastically taken up or lampooned by the media (take for example the dubbing of Torquay as the 'English Riviera')

There is a certain amount of literature on the development of place images and, overall, this is probably the best understood of the marketing areas among city/town marketers. Hedley Smyth in his book 'Marketing the City' describes the impulse to 'civic boosterism' which leads local authorities to adopt advertising and PR techniques in order to generate local confidence and thereby generally improve the perception of the city. This model emphasises the importance of self-image in the attraction of visitors to a place and can be observed in Coventry amongst other places. The simultaneous policies of shaping conditions within the city to encourage new product development and seeking out new markets for the city product is directed at attaining a virtuous cycle of material and image improvements.

In the case of many cities and towns the role of co-ordination of the different roles and products has been given over to Town Centre Management organisations funded through a mixture of public and private funds. The position of TCMs is an evolving one and its multiple facets have proved difficult to grasp. First we have the tensions and contradictions of the public and private stakeholders providing funds. Then there is the interplay of other stakeholders: residents, tourists and the commercial sector. Finally, there are the multiple of the functions of TCMs with the need to consider the marketing and branding of the centre along with the everyday policing of public nuisance, vandalism and crime in the public spaces.

As mentioned earlier, maybe the different agencies involved in selling cities are adding to the confusion. At any one time a city can market and sell itself in many different ways. For example, the city of Coventry currently attempts to portray itself simultaneously as:

- An important historic city - 'The city in Shakespeare Country'

- An important sporting venue

- An excellent place to invest in and relocate to

- The home of the motor industry

This is one example that illustrates the complex and multi-dimensional nature of the place product.

So, are the traditional skills of a brand manager, of trying to create a clear identity for his brand in a competitive market place, relevant here? Is the place brand too complex to mould into one brand identity? Or, if there are too many individual brands, can one overall corporate brand be developed for a place?

Stephen Ward[9] also notes that 'places are...complex packages of goods, services and experiences that are consumed in many different ways'. He states that this is not a problem in itself, but, 'it raises operational difficulties because it means that marketing's usual clear goal of sales maximisation can easily be obscured. With many place activities, the pattern of 'purchase' and consumption is much more problematic and capable only of indirect measurement.'

Another issue here is whether sales maximisation is the only goal to which marketers aspire. Obviously, sound marketing practice starts with a full audit of your market place, followed by the setting of marketing objectives. Such objectives do not necessarily have to be couched in financial or sales terms, as Kotler et al.[10] would recognise. Not-for-Profit marketing supports non-financial indicators such as perceptual indicators - that is, increasing the positive perceptions or opinions about a place.

Nevertheless, Ward[11] recognises that these types of issues present considerable problems for place marketing, not least in how such perceptions can be measured - i.e. that they are only capable of indirect measurement, via consumer research.

# Methodology

A small, convenient sample of Town Centre Managers was compiled from attendees of a retail management conference which we attended last year. A total of 13 TCMs were contacted by postal questionnaire. The questionnaire contained a total of 11 closed and open-ended questions. The response rate was excellent at 92%, but obviously we realise that some of our findings are based on a very small number of replies.

## Findings

The majority of TCMs were involved in the management and marketing of towns; 8% said they were involved in city centre management. The majority claimed that any marketing was carried out by themselves; however, 75% also said that marketing was carried out in other departments, such as the Borough or Town Council's PR department, the Leisure Services department, or Tourism department.

In answer to the question, 'What are the main responsibilities of the marketing person?' which in most cases was the incumbent TCM, the replies were interesting. The majority (41%) saw promotion of the town centre (as a shopping destination) as their main responsibility. The next most important responsibility was 'events' organisation (29%), followed by marketing of the town as a regional destination (12% of replies). The remaining areas of responsibility included attracting inward investment, town centre management (!) and public relations.

Respondents were then asked for their comments on the general objectives of their organisation. There was quite a broad spread of replies, but two main objectives seemed to stand out, which were to attract more visitors (31% of replies) and to encourage more inward investment (27% of replies).

For the next question we were interested in finding out the identities of the main stakeholders, with whom TCMs had to communicate. Many stakeholders were mentioned, but broadly speaking, the local authority/council (30% of replies), and retailers/traders (30% also) were perceived as the main ones. Others included community/voluntary groups (12% of replies), property owners/developers (8%), residents (8%) and local businesses (2%).

The next question related to particular challenges facing the organisation, replies to which were bound to be specific to each town, however the replies seemed to fall into four main areas. They were re-development of town centre, the challenge of out-of-town developments, lack of funds and lastly, lack of credibility of the TCM organisations.

We were also interested to know whether the TCMs had any previous marketing experience. 75% of respondents said that they had previous experience, whilst 25% said no. Of those with previous experience, 55% said that it had been gained in commercial organisations, and 45% had gained experience in local authorities. Significantly, the majority did not possess any formal marketing qualifications, although two respondents were currently studying for the Chartered Institute of Marketing certificate.

Lastly, we wanted to find out how many TCMs relied on the services of external marketing agencies. Just over half of TCMs claimed to use an agency, with 43% of them using an local advertising agency, 29% using a PR agency, 14% using marketing services consultants, and 14% using graphic designers.

## Discussion and conclusions

So, do the traditional skills of a brand manager of a manufactured product apply in place marketing? The evidence from our research would show that it is still patchy. Instead of having clear marketing objectives, e.g. tangible targets to aim for, the emphasis is still vague, and tends to be towards promotion. The locus of marketing effort remains vague for the most part and it is easy to see how the divergent aims and operations of the various authorities involved could result in confusion and/or duplication.

Further research is needed to probe in more detail the exact nature of any objectives that have been set, and whether having perceptual indicators is viable.

However there were some encouraging signs in the area of product definition. Two TCMs are grappling with such fundamentals of marketing - i.e. one said that there is a 'need for all stakeholders to agree what the 'product' is', whilst another stated that they were trying to establish the nature of the brand. The place 'product' is complex; in most cases, several sub-brands exist within a town or city. There is a product for the residents, a product for visitors and tourists and a product for businesses to invest in.

This lack of agreement about the nature of the product is probably made even worse by the power of the various stakeholders, each with their own agenda.

The promotional aspects of marketing appear to be strong. The advertising and promotional campaigns used by towns and cities are becoming 'increasingly professional' (S. Ward[12]). The use of external agencies as indicated in our own research, is quite widespread. However, there still exists a confusion of messages emanating from one town, so consensus is still required on product definition and producing one corporate brand, to avoid such confusion.

Our research demonstrates that there is a lot of agreement on who the main stakeholders are in this area. With so many stakeholders, maybe the decision-making process is longer and may account for difficulties in getting things done? This needs to be verified in further research.

The next stage, therefore, is likely to be structured interviews with TCMs to check out our findings in more detail, and to find out whether it is possible to produce one brand and one corporate identity for a town or city.

# Endnotes

1.  Ward, S. (1998), 'Selling Places. The Marketing and Promotion of Towns and Cities 1850-2000', Routledge.

2.  Page, S. (1997), *Urban Tourism* Routledge.

3.  Guy, C. (1994), *The Retail Development Process* Routledge.

4.  Burgess, J. (1982), 'Selling Places: environmental images for the executive' Regional Studies, 16(1), 1-17.

5.  Ashworth G. and Voogd (1990), *Selling the City: Marketing Approaches in Public Sector Urban Planning*, Belhaven Press.

6.  Ibid.

7.  Ibid.

8.  Warnaby, G. and Davies, B. J.(1997), 'Cities as Service Factories? Using the Servuction System for Marketing Cities as Shopping Destinations' International Journal of Retail and Distribution Management.

9.  Ibid.

10. Kotler, P. Haider, D. H. and Rein I. (1993), Marketing Places: Attracting Investment, Industry and Tourism to Cities, States and Nations New York Free Press.

11. Ward, S. (1998), 'Selling Places. The Marketing and Promotion of Towns and Cities 1850-2000', Routledge.

12. Ward, S. (1998), 'Selling Places. The Marketing and Promotion of Towns and Cities 1850-2000', Routledge.

# References

Ashworth G. and Voogd (1990), *Selling the City: Marketing Approaches in Public Sector Urban Planning*, Belhaven Press.

Ashworth, G. and Goodall, B. (eds) (1990), *Marketing Tourism Places* Routledge.

Burgess, J. (1982), 'Selling Places: environmental images for the executive'. *Regional Studies*, 16(1): 1-17.

Guy, C. (1994), *The Retail Development Process* Routledge.

Holderness, G. (1988), *The Shakespeare Myth* MUP.

Kotler, P. Haider, D. J. and Rein, I. (1993), *Marketing Places: Attracting Investment, Industry and Tourism to Cities, States and Nations* (New York Free Press).

Law, C. M. (1993), *Urban Tourism, Attracting Visitors to Large Cities*. Mansell.

Masden, H. (1991), 'Place marketing in Liverpool: a review' *International Journal of Urban and Regional Research* 16(4).

Neill, W. Fitzsimmons, D. and Murtagh, B. (1995). *Reimaging the Pariah City* Avebury.

Page, S. (1997), *Urban Tourism* Routledge.

Smyth, H. (1994), *Marketing the City: The Role of Flagship Developments in Urban Regeneration,* E & NF Spon.

Urry, J. (1990), *The Tourist Gaze,* Sage.

Urry, J. (1997), *Consuming Places,* Routledge.

Warnaby, G. and Davies, B. J. (1997), 'Cities as Service Factories? Using The Servuction System for Marketing Cities as Shopping Destinations' *International Journal of Retail and Distribution Management.*

# Morecambe Bay regenerated: A leisure/tourism dichotomy

## Christine Williams

University of Central Lancashire, UK

## Abstract

The planning of facilities will be discussed in relation to the consumption of activities traditionally labelled as 'leisure' or 'tourism'. The theories from both leisure, (Veal, 1994; Torkildsen, 1999) and tourism planning (Gunn, 1988; Butler, 1993; Hall, 1998b and Jansen-Verbeke, 1989) will be considered.

This paper continues by investigating the planning process by which Morecambe, as an example of a British coastal resort in decline, has recycled and restructured its Central Promenade area since 1990, to reflect and accommodate changing consumption practices amongst its visitors and the local community.

Key strategic planning documents are examined for their goals and objectives in terms of an holistic approach to the regeneration of Morecambe.

The author gives specific attention to the regeneration via events, for which the town has earned renown and recognition, and which has fuelled the most recent development, the conversion of the Victorian promenade railway station into the Platform, a large-scale music venue.

The article concludes with reflections on the shift away from the sharp divisions in the consumption of coastal destination areas between leisure and tourism experiences (locals v. tourists) towards a shared, though not always harmonious, experience and use.

## Introduction

Leisure and tourism developments are often seen by politicians as the catalyst for economic regeneration. However, as Getz (1992:768) points out, the planning jargon term rejuvenation 'expresses a state of mind which is manifested in 'initiatives to deal with accumulating problems or pursue new opportunities'. Extending Getz' argument, rejuvenation can also improve the external image and increase residents' optimism about a location, or as Law (1993) puts it, civic pride. When regeneration takes place, leisure and tourism experiences are frequently considered to be consumed by different sections of society. This attitude is prevalent in local authorities when they consider the development and on-going management of these activities within their geographical areas.

There is a lack of recognition not only by practitioners but also by some academics that tourism and leisure have many similarities and that the needs of the local community can overlap with those of the tourist. Although a number of attempts have been made to link the two in terms of socio-cultural impacts and economic sustainability, the boundaries between the users of leisure and tourism products are still implied, for example in the fragmentation approach inherent in statutory local government documents (Weed and Bull, 1997).

The authors examine whether or not the polarisation of facility planning, into those predominantly for the local community and other experiences for tourists, is a valid dichotomy. The strategic planning associated with the regeneration of Morecambe and the associated bay, a seaside resort in the North West of England is the basis for this paper.

## Planning of tourism and leisure facilities

Although not in a pre-determined fashion, Morecambe has integrated tourism and leisure into its regeneration strategy. This follows the DCMS (1998) PAT 10 programme policy of regeneration and social inclusion, states that leisure and culture strategies must take an which integrated approach, and includes tourism and sport.

Veal (1994: 48) describes planning *as "....the process of establishing a programme of action for the medium and long term...."*. Hall (1998b) that it is more complex than maintains Veal would suggest. He sees the planning process as a series of choices with external factors (i.e. other organisations' needs etc.) coming into the equation.

Curry (1994) states that external factors are not always considered where land-use planning is concerned. Most practitioners assume an increase in free time and therefore consumption (i.e. early retirement, socio-demographic changes and increases in car ownership), with no recession or economic cycles. The leisure/tourism dichotomy is one of the main characteristics of the land-use planning approach.

Jansen-Verbeke and van de Wiel (1995) consider the external factor of time, suggesting that the time clustering of facilities is as important as spatial clustering. Many UK cities suggest they are "24 hour cities" but do not achieve this, as visitors find many facilities unavailable late at night (e.g. because of lack of transportation). Jansen-Verbeke and van del Wiel (1995) use of time differs from the traditionally used "length of visit" classifier for day visitors or tourists. The importance placed on this factor (Mathieson and Wall, 1982) the authors would argue, has underpinned the premise that leisure and tourism are different which can obstruct sustainable development. As far as seaside resorts are concerned, a more holistic approach to free time experiences would remove the boundaries between visitors and locals.

Gunn (1988) suggests that the planners should consider all the local amenities, and advocates that as many organisations as possible feed into the process, although be states that this rarely happens. As early as 1985, Murphy proposed that a community approach to tourism developments was needed, to redirect it from purely a business decision process to an open community orientated one. He suggested that 'stewardship of resources' is required (: XVI). This is in order that the needs and priorities of the residents can be maintained in balance with those of the tourists.

Hall (1998b) lists five different approaches to planning: Boosterism; Economic/Industry; Physical/Spatial; Community and Sustainable. Morecambe, in the opinion of the authors, has taken an Economic/Industry approach which means that the emphasis is polarised on the generation of income and job creation, whereas Hall's (1998b) "Sustainable" planning approach would integrate economic, spatial and community dimensions into an holistic strategy which would be more appropriate for Morecambe.

This integrated approach can easily encompass tourism and leisure planning; indeed Ashworth and Dietvorst (1995) promote this strategy. They take Butler's (1993) point of view that leisure and tourism facilities act in mutual support of each other.

Jansen-Verbeke and Van de Wiel (1995) take this a stage further and advocate the integration of play as well as tourism and recreation, observing that this was the key to the successful redevelopment of an area of Amsterdam. They noticed that this type of integration attracts the widest support and fulfils social as well as economic objectives.

There are many similarities between the planning of leisure and tourism facilities: they are both non-essential activities, largely dependent on the economic situation, fashions, trends, government policies, and many facilities are common or interchangeable (Lawson and Baud-Bovy, 1977).

Butler (1993) sees one of the major problems of assessing the impact and implementing a strategic plan for tourism as being the fragmented nature of the industry. Added to this dilemma is the notion that tourism needs to be treated as a "self-contained" activity, which has been shown not to be the case.

Butler agrees with Lawson and Baud-Bovy (1977), regarding the mutual interdependence of tourism and leisure facilities as illustrated below in Jansen-Verbeke's model (1986). The tourism and leisure industry also has a "strong" need for the secondary elements in the model (e.g. catering and shopping). A major factor in the economic success of the regeneration process is the length of stay of either visitors or residents in the area. The longer this is, the more important the secondary elements of Jansen-Verbeke's model become (Hall and Page, 1999). Whilst Morecambe's image is not one that conjures up that of a shopping destination, the location of Morrison's supermarket there is a catalyst for some day visitors (Lancaster and Morecambe College, 1997). This turns a secondary factor into the primary "pull factor" (Jansen-Verbeke, 1986), thus rendering the promenade and beach the secondary element level.

**Table 1    Jansen-Verbeke's Model of Elements Necessary for a Tourism Destination (Jansen-Verbeke, 1986)**

| Primary Elements Activity Place | Primary Element Leisure Setting |
|---|---|
| **Cultural facilities** | **Physical Characteristics** |
| Concert Hall | Ancient Monuments etc. |
| Cinemas | Ecclesiastical Buildings |
| Exhibitions | Historical Street Pattern |
| Museums and Galleries | Interesting Buildings |
| Sports facilities | Parks and Green Areas |
| Indoor and Outdoor | Water, canals and river fronts |
| **Amusement facilities** | **Socio-cultural features** |
| Bingo halls | Folklore |
| Casinos | Friendliness |
| Festivals | Language |
| Night Clubs | Liveliness and Ambience of the place |
| Organised Events | Local customs and costumes |
| | Security |
| **Secondary Elements** | **Additional Elements** |
| Hotels and Catering | Accessibility and Parking |
| Markets | Tourist Information |
| Shopping | |

Jansen-Verbeke (1991) suggests that the tourism/leisure infrastructure needs to be in a spatial cluster which includes a *"wide range"* of shops, cafes etc. These functional characteristics need to be supported by the aesthetic qualities of the environment. Jansen-Verbeke (cited in Hall and Page, 1999) quite rightly sees tourist using "bundles of products" from the lists above. The more elements that form these bundle, the more successful the regeneration processes have been.

Spatial distribution of facilities is one area of contention between tourism and leisure practitioners. Whilst the commercial leisure sector is happy to cluster its outlets (e.g. cinemas, video stores, restaurants etc.) in one specialised area, public sector leisure planners would be criticised for carrying out this strategy when developing facilities other than those which are unique (e.g. a dry ski slope or a leisure pool). Spatial clustering would be seen as favouring one specific section of the community and not embracing equity of provision.

Torkildsen (1999) states that the objective of leisure planners is to "provide the right facilities, in the best location, and at the right time, for the people who need them and at an acceptable cost." He suggests that this has a strong social objective basis and could be seen as an area that distinguishes leisure facilities planning from tourism planning. However this stance omits the commercial leisure sector.

In an integrated regeneration approach, the commercial leisure sector has a vital role which is more akin to the tourism industry members than the enabling public leisure sector. Torkildsen's premise perpetuates the leisure/tourism dichotomy when strong arguments have been made against it.

The authors advocate a holistic collaborative approach to the future regeneration of Morecambe. This would mean a shift away from the notion of sharp divisions in the consumption of leisure and tourism products, moving towards the planning of shared use facilities and experiences by locals, day visitors and staying holidaymakers in Morecambe and the bay. This sustainable strategic planning approach (Hall, 1998b), rather than conventional planning, would give a number of advantages, including that of a single process from planning stage to implementation, ease of allocation of resources. It also allows for external factors to be considered (Gunn, 1988).

## Case-study: Morecambe and the Bay

The resort of Morecambe has a resident population of 50,000. Visitor nights in 1997 were 1, 062,722 (Lancaster City Council, Tourism Department 1998), and three quarters of all tourists are said to be day visitors. It has been estimated that 1000 people are directly employed in the tourism sector (Lancaster City Council, 1997).

As well as providing the traditional seaside experiences, its unique attractions include the Frontier Land theme park; Bubbles, a leisure pool, Marine Land, (an aquarium) and a new promenade incorporating public art: (the Tern project), and Eric Morecambe's statue. Morecambe has also been developing a reputation for music events with the opening of The Platform, a large venue converted from the former railway station.

Morecambe has 'few sports grounds and accessible urban open spaces' (Lancaster City Council, 1997); Happy Mount Park, of some five acres, is the only formal park and Salt Ayre leisure centre, midway between Lancaster and Morecambe, serves both communities.

New commercial leisure facilities include a multi-screen cinema, and ten pin bowling. The closed Winter Gardens, a listed building, has not yet been found an alternative use. (Lancaster City Council, 1997).

The seaside resort of Morecambe is administered by Lancaster City Council, the nearest city some three miles inland. The remainder of the geographical area, Morecambe Bay, is a proposed special protection area and a Ramsar designated site. This is because it is internationally important for wildlife, attracting some 200,000 birds in winter, amongst which are five percent of the world's knots, oystercatchers and redshanks (Morecambe Bay Project, 1996). The bay area provides opportunities for informal and formal countryside recreation activities.

## Decline of Morecambe

In the halcyon days of 1950s and 60s these were 25,000 hotel bed spaces, reducing to 16,000 by 1973, and finally in 1990s down to 6,500. Self catering establishments were not perceived to be important prior to 1990 and comparative data is therefore not available, but at present this provides 10,000 bed spaces. This seems to indicate a change of emphasis on the part of the accommodation services. This dramatic decline in visitor nights can be seen even over a short period of two years, from 1995 to 1997.

Table 2    **Morecambe -- Visitor Nights**

| 1995 | 1996 | 1997 |
|------|------|------|
| 2,315,200 | 1,069,569 | 1,062,722 |

*Source: various*

One issue that was pertinent to Morecambe in 1974 was the reorganisation of local government. Some say that unfortunately this area was subsumed by Lancaster City Council; and this was detrimental to Morecambe's continued development (Urry, 1987, cited in Demetriadi, 1997).

The decline of Morecambe is not unique: Williams and Shaw (1997) state that by the 1970s the seaside tourism product was uncompetitive with the Mediterranean beach packages. They observe that the flow should have been two way but unfortunately for British seaside resorts, tourists, from overseas required heritage, culture and viewing the landscape. These are facets the combination of Lancaster's historical visitor attractions, and the Morecambe Bay area could have capitalised.

Harada (1998) puts forward the analogy that cities are like a human body, degenerating and spiralling down but with the ability to spiral up again. Cooper (1997) is more specific about this downward spiral for a coastal town, going so far as to state what the indicators of decline are normally: lack of appropriate accommodation, reduction in direct tourism employment, rise in car ownership giving more opportunities for day visits; environmental demise due to downward drift of the resort and low priority for some local authorities and central government. These factors can be easily recognised in the tourism strategies covering the Morecambe area (Lancashire County Planning Department 1995; Morecambe Bay Tourism, 1995).

As tourists fail to find the experiences and facilities that they require from a resort, they will go elsewhere. The facility providers do not have the resources to change or refurbish their facility, which is partly due to the reduction in tourists. The economic benefit that Morecambe received from tourism was £46.6 million in 1973, but by 1990 it was down to £6.5 million, (Williams and Shaw, 1997). This is evidence of Harada's downwards spiral.

# Morecambe's regeneration process

According to Hall (1998a) cities constantly regenerate themselves. Applying this to the much smaller urban areas of Morecambe there is a major difference, this being that some of the major cities are utilising tourism and leisure (e.g. Sheffield 'the city of sport', Glasgow 'European City of Culture') as opposed to regenerating their traditional but declining industries. Morecambe's original industry was, and still is, leisure and tourism.

Williams and Shaw (1997) considers that it lacks a distinct tourism product and this is at present holding back the upward spiral. It can be assumed that the natural beauty of the Bay is the major attraction, the potential of which was not addressed in the initial stages of Morecambe's regeneration planning processes.

Traditionally, regeneration through the vehicle of tourism and leisure has required a 'flagship' tourist attraction (McCarthy, 1995: 310; Gibson and Hardman, 1998:38). This acts as a catalyst as well as a focus for lesser developments. This is the model that has been utilised successfully in North America. Pacione (1992) suggests that this inherited regeneration model is rooted in a different system of government and finance and does not translate fully to the UK. Morecambe's Mr Blobby Crinkley Bottom Theme Park (a character from television) lasted only a few months until 1994, leaving the citizens, via the local council, with a legacy of litigation, as well as substantial debt.

This theme park was constructed in Happy Mount Park, a public open space which, due to an admission change being levied, disenfranchised the local people. This attraction was in addition to Frontier Land and Marine Land at the opposite end of the resort. One can assume that if it had been successful it would have been in direct competition with them, rather than complementary.

From the authors' own research the flagship attraction for Morecambe from current user patterns is not a built attraction but rather Morrisons' supermarket, a phenomenon not always considered. The natural beauty of the bay is also not regarded in this context even though the majority of Morecambe's visitors are attracted by it.

The main focus of Morecambe's leisure and tourism regeneration to date is the refurbishment of the promenade, and the development of a small number of commercial ventures (i.e. a cinema and a ten-pin bowling alley). Pump priming of money by the public sector is seen as a requirement for a successful regeneration strategy (Law, 1992 cited in Law, 1993). The promenade work came out of the £20 million allocated for coastal defence works and was funded by the Ministry of Agriculture, Fisheries and Food.

The majority of the monies for other completed projects (e.g. The Platform), has come from the Morecambe Single Regeneration Budget, (£60 million over the ten years from 1990 to 2000), (various sources, Lancaster City Council). Successful regeneration can be found in the staging of music events, due to the development of a performance space, "the Platform", from the Victorian promenade railway station and the multi-use Festival Market. The indoor market is a newly built building adjacent to the Platform, where the stall-holders' leases allow for 12 days of non-trading to accommodate high profile performing arts events (e.g. Royal Shakespeare Co. in 1999).

The very nature of these capital projects, being experiences for both locals and tourists, led the authors to believe that an integrated planning approach had been taken.

## Strategic planning of Morecambe's regeneration

As Morecambe's regeneration has its foundation in leisure facilities as well as tourism, the authors have taken an holistic view when examining the content of strategic plans for the area.

Whilst Weed and Bull (1997) research the integration of sport and tourism policies, the authors have taken leisure *per se* and examined the continuum of tourism and leisure strategies from North West Government Agencies, via Lancashire County Council to the micro plans of Lancaster City Council, both non-statutory and statutory documents (see appendix 1). Interestingly these documents show the emergence of a general pattern: apart from events management very few areas of policy cross the tourism/leisure division.

The documentation by North West Council for Sport and Recreation (1994), together with that of the Lancaster City Council's Leisure Services Strategy (1995), display the most insular strategic planning. Sport is predominant and both organisations adopt the premise that it is only for residents. Standeven (1998:41) cites Weed and Bull: 'although sport-tourism activity by policy makers is rising, examples of genuine collaboration by sport and tourism bodies are few and far between'.

The Leisure Services Department's strategy (1995) only superficially considers countryside recreation pursuits, concentrating mainly on indoor and outdoor urban sports provision. The management of the major resources of Morecambe Bay is left to other organisations. This is carried out in an *ad hoc* fragmented way depending upon which Art of Parliament is relevant, with organisational co-ordination generally on a voluntary basis.

The non-statutory Morecambe Bay Strategy (Morecambe Bay Project, 1996) illustrates this multi-organisational approach with over 100 bodies involved, many from the voluntary sector. Gunn (1988) highlights the increasing importance of the voluntary sector especially when regeneration comes via sporting opportunities.

Unlike the other statutory and non-statutory documents, the Morecambe Bay Strategy (Morecambe Bay Project, 1996) does not distinguish between residents' and tourists' needs. Unfortunately it does not acknowledge the role and responsibilities for the Bay of the local authority's Tourism Services (see appendix 1).

The day-to-day management of the Promenade and the foreshore with its many conflicting informal recreation activities (e.g. water sports, fishing and wildlife in distress) are the responsibility of Tourism Services. They co-operate with the Leisure Services and Arts and Events Services, according to the management plan (Morecambe Bay Tourism, 1996) with regard to life saving (the former) and events (the latter).

The Morecambe Bay Strategy (Morecambe Bay Project, 1996) gives directions on waterspace management, allowing both locals and tourists to enjoy a variety of countryside recreation pursuits (sailing, fishing and bird watching) but since it is an advisory document it has no statutory clout.

Arts-related tourism, another potentially distinctive product, is embraced by a number of documents covering Morecambe's geographical area, especially the Lancashire County Council's and Lancaster City Council's policies for the arts. The Arts Development Strategy (Lancaster City Council, 1995) specifically mentions a companion document on arts tourism, but limited resources have not allowed this to be produced. This is during a period of a declining tourism industry. Both councils' arts strategies embrace the local community in terms of participation in the arts as well as being spectators.

Although the local authority's statutory documents (1993; 1997) report the decline in the central retail area, and tourist accommodation and highlight the need to attract commercial partners in the re-use of the Winter Gardens, with the exception of the Festival Market the strategies contain 'wish' lists rather than a means of implementing a strategic plan.

The structure and local plans of both Lancashire and Lancaster Councils (see appendix 1), although complying with the needs of central government, follow Curry's (1994) premise, in that they are more restraining than developmental. Goodhead and Johnson (1996) suggest that a limitation of planning authorities is that anything that is not development (i.e. informal leisure) cannot be controlled, and therefore is not considered.

Not one document fully addresses the whole regeneration issue for Morecambe. Each strategy follows very definite departmental functional areas or organisational responsibilities. Utilising Bell and Watkins' (1996) typology of inter-organisational relations, it would seem that co-ordination with some degree of competition is in place rather than collaboration. As this is defined as 'participants working together to pursue a meta-mission while also pursuing their individual mission' by Huxham and Macdonald, (1992 cited in Andereck, 1997:45), this would be appropriate for different departments within this local authority. Collaboration would require a 'strategic business alliance' with a 'commitment to resolving problems' (Bell and Watkins, 1996:13).

Although the local newspaper, The Visitor, reports extensively on the need to stop the decline of the tourism industry and the progress that the City Council and other agencies have made, the planning thus far seems to the authors to follow the traditional premise that tourists and residents require different experiences. The authors would suggest the contrary: that it is by accident rather than design that the developments to date have produced multi-user spaces.

## Discussion

Utilising the model of Jansen-Verbeke (1986), it is interesting to carry out a comparative analysis of Morecambe in its transitional phase of the regeneration.

**Table 3    A Comparative Analysis of Morecambe and the Bay with Jansen-Verbeke elements necessary for a tourism destination (Jansen-Verbeke, 1986)**

| Primary Elements Activity Place | Morecambe and the Bay | Primary Element Leisure Setting | Morecambe and the Bay |
|---|---|---|---|
| **Cultural facilities** | | **Physical Characteristics** | |
| Concert Hall | yes | Ancient Monuments etc. | yes |
| Cinemas | yes | Ecclesiastical Buildings | |
| Exhibitions | yes | Historical Street Pattern | yes |
| Museums and Galleries | | Interesting Buildings | art deco |
| | | Parks and Green Areas | one park |
| **Sports facilities** | | Water, canals and river fronts | promenade and bay |
| Indoor | pool only | | |
| Outdoor | yes | **Socio-cultural features** | |
| | | Folklore | yes |
| **Amusement facilities** | | Friendliness | yes |
| Bingo halls | yes | Language | |
| Casinos | | Liveliness and Ambience of the place | |
| Festivals | yes | Local customs and costumes | |
| Night Clubs | yes | Security | yes |
| Organised Events | yes | | |
| | | | |
| **Secondary Elements** | | **Additional Elements** | |
| Hotels and Catering | yes | Accessibility and Parking | yes |
| Markets | yes | Tourist Information | yes |
| Shopping | yes | | |

It would seem that Morecambe fulfils many of the primary and all of the secondary aspects of what is required by a tourist, but the reality is more complex. As Jansen-Verbeke *et al.* (1990) state, a range of facilities within the categories are required and in many cases these are not available. Leisure shopping for example, as Hall and Page (1999) suggest, is a spontaneous activity for many visitors, but Morecambe's shops do not offer this type of experience as they are mainly selling day-to-day commodities.

Although Morecambe is not a very big town the existing leisure and tourism facilities are geographically spread; only the newer elements in the regeneration process conform to Jansen-Verbeke's (1990; 1991) spatial clustering recommendation. This is also a disadvantage when time clustering is considered and adds to the lack of liveliness and ambience which are essential elements for extensive night time use.

The model does not make allowances for market segments other than those whose consumption is in the urban context. Countryside recreationalists and special interest tourists (e.g. bird watchers) need to be considered in a facilities audit of Morecambe. These groups are not catered for in the secondary and additional infra-structural elements of Morecambe, but French (1998) is particularly worried that the commodification of estuaries results in mainstream tourism developments (i.e. hotels), rather than their being looked at as a leisure resource in their own right.

A 'centre of excellence' for countryside recreation would fulfil Morecambe's need for a distinctive product that Williams and Shaw (1997) say is lacking. Two North West of England examples are the sophisticated RSPB visitor centre at Leighton Moss (admission charged) and the free heated hide at the RSPB Marshside Reserve (staffed by volunteers). The bay is large enough to accommodate both levels of facilities. Morecambe's external image needs to be repositioned from being a poor substitute for Blackpool (20 miles to the south), to be being more akin to the passive outdoor activities of the Lake District National Park (30 miles to the north).

Alternatively, a 'centre of excellence' for watersports could also meet a range of needs, again moving towards the image of Lake Windermere in the Lake District National Park. It is however recognised that a tidal estuary gives operational problems for this type of development and that conservationists would most certainly object (French, 1998).

Many writers have commented on the potential for diversity in the tourism product. Agarwal (1997) advocates the development of sport and recreational facilities as well as special interest and activity holidays. The authors' recommended strategies would fulfil those needs.

## The use of events in Morecambe's regeneration process

Events are one of the growth free time experiences to cross the divide from being something for the local community to being a component of tourism. Morecambe is utilising performing arts events to act as a catalyst for its regeneration (e.g. WOMAD). Arts festivals tend to be the domain of wealthier individuals, whereas Morecambe has included more popular culture in the programming of the Platform (e.g. National Theatre, with folk music, pop groups, and community art).

Hall (1989) considers that events are a way for a tourism destination to gain prominence for a short period of time. He expands on this by stating that events may be the response to a problem, as in the case in Morecambe. Getz (1991, cited in Law, 1993) is more specific, suggesting that one of the six reasons for holding an event is to add animation and life to an existing destination. This confirms Jansen-Verbeke's opinion that liveliness and ambience of a location are essential elements of a tourism destination.

Van Der Lee and Williams (1986) divide the impact of events into short and long term. Whilst these differ depending on the type of event, they are worthwhile considering in relation to Morecambe's regeneration.

**Table 4    Social Costs and Benefits of Events**
adapted from Van Der Lee and Williams (1986:28)

| Short term social costs | Long term social costs |
|---|---|
| traffic delays | long term debt |
| loss of low cost housing | |
| crime | **Long term social benefits** |
| loss of an amenity | increase tourism |
| | image improvement |
| **Short term social benefits** | expanding trade and industry |
| psychological for the host community | increased participation by the local community |
| business opportunities | |

Morecambe has circumvented most of the short term costs identified by Van Der Lee and Williams (1986) although it has traffic problems due to changes to the promenade road. Additional car parking provision is being sought to try to alleviate this. To date the events management strategies utilised in Morecambe have not resulted in the loss of housing or amenities in the short or long term. The Platform has the dual benefit of not only creating an additional amenity but it also re-uses a redundant building. The Mr Blobby theme park has resulted in long term debt for the local authority, and an area of conflict between councillors and residents.

Whilst many of Van Der lee and Williams' (1986) benefits have not been observed in Morecambe's overall visitor numbers as the use of events is a recent initiative. Crompton (1998) states that the economic benefits of an event may be over-estimated, especially if no account is made of 'time switchers' (people going to Morecambe anyway who change the date to coincide with the event) and 'casuals' (people in Morecambe already who decide to buy a ticket).

The use of arts events in the regeneration process, as Morecambe is doing, is a concern of Waterman (1998). He proposes that there are overlapping objectives which are not always compatible with the local community's needs: attracting of tourists, raising the image of a place. This can result in a top down approach which tends to stage elite but economically viable flagship events rather than community arts developments.

These social dilemmas are recognised by Bianchini and Parkinson (1993) when discussing cultural policy and urban regeneration. They conclude that conflict can arise when consumption-orientated strategies take priority. Lancaster's Arts Development strategy (1995) suggests that the local community's needs are a major consideration when staging events. In the past Walton (1997:43) has directly criticised the local authority in Morecambe for 'parsimony towards popular festivals and a preference for showy municipal premises over holiday industry investment'.

Bianchini and Parkinson (1993) see a dilemma between staging one-off events versus permanent performance space, the route Morecambe has taken. Whilst one-off events can be seen as being the least expensive option, capital expenditure is still required to provide the infrastructure to stage them. It is therefore difficult to make a generalisation about which is the most cost effective strategy.

Both strategies have been pursued by many local authorities and organisations in the regeneration process. Gibson and Hardman (1998:38) express concern that if the number of events continued to grow at the current rate, it 'could lead to a reduced share of a possibly finite market.'

# Conclusion

The regeneration of Morecambe has provided additional leisure opportunities for locals and tourists alike. Law (1992, cited in Law, 1993) suggests that increased visitor numbers not only make new facilities viable but help retain and enhance existing ones.

The local community will not only benefit from the economic growth caused by attracting visitors but they have gained by having a much improved infrastructure and a diversity of leisure opportunities. Part of the increased demand for leisure and tourism experiences from residents may come about though the removal of one of the main barriers to participation, the lack of disposable income (Torkildsen, 1999 and Rodgers, 1993 cited in Hall and Page, 1999), as the whole ethos of Morecambe's regeneration policy is focused on income and job creation.

Any gain in the money spend by residents on local facilities is most desirable, and equally as important as attracting day visitors and tourists. Without these facilities residents will look to other towns and cities to fulfil their leisure needs and spend their disposable income wherever their demands can be met. Because of this residents' expenditure should not be overlooked (Jokovi, 1992).

Unfortunately the current fragmented approach to Morecambe and its regeneration may lead to more *ad hoc* approaches, similar to that of the Mr. Blobby theme park, an attempt at the commodification of a public open space. Jansen-Verbeke *et al.* (1990) advocate that the public sector needs to recognise the conditions required for successfully regeneration and to "encourage opportunities through the complementary and compatibility of varied facilities."

The authors' on-going research into the leisure/tourism dichotomy has led them to believe that a convergence of facility use is taking place. To facilitate the integration of visitors and residents when considering seaside resort regeneration and long term sustainability via leisure and tourism developments, a new consumption model is needed: the Leisure/Tourism Consumption Convergence model.

# References

Agarwal, S. (1997), The Public Sector: planning for renewal? in Shaw, G. and Williams, A. (Editors) *The Rise and Fall of the British Coastal Resorts,* Mansell, London, pp. 137-158.

Andereck, K. L. (1997), Case-Study Of A Multi-Agency Partnership: effectiveness and constraints, *Journal of Parks and Recreation Administration*; 15 (2): 44-60.

Ashworth, G. J., and Dietvorst, A. G. J., (1995), Conclusion: challenge and policy response in Ashworth, G. J. and Dietvorst, A. G. J.(Editor) *Tourism and Spatial transformations: implications for policy and planning.* CABI, Wallingford, pp. 329-359.

Bell, B. and Watkins, M. (1996), Interorganisational Relations in Regional Tourism: a exploratory study. ANZALS Conference Proceedings, *Leisure, People, Places and Spaces;* University of Newcastle, NSW, Australia.

Bianchini, F. and Parkinson, M. (1993), *Cultural policy and Urban Regeneration.* MUP, Manchester.

Butler, R. W., (1993), Pre- and Post-impact Assessment of Tourism development in Pearce, D. G. and Butler, R. W.(Editor) *Tourism Research: critiques and challenges.* Routledge, London.

Cooper, C. (1997), Parameters and Indicators of the Decline of the British Seaside Resort in Shaw, G. And Williams, A. (Editors) *The Rise and Fall of the British Coastal Resorts,* Mansell, London, pp. 79-101.

Crompton, J. L. (1998), Analysis of Sources of Momentum that Underlie the Investment of Local Public Funds on Major Sporting Facilities and Events, Conference Proceedings *Sport in the City,* Sheffield Hallam University, UK.

Curry, N. (1994), *Countryside Recreation, Access and land Use Planning.* Spon, London.

DCMS (1998), Annual Report, HMSO, London.

Demetriadi, J. (1997), The Golden Years: English seaside resorts 1950-1975 in Shaw, G. And Williams, A. (Editors) *The Rise and Fall of the British Coastal Resorts,* Mansell, London, pp. 49-78.

French, P. (1998) *Coastal and Estuarine Management.* Routledge, London.

Gibson, C. and Hardman, D. (1998) Regeneration Urban Heritage for Tourism, *Managing Leisure;* 3 (1): 37-54.

Goodhead, T. and Johnson, D. (1996), *Coastal Recreation Management.* Spon, London.

Gunn, C. A. (1988), *Tourism Planning,* 2nd Ed., Taylor and Francis, London.

Hall, C. M. (1998), Image, Tourism and Sports Event Fever. Conference Proceedings *Sport in the City,* Sheffield Hallam University, UK.

Hall, C. M. (1989), The Definition and Analysis of Hallmark Tourist Events, *Geo Journal;* 19 (3): 263-268.

Hall, C. M., (1998), The Politics of Decision Making and Top-down Planning: Darling, Harbour, Sydney in D. Tyler, Y. Guerrier, and M. Robertson, (ed.) *Managing Tourism in Cities: policy, process and practice.* Wiley, Chicester, pp 9-25.

Hall, C. M. and Page, S. J. (1999), *The Geography of Tourism and Recreation.* Routledge, London.

Harada, M. (1998), Urban Development Based on Major Sports Events: escape from the downward spiral of degeneration. Conference Proceedings, *Sport in the City,* Sheffield Hallam University, UK.

Jansen-Verbeke, M., (1986), Inner City Tourism: resources, tourists and promoters. *Annals of Tourism Research;* 13 (1): 79-100.

Jansen-Verbeke, M., and Ashworth, G., (1990), Environmental Integration of Recreation and Tourism, *Annals of Tourism Research;* 17 (2): 33-45.

Jansen-Verbeke, M. (1991), Leisure shopping; a magic concept for the tourism industry? *Tourism Management;* 12, (March), pp.9-14.

Jansen-Verbeke, M., and van de Wiel, E. (1995), Tourism Planning in Urban Revitalisation Projects in G. J. Ashworth and A. G. J. Dietvorst (ed.) *Tourism and Spatial transformations: implications for policy and planning.* CABI, Wallingford, pp.129-145.

Jokovi, E. M. (1992), The Production of Leisure and Economic Development in Cities, *Built Environment;* 18 (2): 138-154.

Lancashire County Council Arts Sub Committee (1996), *Arts Policy and Plan 1996-1999,* Lancashire County Council.

Lancashire County Planning Department (1988), *A Countryside Recreation Strategy for Lancashire,* Lancashire County Council.

Lancashire County Planning Department (1990), *Landscape and Wildlife Strategy For Lancashire,* Lancashire County Council.

Lancashire County Planning Department (1994), *Structure Plan 1991-2006,* Lancashire County Council.

Lancashire County Planning Department (1995), *A Tourism Strategy For Lancashire,* Lancashire County Council.

Lancashire County Planning Department (1997), *Structure Plan 1991-2006*, Lancashire County Council.

Lancaster Arts and Events Services (1995), *An Arts Strategy for Lancaster District Part 1: Arts Development,* Lancaster City Council.

Lancaster and Morecambe College (1997), Survey of Morecambe Visitors, Unpublished.

Lancaster City Council (1993), *Morecambe and Heysham Local Plan: deposit edition 1991-2001*, Lancaster City Council.

Lancaster City Council (1997), *Lancaster District Local Plan: deposit edition.* Lancaster City Council.

Law, Christopher M. (1993), *Urban Tourism: attracting visitors to large cities.* Mansell, London.

Lawson, F., and Baud-Bovy, M., (1977), *Tourism and Recreation Development: a handbook of physical planning.* The Architectural Press, London.

Leisure Services (1995), *Leisure Into The Next Millennium,* Lancaster City Council.

Mathieson, A, and Wall, G., (1982), Tourism: economic, physical and social impacts, Longman, London.

McCarthy, J. (1995), The Dundee Waterfront: a missed opportunity for planned regeneration, *Land Use Policy*; 12 (4): 307-319.

Morecambe Bay Project (1996), *Morecambe Bay Strategy,* Cumbria County Council and English Nature, Cumbria.

Morecambe Bay Tourism Department (1995), *A Strategy For Tourism In Morecambe 1995-2000,* Lancaster City Council.

Morecambe Bay Tourism Department (1996), *Interim Promenade and Foreshore Management Plan 1996-2000,* Lancaster City Council.

Murphy, P. E. (1985), *Tourism: a community approach.* Routledge, London.

North West Arts Board (1998), *Review 1997-1998,* North West Arts Board.

North West Council For Sport and Recreation (1992*), Into The Wild Country,* North West Council For Sport and Recreation, Manchester.

North West Council For Sport and Recreation (1994), *Sign Up For Sport 1994-2000*, North West Council For Sport and Recreation, Manchester.

NWTB (1992), *Building on Success; the strategy for tourism in the North West*. North West Tourism Board Tourism, Wigan.

NWTB Tourism Development Services (1995*), North West Coastal Resorts Initiative Phase 2*, North West Tourism Board Tourism, Wigan.

Pacione, M. (1992), Citizenship, Partnership and The Popular Restructuring of UK Urban Space, *Urban Geographer*; 13 (5): 405-421.

Page, S. (1995), *Urban Tourism*, Routledge, London.

Standeven, J. (1998), Sport Tourism: joint marketing-a starting point for beneficial synergies, *Journal of Vacation Marketing*; 4 (1): 39-51.

Torkildsen, G., (1999), Leisure and Recreation Management. Spon, London, (4 Ed.)

Van Der Lee, P. and Williams, J. (1986), The Grand Prix and Tourism, in J. P. A. Burns, J. H. Hatch, and T. J. Mules (ed.) *The Adelaide Grand Prix*. The Centre for South Australian Economic Studies, Adelaide.

Walton, J. K. (1997), Seaside Resorts, 1900-1950 in Shaw, G. And Williams, A. (Editors) *The Rise and Fall of the British Coastal Resorts*, Mansell, London, pp.21-48.

Waterman, S. (1998), Carnivals for Elites? The Cultural Politics of Arts Festivals, *Progress in Human Geography;* 22 (1): 54-74.

Weed, M. E. and Bull, C. J. (1997), Integrating Sport and Tourism: a review of regional policies in England, *Progress in Tourism and Hospitality Research*; 3, pp.129-148.

**Appendix 1 Contents of Strategic Plans Specifically Related to Morecambe**

| Document | Integration of Tourism with Leisure | Integration of Locals and Visitors | Existing Facilities in Morecambe | Proposed Facilities for Morecambe | Over-lapping Responsibilities | Work of Other Organisations | Other Strategies Mentioned |
|---|---|---|---|---|---|---|---|
| **Lancaster City Council** | | | | | | | |
| Morecambe and Heysham Local Plan (1993) 1991-2001 | Sports and arts provision not included | ✓ | ✓ | Public open space, Coastal Way and National Cycle Way | X | X | X |
| Lancaster District Local Plan - Deposit Version Oct. 1997 | X | ✓ | Including bingo halls, pubs, fast food, amusement arcades | New bus station | X | X | X |
| Leisure into the Next Millennium (1995) Leisure Services | X | X | Only sports related | Refurbishment of the Dome Theatre and Waterfront bar within Bubbles Leisure Park | 1. Safety on the Foreshore 2. Children's holiday play schemes 3. Events 4. Countryside Recreation | Voluntary Sector | National and Regional Sports Related ones |
| Strategy for Tourism in Morecambe 1995-2000 Tourism Services | ✓ | ✓ | ✓ | All Weather Attractions; Eco-tourism; Events | 1) Events 2) Countryside Recreation | Arts and Events Service | Morecambe Bay Project |
| Interim Promenade and Foreshore Management Plan 1996-2000 (1996) Tourism Services | X | ✓ | ✓ | Major refurbishment of the Promenade | 1) Watersports 2) Fishing 3) Wildlife in Distress 4) Events 5) Public Art | ✓ | Lancaster City Council's Leisure and Arts Strategies |
| An Arts Strategy for Lancaster District (1995) Part 1 Arts Development Arts and Events Services | ✓ | ✓ | Existing tourism product | X | Playleaders training in arts and crafts | Many especially Leisure Services Children's Festival | Especially The Arts Tourism Strategy (which was not produced). |
| **Lancashire County Council** | | | | | | | |
| Structure Plan (1994) 1991-2006 | Integration in the rural areas | X | X | X | X | X | Other Lancashire County Council Strategies |
| Structure Plan (1997) 1991-2006 | Ditto | X | X | X | X | X | Ditto |
| A Strategy for Tourism in Lancashire (1995) | Via District Councils | ✓ | General statements | General statements | Frequently | Partnership Possibilities | Including non-statutory ones |
| Landscape and Wildlife Strategy for Lancs. (1990) | X | X | X | X | Ecological rather than recreational | Yes | Only Lancashire County Council's |
| Countryside Recreation Strategy for Lancs. (1988) | Co-operation and partnership | ✓ | Long Distance Coastal Path | X | X | X | X |
| Arts Policy and Plan 1996-1999 | Arts-led tourism | X | Arts related events, The Dome | X | X | District Councils | X |
| **Statutory Agencies** | | | | | | | |
| NW Council for Sport and Recreation (1994) Sign up for Sport 1994-2000 | X | X | X | X | X | Including District Councils | Local Sports Councils |
| NW Council for Sport and Recreation(1992) Into the Wild Country | X | Watersports only | General | X | X | ✓ | ✓ |
| NW Arts Board Review 1997/98 | X | X | X | Tern project | X | Events / music related | X |
| NWTB (1992) Building on Success: The Strategy for Tourism in the N. W. | Via sports and the arts | X | Not specifically | X | X | X | National only |
| NWTB Tourism Development Services (1995) NW Coastal Resorts Initiative Phase 2 | Parks and open spaces only | X | In-depth analysis | X | X | Events management | X |
| Morecambe Bay Strategy (1996) Morecambe Bay Project Office | ✓ | ✓ | ✓ | Caravan sites and public art | X | Lancaster Tourism Services foreshore role omitted. | Local Plans |